"Alvord's perceptive gloss of the late, great, 20th century's pitiful auto intoxication is a fascinating read and a stunning contradiction of the fatuity that technology is neutral ... Her gathering of stories illuminates the existence of a vital planet-wide, counter-car-culture ... Witty, substantial and penetrating, *Divorce Your Car!* is a mighty persuasive job of work."
— Stephanie Mills, from the Foreword

"A clear-headed, approach to reducing — or even eliminating — our dependence on cars, *Divorce Your Car!* points the way to a greener world and maps out how we can live happily ever after by breaking free of auto-cracy. I found the book informative and inspiring, full of common sense and fresh insight for the person who wants to simply walk and bike more as well as hard-core folks like me who bike to work every day, even through Minnesota's legendary blizzards and wind chill."
— Jay Walljasper, editor-at-large of *Utne Reader* and frequent writer on urban issues.

"This is an amazingly well-informed book. It's also fun to read."
— Noel Perrin, author of *Life with an Electric Car*

"Finally, an anti-car book for everyone!
Divorce Your Car! is trenchant, funny, and ready-to-use."
— Charles Komanoff, Right Of Way pedestrian rights group, New York City

Divorce your Car!

Divorce your Car!

Ending the love affair with the automobile

KATIE ALVORD

Foreword by Stephanie Mills

NEW SOCIETY PUBLISHERS

Cataloguing in Publication Data:
A catalog record for this publication is available from the National Library of Canada.

Cover design by Charles Dobson.

Printed in Canada by Friesens.

New Society Publishers acknowledges the support of the Government of Canada through the Book Publishing Industry Development Program (BPIDP) for our publishing activities, and the assistance of the Province of British Columbia through the British Columbia Arts Council.

Paperback ISBN: 0-86571-408-8

Quotations from *Automania: Man and the Motor Car* by Julian Pettifer and Nigel Turner are used courtesy of Carlton International Media Limited.

Quotations from "Car-free living in Chevy Chase, D.C." by Ellen Jones are used courtesy of Ellen Jones and of *Audubon Naturalist News*, a publication of the Audubon Naturalist Society.

The information and recommendations in this book are for reference and guidance only. Information related to health or law is intended to supplement, not replace, advice from professionals in these fields. Consulting an appropriate professional before acting on such information is recommended. The author and publishers disclaim any liability arising directly or indirectly from the use of this book.

Inquiries regarding requests to reprint all or part of *Divorce Your Car! Ending the Love Affair with the Automobile* should be addressed to New Society Publishers at the address below.

To order directly from the publishers, please add $4.00 shipping to the price of the first copy, and $1.00 shipping for each additional copy (plus GST in Canada). Send check or money order to:
New Society Publishers
P.O. Box 189, Gabriola Island, B.C. V0R 1X0, Canada

New Society Publishers aims to publish books for fundamental social change through non-violent action. We focus especially on sustainable living, progressive leadership, and educational and parenting resources. Our full list of books can be browsed on the worldwide web at: http://www.newsociety.com

NEW SOCIETY PUBLISHERS
Gabriola Island, B.C., Canada

CONTENTS

CONTENTS

continued

ACKNOWLEDGMENTS

Many, many thanks to everyone who has contributed to this effort. Thank you first to three special people who played pivotal roles in making this book happen: to Rick Theis, for the rich discussions that helped birth the book's title and concept; to Daniel Melcon, for believing I could write this even before I did and for being the first to actually mention its title to a publisher; and to Angela Bischoff, for helping to inspire my first car divorce and, later, helping to connect me with New Society. Major thanks also to Stephanie Mills, ever an inspiration, for sharing invaluable writing wisdom and encouragement; to Craig Scarborough, for the preface and more; and to Chris and Judith Plant, Heather Wardle, and Lisa Garbutt at New Society for having enthusiasm for this project and great patience with my learning curve.

Thanks to the many people who so generously provided their time to review draft chapters: Adrienne Alvord, Marjorie Alvord, H. B. Alvord, Jean Alvord, Carol Bennett, Angela Bischoff, Mary Been, Kristine Bradof, Dan Burden, John Carpenter, Mark Delucchi, George Ellman, David Engwicht, Randy Ghent, Stephen Goddard, Tooker Gomberg, Jim Gregory, Michael Hackleman, Keith Hammer, Ed Hancock, Dorothea Hass, John Holtzclaw, Jackie Huntoon, Joe Kirkish, Karla Kitalong, Kraig Klungness, Charlie Komanoff, Todd Litman, Carol McLennan, Mike Medberry, Jim Mihelcic, Stephanie Mills, Patricia Mokhtarian, Carolyn Nickerson, Jackson Nickerson, Jill Nussinow, Lyssa Pacas, Kurt Paterson, Betzi Praeger, Frank Praeger, Richard Reese, Preston Schiller, Bruce Seely, Robert Sanoff, Craig Scarborough, Robert Silverman, Joan Stein, Suzanne Van Dam, Tom Van Dam, Ellen Vanderslice, Bethanie Walder, Joel Woodhull, and Mary Ann Wright. Thanks to staff members at the Portage Lake District Library and Michigan Technological University's Van Pelt Library who so often provided assistance above and beyond the call of duty. Thanks to the many authors whose books and papers have made invaluable contributions to this work. Thanks to all the car-free folks who've been such an unending source of inspiration. Thanks to everyone who provided interviews or information for this book, and my apologies to those whose quotes or information didn't make it into these pages; regrettably, I ran out of space for all the great material everyone provided. Thanks to the people who've helped me with fact-checking; remaining errors are my responsibility (and I welcome having them pointed out, in case there's an opportunity to correct them in future editions). Thanks to my friends for tolerating my absences, and for still being there despite them. Thanks to so many others who have graced me with experiences and ideas that have fed this book, and to anyone else I may have forgotten to mention.

Finally, thanks to my family for love, humor, boundless encouragement, and intelligent advice; and to my long-suffering spouse, for all that as well as for patience, support, insight, and — especially — for being my partner in car divorce. I'm grateful, and very lucky to have had help from you all.

FOREWORD

by Stephanie Mills

My car invests me with a dual personality: outside it, I'm a noble cyclist or pedestrian-in-the-crosswalk, but in it I demonically switch into a foul-tempered, arrogant driver waiting for those slowpokes to get that baby stroller across the intersection. What's more, my car keeps me in an ethical bind. I could be seriously self-propelled if I had one horsepower for every time I've skulked, in my Toyota, through the gas station to purchase more fuel for a vehicle whose use as my primary mode of transportation implicates me in a vast complex of destruction, from the havoc wrought on the lands and lives of the last frontiers of oil exploration to the damage to my neighbors' repose when I drive home late at night, giving their dogs something to bark about.

Whatever the ideals, walking the talk is always the hard part. When the talk has to do with voluntary simplicity, the restoration of human health and community, and the protection of such planetary commons as natural diversity and the atmosphere, getting out of one's automobile is surely the most obvious first step on that integrity walk. Obvious yes, but possible?

Katie Alvord, among many thousands of others, is living proof that it's possible, here and now. Happily for those of us in need of some instruction in the ways and means of car divorce, Alvord, a car divorcee who has for years walked, pedaled, and otherwise pursued that ideal, has now articulated it in book form, and wonderfully well.

Divorce Your Car! does not insist that we in car-dependent countries quit our automotive addiction instantly. Still, anyone who reads the accounts of the relentless propagandizing for cars and of their polymorphously adverse effects, which constitute the first half of the book, will be eager to read of the moves for making the segue away from the sedan or the SUV that bring the book to a satisfying conclusion.

Alvord nimbly articulates the connections between automobiles, their arteries, their effluents, and the increasing number and severity of "natural" disasters; between the urban renewal and freeway construction ("white roads through black bedrooms," as one of her sources put it) that helped ignite the Watts, Newark, and Detroit riots. Alvord's elucidation of the civilizational and geophysical effects of the car — the late, great 20th century's pitiful auto intoxication — is a fascinating read and a stunning contradiction of the fatuity that technology is neutral.

Divorce Your Car! compiles such a mountain of evidence of the systemic abuse of the planet and the body politic attendant upon mass automobile use that no reasonable justification for not making a major policy and (gulp) personal shift away from cars would seem to remain. Still, because of its determining role in our infra-structure, and thus our culture, the car is tenacious — it malls and mauls.

I was once a passenger in a head-on automobile collision. Although none of the three persons in the two little cars that crashed was killed, our bodies and our lives were not much fun for years afterwards. Reflecting on that life event now, I think how much nicer it would have been for us to make that 150-mile or so journey downstate by bicycling to a rail depot, loading our bikes into the baggage car, taking our seats and settling in for a little picnic with our fellow travelers, followed by some conversation and perhaps a nap.

Even without benefit of an educational experience like a serious accident, most of us are aware that reliance on the individual passenger automobile as the princi-ple means of personal transportation has proved to be a ruinous idea for everyone. Even the members of Detroit's auto-plutocracy break and bleed when they're thrown through windshields. We Michiganers, which Alvord and I both happen to be, can see that the auto is not only the linchpin of American industrialism and resource extraction, it's also the chief suspect in a century-long theft of time, conviviality, and beauty. No place is enhanced by the presence of cars. If it's difficult to picture a car-free existence, to devise a scenario whereby such great change could come about boggles the mind.

Nonetheless surprisingly many activists around the world have developed the conceptual and organizational technologies to liberate their communities from autocracy. Their initiatives, catalogued in *Divorce Your Car!*, can direct us to walk, bike, bus, and rideshare on that path — not the Interstate — as yet less taken. So we're not necessarily doomed to a future of being suffocated, chagrined, and pau-perized by our cars. Alvord's gathering of stories illuminates the existence of a vital planet-wide counter-car-culture. Thus *Divorce Your Car!* ends on a high note, with a plausible, practical vision.

As the post-petroleum era dawns, *Divorce Your Car!* is just the kind of advice we should be taking. As I read the manuscript, with interest piqued by fractures and scars, I wished that every road commissioner and township planner in my region and everywhere could be required to read and heed *Divorce Your Car!* That way we'd get the millennium off on the right foot!

In the course of about a century — a flicker of historic time — society amalga-mated itself with the automobile. Given a sudden outburst of common sense, in another flicker, our bum romance with cars could be relegated to the learning expe-rience bin. The air could be cleaner, the countryside greener, and our bodies leaner. En route to those attractive outcomes, careers in depaving will burgeon, bicycle repair will be a growth industry, and working on the railroad could be back in style, while the demand for volunteers to care for moribund, oil-soaked marine life will plummet.

Witty, substantial, and penetrating, *Divorce Your Car!* is a mighty persuasive work. So persuasive that, despite the fog, damp, and cold of a recent post-Alvord

December morning, I could not help but do my Saturday errands on my bike. Not quite a divorce, but a satisfying trial separation in a marriage that shouldn't be saved.

Stephanie Mills
Maple City, Michigan
December 1999

PREFACE

by the Author's Ex

Who more appropriate to offer a preface to (and a ringing endorsement of) *Divorce Your Car!* than the "car" itself? You see, ten years ago the author and I formally ended our apparently happy marriage having poignantly realized that we were growing in different directions. Those directions were different enough to render our marriage, well, inappropriate. Mind you, ten years earlier when we began the marriage it seemed completely appropriate. But guess what? Things change!

Katie was intent on (literally) walking her talk in an effort to improve the living conditions for everyone on this planet. I was intent on making lots of money in an effort to improve *my* living conditions on this planet, which involved, naturally, adding to my collection of fun things with internal combustion engines. You won't need to read far into this book to understand why we reached the conclusion we did. It just wasn't going to work!

In the past ten years I'd have to say that I've been more successful in accomplishing my goals than Katie has in accomplishing hers. That is, while I've got more toys with internal combustion engines, the global environment is significantly worse than it was then. So if I'm more successful, then why is it that I'm *proud* of Katie but she still thinks I'm a bit *misguided?* Go figure.

The fact is, I know that Katie's basic premise is right: we *are* addicted to our cars, and the relationship is fundamentally unhealthy for ourselves, our environment, and ultimately (and ironically) our economy. Chances are that you know it too, but we are all probably at different stages in the process of doing something about it. This book is not only a compelling diagnosis for those addicts still in denial, it is a compassionate prescription of potential remedies, ranging all the way from trial separation to divorce. Personally, I don't think I could make it going cold turkey. But I now ride a bike to work, and that's a start.

Craig Scarborough
Sonoma Valley, California
November 1999

What Does It Mean to Divorce Your Car?

"The long and continuing relationship between man and the automobile has ... become so much a part of our lives that it is perhaps now more akin to a marriage than a love affair."

HENRY FORD II, IN JUDITH JACKSON, *MAN AND THE AUTOMOBILE: A TWENTIETH-CENTURY LOVE AFFAIR*

"Just because [people] are wedded to their cars, we need not assume they cannot be divorced."

A.Q. MOWBRAY, *ROAD TO RUIN*

CARTOON, 1993: A MAN STANDS AT A PUBLIC AGENCY WINDOW, under a sign reading "Marriage Licenses." The clerk at the window turns down his request. The man leans forward, gripping the counter, and pleads: "But why not?!! I love that car!!!"

NEWS STORY, 1999: A Tennessee man tries to marry his car. His license application lists the Mustang's birthplace as Detroit, father as Henry Ford, and blood type as 10-W-40. When officials reject the application, he vows to keep trying.

Life imitates art, and people mirror society. Licensed or not, our love affair with the car is a marriage in many senses. Like the cartoon fellow and the Tennessee man, we've taken our romance with the car to an extreme. And why not, indeed? Cars give us mobility and speed; they can be useful and convenient; they have psychological benefits, reflecting our personalities, giving us status, and providing at least a feeling of privacy in an increasingly crowded world. But the price we pay is high. Car crashes are the top killers of children in the U.S. and elsewhere. Auto emissions are implicated in global warming. Our surroundings are overwhelmed with car-induced sprawl. From miles-long traffic jams in Bangkok to deadly smog in Mexico City, from the cities crammed with cars to the countryside wounded by their overflow, no place on earth is untouched by the negative effects of automobiles.

Given how much we drive despite its costs and problems, any candid self-help book might assess our automotive marriage and pronounce, "This isn't love, this is addiction!" At some point in the last 100 years, the love affair has become a dysfunctional relationship — one we're stuck in and don't quite know how to leave. Somehow we do need to leave it — given cars' problems, we desperately need to change the role they play in our lives — but once we realize that, can we? The extent of our auto-dependence has made alternatives harder to find and tougher to use. Despite this, choices do exist, and making these choices can help solve the problem.

Even in auto-dependent countries, there are people out there showing that we can divorce our cars ... and live happily ever after.

What does it mean to "divorce" your car? It means leaving behind the kind of relationship in which the car is like a spouse in a dismal marriage — familiar but burdensome, used too often, as hard to shake as a bad habit — and replacing it with something better. Simply put, divorce means *not being wedded to our cars.* These days, it might be hard to imagine being mobile without ever getting inside a car. But using one occasionally, when there may be no other viable choice, is different from treating a car as your partner in life.

Just as divorce from a spouse can take many forms, so can divorce from a car — from selling the car (and never seeing it again) to joining a car-sharing co-op (a sort of joint custody arrangement) to simply driving less (an amicable divorce involving occasional get-togethers). Divorce from a car might mean living car-free — not owning a car, taking transit, walking, biking, and perhaps occasionally borrowing or renting a car when a need arises. It might mean living car-lite — owning a car, but using other travel modes more often. It might mean moving so you can be either car-free or car-lite more easily. However a car divorce comes about, its most important aspect may be a shift in attitude, away from the assumption that when you go someplace you'll have to drive. That's a shift that can open a new range of options in your life — as it did in mine.

In 1992, I decided to divorce my car. I'd considered this from time to time before then — uneasy with the knowledge that cars polluted, wasted energy, generated sprawl, cost lots of money, and vastly complicated international relations in places like the Middle East — but in our car-dependent culture I feared not driving might limit me. Then, in 1992, I attended a series of environmental conferences and met some inspiring people who lived full and happy lives in car-dependent countries, without owning cars. I began to ask myself: if they can do it, why can't I? By midyear, I was ready to try not driving — just try it.

I left my car in the garage and took out my bicycle instead. That became my vehicle of choice, supplemented by bus rides for longer distances, and occasional taxi rides or carpooling with helpful friends and neighbors. Especially since I lived in a rural area, choosing not to drive presented challenges, but in balance it turned out to be easier than I'd imagined. It helped that I made my living by writing and editing, working at home with a flexible schedule. When I traveled, usually by bicycle, I planned ahead a bit more. I rode my bike to meetings, to grocery stores, to the library, and to see friends. I outfitted my bike for rain and darkness. I installed a rack over the back wheel that could hold grocery bags or packs full of books and papers. Although the nearest bus stop was three miles from my home, I often combined biking and transit to get places and came to greatly appreciate that ours was one of a growing number of bus systems allowing passengers to bring bikes along. I learned that this combination of bike and transit could help me travel with a range and a convenience rivaling those of cars, for far less cost. The longer my car stayed in the garage, the more I realized I didn't need it as much as I'd thought.

Sometimes not driving simplified my life. I didn't take trips unless they were wonderfully compelling or absolutely necessary, and I found that I just didn't have to go places as much. Instead of darting to the store to fill some craving for dinner, I got creative with what was already in the cupboard. I attended meetings only when face-to-face contact was essential, otherwise doing business by phone, fax, or e-mail. Yet I discovered downsides to living without a car; it became even more painfully obvious that modern communities are structured more for cars than for people, and that non-drivers have been disenfranchised. Where I lived, as in so many car-dependent places, homes and businesses were far apart, bike lanes sparse, bus schedules limited. Almost everywhere, cars dominated. With fewer facilities provided for walkers, cyclists, and transit riders, I sometimes felt like a second-class citizen.

On the plus side, I immediately noticed that I had cut my expenses and was saving money. I got more exercise, my health improved, and I dropped a few pounds without watching what I ate. My stress level went down and I slept better at night. And I felt great! Bicycling was a blast. Taking transit relaxed me. I'd always liked walking and loved doing more of it. Being in shape raised my confidence, and living consistently with my principles gave me great satisfaction. Overall, I realized, divorcing my car was a lot of fun.

Being three miles from the nearest small town and 17 from the county's main population center, I had at first been uncertain how I'd do without using my car. Rather than sell it right away, I'd opted for a sort of trial separation: I kept the car for a year and let myself use it in a pinch. But after that year had passed, I counted the times I'd driven and didn't make it from my fingers to my toes. This was hardly enough driving to justify the insurance, registration, maintenance, and depreciation costs of owning the vehicle — so in 1993, I sold my car.

A couple of years after my first car divorce, my life changed again. I moved to the Upper Peninsula of Michigan, and married a man who owned a car. We set up house on the land where he lived, again in a rural area, 11 miles from the nearest town. With the area's flat topography, I figured that I'd continue my biking lifestyle and that we could both move toward ridding the world of another car. We upgraded our bikes, bought bike trailers, and got snow tires for winter riding. But there were obstacles we hadn't counted on. With winters bringing anywhere from 100 to 400 inches of snow, our ice-biking abilities were sometimes overwhelmed. The nearly complete lack of transit proved more limiting than we had expected. And we were frequently plagued by loose and lawless dogs.

We decided our location might call for a car-lite divorce. We continued to bike when we could, keeping the car in the garage to be used for longer-distance travel, some cargo-carrying trips, and during severe weather. We also kept our eyes open for pedal-powered or alternatively fueled vehicles that could at least help us reduce our use of gasoline. In the process, we came across a small home-converted electric vehicle at a good price and decided to give it a try. We added to our supply of photovoltaic panels, and charged the vehicle with solar energy when the sun allowed.

The electric vehicle didn't get us to the point of getting rid of an internal combustion car, but did allow more of our journeys to be gasoline-free. At the same time, having an electric vehicle has actually reconfirmed for us how much we like biking and appreciate its health, simplicity, and cost-saving benefits. We find ourselves gravitating to bikes as our first choice as we continue to experiment with various ways of reducing our travel and its impacts.

In going through these car divorces, first one way and then the other, I've learned that there are opportunities for car-free travel even in some of the most car-dependent places. I've also learned that there are a lot more people out there who have already divorced their cars, a small legion of folks who are quietly (or not so quietly) car-free or car-lite by preference. This book shares some of their stories and is enriched by their experiences — it is a celebration of their choices. That there are so many of them is especially impressive given the ways that our economy and infrastructure favor car use.

Even if the deck weren't as stacked in the car's favor, our society would still use cars, but we would use them less — and enjoy life more. If you're ready to move in this direction — if you're tired of being stuck in traffic, tired of automotive pollution, just plain tired of driving — *Divorce Your Car!* is written for you. Maybe you're a soccer parent, weary of chauffeuring your kids everywhere they want to go. Maybe you're a frustrated commuter, sick of the time you've wasted, the fumes you've breathed, the road rage you've experienced. Maybe you're concerned about smog or climate change and want to cut down on driving, but aren't quite sure how to do so. Maybe you're already car-free or car-lite and want to use this book as a resource to help others follow a similar path.

Whatever your case, this book will give you ideas for driving less or even not at all, as well as background on our automotive entanglement that argues for making that choice. Part I explores a few of the factors that led us to become so dependent on cars. It examines the ways in which a number of forces beyond free will or the "free market," including some government policies and business practices, helped propel our affair with the car into the marriage of today. Part II shares some of the compelling reasons for ending the marriage, providing details about damaging aspects of the relationship. Part III surveys the range of alternatives we can use as we divorce our cars and move to healthier means of mobility and access, and includes examples from car-free and car-lite folks who have done so. It also takes a quick look at some ways, including policy changes, that we can get support for divorcing cars; delves into the way our individual choices can build into collective change; and includes a vision of a less car-dependent world. The book ends by listing a few of the resources that can help get us closer to such a world.

I hope this book — part fact, part philosophy, part how-to — will demonstrate both the pressing need to drive less and the many opportunities we have to do so. I hope it will give you enough information and inspiration to pursue those opportunities. To those still tightly entangled in the auto-driver relationship, divorcing a car might seem the height of impossibility, or even foolhardiness. But venture into the territory of those who've done it and you'll find that divorce from a car is not only possible, it can bring unexpected delights and great rewards. On a collective level, divorcing cars can bring us cleaner air, clearer water, less noise, and friendlier communities. It can foster better transportation options, more compact cities, and correspondingly more farmland, wildlife habitat, and parks. On a personal level, it can be incredibly liberating, bringing less stress, more money, better health and fitness, reduced risk of accidental death, and a simpler lifestyle. Perhaps best of all, by divorcing your car you can gain the deep personal satisfaction of knowing you've helped to nurture not only yourself but also your community and the entire planet. By divorcing your car, you really can live happily ever after.

PART 1

Love's Been Blind:
How We Ended Up Married
to Cars

*"Since we love our cars with such passion,
it is only natural that we shut our eyes to their flaws."*

WOLFGANG ZUCKERMANN, *END OF THE ROAD*

From the infatuation of the 1890s to the entanglement of today, we've had over 100 tumultuous years of romance with the car. Part 1 explores the development of our automotive affair and a few of the factors that have influenced its current state. As a marriage counselor might tell you, it can help to review a relationship's track record before trying to solve its problems. With that in mind, this brief, eclectic chronicle focuses on some of the love affair's key trouble spots; as with most romances that end up on the rocks, ours with the car encountered bumps from the beginning. And sometimes, love's been blind. These first few chapters look at ways in which we've been seduced not just by automobility but also by car-favoring government policy, industry practice, and media promotion, ways in which our union with the car is in part a forced marriage and not simply a free-market choice.

CHAPTER 1

Falling Head Over Wheels:
The Advent of Cars

*"If you're married, there'll have been times when
you've said to yourself, 'Why the hell did I do it?'"*

GEORGE ORWELL, *COMING UP FOR AIR*

IN 1882, GERMAN ENGINE-BUILDER KARL BENZ took his fledgling internal combustion
carriage out for a spin on the streets of Stuttgart. He was promptly arrested. Benz,
though, did not let apprehension by the law stand in his way. Once home in
Mannheim, he did the same thing as many young lovers forbidden from flirtation:
he snuck out at night for testing trysts with his experimental auto. About the same
time and also in Germany, engineer Gottlieb Daimler began pursuing his own dalliance with the car, building four prototypes between 1885 and 1889. Benz was first
to announce a car for sale, advertising his gasoline-powered three-wheeler in an
1888 prospectus claiming the vehicle posed "no danger whatever." French agents,
entranced by automobility, soon started selling Benz buggies and cars with Daimler
engines to wealthy Parisians who used them for status-displaying promenades
along the Champs d'Elysees. And across the Atlantic, an 1889 *Scientific American*
article on the Benz car caught the rapt eyes of American inventors who'd been toy-
ing with their own steam-, electric-, and gasoline-powered versions of the horseless
carriage.[1]

The 19th century had already seen major changes in human travel. Passenger
trains started running in 1825 in England, quickly spreading to other countries.
Cable cars and then electric trolleys came to cities in the 1870s and 1880s, soon carrying loads of urban passengers. When bicycles showed up around the same time,
the public marveled at the personal freedom they allowed. Expectations of travel
changed; horizons broadened. Then cars motored into the mix. Even before Daimler
and Benz began romancing the car, several other inventors had dabbled with "loco-
mobility," though reactions to these early experiments were often less than enchant-
ed. Several places, including New York and Chicago, banned self-propelled vehicles
for periods in the 19th century. In 1865, an alarmed British Parliament passed the
Red Flag Act, placing two- to four-m.p.h. speed limits on "road locomotives" and
requiring they be preceded by a walking attendant carrying a red flag. When
Siegfried Marcus tested a motorized handcart on Austrian roads, he was called a
public nuisance and sent home by police. In France, Count Albert de Dion developed
a steam quadricycle; when he tried to produce it commercially, his own father won
a court order to restrain him.[2]

By the 1890s, though, public response began to shift. In 1893, cars displayed at Chicago's Columbian Exposition got scant attention. But in 1895, the first auto road races began to turn heads. A French car took only 48 hours to complete a 732-mile course from Paris to Bordeaux and back, averaging an astounding 15 miles per hour. Later that year, the *Chicago Times-Herald* sponsored a race which got publicity perhaps more dramatic than the contest itself; after several postponements, the cars finally ran in a snowstorm and only two finished the course. Still, newspapers worldwide trumpeted excited race reports, and the public began to swoon. French motoring enthusiasts founded the Automobile Club of France. The British, eager to pursue their own auto romance at faster than four m.p.h., lobbied to repeal the Red Flag Act and succeeded the following year. The flow of motor-vehicle-related applications into the U.S. Patent Office accelerated, growing to 500 on file by September 1895. That same year, Thomas Edison told reporters: "The horseless vehicle is the coming wonder." By the end of the century, scores of small carmakers in France and the U.S. made those nations the world's two top auto producers — the love affair with the car was underway.[3]

In many ways our romance with the car has followed a pattern common to human courtship, something we might call "The Early Flash of Insight that Soon Gets Forgotten." It happens when you meet someone, feel some attraction, and go out, but early on a red flag goes up and you have an intuitive flash that this person is unsuitable for long-term partnership. At first, the headiness of attraction leads you to forget this insight. You go out again and pretty soon have a full-fledged relationship on your hands, maybe even marriage. Eventually, though, the relationship develops problems for the very reason you foresaw. At this point you remember your insight with a big, loud "Oh, yeah," and re-examine why you ever got involved in the first place.

We are now collectively at this stage with the car. Some of us, in fact, have been asking: How did we end up *married* to motor vehicles? Many factors led us down the aisle — desires for improved independent mobility, idealism about the changes cars might bring, and fascination with automotive technology among them — but as they did, we lost sight of some initial red flags. Maybe we dismissed bad news that might have interfered with the infatuation, maybe encouragement of the love affair by media, industry, and government policies distracted us from drawbacks that might otherwise have cooled our automotive ardor. Whatever the case, what's interesting is just how many early warnings there were about motor vehicles, and how frequently we seem to have forgotten them. As this chapter explores the early romance, it serves in part as a reminder — a kind of "Oh, yeah" — that although cars can be quite seductive, we've known on some level from the beginning that they'd be problematic as a long-term love match.

Love Letters to the Car

"From the outset of its diffusion in the United States," writes historian James Flink, "the motor vehicle was given extensive and overwhelmingly favorable coverage in popular periodicals — coverage well beyond what an objective appraisal of the innovation's importance and potential at the time could have justified." He adds: "Close cooperation between the press and the automobile industry was established early." Besides the races co-sponsored by carmakers and the press, one famous early collaboration was that of car-builder Alexander Winton and Cleveland reporter Charles B. Shanks. In 1899, Winton took an auto-endurance trip from Cleveland to New York with Shanks in tow; around a million people saw them motor into New York, and the reporter's dramatic dispatches got credit for bringing these crowds. Others, too, credit the press with much of the early positive attention paid to cars. Historian Kenneth Richardson describes the British press as "one of the most powerful auxiliary forces in forwarding the development of motoring." The same was apparently true in France, where enthusiasts could choose from 25 different car publications by 1900.[4]

Many early reports about cars glowed with enthusiasm. "With the glitter of polished nickel and the sheen of many-colored enamels," wrote the *New York Times* in November 1900, "the first show of the Automobile Club of America was opened last night at Madison Square Garden." The next day, the paper gushed about the "neverending whirl of animation" and "sweeping curves of the self-propelled vehicles" displayed at the show. Such early descriptions of autos abound with the language of love. *Motor World* wrote of the automobile's "charm"; a 1900 *Scientific American* article waxed eloquent about the "great beauty" of one car and the "distinctive details ... dear to the heart" in another.[5]

The press helped the public open its arms to cars even before many cars were built. When *Horseless Age* premiered in 1895, pre-dating the U.S. auto industry, its editors wrote: "The appearance of a journal devoted to a branch of industry yet in an embryonic state, may strike some as premature." But, the magazine said of the impending auto, "the growing needs of our civilization demand it; the public believe in it, and await with lively interest its practical application to the daily business of the world." If people needed cars, though, not everyone knew it at that time. In 1896, at the first U.S. auto track races, bored spectators invented the cry "Get a horse!" and left in disgust.[6]

Press descriptions of the car's unending benefits continued nevertheless.

- "It is the greatest health-giving invention of a thousand years," Frank Munsey wrote in 1903.

- Car trips were considered good for the liver and were prescribed to treat tuberculosis; a New York City health commissioner wrote that drivers got "actual physical exercise" from "the slight, but purposeful effort demanded in swinging the steering wheel."

- Driving offered "a brisk activization of the entire organism," advised a German writer.

- "In cities and towns the noise and clatter of the streets will be reduced, a priceless boon to the tired nerves of this overwrought generation," forecast

Horseless Age in 1895. And, the magazine claimed, "streets will be cleaner, jams and blockades less likely to occur, and accidents less frequent."

🚗 *Scientific American* predicted in 1899 that cars would "eliminate a greater part of the nervousness, distraction, and strain of modern metropolitan life."[7]

Replacing horses with motors did solve some problems, among them that of city streets filled with manure. But many early writers also believed cars would make families closer, resolve overcrowding and pollution in cities, save money, eliminate class distinctions, and abolish slums.

🚗 They idealized commuting by car: "Imagine a healthier race of working-men ... who, in the late afternoon, glide away in their own comfortable vehicles to their little farms or homes in the country or by the sea twenty or thirty miles distant! They will be healthier, happier, more intelligent and self-respecting citizens."

A Quick (and Sometimes Dirty) Scrapbook of Our Affair with the Car Page One[8]

1888 Berta Benz (wife of Karl) and sons make the first long motorcar trip (62 miles) pushing the car up hills and stopping for several repairs — among them, Berta clears the fuel line with her hairpin and fixes an electrical short using her garters as insulating tape.

1896 Brothers J. Frank and Charles Duryea birth the U.S. auto industry, offering 13 gasoline cars for sale in Springfield, Massachusetts.

Bridget Driscoll becomes the first pedestrian killed by a car in London.

1899 The Automobile Club of Great Britain hosts its first major motor show, featuring a race between a horse and a motorcycle; the horse wins.

New York realtor H.H. Bliss becomes the first U.S. auto casualty when he steps off a trolley and is run over by an electric taxi trying to pass on the right. The taxi driver is not held responsible since he attempted to stop.

1900 The first European auto movie is produced: "How It Feels To Be Run Over."

1901 Discovery of the Spindletop oil gusher in Texas ushers in an era of cheap gasoline for American internal-combustion cars; some who hear the gusher blow believe it signifies the end of the world.

1903 Nelson Jackson makes the first successful car crossing of North America, then becomes the first traffic violator in Burlington, Vermont, for exceeding the six m.p.h. speed limit.

1906 A Stanley Steamer sets a speed record, breaking 124 m.p.h., then blows up.
A New York newspaper editorial warns that the car "stirs up primitive emotions."

1907 British prime minister Herbert Asquith recommends a heavy auto tax, calling the car "a luxury which is apt to degenerate into a nuisance."

🚜 They lauded cars as generators of serenity, forgiving less gentle attributes: "Instead of being a disturber of the peace, the automobile encourages the calm pleasures of repose and reflection. To be sure it is an occasional breaker of bones; but that is due alone to man's propensity to blunder."

🚜 They predicted cars would enhance access to fresh air: "The possession of a car ... Think of what it means. Every friend within 3,000 square miles can be visited, any place of worship or lecture or concert attended ... and with it all fresh air inhaled under exhilarating conditions."

🚜 The car, echoed *Country Life* in 1911, "has brought God's green fields and pure air seemingly nearer."[9]

By 1906, magazines frequently referred to cars as necessities. In 1907, *Harper's Weekly* stated as "fact" that "the automobile is essential to comfort and happiness" (perhaps helping readers realize they'd been uncomfortable and unhappy until the late 19th century). Composers began writing love songs about cars. "Come away with me Lucille, in my merry Oldsmobile," urged 1905's most popular tune. "The automobile is the idol of the modern age," commented one writer praising the car's romantic utility. "The man who owns a motorcar ... is a god to the women." Others claimed religious benefits for cars, as when E.C. Stokes declared, "Next to the church there is no factor in American life that does so much for the morals of the public as does the automobile ... If every family in the land possessed an automobile ... many of the problems of social unrest would be happily resolved ... The automobile is one of the country's best ministers, and best preachers."[10]

The Romance Heats Up

In 1900, bike and carmaker Col. Albert Pope declared his 15,000 dealers were "fairly howling" for cars in response to "enormous demand." A few years later, Ford Motor Company investor John W. Anderson wrote his father: "Now the demand for automobiles is a perfect craze." By 1901, 130 car manufacturers clustered around Paris; by 1905, 280 had started in Britain; from 1900 to 1908, 485 companies entered the U.S. auto business. There was money to be made there, and since early auto builders bought components from parts makers and assembled cars instead of constructing them from scratch, it was easy to get started without much capital. Car sales skyrocketed, especially in the U.S. where motor vehicle registrations swelled from 8,000 in 1900 to more than 458,000 by 1910.[11]

Around the turn of the century, steam, electric, and internal-combustion cars all received about equal attention from carmakers and the public. But developments like Texas oil discoveries and Detroit carmakers' use of gasoline power helped internal combustion pull ahead of the pack. As gasoline cars gained ground, the U.S. made advances in mass production and overtook France in 1904 to become the world's top auto producer. Low raw materials costs, the world's best machine tool industry, and favorable tariffs all fostered the auto industry in the U.S., which also had the world's biggest market for cars with its sizable middle class living in communities dispersed over a large area. The Ford Motor Company played crucial roles both in expanding U.S. car production and in encouraging mass consumption of cars, by mass-producing inexpensive Model Ts in 1908, then making them even cheaper in 1913 by using a moving assembly line. Cars rolled off the line at the astonishing speed of one every three minutes. Mesmerized by mass production and agog with the affordability it gave the Model T, the public flocked to dealers. By 1920, fully half the world's motor vehicles were Model T Fords. Model T sales sparked car cultures in Canada, Australia, and New Zealand, too, where — as in the U.S. — long distances between communities and relatively high, equitably distributed incomes encouraged car sales.[12]

As production picked up in the U.S. and Canada, car culture in North America and Europe began to diverge. While Europe imposed horsepower taxes, the U.S. had none; North America had cheaper, more plentiful gasoline; and both factors promoted the manufacture of more powerful but less efficient engines in the U.S. and Canada. Industrial culture also differed; American carmakers focused on quantity while Europeans retained a labor-intensive, quality-oriented but low-volume production style. And U.S. carmakers were more aggressive than Europeans about not only satisfying car demand, but expanding it. By lowering prices on mass-produced vehicles like the Model T, paying auto workers wages that helped them afford cars, advertising extensively, and selling cars on buy-now-pay-later plans more widely available than in Europe, U.S. carmakers induced more and more consumers to desire and buy cars.

> *"Once upon a time, the American met the automobile and fell in love. Unfortunately, this led him into matrimony, and so he did not live happily ever after."*
>
> JOHN KEATS, THE INSOLENT CHARIOTS

As of a few years after World War I, auto manufacturing was North America's top industry and the power and wealth of the auto business had become immense.[13]

Letters Not So Lovely

Despite automotive attractions and amorous write-ups, dissatisfaction with cars crept into the early romance, hinting of conflicts to come. Sometimes short-term solutions reduced these problems, but from the perspective of decades later, it's clear that few of them went away for good.

Early road rage: "Never in my life have I been cursed at so frequently as on my automobile trip in the year 1902," wrote Otto Bierbaum of his journey between Berlin and Italy. "Every German dialect from Berlin through Dresden, Vienna, and Munich to Bolzano was represented, as well as all the idioms of the Italian language ... not to mention all the wordless curses: shaking fists, stuck-out tongues, bared behinds, and others besides." Early driving habits often gave reason for anger. Some road rudeness occurred between drivers — such as leaving another motorist in one's dust (and in those days the dust was considerable) — but most took place between drivers and non-drivers. A French pedestrian wrote this open letter to the Parisian Chief of Police in 1896:

Yesterday evening at six o'clock on the rue de Courcelles, I, my wife, and my children were nearly run over by a gentleman in an automobile who came racing by at the speed of a train ... I must count myself among those who believe there is no safety anymore on the streets of Paris ... From this day on I shall carry a revolver in my pocket whenever I go out, and I will shoot at the next crazy idiot who tries to flee after he was on the verge of running over my family and me.[14]

After this ran in Parisian papers, the French car magazine *La Locomotion Automobile* fired back. If pedestrians armed themselves with revolvers, it wrote, drivers would carry machine guns.[15]

M.M. Musselman, writing of a 1904 trip in his father's horseless carriage, recounts: "We overtook prancing horses that sometimes veered off in terror; we passed the Del Prado Hotel ... where an old gentleman shouted imprecations and shook his cane at us as we chugged too close to his coattails; and finally we passed a bicycle cop who gave us a severe warning to slow down to ten miles per hour." Of another ride, he recalls:

We encountered a skittish horse attached to a rather elegant-looking surrey. The horse reared up on its hind legs and backed the surrey sidewise across the road. In a twinkling father swung the Marmon off the road and through a barbed-wire fence. Then instead of slowing down, he plowed through a cornfield for a hundred feet, then finally swung back through the fence and regained the road.[16]

Little wonder that *Overland Monthly* wrote in 1909 that "it is no secret that the average farmer has more or less antipathy for the motorist." A speaker at 1905's National Grange meeting gave reasons for this aversion: "Accidents of the most shocking nature have been of common occurrence. In some sections of the country travel upon the country roads [with horses] has been reduced to the driving absolutely necessary, cutting out all [horse and buggy] pleasure driving." Touring cars that began cruising country roads in the summer of 1904 further outraged farmers by frightening livestock and raising dust, which damaged crops and dirtied clean laundry on the line. Auto tourists also trespassed and plucked farmers' fruits for picnics. Some country residents responded with hostility. In parts of the U.S. and Canada, they tossed broken glass and nails onto roads to ruin cars' tires. Farmers near Rochester, Minnesota, plowed their roads so a car couldn't travel them but a horse and buggy could. Ohio farmers threatened to boycott businesses whose owners purchased automobiles. New Jersey farmers passed a resolution withholding support from any car-owning political candidate.[17]

The antipathy was intense, but ultimately farmers began defecting from these car wars. As low-cost cars became available, they got their own Model Ts and began using them for trips to town and market. Reports of automotive animosity, for the time being, faded.

Rich vs. poor: Early on, the car served mainly as a dalliance for the upper class. Well-to-do sportsmen, engineers, and businessmen became the first car buyers in most countries. Doctors, too, were among early auto-buyers, as cars provided fast transport to medical emergencies. Coming after railroads, cars acquired what Wolfgang Sachs calls "a restorative significance" for the rich. The train, he writes, had threatened the wealthy's sense of place and power: "What the common people welcomed as a democratic advance, individuals of more privileged position greeted with a snort." Indeed, the Duke of Wellington expressed disapproval of railroads in 1835, saying "they only encourage common people to move around needlessly." The automobile, though, was welcomed by the rich, who "used its speed and power to display their social superiority," Sachs adds. The automobile "served better than any other object as a status symbol, because by its very nature it commanded public attention: one drove on the streets in clear view of everyone."[18]

Not only were the less fortunate reminded publicly of their poverty when wealthy motorists drove by, but cars also began taking some of what little they did have: public street space. In places, lower-class resentment of autos and their owners inspired stone-throwing sprees. In some New York neighborhoods in 1904, stone-throwing at motorists became so rampant that the city called out special police to stop it. In 1906, Princeton University president Woodrow Wilson expressed concern that automobiles allowed their owners to display wealth so ostentatiously, the poor would be driven past envy to socialism.[19]

This split between rich and poor was mitigated as low-cost cars emerged. There continued to be those who couldn't afford cars, but as auto ownership grew, their voices faded.

Dominating the streetscape, changing the landscape: As people noticed cars taking over public streets, some objected. In 1903 British Parliament minister Cathcart Watson harangued motorists for presuming "the right to drive the public off the roads. Harmless men, women and children, dogs and cattle, had all got to fly for their lives at the bidding of one of these slaughtering, stinking engines of iniquity."[20] In 1912, Austrian Dr. Michael Freiherr von Pidoll wrote:

> Where does the motorist get the right "to master" — as he boasts — the street? It in no way belongs to him, but to the population as a whole ... Automobile traffic in its present-day form involves, as we have seen, the constant endangerment of passersby or other vehicles, as well as a severe infringement on those community relations that correspond to an advanced culture.[21]

Parked cars, too, created problems. By 1916, *Automobile* magazine lamented that "the parking problem" in cities was every day growing "more acute ... We are facing something which was never foreseen in the planning of our towns, a thing which has come upon us so swiftly that there has been no time to grasp the immensity of the problem till we are almost overcome by it." By the 1920s, parked cars filled 30 percent of Washington, D.C.'s downtown street space.[22]

Those fed up with car-induced urban problems could, of course, use cars to get out of cities and, at first, many apparently agreed with demographer Adna Ferrin Weber's 1898 remark that "the 'rise of the suburbs' is by far the most cheering movement of modern times." But by the 1920s, drivers began to shun auto problems even as the populace became more auto-dependent. House buyers sought and paid more for homes on quiet, narrow streets to avoid wider car-filled boulevards. And commentators like conservationist Benton MacKaye began to complain: "The motor slum in the open country is today as massive a piece of defilement as the worst of the old-fashioned urban industrial slums."[23]

Rattletraps and repairs: Early cars required repairs so often it became the topic of songs: "He'd Have to Get Under, Get Out and Get Under (To Fix Up His Automobile)," crooned one popular early-20th-century ballad. The wealthy handled frequent repairs with chauffeurs who served as mechanics. Until a repair industry developed, other motorists corrected mechanical maladies themselves or hoped to find a progressive blacksmith or bicycle engineer. Flats and punctures were so common that turn-of-the-century motorists went through an average 37.5 tires each year.[24] Other problems arose, too, as recorded in this motor-diary entry about a 1903 drive through North Wales:

> Left Menai 9 a.m. Called at Bangor for a new tyre, could not get one: ran over a sheep: at Bethesda changed gears so rapidly that I broke the connecting rod of the steering gear: being at the top of a long hill there was nothing for it but to go down the hill backwards in the hope of getting to the bottom alive, and finding a blacksmith: this was done ... after wait of 2½ hours blacksmith finished his job, but the product of his labour was ¹⁄₁₆th of an inch too small: waited another 2½ hours ...[25]

Early cars were also uncomfortable, "intended evidently for people with rubber back bones," wrote Booth Tarkington in 1903. Drivers and passengers wore layers of protective clothes to ward off discomfort. Tarkington also recorded the typical exhaustion of travelers after auto journeys; once arriving at hotels, they "retired instantly to bed and did not rise again until noon of the next day."[26]

"A very shaky and disagreeable conveyance altogether ...."

QUEEN VICTORIA'S OPINION OF THE MOTOR CAR, IN RAYMOND FLOWER AND MICHAEL WYNN JONES, *100 YEARS ON THE ROAD*

Why not give it up after all this trouble? For one thing, some clever entrepreneurs turned car problems into opportunities: not long into the 20th century, support industries evolved to compensate for driving's discomforts. Yet while new technologies eased driving somewhat, car maintenance and repairs continued to be time-consuming. But perhaps many motorists felt like Rudyard Kipling when in 1904 he wrote, "I like motoring because I have suffered for its sake."[27]

Speed and carnage: Early auto magazines admitted motorists were obsessed with speed. Speed limits were frequently broken, and authorities soon established speed traps. Early speedsters often disregarded traffic cops' summons to stop; in Chicago, the situation became so bad that policemen began shooting at drivers who ignored speed traps. Beyond such cat-and-mouse games, speed had serious consequences. Road races horrified many with their carnage. The 1903 Paris-Madrid-Paris race killed five drivers and several spectators; labeled the "Race of Death," it was canceled before completion. Every-day driving took its toll, too. As car use grew, newspapers carried reports of serious crashes nearly every day. In 1908, *Horseless Age* rationalized: "When the speed craze dies out ... accidents will become so rare as to stamp the automobile the very safest of road vehicles." The very next year, though, the magazine admitted "the 'automobile hazard' is not likely to decline."[28]

Non-motorists, fearing for their safety, began deserting the streets. No wonder: by 1924, cars killed over 20,000 people a year in the U.S., almost half of them children. Another 700,000 were injured, and over a billion dollars in property was damaged. Auto death rates went from 1.8 per 100,000 in 1910 to 26.0 per 100,000 in 1929. Cars slaughtered animals, too, in great numbers: a 1924 Iowa investigation found 225 roadkills of 29 wild and domestic species on one 632-mile journey. But over time, habituation to driving's dangers seemed to set in. Ultimately, safety improvements shaved down crash and death rates, but absolute numbers of deaths and injuries have remained high.[29]

Traffic congestion: As some journals championed cars as a cure for road congestion, others noticed they didn't quite work that way. Experience soon showed that cars clogged roads as much as other vehicles. Traffic jams became "the norm" by 1912, probably earlier in some places. By the 1920s, congestion dropped speeds on New York's Fifth Avenue to under four miles per hour; in Atlanta, merchants complained congestion was causing a decline in downtown business.[30]

Bigger roads were quickly proclaimed the answer, but some noticed that didn't work either. As early as 1907, a writer in the *Municipal Journal and Engineer* observed that, though early road-widening projects had been expected to relieve congestion, "the result has appeared to be exactly the opposite." As pieces of the coast-to-coast Lincoln Highway were built across the U.S. in the teens and twenties, recounts one history, "each improvement stimulated traffic; motorists making up that traffic compared improved with unimproved sections of highway and demanded more improvements, which brought more traffic, and so on, down to the present and seemingly on to an indefinite date in the future." In 1916, Woodrow Wilson commented that burgeoning numbers of U.S. motorists "use [roads] up almost as fast as we make them." Road-building not only failed to keep up with quick growth in car numbers; as paving accelerated, it encouraged more car-buying and driving. As historian John Rae observed, the building of new streets and highways to accommodate cars touched off "a race between road and vehicle that is still in progress, with the vehicle consistently ahead."[31]

Fouling the air: In 1896, electric-car maker Pedro Salom wrote that "all the gasoline motors we have seen belch forth from their exhaust pipe a continuous stream of partially unconsumed hydrocarbons in the form of a thick smoke with a highly noxious odor. Imagine thousands of such vehicles on the streets, each offering up its column of smell!" Even General Motors founder W.C. Durant called gasoline cars "noisy and smelly" at one point. As early as 1912, *Country Life in America* wrote: "Physicians are now announcing that the opaque smoke exhausted from the rear of some automobiles is not only nauseating, but that large quantities of it are actually dangerous to the health of the community." Adding to farmers' complaints of crop damage, doctors reported that road dust, too, was bad for health in that it increased throat and eye infections. Eye drops were advertised as "a tonic for the 'auto eye'."[32]

In 1904 an Austrian anti-pollution cartoon showed a pedestrian wearing an elaborate gas mask to navigate through the dust-and-exhaust clouds left by a motor-car. "Wandering machines, traveling with an incredible rate of speed, scramble and smash and shriek along all the rural ways," bemoaned C.F.G. Masterman in *The Condition of England 1909*. "You can see evidence of their activity in the dust-laden hedges of the south country roads, a grey mud colour, with no evidence of green." Even drivers admitted to this side effect:

> What a dust storm we stirred up leaving Italy! ... Georg raced along, demanding from the car all it had to give ... and behind us there swelled a colossal cone ... We outraged the pedestrians with a gas attack — their faces pulled into a single grimace — and we left them behind in a world without definition, in which the fields and the trees in the distance had lost all color to a dry layer of powder.[33]

As paved roads became more common, dust problems dropped from view. Though concern over car exhaust continued, it was vastly overshadowed as a pollutant by industrial smokestacks. While some continued to complain of reeking gasoline fumes, no campaign against them mounted until decades later.

"Within only two or three years, every one of you will have yielded to the horseless craze and be a boastful owner of a metal demon ... Restfulness will have entirely disappeared from your lives; the quiet of the world is ending for ever."

OVERHEARD IN PARIS BY BOOTH TARKINGTON AROUND 1900, IN JULIAN PETTIFER AND NIGEL TURNER, *AUTOMANIA*

Money: When it came to money and cars, love was especially blind. Many publications extolled the money-saving qualities of motor vehicles, even when new cars, priced from $1,000 to $5,000, cost about ten times more than a good horse. "Any man who can afford a horse can better afford an automobile," wrote *Horseless Age* in 1903. "So far as we can at present see, the displacement of the horse will cheapen living and travel, certainly not increase them," said another writer that year in the *Independent*. Yet later, after more people had actually used and maintained cars, stories changed. "According to my experience and that of my friends," one driver wrote in 1906, "it is impossible to maintain an automobile as cheaply as horses ..." In 1909, when cars cost about five times what a horse did, the "indefinite" life of cars argued for their economy, said *Country Life in America*. Actually, cars lasted only around five years on average at that time.[34]

As automobile owners began realizing that cars often cost more than a horse and carriage, they seemed to slip blithely into denial. They ignored comparative costs and focused instead on economies stemming from the car's speed, endurance, and range. Car buyers also overlooked the fact that economies only applied if one drove many miles, but at that time average families did not travel by horse and buggy enough to actually save money by purchasing a car. Even the costs of going into debt to purchase cars were overlooked, as a 1907 committee report from a Pittsburgh women's club complained: "So mad has the race for social supremacy become ... that owners of houses are mortgaging them in order to buy as many and as speedy automobiles as their neighbors. Extravagance is reckless and something must be done before utter ruin follows in the wake of folly." In 1908, another car critic noted that "many who never felt that they were in a position to purchase a horse and carriage ... now indulge in automobiles costing several thousand dollars originally ... A resident of Boston said a year ago that one would be astonished to know the number of second mortgages that had been placed upon houses in the vicinity of his city to enable the owners to procure cars." As historian James Flink observes, this was "indeed a strange outcome from the adoption of an innovation whose advocates had praised economy as one of its main advantages."[35]

Through at least 1910, there was little public discussion of potential collective costs of mass conversion to private car ownership, or of the possibility that the total spent on roads, fuel, and cars per person could well exceed what might otherwise need to be spent by society on rail and mass transit. By 1933, however, the President's Research Committee on Social Trends recognized that the "taking to wheels of an entire population had a profound effect on the aggregate burden of taxation."[36] By that time, though, the idea that cars provided cheap transport had become too ingrained to be dislodged by any government report.

"Many a family that has lost its car, has found its soul."

1932 NEWSPAPER COMMENT ON DROP IN CAR OWNERSHIP DUE TO THE DEPRESSION

The Crash of a Whirlwind Courtship

As love-struck auto buyers continued to disregard discouraging words about the car, the 1920s roared with the sound of millions of new internal combustion vehicles in an auto-induced boom especially intense in the U.S. From 1920 to October 1929, the country's motor vehicle registrations nearly tripled from ten to 26.7 million. But some believe, as James Flink writes, that the automobile boom "sowed the seeds of its own demise." Flink argues:

> Mass motorization played a key role in creating the most important necessary conditions underlying the Depression ... The steep decline in aggregate spending evident by the late 1920s ... can be shown to have resulted from the economic dislocations that were an essential ingredient of the automobile boom, and from the inevitable drying up of that boom.[37]

One contributor to these economic dislocations was the shift from savings and cash purchases to buying on credit. Cars more than any other product led to the abandonment of thrift as a value, generating unprecedented growth in credit purchases; before 1920, few items had been bought this way. Installment buying for cars, first offered by French banks in 1906, spread to U.S. banks in 1910. Then, despite a 1916 National Auto Chamber of Commerce proclamation calling installment plans unethical, car companies followed banks into the financing business, making car loans even easier to obtain and expanding the market for cars. General Motors Acceptance Corporation (GMAC) was founded in 1919 and wrote $2 million in car loans within a year. By the mid-twenties, an estimated 75 percent of new cars across the country were bought using loans and installment plans. The National Association of Credit Men, concerned that too much was being spent on cars, passed a resolution condemning the growth of car sales on credit.[38]

Government, too, was spending more on cars. Road construction absorbed increasing amounts of government budgets at all levels, finally becoming the second-largest category of public expenditure for the '20s. In 1929, U.S. government expenditures on roads totaled $2.237 billion but revenues collected from various special motor vehicle taxes came to only $849 million, requiring about 62 percent of road spending to come from other sources.[39] Cars helped drive us further into debt, writes M.M. Musselman, at many levels:

> The automobile became the biggest customer of the coal and iron mines, the steel mills, the plate-glass and the rubber factories and many others. When the motor companies borrowed money to expand in order to build more cars, all the companies that supplied them had to do the same. In addition we built roads and filling stations and suburbs at a terrific pace — all on the installment plan — to take care of the growing auto industry. And the more people there were who had cars, the more there were who needed them, or thought they did. When, finally, almost everybody owed money to a bank or a finance company and almost every business was expanding on borrowed money or floating stock issues to meet the demands of this constantly expanding credit the actual cash money of the land was spread mighty thin. The place where it was spread thinnest of all was in Wall Street.[40]

Adding fuel to the fire, the auto industry vastly expanded advertising within the decade and became one of the heaviest users of ad space in magazines, newspapers, and other media. Just in magazines, auto ad spending went from $3.5 million in 1921 to over $9 million in 1927. "Advertising," writes James Flink, "also undoubtedly helped push automobile sales beyond the bounds of sanity in the 1920s."[41]

As all this car-buying saturated the market, many carmakers acted as if the boom would never end and overproduced heavily in the late 1920s. In autumn 1929 as the stock market plunged, auto sales manager Clarence Eldridge condemned his own industry for its role in the mess. In a speech to the Minnesota Automobile

Dealers Association, he chastised the auto business for not recognizing and "more intelligently [adjusting] production to the absorptive capacity of the market." He reproached his industry for exploiting "all of the methods, sound or unsound, which might sell new cars." He placed responsibility "with the automobile manufacturers. It is they who by their blind worship at the shrine of the goddess 'quantity production,' have created this situation." [42]

The whirlwind early car courtship ended. Luxury car sales, which had peaked at 150,000 in 1927 in the U.S., plummeted to less than 20,000 by 1933. Employment in the auto industry dropped to 40 percent of mid-1920s levels. U.S. new car production dropped 75 percent from 1929 to 1932, and a number of small car producers went out of business. During the Depression, car registrations dropped slightly in the U.S. They dropped more sharply in Canada, where farmers who couldn't afford gasoline hitched their horses to cars which had the engines removed.[43]

> *"By the end of the first decade of the twentieth century the automobile ... was already potentially what it would become in fact — an item of incredible mass consumption."*
>
> JOHN RAE, *THE AMERICAN AUTOMOBILE*

But despite the crash, the car had already snared us. The auto boom, however much it contributed to the Great Depression, profoundly affected culture and economics. Of all the world's countries, the U.S. fell hardest for the car: by 1927, there was one car for every 5.3 U.S. residents. Not far behind came New Zealand, with a car for every 10.5 people; Canada, with one for each 10.7 citizens; and Australia, with one for every 16 residents. No other country at this time had more than one car for every 43 people (Argentina) or one for every 44 residents (France and Great Britain).[44]

Automobility helped usher in consumerism, allowing the car and consumer culture to roll hand-in-hand through the rest of the 20th century. And almost without knowing it we had betrothed ourselves to the auto. As the 1933 report of the President's Research Committee on Social Trends stated: "Imperceptibly, car ownership has created an 'automobile psychology.' The automobile has become a dominant influence in the life of the individual and he, in a real sense, has become dependent upon it."[45] We were hooked, and about to get even more so.

CHAPTER 2

Other Suitors Drop by the Wayside: The Decline of Non-Car Transport

"The future that lies before the motor car is big enough to require no fear of rivals."

HENRY FARRAND GRIFFIN, 1913, IN KENNETH AND BLANCHE SCHNEIDER, *THE QUOTABLE CAR*

THROUGH THE 20TH CENTURY'S EARLY DECADES, we weren't yet trapped in monogamy with the car. Until at least the 1920s, even North America still had an array of transportation choices: streetcars, bicycles, horse-drawn wagons, electric cars, gas cars, and interurban as well as long-distance trains. But the car increasingly replaced these other travel means and, rather than public fervor for automobiles taking its own course, government and business in effect lent the love affair a hand; especially in the U.S., certain regulatory policies and industry practices also fostered the decline of non-car travel. As we abandoned other transport suitors, we marched further down the aisle toward a union some have called "a match made in Detroit."[1]

Good-bye to the Horse and Buggy

Until the 1920s, horses provided significant transport, especially to those who couldn't afford autos. More horses than cars roamed St. Louis, for instance, until 1916; in 1920, that city still housed close to 20,000 horses. The horse, though, could be a sloppy escort. Manure turned crowded city streets into avenues of muck, breeding flies and disease. Every day in 1900, New York City's horses dropped 2.5 million pounds of manure and 60,000 gallons of urine into streets. British communities swept up an estimated 20 billion pounds of manure a year. So-called "street dust" — germy particles of dried horse dung — irritated noses and throats. Aromatic stables often occupied crowded tenement neighborhoods, making such places even less livable. When horses died, disposal of their carcasses was difficult and they sometimes drew predators into cities.[2]

Reformers of the day thus quickly embraced technologies that could dump the dirty horse. First electric streetcars displaced the horse-drawn omnibus; by 1908, around 500,000 horses had been retired by electric trolleys in U.S. cities. Bicycles, too, replaced horses, especially in the 1890s. As the car drove in around the turn of the century, horse populations hit an all-time peak — 30 million in the U.S., 3.5 million in Britain, a horse per person in Australia — but their numbers soon fell. Buggy makers became concerned about their future and entered the auto business as a hedge. Livery-stable owners switched to running garages or car-rental businesses. By 1910, the value of cars to the U.S. economy had surpassed that of the carriage and wagon trade. By the 1920s, horses on city streets had become the exception.[3]

In the country, meanwhile, as the press forecast a host of benefits farmers would reap from motor vehicles, rural residents got over their earlier distaste for cars enough to consider putting horses out to pasture. For one thing, switching to cars would free millions of acres — 100 million just in the U.S. — devoted to horse fodder: horses consumed 40 percent of the U.S. grain crop. The car would "remove the last serious obstacle to the farmer's success," said one writer in *Harper's Weekly* in 1907. "It will market his surplus product, restore the value of his lands, and greatly extend the scope and pleasure of all phases of country life." By eliminating isolation, said the press, cars would encourage succeeding generations to stay on the farm. The car's engine, with the strength of several horses in one small (albeit noisy) package, would ease farm labor. Motor vehicles would move food to market more cheaply, giving consumers lower prices as farmers gained more profits — the best of all possible worlds.[4]

Model Ts and mass-produced tractors increasingly displaced real horsepower on farms especially after World War I. During the war, the British government purchased tractors to help combat food shortages. U.S. farmers, too, prompted by government slogans like "Buy Tractors and Win the War," bought tractors to increase crop production. But after the war ended, farmers found themselves in a bind. Food prices dropped, but farms had to continue using tractors and maintaining high production in part to cover higher costs of tractor payments and the artificial fertilizers they had to use in place of manure.[5]

Thus the mechanization touted to bring farmers prosperity ultimately brought many just the opposite. Farmers first bought cars and tractors mainly for their supposed economic advantages. But as early as 1928, analyst Harvey Peck determined that motorization decreased the average farmer's net income.[6] Tractors raised farming's capitalization and fixed operating costs, so to stay competitive a farmer had to invest more money and raise more crops. The overproduction encouraged by tractors led to a food glut in the 1920s and depressed conditions for farmers. At the same time, new roads and suburbanization increased property taxes near cities and encouraged farmers to sell their acreage, as they realized they could make more money auctioning land for development than by continuing to work it.

The number of cars on U.S. farms went from 85,000 in 1911 to two million in 1920 to almost five million in 1930. Tractor numbers multiplied, too. In 1929, as tractors on U.S. farms grew to five times the 1919 level, the Hoover Committee on Recent Economic Changes noted that farm mechanization allowed "enormous economies in the production of staple agricultural products, but its effective utilization demands larger operating units and a more specialized type of economic organization; it permits also of a considerable release of manpower." The "release of manpower" from farms led to migration into cities, the reverse of what car advocates had promised. Tractor-generated overproduction and drought fed the 1930s dustbowl and even more farm failures. "The family farm was being killed off by automobility," writes James Flink. By 1965, more than 30 million Americans had moved from the country to the city.[7]

In replacing the country horse with Model Ts and tractors, we decreased the isolation of country dwellers and increased the production of food. In replacing city horses with cars, we cleaned streets of manure, eliminated horse-related accidents, and quieted the noise from iron-shod hooves clattering on cobblestones. But as we cleared up one set of social, economic, health, and pollution problems, we substituted another. Among those who recognized that abandoning hooved transport might not be altogether positive was Winston Churchill, who declared: "I have always thought that the substitution of the internal combustion machine for the horse marked a very gloomy milestone in the progress of mankind."[8]

"I Love My Horse and Wagon But Oh! You Buick Car."

EARLY 20TH-CENTURY SONG TITLE

Renouncing the Railroads

Before mid-19th century, it was rail that captured the public's heart, changed lifestyles, and altered landscapes. Knowing that a rail line could make or break a community's economy, local politicians were eager to embrace the train and at first did almost anything they could to get tracks through their towns. On both sides of the Atlantic, railroads grew so quickly that some soon dwarfed the governments of places they served.[9]

In the U.S., however, the relationship between people and railroads soured fast. Rail magnates soon gained reputations as powermongers. They bought off politicians and manipulated prices to put competitors out of business. Where they had monopolies, they sometimes gouged shipping customers, particularly farmers, to make up for losses in more competitive locales. Shady stock manipulations by railroads caused small stockholders, again including farmers, to lose money. Tabloids of the time painted pictures of fat-cat corruption, arrogance, and lavish lifestyles among rail tycoons. Periodicals carried color spreads of William Vanderbilt's two-million-dollar vacation "cottage," for example, along with reports of Vanderbilt's response when asked if his railroad would be willing to suffer a loss in the public interest: "The public be damned!"

The public responded with anger, and anti-rail sentiment was still high as cars entered the transport scene. By the end of the 19th century, railroads, cars, and the public fell into roles not unlike the players in an 1890s melodrama. The good public, itself the damsel in distress, saw railroads (run by robber barons) as the greasy, mustachioed villain. The car, on the other hand, was widely perceived as the clean-cut hero arriving to pluck the bound-and-gagged damsel off the tracks. Instead of being tied by the villainous trains, the public would find freedom with the heroic car. Auto interests played up these contrasting images of cars-good and trains-bad, and U.S. government policy often reflected this perspective, too. In 1887, Congress had created the Interstate Commerce Commission (ICC), which layered increasingly complicated regulations on railroads. The ICC also refused repeatedly to grant significant rate increases to trains and, not long into the twentieth century, this began cutting deeply into rail profits. About this time Congress decided to help autos and trucks by passing the first Federal Aid Road Act of 1916, and then the Federal Highway Act of 1921.

Railroads suffered even more as trucking, initially unregulated and helped by government road handouts, began to take over much of rail's profitable long-distance freight business. When railroads finally complained about trucking's unfair advantages, they caught the ear of President Warren Harding who told Congress that only subsidies made trucking profitable. Still, the first serious regulation of trucking didn't come until 1935. Even then, the U.S. government's different attitudes toward roads and rail persisted, manifesting during the Depression in the support each received: the government gave railways loans to upgrade rights-of-way, for instance, but paid entirely for road rights-of-way. The Depression-era Works Progress Administration gave ten times the funding to roads as to rail.[10] Thus, by the 1930s, a pattern of government subsidy for motor vehicles had been established and, in the meantime, serious damage had been done to U.S. trains.

In some other countries, policy and practice encouraged rail and road modes to work together, each taking on roles at which they were most effective and efficient: railroads handled long hauls and truckers took short shipments and door-to-door deliveries. Britain and Canada developed public-private partnerships overseeing rail service, and European countries nationalized their railroads. Trains in these countries fared better, but beginning in the 1920s, U.S. trains hemorrhaged passengers. Interurban railway ridership in Ohio, for example, dropped from a 1919 high of 257 million passengers to less than 40 million in 1933.[11] U.S. rail passenger travel had reached a peak of 47 billion passenger-miles in 1920.[12] As of 1916, U.S. railways had employed 1.7 million people and were worth $21 billion. But during the Depression about a third of U.S. rail carriers went bankrupt, and passenger rail, traditionally underwritten by freight operations, suffered accordingly.[13]

While trains did rebound during World War II, decades of unfavorable policies and poor returns took an even more serious toll after the war. By the 1970s, U.S. trains were gasping for breath — not surprisingly, since in preceding decades the U.S. government had spent 62 times as much on roads as on rail. Even so, 1970s trains still carried millions of commuters to work and accounted for twice the freight ton-miles carried by trucks. To save some semblance of rail service, the U.S. government deregulated rail freight and partially nationalized passenger rail by creating Amtrak. Since then, U.S. freight and passenger lines have recovered somewhat, despite still being saddled by a governmental double standard that subsidizes cars but only reluctantly invests in rail.

> "I am even inclined to go a step further and hazard the opinion that the motor will kill the railway."
>
> HENRY NORMAN, BRITISH M.P., 1903,
> IN KENNETH AND BLANCHE SCHNEIDER,
> *THE QUOTABLE CAR*

Breaking Up with the Bike

In the 1890s, robust demand for bikes made them an important economic force. More than four million bicycles wheeled around North America by 1896, for an increasing array of transport purposes. Bicycle touring supported numerous country inns. Police officers and telephone linemen used bikes. In Chicago, the postmaster hastened mail delivery and saved $5,000 a year by switching postal carriers to bicycles, and at least one bike ambulance carried patients to hospitals at speeds the horse-drawn equivalent couldn't match.[14]

Some, however, complained that the bicycle affected the economy too much. The bicycle's popularity rose so quickly it was soon accused of draining money from other industries. Shoemakers sat idle, lamenting that hardly anyone walked anymore. Saloonkeepers complained that drinking had declined due to cycling. Consumption of cigars dropped by 700 million a year during bicycling's peak. Instead of spending Sunday afternoons in taverns over a smoke and brew, writes historian Robert A. Smith, "the young bloods were out on their bicycles, scorching through the streets and breathing nothing but clean air." The bicycle became a sort of multi-purpose scapegoat. *Bicycle World* wrote in 1898: "Nowadays, if there is an elopement, a stagnation in the peanut market, a glut in smoking tobacco, or a small attendance at the theaters, everyone who is a loser points to the bicycle and says, 'You did it.'"[15]

Besides contributing to early declines in demand for horses, the bike threatened trolleys and interurban trains, and some even sued to stop the bicycle. Construction of the Pasadena Cycleway, for instance, an elevated nine-mile bike path from Pasadena to downtown Los Angeles, was halted two years after construction began in 1898 by the Southern Pacific Railroad, which feared losses of Pasadena-to-L.A. passenger fares. Teamsters and cab drivers, too, waged wars with bikes. As conflicts for street space increased, laws were passed banning cyclists from certain areas, including parks and sidewalks.

While these conflicts may have dimmed some of bicycling's luster, the bike rolled even closer to its undoing by unwittingly furthering the adoption of the automobile, particularly with cyclists' support of good roads. In North America especially, cars drew attention from bikes and ultimately crowded them off the now-paved roads that bicyclists had helped to win. Socialites in summer resorts who had once ridden bikes began driving electric runabouts. Magazines like *Outing* and *Wheel* that had championed bikes began defecting to cars. One article pointed out a feature of motor vehicles that the bicycle could never hope to equal: "The love-making possibilities that are shadowed forth in the horseless carriage will cause it to be the vehicle more favored by those sentimentally inclined."[16]

A few factors may have kept the bicycle in wider use for longer periods in Europe. With more compact, closely spaced communities, Europeans had more and easier bicycling opportunities than people in more sparsely settled North America, Australia, and New Zealand. And European car and gasoline prices stayed high, so bicycles remained an important low-cost means of transport for more people for a longer period. But in the U.S., where the automotive love affair was strongest, the bicycle was set aside almost as precipitously as it had been embraced.

A major blow to the bike was dealt by business interests that had already begun defecting to cars. In 1897, Col. Albert Pope — whose Pope Manufacturing Company was the biggest bicycle builder in the U.S. — began offering electric cars for sale. He also started a bicycle price war that ultimately dropped bike prices from around $125, typically, to as low as $16. That led to a sales boom in 1897, and a bust in 1898. Reworking the weakened bicycle industry, Pope joined John D. Rockefeller and other financial powers in 1899 to form the American Bicycle Company, a monopolistic trust that controlled major U.S. bicycle builders, dealers, and patents. After a series of financial maneuvers, Pope and Rockefeller solidified control of the ABC in 1902; ten months later the company defaulted on its bonds and went into receivership. The affair tarnished the bike industry's image, depleted much of its capital, and put about 400 small bicycle makers out of business.[17]

As the hundred or so independent cycle builders still remaining suffered through a recession, the big manufacturers went into car-building, motorcycle-making, and development of military machines, draining capital, intellectual talent, and

---

A Quick (and Sometimes Dirty) Scrapbook of Our Affair with the Car Page Two[18]

1908 Ford Motor Company introduces the Model T.

William C. Durant unites 23 businesses in a holding company called General Motors.

1911 The London General Omnibus Company retires its last horse-drawn vehicle.

1914 Ford Motor Company raises wages to $5 a day, double the prevailing rate, in part to combat 370 percent worker turnover due to the rigors of working on an ever-faster moving assembly line.

1917 Woodrow Wilson is the last U.S. president to ride to his inaugural in a horse-drawn carriage.

In Russia, Lenin rides to power in the czar's Rolls Royce.

1921 The Pig Stand, first drive-in restaurant in the U.S., opens in Texas.

1922 Model T sales break one million yearly for the first time.

1924 U.S. Treasury Secretary Andrew Mellon tells *Collier's* magazine that the Washington Monument should be moved to build more parking. In downtown Washington, both trolleys and pedestrians travel at higher average speeds than cars.

1925 U.S. refiners start adding tetraethyl lead to gasoline, in spite of pleas by Dr. Harriet Hardy and others not to do so. Background levels of lead increase 100-fold in the next 60 years.

1928 Herbert Hoover promises "two cars in every garage" to U.S. voters.

1932 Ford introduces a low-cost V-8 sedan which quickly becomes a favorite of gangsters; later, John Dillinger and Clyde Barrow both write Ford praising V-8s they've stolen. Says Barrow's letter: "I have drove Fords exclusively when I could get away with one."

leadership from the bike business. Bicycles became children's toys and, to some extent, women's transport. "The bicycle became an outsider in the plans of corporate interests," writes David Perry. "Some have even described the bicycle as the martyred saint of the machine age."[19] While bikes remained a transport mainstay in other parts of the world, they faded into the background in North America, unsung and often unseen.

Selling Out the Streetcars

"There is probably no single influence that has contributed so much to the pleasure and comfort of the masses as the trolley car," wrote muckraker Burton Hendrick in 1919. Inventor Frank Sprague had built the first electric trolley in Richmond, Virginia, in 1887. Cleaner than horses, cheaper than cable cars, the trolley quickly became the urban transportation mode of choice. Within two years of demonstrating his successful Richmond trolley, Sprague received orders for building an additional 200 systems. The success of electric streetcars spurred development of interurban rail lines, the latter proliferating at about the same time automobiles emerged. At first, interurbans grew much more quickly than auto sales. Interurbans offered transport to a broader segment of the population than did cars, and cars required expensive road construction to be truly practical. In the 1890s, an interurban line could be built for as little as $10,000 per mile.[20]

Streetcar use peaked in the early 1920s but, despite providing efficient and relatively cheap travel, streetcar companies suffered numerous problems. To some extent, the same sort of stock manipulations, corruption, and power-peddling that had plagued railways took root in the streetcar business. Some trolleys also had money problems due to poor management or overbuilding. And as cars proliferated, streetcars increasingly had to compete with them and the government assistance they received. While governments approached transit as a business to tax and regulate, they treated roads as a public service to subsidize. Streetcar owners constructed, maintained, and paid taxes on their rails, but car owners drove on untaxed roads whose construction was financed by everyone whether they owned cars or not. This inconsistency in policy amounted to a *de facto* choice by government of one mode over the other, and made it difficult for streetcars to compete. As government support flowed to asphalt and automobiles, starting with federal aid in 1916, transit ridership fell. Through the '20s, streetcars also battled fare caps, heavy debts, over-competition between lines, heavy regulation, rising costs, and a popular — but inaccurate — perception that cars cost less than trolleys. The 1935 passage by Congress of the Wheeler-Rayburn Act, which forced electric utility conglomerates to sell off peripheral businesses such as streetcars, also hurt streetcar survival.[21]

Despite such handicaps, streetcars did do well in some cities; those that survived were mainly city lines sold to local governments. Many city people were served well enough by these trolleys that they didn't require cars; in 1927, the lowest rate of U.S. car ownership was in cities of 100,000 and up, where only 54 percent of families owned autos.[22] But some surviving streetcar systems would soon face another challenge. In the early 1930s, General Motors decided the only way a "market for [city] buses could be created was for it to finance the conversion from streetcars to buses in some small cities," according to later testimony by GM general counsel Henry Hogan. In 1932, GM formed a company called United Cities Motor Transit (UCMT) which bought streetcar lines, dismantled them, and substituted buses. After the American Transit Association censured UCMT for attempting this with the electric transit system in Portland, Oregon, the company disbanded.[23] But GM soon formed another similar company with a few partners.

Working with small businessman and bus operator Roy Fitzgerald, GM, Firestone, Standard Oil of California, and others formed National City Lines (NCL) in 1936 (later, Phillips Petroleum and Mack Truck would join). This auto-oil-rubber-controlled holding company began to systematically eliminate its competition. On behalf of NCL, Fitzgerald bought trolley lines, dismantling them and replacing them with buses. This conversion to motor buses, mostly GM diesels, took place despite the fact that streetcars, and especially trolley coaches, were often NCL's biggest net revenue producers, more economical and profitable than their internal combustion replacements. NCL operated under written agreements requiring it to buy buses, fuel, and tires for the new systems exclusively from its backers and suppliers. As some replacement bus systems began losing money, NCL and its affiliates (American City Lines and Pacific City Lines) sold them to municipalities for high profits — netting, for example, $6.5 million on the Los Angeles system after it had ripped up hundreds of miles of track and left buses in their place. And when it sold such converted systems, NCL's sales contracts generally required that buyers never convert the systems back to electricity.[24]

Altogether, UCMT, NCL, and its affiliates converted or destroyed about a hundred electric rail systems in 45 cities from 1932 to 1956. GM also controlled Omnibus Corporation, which motorized New York City's electric streetcars in 1935. "The New York system was one of the world's largest," writes historian David St. Clair, "and its motorization is often cited as the turning point for electric railways in this country." In 1949, by the time many conversions had already taken place, a federal court found NCL, GM, Standard Oil, Firestone, Phillips Petroleum, Mack Truck, Roy Fitzgerald, and others guilty of criminal conspiracy for violating the Sherman Anti-Trust Act, in essence "ganging up to restrain a competitor."[25]

The record indicates that at least some participants knew they would benefit long-term from the motor vehicle markets National City Lines would open for them. An internal memo from Mack Truck, for instance, predicted the company might lose money on its NCL investment but future truck and bus sales would make the involvement "more than justified" in the long run. It also appears some participants knew well before the 1949 court case that NCL activities might be illegal. Both Firestone and Standard Oil used fronts to help maintain anonymity as they participated in NCL transactions. Testimony from Standard Oil's treasurer indicated the company didn't want to be held responsible for motorizing streetcar lines. In addition, a 1943 letter from Phillips Petroleum to GM vice-president and treasurer H.C. Grossman questioned the "propriety and perhaps legality" of the NCL agreements.[26]

National City Lines and colleagues appealed the criminal conspiracy conviction, but an appeals court upheld the original guilty charge. The streetcar systems, however, were not restored, and the investors had already made an estimated $30 to $50 million on NCL's trade, with more to come as cities fell to auto-dependence. The court fined the guilty companies $5,000 each for their roles in decimating the streetcars, and fined each guilty individual one dollar.[27]

Although "criminal conspiracy" was the finding of the U.S. courts, historians and transportation experts continue to debate just how much of a conspiracy the National City Lines affair really was, and just how much it contributed to the overall decline of American public transit. Some assert that the conspiracy did not do much to trolleys that they weren't already doing to themselves; some say "free market choice" of autos by so many caused the demise of trolleys (and, later, of their motorbus replacements). However, as David St. Clair writes: "The automobile was popular, but that alone was probably insufficient to explain the fate that befell transit."[28] Already, government regulations had forced streetcar service cuts, and government road subsidies had made car travel seem cheaper than it really was. Auto interests had worked hard to seduce public opinion, even using ads that linked value-laden terms like "wrong" or "not fair" with trolley-riding. Dismantling trolley systems may have been just the next in a series of steps to ensure the market for motor vehicles, a step that effectively narrowed consumer options for urban transport. As Stephen Goddard writes: "In a sense, whether the GM conspiracy killed the street railways is beside the point ... GM argues that it simply followed the capitalistic impulse. However, its resources and partnerships were such as to subvert the choice implicit in such a free market." Ultimately, adds Goddard, while "the trolley industry was already on life-support by the 1930s, the highwaymen deserve the credit for pulling the plug."[29]

> "In many places, mass transit didn't just die — it was murdered."
>
> JONATHAN KWITNY,
> HARPER'S, FEBRUARY 1981

Dumping Transport Diversity

By forsaking the horse, abandoning the bike, running down the railroads, and trashing the trolleys, we ended up with little choice but to embrace the auto for nearly all our transportation needs. Now, as some areas strive to restore non-car mobility, we've discovered that our earlier scorning of other transport suitors was a costly mistake. Los Angeles, for example, has spent billions to reconstruct a rail transit system much smaller than that removed by GM, Roy Fitzgerald, and colleagues in the 1940s. By resulting in the destruction of tracks and selling of rights of way that could have formed the basis for modern transit in dozens of cities, the dismantling of electric streetcar systems has ultimately cost us billions more.[30]

In the U.S. in particular, the matchmakers that turned us away from non-auto transport — government policymakers as well as automotive interests pushing hard to expand markets — were too persuasive to resist, especially when we were already so infatuated with the car. Growing car-dependence bred more car-dependence as cars took over U.S. travel in the 1950s and '60s. "Car ownership meant not having to depend on anyone else," writes Stephen Goddard, "unless, of course, the car broke down. For no longer could the car owner catch the trolley instead ... The answer was simple: buy a second car."[31] By dumping transport diversity, we tied our destiny that much more tightly to the automobile.

CHAPTER 3

The Possessive Auto
Takes Over the Landscape:
The Proliferation of
Roads and Suburbs

"It is doubtful if the present general exodus to country homes
would be in progress but for the automobile and the good roads
which it has been instrumental in causing to be built."

CHARLES GLIDDEN, 1911, IN JULIAN PETTIFER AND NIGEL TURNERS', *AUTOMANIA*

RIBBON-CUTTING CEREMONIES — those gatherings of dignitaries spouting speeches and bearing giant scissors, flanked by marching bands and beauty queens like "Miss Blacktop" or "Miss Asphalt" — rose in frequency as we built new roads and gifted more space to the car. The Bronx River Parkway, the first publicly funded limited-access highway, opened in 1923. Soon after, Italians built the first leg of their Autostrada, another limited-access road. As motorization spread, we gave the car more space for its exclusive use — and the more we gave it, the more it seemed to want. Ribbon-cuttings began to cascade: Hitler opened the initial stretch of Autobahn in 1935; Canada's first superhighway, the Queen Elizabeth Way, opened in 1939; the Arroyo Seco Parkway, California's first freeway, and the Pennsylvania Turnpike, the first modern auto toll road, opened in 1940.

From the beginning, our love affair with the car needed road-building help to flourish. As one 1930s book explained, "the automobile is worthless without the improved road."[1] Increasingly, this help took the form of huge government dowries to the car: billions of dollars for roads, and billions more in guaranteed loans for the suburban homes to which many of them led. The U.S. took the lead in granting these dowries and enacting policies that ultimately helped cars take over the landscape; it continues to be the most extreme example of massive highway building and car-dependent suburbanization. But the U.S. has not been alone; policies in other countries, too, have consummated our automotive courtship by encouraging more car use and loss of land to pavement and sprawl.

The Longing for Good Roads

How could motorists pursue their horseless fancy without good roads on which to drive? They tried, but paid for the effort with frustrating hours spent stuck in mud. In 1903, fewer than ten percent of U.S. roads were paved; drivers expected mudholes on most journeys and generally carried tow-ropes. In Australia, roads from outback stations to cities were so bad that at times even sturdy ox teams hauling wool could travel only 40 miles per week.[2]

Even before muddy motorists became common, cyclists and others had made changes as they agitated for better roads. Ontario appointed an "Instructor in Roadmaking" in 1896 who, by 1901, talked the Ontario government into a million-dollar allocation for road-building; provincial funding for roads throughout Canada expanded from there. In the U.S., the League of American Wheelmen (LAW) got the government to spend $10,000 to open an Office of Road Inquiry in 1893. This gave good-roads advocate General Roy Stone, who headed the office, a state-funded platform from which to "preach the gospel of good roads." Stone's activities included urging support of taxes for road-building, giving teachers materials to sway school children to the good-roads cause and, aided by "Father of the Good Roads Movement" Col. Albert Pope, getting donations to build sample roads a few hundred feet long (enough to entice people into wanting more) around the country.[3]

Farmers also began showing interest in better roads for horses and wagons. Getting to market was one concern; plus, the postal service started rural free mail delivery in 1893 but let carriers skip routes if roads were impassable. Pleas from farm families waiting for mail joined agitation by eager cyclists, and calls mounted to "lift our people out of the mud." Even railroads campaigned for good roads, anticipating higher profits if farmers could more easily get wares to train stations (but not that public roads funding might subsidize their competition). The advent of cars added decisive momentum to good-roads pressure. By 1903, when the National Good Roads Convention endorsed U.S. government funding for roads, cars had overtaken bicycles as the main vehicles both motivating and benefiting from the change. At least three national car associations had formed and they began lobbying for roads, "at first without much public fanfare," writes historian James Flink, "to avoid associating road improvements too closely with the special needs of the motorist."[4]

In the end, though, the needs of motorists prevailed, or what appeared to be needs of motorists. Also at this time, needs of motorists and automakers began commingling. Shortly after forming in 1902, for instance, the American Automobile Association (AAA) received $5,000 from the National Association of Automobile Manufacturers "in return for three seats," Flink writes, "on [AAA's] board of directors." The Good Roads Movement that had begun in part as a populist effort increasingly became an industry initiative. As more business members joined groups like AAA, highway engineers and road contractors formed groups of their own. This emerging highway lobby pressed government to fund the roads that would allow them to sustain their profits and prosperity.[5]

> *"A powerful force had evolved, wedding road builders and the motor industry, in which government and business joined happily in promoting one mode of travel over all others."*
>
> STEPHEN GODDARD, *GETTING THERE*

Government Dowries for Road Construction

That national governments should pay for road building was not a foregone conclusion in the early 20th century. Before then, road funds came mostly from local property taxes or tolls. So Carl Fisher, founder of the Indianapolis Motor Speedway, began seeking private donations when, in 1912, he proposed a coast-to-coast highway. Supporters of this Lincoln Highway effort first wanted automakers to finance the proposed road, since they'd gain most if more people had access to easier car travel. But Henry Ford refused to donate, stating that taxpayers ought to fund such a project. Though the Lincoln Highway Association (made up mainly of auto, oil, and cement industry representatives) continued collecting donations which they spent on "seedling miles," much of the highway was ultimately built with federal funds. Like other similar efforts, the Association's legacy was less an actual road than the generation of support for government road-building dollars, just as Ford — and the Association, it turns out — had wanted. As Association leader and Packard Motor Car Company president Henry Joy later noted, "What we really had in mind was not to build a road but to procure the building of many roads."[6]

As efforts like these mounted, national governments increasingly levied new taxes or allocated money for roads. Some road-funding measures failed at first, partly as taxpayers resisted paying for something that would mostly benefit special interests. In the U.S., it took 13 years of lobbying before Congress approved the Federal Aid Road Act of 1916. In Canada, it took proponents eight years to get Parliament to fund roads with Cdn$20 million in the Canada Highways Act of 1919. As national governments began requiring states and provinces to form highway departments, the latter levied gasoline taxes. By 1929, all 48 states had gas taxes; but in at least 27 states and throughout Canada's provinces, road building still cost more than gas taxes brought in, so the balance was paid from property taxes and general funds.[7]

U.S. road building accelerated under Thomas MacDonald, a highway engineer who led the Bureau of Public Roads from 1919 until 1953. MacDonald, a skillful administrator and effective roads promoter, gave radio speeches using statements like "the open road is symbolic of freedom." He also expanded the highway lobby by founding quasi-governmental groups like the Highway Education Board (HEB). Funded partly by auto-highway interests, the HEB awarded scholarships, sent speakers to schools, gave booklets to students that praised highways' effects on domestic life, and suggested essay topics to classes like "How good roads help the religious life of my community." It predicted such efforts could in the future be "a mighty influence at the ballot box when road bond issues and highway programs [are] up for rejection or approval."[8]

As the Depression hit, some governments wanted to use gas taxes for economic programs. In Britain, Winston Churchill had no qualms about sidestepping the theory that motor vehicle revenues should only fund motor vehicle infrastructure — an idea he considered "an outrage ... upon common sense" — and using gas and horsepower taxes for other purposes. But in the U.S., the strengthened auto-highway lobby flexed its muscle and blackballed such diversions, getting the U.S. government to stop aid to states that spent gas taxes on anything besides roads.[9]

So the U.S., instead of diverting funds from road-building, used road-building itself as an economic program. Like a drunk who swigs martinis as a hangover cure, the government poured money into roads in an attempt to get out of a Depression partly set up by the earlier auto boom and bust. Some road building to ease unemployment began under President Herbert Hoover, but truly massive programs came when Franklin Roosevelt succeeded Hoover and founded New Deal agencies which supported extensive road construction. The Civic Works Administration built 500,000 miles of roads during the 1930s. Nearly half the Public Works Administration's two million laborers were hired to build roads. By the time it was shut down in 1942, the Works Progress Administration had built or surfaced over a million miles of roads. All this doubled U.S. paved road mileage by 1940.[10]

As businesses struggled through the '30s, U.S. automakers were helped at least indirectly by these road programs. Roads spurred Germany's economy, too, as Adolf Hitler, admired for his highway-building by Roosevelt and MacDonald, set out to construct 4,500 miles of Autobahn.[11] These efforts not only gave people jobs. In Germany,

---

A Quick (and Sometimes Dirty) Scrapbook of Our Affair with the Car Page Three[12]

1933 First U.S. drive-in theater opens in Camden, New Jersey, to mixed reviews.

At the Berlin Auto Show, German chancellor Adolf Hitler announces plans to build the German Autobahn, stating, "A nation is no longer judged by the length of its railways but by the length of its highways."

1939 Maurice and Richard McDonald open their first drive-in restaurant in San Bernardino, California.

1942 U.S. government stops civilian car production and automakers become military contractors, building 20 percent or $30 billion worth of all defense hardware for World War II; they keep advertising through the war years, promising "a Ford in your future" and "better Buicks" as soon as the war ends.

1946 An ad for Chevrolet becomes the first car ad to appear on network television.

1948 First car wash in the U.S. opens in Detroit.

Tail fins introduced by Harley Earl, GM vice president of styling.

1953 Charles E. Wilson, GM president from 1941 to 1953, is appointed U.S. Secretary of Defense, telling Congress, "What's good for our country is good for General Motors and vice versa."

1955 Foresters begin to notice that smog is causing pine trees to yellow and die in U.S. National Forests above the Los Angeles Basin.

1956 U.S. President Dwight Eisenhower signs the Interstate Highway Act of 1956.

Reverend Robert Schuller opens a drive-in church in Garden Grove, California.

they supplied avenues for Hitler's military, helping set Europe up for World War II. In the U.S., they provided access to unsettled areas, helping set North America up for post-war sprawl. In both places they further cemented the marriage to a system based on auto-industry expansion as a requirement for economic prosperity.

From Autobahn to Interstates: More Asphalt Offerings to the Automobile

While the Autobahn represented 1930s state-of-the-art highway construction, road infrastructure reached its apex with the coming of U.S. interstate highways. General Motors primed the public for post-war paving with its 1939 Futurama at the New York World's Fair, forecasting 14-lane superhighways with 100 m.p.h. speed limits and describing how bulldozing slums and old downtowns for urban freeways would improve cities. Car companies also saw urban freeways as a way to help sell more cars in cities. As Studebaker president Paul Hoffman wrote in 1939, "If we are to have full use of automobiles, cities must be remade. The greatest automobile market today, the greatest untapped field of potential customers, is the large number of city people who refuse to own cars, or use the cars they have very little, because it's such a nuisance to take them out." To get at that urban market, Hoffman continued, "We must dream of gashing our way ruthlessly through built-up sections of overcrowded cities." Automakers thus supported city-oriented freeways and opposed toll roads, which generated only half the traffic as freeways.[13]

The 1956 Interstate Highway Act ultimately funded a significant amount of urban freeway building. The years of lobbying leading to passage of the Act included extensive pro-highway press from William Randolph Hearst, for one, who received an award from the American Road Builders Association for his "forceful and inspiring public interest campaign for adequate roads." Lobbying also came from a bevy of auto, cement, steel, and rubber interests, including the National Highway Users Conference (NHUC) and that group's "Project Adequate Roads." These lobbyists found themselves dealing with an administration under President Dwight Eisenhower that included such officials as Secretary of Defense Charles E. Wilson, previous president of GM; Bureau of Public Roads head Francis Dupont, whose family still owned significant GM stock; and key Eisenhower advisor General Lucius Clay, concurrently on GM's board of directors.[14]

Some who lobbied for interstates argued outright that they were needed to expand car markets. Studebaker-Packard president James Nance told Congress: "Obviously we have a selfish interest in this program, because our products are not good except on the road ... We have to have the roads if we are going to make ... car buyers out of ... people." But mostly, this was less discussed than other rationales. Besides urban renewal, interstate advocates stressed national defense. Eisenhower himself had seen how bad roads could hinder the military and how good roads, like Autobahns, could aid it. Invoking the Cold War, interstate supporters extolled how well these highways would allow cars to carry us to safety in nuclear attacks. An NHUC pamphlet lauded both highways and cars as defense assets, claiming autos themselves might "even [afford] some protection against nuclear fallout." Vice-

President Richard Nixon called interstates a solution to congested roads and traffic courts, and to the "annual death toll comparable to the casualties of a bloody war" on highways.[15]

Eisenhower's administration proposed spending $50 billion to build 40,000 miles of interstates over ten years. In comparison, the yearly U.S. budget was $71 billion; the Marshall Plan had used only $17 billion to rebuild much of Europe's infrastructure after World War II, including subways and train systems. The final bill, as passed in 1956, budgeted $25 billion for 38,000 miles of highway, funded primarily by gas taxes dispensed from a new Highway Trust Fund. Heavy lobbying had also included an offer states couldn't afford to refuse: nearly free money for interstates, as the federal government would cover 90 percent of their construction costs. "Conceived as a capitalistic milestone," writes Stephen Goddard, the Interstate Highway System was "transmuted by Congressional alchemy into a quasi-socialistic program."[17] Congressional testimony shows that backers of the Act intended such road-aid to be ongoing. During hearings on the legislation, Representative Brady Gentry of Texas, a highway booster, had asked: "Is it not true that the highway system needs of the United States of America are almost without limit, and will they not be almost without limit on and on?" Bureau of Public Roads chief (and GM stockholder) Francis Dupont had replied: "I hope so."[18] By the late 1990s, more than 45,000 miles of interstates had been built.

Eisenhower later lamented the effect of his own Interstate Highway Act. Apparently he hadn't realized that some interstates would slash through cities,

> ## Recipe for an Interstate Highway System
>
> The National Highway Users Conference estimated during the 1960s that road-builders used the following quantity of materials for every million dollars spent on the Interstate Highway System:[16]
>
> - 16,800 barrels cement
> - 694 tons bituminous materials
> - 485 tons concrete and clay pipe
> - 76,000 tons sand, gravel, crushed stone, and/or slag
> - 24,000 pounds explosives
> - 121,000 gallons petroleum products
> - 99,000 board feet lumber
> - 600 tons steel
> - 57 new bulldozers and other items of construction machinery
>
> Appropriate land, add labor, mix well, and you, too, can have an Interstate Highway System. The U.S. has now spent well over $100 billion on its interstate highways.

instead believing they would, like Autobahns, go around them. In 1959, Eisenhower reportedly saw bulldozers razing city buildings for a highway and quickly ordered an inquest to see if this might be stopped, but urban road-building had already run too rampant. In the end, Eisenhower could only regret the waste of having motorists "driving into the central area and taking all the space required to park the cars." Former roads chief Thomas MacDonald, too, voiced hesitations about the road-building he'd earlier promoted. In 1947, approaching age 70, MacDonald became concerned about our monogamy with cars. He called on state highway officials to end "the preferential use of private automobiles" in cities and suggested they "promote the patronage of mass transit ... Unless this reversal can be accomplished, indeed, the traffic problems of the larger cities may become well nigh insoluble."[19]

The Overgrowth of the Suburban Jungle

But who cared about city traffic when it was so easy and cheap to get to suburbs? In addition to road-building dollars, the U.S. government gave inadvertent dowries to cars in the form of guaranteed loans for suburban homes, starting under Roosevelt's New Deal. This, too, wedded us more tightly to driving. Though suburbs existed before cars, early ones were limited in scope by the conveyances used to reach them. Brooklyn, for instance, began as a ferry suburb of New York, and initially spread no farther than walking distance from the terminal. Likewise, homes in streetcar suburbs sprouted within walking distance of stations, generally on cozy one-tenth acre lots. Automobiles, however, vastly extended the range of suburbs and began turning them to sprawl. Cars forced lots to swell for driveways and garages, and homes began to spread out. Suburbs designed around cars held only half as many homes, or less, per unit area as those designed around trolleys.[20]

"The automobile has caused the word 'suburb' to carry miles further than it used to until now it has come to signify to the motorist almost any place where gasoline may be readily obtained."

SUBURBAN LIFE MAGAZINE, 1907, IN JANE HOLTZ KAY, *ASPHALT NATION*

U.S. suburbanization accelerated with formation of the government Home Owners Loan Corporation in 1933 to refinance mortgages, and the Federal Housing Administration (FHA) in 1934 to guarantee mortgages, both of which favored suburban over inner-city home sales. Even bigger government stimuli for suburbanization came after World War II. When returning soldiers found a post-war housing shortage, the U.S. government quickly allocated billions more to FHA mortgage insurance, and created yet another mortgage program within the Veterans Administration (VA). The bounty of FHA and VA mortgage guarantees "at whatever price the builder set," writes Kenneth Jackson, "stimulated an unprecedented building boom." Builders quickly started turning out assembly-line houses the same way Ford had churned out assembly-line cars. Where 1944 had seen 114,000 single-family housing starts, the level hit 937,000 in 1946 and jumped to 1,692,000 in 1950. FHA and VA policies continued favoring suburban over city homes; in 1955, for example, over three-quarters of all new metropolitan housing went up in suburban subdivisions.[21] It became cheaper to buy a new suburban house and drive to it with cheap gas than to buy an older city house. Government loan subsidies sometimes made suburban houses even cheaper than renting.

Wartime and then Cold War contracts to industry also supported sprawl and more driving by funding businesses located outside cities. And laws like the Housing Act of 1949 destroyed downtowns in the name of alleviating slums, pushing more residents to urban fringes. Municipalities paid for suburban streets and services and delivered the bill to all taxpayers, in effect forcing inner city residents to subsidize suburbs. As federal funding of road construction continued, roads spread like varicose veins across the land. The process "yet again," writes Jane Holtz Kay, supported "the car-bred exodus of the American dream." By the end of the 1950s, she adds, "subsidized home owners had taken their subsidized cars from their subsidized homes on their subsidized roads to their malls ... The publicly funded private car had established the auto age."[22] Parts of this process have been repeated in some other countries, but in the U.S., suburbanization has reached a pinnacle.

Reshaping the Landscape

In city and country, the spread of roads and the proliferation of cars has reshaped the landscape as we've converted once-proud civic structures to parking lots, and rural landscapes to mazes of asphalt and multiple-car households. In effect, we've made sacrificial offerings to the car out of cities, farms, and wilderness.

Ruined cities: Gracious central cities have been overrun by cars, razed to make more room for cars, and left behind as cars encouraged flight to suburbs. In North American cities, motorists destroyed livable qualities built into 19th century neighborhoods, writes historian Clay McShane, by "converting their gathering places into traffic jams, their playgrounds into motorways, and their shopping places into elongated parking lots." With the Interstate Highway Act, freeway-building came to cities. Yet few of the people displaced by new urban freeways even expected to use them. In the 1960s, only 40 percent of U.S. city dwellers owned cars. Interstates took homes from these residents, ruining neighborhood businesses on which they relied and favoring chain stores, which could afford the high price of locating near freeway exits.[23]

> *"Like locusts eating the fields, so do cars take possession of our streets and squares."*
>
> GERMAN WRITER W. FORST, 1962, IN CLAY MCSHANE, *THE AUTOMOBILE*

U.S. interstate construction leveled so many African-American homes for highways that interstates were called "white roads through black bedrooms." Urban highway building also contributed to 1960s riots in several cities. After riots in Newark, an unsigned letter sent to Daniel Patrick Moynihan pleaded: "Dear Sir ... They are tearing down our homes and building ... motor clubs and parking lots and we need decent private homes to live in. They are tearing down our best schools and churches to build a highway ... There are supposed to be justice for all. Where are that justice?" As it poured money into highways, the government spent little for transit; this, too, fed 1960s riots by limiting the ability of inner city residents to get to jobs and meet other needs. Lack of transit contributed to riots in Watts, concluded a California commission, by creating "a sense of isolation, with its resultant frustrations, among the residents of central Los Angeles." While the riots ultimately generated more support for transit, they had little effect on road-building. Unjust or not, we continued gifting roads and land to the automobile, ending up with cities minus traditional housing and historic structures, blighted by concrete and the proliferation of cars.[24]

Shrinking farmlands: Cars, road-building, and suburbanization have also claimed significant farmland. As cars have encouraged sprawl, land values on farms near cities have risen. Not only have farmers found themselves able to make more money by selling out to developers, some have been forced to sell as rising land values have increased property taxes. As one farmer sells and housing goes up near other farms, land values rise farther out, inducing more farmers to sell. This spiraling development pattern is acute in several U.S. agricultural states, where some of the best farmland has been sealed under homes, malls, and asphalt. The American Farmland Trust estimates that one million acres per year is lost to U.S. suburbanization. Of over 13 million acres of U.S. farmland converted to urban use from 1982 to 1992, close to a third was prime or unique farmland.[25]

> *"Thanks to the interstate highway system, it is now possible to travel across the country from coast to coast without seeing anything."*
>
> CHARLES KURALT

Population growth has been rightly identified as one culprit causing sprawl and farmland loss, but the extent to which the car encourages development to spread is sometimes overlooked. In southeast Michigan, for example, as population increased by 420,000 from 1975 to 1995, car numbers increased five times that

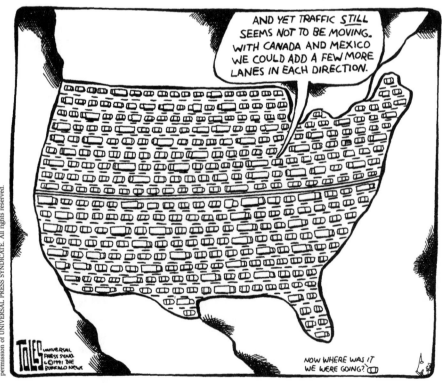

amount, and land consumed by sprawl increased accordingly. As the trend continues, predicts the Southeast Michigan Council of Governments, population will increase by six percent through 2010 but land area covered will increase by 40 percent — nearly seven times faster. Throughout Michigan, where crop diversity rivals California's, car-induced sprawl has already been devouring farmland at the rate of ten acres per hour.[26] This scenario is being replicated on urban fringes worldwide.

Disappearing wildlands: The car began shrinking North American wilderness in 1903 and 1904 with the first cross-continent auto trips and the early spread of auto-touring. National parks give a telling example of the way cars have diminished wilderness. Railroads provided early transport to national parks; once there, visitors hiked or traveled by horse-drawn wagons on rough roads. Car drivers began using those roads as soon as parks let them: Mt. Rainier opened to cars in 1908, Yosemite in 1913, and Yellowstone in 1915. Letting cars in was like opening floodgates; by 1922, two-thirds of Yellowstone tourists came by car. In the 1930s, as $220 million in New Deal money went to road-building within parks, Lewis Gannett complained that Yosemite traffic had become as bad as New York City's.[27] While 128,000 cars had motored into national parks in 1920, the number mushroomed to two million by 1940 and exploded to more than seven million in 1947. As cars took over the parks, Edward Abbey noted that the slogan "Parks are for people" really meant "Parks are for people-in-automobiles."[28] Paving to service all these cars expanded. As of 1994, Yellowstone counted around 12,000 parking spaces; Yosemite had 350 road miles and over 7,000 parking slots, more than the number of campsites and lodging units combined. Over 5,000 were packed into seven-mile-long Yosemite Valley, more than 700 parking spaces per mile.[29]

Outside of parks, motor vehicles — combined with resource extraction like logging — have changed the shape of many wild forests. In 1916, U.S. government funding of forest road-building began; by 1998, the U.S. Forest Service acknowledged that over 440,000 miles of roads had been built in National Forests — nearly ten times the length of the Interstate Highway System.[30] While many forest roads get built initially for temporary logging access, the Forest Service often leaves these in place (rather than closing and replanting them) for use by motorists, including off-road vehicle users. In Canada, too, logging roads have chopped through forests. In British Columbia, the Ministry of Forests has built more roads — nearly 25,000 miles (40,000 km) of them — than the roughly 17,000 miles (27,000 km) of paved road managed by the Ministry of Transportation and Highways.[31] Park, forest, and other roads have thus shrunk roadless areas significantly, eliminating wilderness quality not only from land on which vehicles drive, but also on territories within earshot of engines. In the U.S. east of the Rocky Mountains, only a few roadless areas greater than 100,000 acres remain. Even in western North America, roadless land has shrunk to a fraction of what it once was as motor vehicle use in wild areas has increased.[32]

The Sprawl Spiral

By funding roads for cars and favoring suburbs, government policies have fed a sprawl spiral. Building of roads has supported more car purchases, driving, and suburban home sales. Suburbanization in turn has encouraged more driving and more congestion; that in turn has inspired more road-building and sprawl. It's a pattern that continues to repeat: more cars lead to more sprawl, more sprawl leads to more cars, and the land area consumed by roads and development spirals out of control.

How much land in the "typical" city is now devoted to cars? Estimates for North America vary, ranging most often between 15 and 50 percent. Globally, says Michael Renner of Worldwatch Institute, "at least a third of an average city's land is devoted to roads, parking lots, and other elements of a car infrastructure."[33] Statistics on just how much land has been paved are difficult to verify, but it's likely the U.S. alone has covered over 60,000 square miles — an area about the size of Georgia. Yet still we give cars more. In the 1960s, the ongoing spiral of highway building and motor travel was described and advocated by the Asphalt Institute:

> It is the purpose of travel development to encourage motorists to ... drive longer distances ... the more motorists travel, the more funds for road construction are produced, enabling highway departments to build and improve still more mileage ... We have a self-perpetuating cycle, the key element of which is new paved roads ... Scratch the new roads and the cycle ceases to function.[34]

Despite some progress toward funding alternatives, most U.S. transportation money still funds road construction. In 1998, Congress authorized $218 billion for transportation over the next six years — the biggest single public works bill ever — and earmarked about $170 billion of that for highways. In Canada, some provinces — such as Ontario — are increasing road appropriations as they cut transit funding. The European Union has increased road spending. The World Bank sends 60 percent of its urban transport loans into road-building in developing countries.[35]

> "The current division of market share between the automobile and mass transit is in no way the product of a free market. On the contrary, it reflects massive and sustained government intervention on behalf of automobiles."
>
> PAUL WEYRICH AND WILLIAM LIND,
> CONSERVATIVES AND MASS TRANSIT:
> IS IT TIME FOR A NEW LOOK?

At the same time, increasing evidence shows this road-building won't solve congestion problems. As the popular analogies go, you don't fight obesity by loosening your belt, or cure nasal congestion by widening your nose. Various computer models, mathematical theorems, and studies indicate that if you build or widen roads, cars will come. It's such a common occurrence that transportation engineers have names for it like "latent demand" and "generated traffic." A 1998 Surface Transportation Policy Project analysis found that cities that had spent billions for new road capacity had the same congestion levels as those which had not.[36] A mathematical theorem called Braess's paradox demonstrates that adding capacity to crowded roads can actually slow traffic. And a few studies show the reverse is true: if you take roads out or keep streets narrow, allowing compact placement of buildings and encouraging walking, traffic diminishes. For instance, a study comparing the narrow streets of Portsmouth, New Hampshire, to a conventional, low-density subdivision of the same size found that the subdivision and its wide roads generated three times the car trips.[37]

But the forces behind ongoing road construction may be too vested to be easily overruled by such studies. These forces, institutionalized in widespread government subsidies for pavement and suburbs, have made the cost of car transportation artificially low. And the extent of new roads, now snaking miles farther than ever before, accompanied by sprawl and degradation of transit, have gone beyond encouraging car ownership to nearly forcing it.

CHAPTER 4

Keeping the Romance Alive:
The Role of Marketing
and Advertising

*"Nothing has been so responsible for promoting our automania
than the image-building efforts of Madison Avenue."*

JULIAN PETTIFER AND NIGEL TURNER, *AUTOMANIA*

"YOU CAN'T GET PEOPLE TO SIT OVER AN EXPLOSION," declared Col. Albert Pope in yet another turn-of-the-century critique of internal combustion cars. Many people did indeed fear getting too close to early autos, given their resounding rumbles, choking fumes, frequent breakdowns, and disastrous crashes. Even adventuresome Teddy Roosevelt had doubts about them and had his first motor trip, in 1902, tailed by a horse and buggy just in case. But automotive entrepreneurs found ways to answer these anxieties. One of them was advertising.[1]

Before the 1890s, advertising consisted mainly of simple announcements. But then advertisers discovered the power of emotional appeals and started using subliminal suggestions, imperatives, and images to persuade both subtly and forcefully. Slogans became more important. Ads began to feature fetching females. About this time cars emerged and, from the Gay Nineties to the Roaring Twenties, automobiles and advertising — each profoundly affecting the other — came of age together.

Besides the extensive editorial coverage already given to cars by both mainstream press and specialized periodicals, the media began selling, and carmakers began buying, an increasing amount of advertising. Automakers started out using ads to counteract negative motoring experiences and persuade the public of cars' safety and durability. Because they also had to boost sales enough to bolster their often hand-to-mouth financing, they advertised fast, hard, and big. While other businesses bought ads of only a few inches, automakers used quarter, half, and full pages to display their claims with impact and urgency.

"Practically noiseless and impossible to explode," blared an 1897 Oldsmobile ad. "Safe, simple, and durable. Boiler is absolutely non-explosive," reassured a 1900 ad for the Porter Stanhope steamer. "The only gasoline car that ran the contest from New York to Boston and back without repairs or adjustments OF ANY KIND," asserted a 1903 ad for Haynes-Apperson. Perhaps insecure about whether these claims would convince the dubious, the makers of the Hupmobile ran ads which stated outright that it had been "built for the express purpose of battering down the defenses of the man who hesitates about buying a car."[2]

Once the public started believing horseless buggies actually functioned, auto ads shifted their focus to image. The value of elegant appearance became one of the first new car ad themes. People started seeing cars as symbols of class, status, and freedom in direct response to the ways they were advertised; this built demand. At the same time, advertising for individual car brands bolstered demand for cars in general. Advertising became increasingly powerful; as it brought greater profits to the auto industry, automakers poured more money into advertising and both industries grew. Publishers, too, began to see how much money ads could bring them. While they'd considered advertising disreputable up to the late 19th century, that attitude shifted as magazines and newspapers became more dependent on ad revenues. Magazines soon began to promote advertising to businesses as a means of creating product demand. Previously confined to back pages of periodicals, ads moved into the body of publications, fraternizing with editorial content.

The sheer quantity of advertising skyrocketed — from 1918 to 1920, spending on national advertising in the U.S. doubled; it doubled again by the mid-twenties — as did magazine circulation. By 1915, one-seventh of all U.S. magazine advertising was for cars or car accessories. By 1917, the U.S. auto industry was buying a quarter of all the ad space in national magazines. By 1923, one-third of ads in the *Saturday Evening Post*, the number one U.S. magazine, were for cars.[3] All this advertising, writes Frank Rowsome Jr., "was in considerable degree responsible for the astonishing growth of the auto industry." Along with automakers' marketing gambits, it fueled our desire for cars and helped to keep us coming back for more.

> *"Early to bed and early to rise. Work like hell and advertise."*
>
> MOTIVATIONAL INSTRUCTION TO CAR SALESMEN, *FORD TIMES*, 1911

Immersed in Car Ads

It's estimated people in the western world see 3,000 to 16,000 ads and commercial images every day, or roughly three to 17 of them every waking minute.[4] Close to a fifth of those relate to cars. U.S. car and car-product sellers are the number one advertisers on TV and in magazines, number two in newspapers. Car and car-product ads account for about a quarter of newspaper ads, close to 20 percent of TV ads, 15 percent of magazine ads, and ten percent of radio ads.[5] Car ads fill billboards, sports stadiums, web pages, and even show up on transit buses.

Every year, more is spent on car and car-accessory ads than on any other product category. U.S. ad spending for autos, auto accessories, equipment, and supplies topped $14 billion in 1998. Worldwide that year, automotive industries spent at least $24 billion to entice us with ads. Five of the top ten advertisers outside the U.S., and three of the top six in the U.S., were auto companies. GM spent over $3 billion on ads in 39 countries around the globe; Ford spent over $2 billion; and Daimler-Chrysler, Honda, Nissan, Toyota, and Volkswagen each spent one to two billion on advertising worldwide. In Canada, GM spent $166 million in 1998 — up nearly 80 percent from the previous year — and was the country's top advertiser.[6]

Magazines depend so heavily on car ad revenue that a 1998 advertising cut by GM sent "shockwaves" through the magazine world, said trade journals. Giant ad budgets can affect what we see editorially, too. In 1992, the *Journal of Advertising* reported a finding that advertisers had tried to influence editorial content in nearly 90 percent of U.S. daily newspapers; in 37 percent, they succeeded. The study didn't say who exactly was trying to exert this influence, but retail stores and car dealers are the two top newspaper advertisers. Populist radio commentator Jim Hightower has had his show cut because oil companies didn't like what he was saying. At least one broadcaster in Detroit has reportedly cut programming unfavorable to automobiles. So we're not only immersed in car ads, the ads themselves are immersed in a media context that tends not to contradict their message, and even reinforces it. Cars appear often and favorably in TV programs and movies, for instance.[7]

"The giant dimensions of current advertising and the increasingly devious techniques at its disposal occasionally give alarm to thoughtful citizens."

FRANK ROWSOME JR.,
THEY LAUGHED WHEN I SAT DOWN

Auto companies often state that they just provide what the market demands. But as John Kenneth Galbraith argues, the industry's oligopolic structure already allows the largest companies to direct if not dictate consumer choices.[8] On top of that, billions of dollars in car ads do even more to nurture consumer demand, expanding it and sometimes creating it outright. After all, that's the point of advertising.

Car Ad Claims

Since the industry's early days, car ads have promised buyers much more than a motorized metal box with four wheels. In fact, many car ads say little about actual product features. Instead, the ads sell images and illusions, maneuvering cars into position as symbols of status, influence, sexual prowess, freedom, fulfillment, and more. Buy me and these things will be yours, the ads say. They also use wording techniques such as vague claims to evoke impressions without promising anything specific (e.g., "more power," but more than what?); flattery ("this automobile is an elegant display of your own personality traits"); or leading rhetorical questions ("Isn't that the kind of car America wants?"). With tools like these that can work on a subconscious level, cleverly crafted ad campaigns can have significant effects even on people who believe themselves immune to ads.[9] Whether you're interested in cars or not, on some level your brain will associate the positive feelings these ads evoke with cars.

Car ads have long featured cars in idealized situations: you rarely see a traffic jam in a car ad, for example, but instead see cars zooming along deserted country roads. This, such ads imply, is the driving experience you'll get if you buy the featured car. Car marketers also use a range of images to court different buyers: cars in the woods for outdoorsy types, ads full of happy children for soccer parents, scenes filled with pride, hope, and social advancement for minorities. And they employ some favorite themes to, as trade journals sometimes put it, "snare" buyers and increase sales.[10]

Love, romance, sex: Perhaps nowhere are the promises more notoriously outright as when car ads promise love and sex. Take one 1964 print ad, which tells us: "Two weeks ago this man was a bashful schoolteacher ... Now he has three steady girls, is on first name terms with the best headwaiter in town, is society's darling. All the above came with his Mustang."[11]

In earlier decades, car companies gained a reputation for draping scantily clad women over new car models to entice male buyers. With increased car purchasing by women, love and sex themes in auto marketing have often become more subtle and less gender-specific, but remain just as pervasive. "Passion for the road." "ROMANCE chiseled in STEEL." "It's not a car. It's an aphrodisiac ...." These are just a few of the slogans contemporary ads have used to associate cars with love and sex. "Great cars appeal to a more passionate side," purrs one TV ad. "One part love, two parts lust, and under $550 a month," another ad says of a luxury car. "While some cars can hug the road, very few can actually seduce it," is the husky claim of yet another.[12]

> "This baby can flick its tail at anything on the road!"
>
> SEX AND DOMINANCE PACKAGED NEATLY IN ONE CAR AD SLOGAN, 1957, IN JULIAN PETTIFER AND NIGEL TURNER, *AUTOMANIA*

Copywriters fill love-and-sex car ads with innuendo. One magazine ad features a photo of a woman applying lipstick, the car a tiny image in her compact mirror. The text purposefully confuses the image of the car with that of the woman, describing "catlike eyes ... muscular lines ... a sleek interior design." It finishes: "The high performance suspension system lies waiting for the next curve ... only when you drive it will all its secrets be told." Another ad, this one for TV, features the lyrics of an old love song accompanied first by the image of an amorous couple, then the couple in a car and, finally, as the song reaches its climax — "the very thought of you, my love!" — just the car. Juxtaposing a lyric of love with the image of the automobile, the ad reinforces the idea not only that love comes with an auto purchase but also that it's desirable for us to feel passion for a car.

Speed, power, dominance: In 1936, to assuage concern about speedsters and wrecks, the Automobile Manufacturers Association promised that its members would refrain from emphasizing speed in their ads.[13] Today car ads regularly carry text like: "How fast are you going? ... Maybe it's time to punch it," "Faster. Sleeker. Meaner," or "When you hit the throttle ... you'll not only carve up the road, you'll eat it."

Ads sell power with speed: "Experience a power surge," and "Keep America Powerful," urge print ads for trucks and truck parts. "INVINCIBLE," reads the headline of a sport utility vehicle (SUV) ad — "That's how you feel behind the wheel ... like a hero all over again." In some car ads, power equates with aggression. One carmaker has advertised "The ideal vehicle for 'Type A' personalities. Aggressive on the outside. Uncompromising on the inside." Another boasts that its brand "Gives traditional luxury cars a swift kick in the ascot."

From here it's just a short step to dominance. "As a matter of fact, I do own the road," blares a two-page truck ad. "It doesn't just say you've arrived, it says you got there any way you darn well pleased," asserts a newspaper's full-page SUV layout. Such "break-the-rules" ads have become a common ploy for targeting aging baby boomers who may still consider themselves rebels.[14] As these ads suggest scorning road rules, they feed road rage and endorse anti-social behavior. Buy our car, say the ads, and you no longer need to consider the other guy — you're fast, you're powerful and, just as in the early days of cars, you can leave everyone else in your (now figurative) dust.

Status and wealth: Shortly after 1910, car ads began to incorporate background scenes of grand mansions, imposing country homes, and elegant city districts, full of the implication that social status would flow from owning an automobile.[15] The setting shown with a given vehicle was often beyond the means of target buyers, but associating a certain car with high-class settings inferred that if you bought one, you'd raise your status and be like the rich folks living in big houses. Status has continued to be one of the prime intangibles carmakers sell in ads.

Status ads often encourage and endorse elitism. An early ad for the Jordan Playboy read: "Strangely, we have always underestimated the Playboy demand. We have never built enough. But we never will — you may be assured. There's too much fun in building a few less than the people want. It's friendly, human — you know — to want to have something the other fellow can't get."[16] More contemporary ads repeat the same theme: "It's not for everyone. But isn't that the beauty of it," says one ad, and continues: "It's one thing to be wanted by all. It's quite another to be obtainable by only a few."

Safety, serenity, and family: For years, carmakers resisted safety improvements and regulations with the rationale that "Safety doesn't sell." But now that consumer campaigns and government regulations have made safety features a requirement, the auto industry uses ads to take credit for safety innovations and saving lives. One ad claims, "Its arsenal of safety features will give you a sense of inner peace. Make you feel almost invulnerable." And from "inner peace" it's not far to get a more complete religious experience with the purchase of an auto, as yet another ad touts "a car that can not only help save your life, but help save your soul as well." Then there are ads that tell harrowing real-life stories of people who've lived through serious car wrecks, with the result, the ads say, that the survivors believe their cars saved their lives. These ads don't generally mention that what these cars offer, at most, is only safety relative to other cars, not relative to other forms of transportation.

Car ads also tout cars as solutions to other problems cars create. Sit in our car, says one ad, and "experience an overwhelming sense of relaxation." Psychological studies, on the other hand, tell us that getting behind the wheel causes more adrenaline to flow and driving, especially in congestion, is generally recognized as a generator of stress. "Is it just us, or is it loud out there?" says another ad, promoting a new model's quiet interior. "Because, boy, it sure seems like wherever we go, all we hear is noise, noise, noise." Might that be traffic noise?

Safety and serenity often feature in car ads alongside family values. One ad features a photo of a young boy sleeping; part of his bedsheet is crumpled into the shape of the car company's logo. Without text or a car, the ad associates its brand with security (the boy safely home in bed), serenity (sleeping peacefully), and family values (this could be your child). "It's not a family car. It's family," says another ad. "We believe a family car should be more like one of the family than just mere transportation." In one more, we look down on a father and son sharing a refreshing moment on an inflatable raft in a sparkling blue swimming pool. "I want to appreciate the times when moments are made into memories," the accompanying text tells us, apparently the voice of the father. "They remind me of what's truly important." The only mention of a car is the company's logo at the end. By implication, this ad tells us that buying a car will provide the serenity and contentment we truly crave.

"Concepts have a way of surrounding us ... it's very easy to get stuck inside them. Of course, the $100 billion per year North American advertising industry exists to ensure that we stay stuck in our concepts, stuck in our metaphorical cars, and our real cars."

JOYCE NELSON, IN GORDON LAIRD AND SUE ZIELINSKI, *BEYOND THE CAR: ESSAYS ON THE AUTO CULTURE*

Freedom and escape: "I am tired of going to stores and helping with meals," lamented a 1920s ad by car builder and copywriter Ned Jordan. "I am going somewhere if it is the last thing I ever do ... Give me a Blue Silhouette Jordan ... far silhouetted plains — freedom ... moonlight on the open road ..."[17] Jordan became well-known for his evocative ads that said little about the vehicle and a lot about yearnings and desires; his ads frequently touted cars as gateways to freedom.

Another early advertiser of freedom, Jowett automobiles in Britain, used ads equating cars with the English battle for freedom: "Freedom is waiting for you at the bang of your front door ... For sixteen years the Jowett Car has been bestowing 'This Freedom' on grateful folk, at a price you can easily afford. Freedom! at less than you pay for the humdrum, crowded railway train."[18] It's a theme that's continued as a major car ad feature. "Cast your worries aside .... You are free," proclaims a 1960s sportscar ad.[19] "Life. Liberty. And the pursuit of just about anything you please," says a 1990s car ad.

Then there are escape ads, as in "You don't have to blaze through the forest, hug trees and grow a beard to escape the cruel grip of civilization." This ad assures that an SUV purchase will bring "solace from all things urban." Perhaps this means solace from the profusion of freeways, parking lots, and automotive din that have made cities unlivable because they are inundated with cars like the one the ad is selling? Such ads don't mention that proliferation of cars and their infrastructure is often the very thing from which people need to flee when they feel they must "escape civilization."

Nature and environment: "Bluer sky, greener grass, cleaner air. These are elements we see in the vehicles we're developing," says one car ad. Besides running ads promising a cleaner environment with a car purchase, car marketers team up

with national parks, national forests, and some environmental organizations to produce marketing materials that further pair their products with nature. Ads picturing
cars in natural (unpaved) settings are common; some ads picture cars in places no
car ought to go, then encourage drivers to go there.

Pristine watersheds, sensitive geologic formations, delicate meadows, and forest floors have all been settings for car ads. "Want to drive where there are no people? And no pavement? No problem," urges copy under an SUV pictured on the very
edge of an otherwise untrammeled canyon. "If it were any bigger, it would be
declared a National Park," trumpets the headline over a new SUV parked right next
to a trout stream. Another four-wheel-drive maker advertises that, to its engineers,
"This is a pothole" [shown over an image of a canyon] and "This is a speed bump"
[shown over a photo of a mountain peak]. Still another advertises that "millions of
acres" will be yours if you buy their four-wheel-drive.

Ads To End the Auto Age

What might happen to demand for cars if we saw anti-car ads instead? The Media
Foundation wants to find out. A global network of artists, writers, teachers, and other
"culture jammers" that battles consumerism with guerrilla media tactics, they publish
Adbusters magazine and have produced a series of anti-car ads:

- a 30-second spot featuring an Autosaurus (a dinosaur-like creature built of cars);

- a print ad picturing a car and headlined: "At this price, it'll take your breath
  away." The small print lists the true health and monetary costs of cars;

- an ad showing only a bicycle, offering: "If you polluted the air in the '80s,
  here's your chance to redeem yourself. Riders wanted;"

- a mock movie poster: "Jurassic Parking Lot — The Motionless Picture," with an
  Autosaurus superimposed over a gridlocked highway;

- an ad headlined "Spot the Serial Killer" picturing a family photo next to a red
  roadster (the killer is the roadster);

- a billboard layout featuring a silver-gray sedan framed by the words: "Power,
  Comfort, Prestige ... & Pollution."

Some broadcasters have refused to run the Autosaurus spot. On February 27, 1993,
the spot aired once during a Canadian Broadcasting Corporation (CBC) program
called "Driver's Seat," normally sponsored by auto manufacturers. Then the CBC
pulled it. In justifying the network's action, CBC director of communications Tom
Curzon stated: "We have and reserve the right not to embarrass an advertiser." The
Media Foundation has sued the CBC for violating its right to free speech and for
breach of contract.[20]

If you want to try getting your local station to run an *Adbusters* spot, contact the
Media Foundation, and they'll send you a video clip and instructions. They've also got
postcards and calendars featuring their various anti-ads, automotive and otherwise.
See "Selected Resources" for more information.

"A gift of the great outdoors," echoes another ad, is "a gift you can now give to your family with [our] all-new 1990 4-door 4-wheel drive." Buy this car, the ad implies, and you'll get "a place where Mother Nature whispers softly in your ear ... a sound that soothes the soul. A sound that ... can drive the maddening music of the city from your minds." With repeated messages like this, it's easy to forget that cars do plenty to destroy that "gift of the great outdoors."

Annual Models and Other Marketing Maneuvers

Carmakers use many other marketing strategies besides ads. They range from the simple, like car names that seduce us by evoking feelings or suggesting characteristics carmakers want associated with their models, to the more elaborate. Auto shows and races have been used since the car's inception; in 1998, more than 30 major auto shows were held in at least 27 countries drawing over six million people and 60,000 visits from the press. Carmakers get attention with publicity stunts, outlandish prototypes, or grand announcements of new models. Auto shows have introduced new SUVs by crashing them through plate glass windows; dropped trucks from ceilings; and set up Disneyesque rides through automotive fantasy lands. Carmakers have also used traveling mall shows, film appearances by cars, and sponsorship of concerts, sports events, children's reading programs, Earth Day activities, and charity events to market cars. To launch one new model, Nissan sponsored a contest in Atlanta to see who could live in the car the longest; the winner got the car, and Nissan got lots of media coverage. In case such things don't grab enough buyers, dealers advertise rebates, bonuses, coupons, and special loan rates.[21]

Like many businesses, carmakers also provide curriculum materials to schools. Logo-stamped materials induce "imprint conditioning," say critics, lulling children into feeling friendly toward particular brands. Curriculum materials have been used as public relations to counteract image problems, too, as with one carmaker's 1972 booklet, "Professor Clean Asks ... What Is Air Pollution?" The booklet, two million copies of which were distributed to 8,000 schools, downplayed air pollution's risks and assured students that pollution control devices would solve the problem "in the near future."[22]

One of the most famous and effective car marketing strategies has been the annual model change. In the auto's youth, carmakers learned to save up technological improvements over twelve months, then include them all at once in new models released at the beginning of the year. But some carmakers kept putting out yearly models even when they had no new technology to include. As early as 1914, Reginald Cleveland wrote that "'Last year's car' has come to be as much a phrase of reproach as 'last year's hat'."[23]

Annual model changes became a true institution after 1923, when Alfred P. Sloan became head of General Motors. Sales growth to that date had been phenomenal, but the car market showed signs of saturation. To keep growth at high levels, Sloan decided the company needed a new sales strategy. In 1926, he hired designer Harley Earl for a new GM department: Art and Color. Realizing that most vehicle

Calvin and Hobbes   by Bill Watterson

purchase decisions are steeped in emotion and profoundly affected by factors like a car's color, GM made mainly cosmetic changes to each year's models. Sloan called it "constant upgrading of product," but it was really a planned obsolescence that encouraged owners to trade cars in because they were out of style, well before their functional lives had ended. Heavy advertising played an important role with annual model changes, since the minimal changes each year needed help to appear more exciting and desirable. In the face of annual model changes, ownership of a Ford Model T (which was the same every year) became akin to a public mark of failure by the mid- to late-1920s. Ford, too, soon started changing styles each year.[24] By the 1950s, opulent annual style alterations were making older cars look dated in a hurry, accelerating turnover and boosting sales. About this time, GM's Harley Earl told his staff that turnover should be faster still. "Our job is to hasten obsolescence," Earl said. "In 1934, the average ownership span was five years; now it is two years. When it is one year we will have a perfect score."[25]

GM also coordinated yearly model changes with segmentation of its divisions into a hierarchy of price ranges so that, as new models came out, car buyers could be encouraged to step up to the next higher division. Even if buyers couldn't afford a more expensive car, model changes could provide them with renewed esteem for buying this year's version of the car they already had. Annual model changes thus both magnified class distinctions and reinforced the role of cars as status symbols: the better and newer your car, the more successful you apparently were. In this way they set up a "ladder of consumption" that still persists.[26]

Truth in Advertising

Would we still buy cars if there were no advertising? It's never been tested with automobiles, but some 1970s milk ad experiments explored the question. Advertising for milk was stopped in certain test markets; at first nothing happened to sales but, after about a year, they went into a dizzying decline. Advertising was restarted, but it took 18 months for the decline in milk sales to reverse. The researchers concluded that advertising does indeed keep sales higher than they'd be without it.[27]

Would we buy cars so often if, when we did, we bought only a machine with four wheels and an engine, rather than love, sex appeal, power, freedom, and status?

Ecopsychologists Mary Gomes and Allen Kanner argue that large-scale advertising creates psychological patterns in us that predispose us to buying more and more often.[28] Since auto ads convince us that buying a car helps meet our unmet needs, many of them emotional, new car purchases at first provide pleasure and a sense of achievement. These feelings usually wear off quickly; then advertising convinces us that we must get them back by making another purchase (notice how well this pattern fits with annual model changes for cars).

Car ads thus play an important role in keeping the romance alive by continuing to promise a range of intangible qualities that bring people various kinds of fulfillment. But do you really get "love" when you buy a car? You might more likely get glares and gestures if you zoom out on the road and do something your fellow drivers don't like. What about security and safety? Even in the safest car, say National Safety Council figures, your chances of injury and death are higher than in other forms of transport. And do you get "freedom" by owning a car? On average, new car owners spend half a year working to pay for their purchases, and drivers spend increasing numbers of hours trapped in traffic jams; this kind of freedom isn't free. Auto advertising serves as a multi-billion-dollar-a-year demand generator as well as a counterforce to the problems cars impose and, for better or worse, it works.

A Quick (and Sometimes Dirty) Scrapbook of Our Affair with the Car Page Four [29]

1957 Ford introduces the first car model based on marketing research: the Edsel. It fails.

1958 Cadillac releases its 1959 model; its record-setting tail fins are 107 centimeters high.

1959 "The primary function of the motor car in America," says sociologist Vance Packard, "is to carry its owner into a higher social stratum."

1960 Elvis has his Cadillac gold-plated, trimmed with white fur seats, and outfitted with a phone, TV, record player, bar, and electric shoe buffer.

1961 Author Jean Gottman uses the word "megalopolis" to describe the way cities have begun to sprawl together into one auto-dependent urban-suburban mass.

1965 Ralph Nader publishes *Unsafe at Any Speed*; General Motors has Nader tailed by private detectives, who get caught in the act.

1967 Los Angeles police apprehend author Ray Bradbury for suspect behavior: walking in a suburban neighborhood.

1969 An oil spill in the Santa Barbara channel off California's coast raises environmental concerns about offshore drilling.

1970 On Earth Day, Florida Tech students put a Chevrolet on trial and convict it for poisoning the air.

CHAPTER 5

This Isn't Love, This Is Addiction!
The Relationship Today

*"What is the purpose of life? For us, the answer will be clear,
established, and for all practical purposes indisputable:
The purpose of life is to produce and consume automobiles."*

JANE JACOBS, *THE DEATH AND LIFE OF GREAT AMERICAN CITIES*

IN ONE SCENE OF MONTY PYTHON'S *The Meaning of Life,* the Grim Reaper talks his way into a dinner party at a small English manor. The six guests at the table react with denial at first, but the Reaper convinces them they have perished; their hostess has served a contaminated seafood mousse. "Follow me," says the Reaper, and the specters of the diners rise, leaving their bodies slumped at the table. As the group drifts out the door and through a yard where three expensive vehicles sit in a row, one of the just-deceased asks lightly, "Shall we take our cars?"

Monty Python's comic vision of luxury cars pursuing the Grim Reaper to heaven is not so different from reality. We drive often, we drive nearly everywhere, and we drive even unto death. It's almost reached the point where we don't need to leave our cars at all: from the time we're conceived (a few of us in back seats) to the time we die, we can do nearly everything there is to do while inside an automobile. Or so it seems. Some of us are born in cars. We spend much of our early lives strapped into car seats. Parents drive us around until we're old enough to go through what's become the primary rite of passage in many western countries — getting a driver's license — and then we drive ourselves. Soon we find ourselves driving to work, and working to drive. We eat while driving, dress while driving, shave, put on makeup, talk on the phone, and read books while driving. Without leaving our cars, we can bank, watch movies, purchase food, purchase gas, get flu shots, get married, and attend funerals. A significant number of us die in cars, and our bodies are carried away in cars to a final resting place — which, for a few of us, *is* a car, as evidenced by folks who've been buried in their cars. This isn't love, this is addiction! And Monty Python's sketch is a classic send-up of just how far the addiction can go.

Overrun by Automobiles

Worldwide in the 1990s, the number of cars grew three times faster than the human population.[1] In the U.S., car numbers increased an astounding six times faster than the population from 1969 to 1995. The global count of motor vehicles was estimated to be somewhere over 700 million by 1999; as of July of that year, over 209 million of those were U.S.-registered passenger cars and light trucks. There are now more cars in the U.S. than licensed drivers, and more cars than adults. The number of U.S. households with three or more vehicles grew six-fold from 1969 to 1995, a change even the Federal Highway Administration considers "startling."[2] Counting unregistered vehicles not included in these statistics, the U.S. may be home to more cars than people.

Vehicles have gotten bigger, too, since the oil-short, small-car 1970s. Sales of light trucks, vans, and SUVs climbed aggressively in the 1990s; by decade's end, they accounted for somewhere around 50 percent of new vehicle sales in the U.S. Large cars generate more profits for manufacturers than small ones, which helps motivate this drift toward bigger vehicles. Some recent models are too big to fit in parking lots and car washes, which may have to remodel to accommodate them. Similar vehicle size increases in the 1950s, when some "intermediate-sized" cars became bigger than "full-sized" cars of a decade earlier, forced taxpayers to pay for revamping roads for the larger cars.[3] Most people think of SUVs and light trucks generically as cars, and use them like cars; only about 14 percent of pickup buyers use them mainly as work trucks.[4] But, on the excuse that they're work vehicles, SUVs and light trucks have been regulated less stringently, allowed to use more gasoline and emit more pollutants than regular cars, and have cut deeply into air quality improvements, bringing average fuel economy down in the U.S. since 1988. "The average car going into junkyards today gets better mileage than the average car in dealers' showrooms," writes Jim Motavalli.[5] More stringent emissions controls imposed in 1999 will address the pollution issue and will eventually apply equally to cars and SUVs, but these will be phased in slowly, over ten years.

More and bigger cars use more land as well. Cars have encouraged developed areas to sprawl at up to ten times the rate of population growth in U.S. cities. From 1970 to 1990, as population in Los Angeles grew 45 percent, developed area expanded 300 percent; in St. Louis, as population grew 35 percent, developed area expanded 355 percent. As a result, the distances we drive have also grown. In 1970, U.S. residents drove one trillion miles per year. By the mid-'90s, that had more than doubled, and nine of every ten miles were being traveled by car. Daily commutes increased nearly 40 percent from 1983 to 1995, to almost 12 miles on average, and are still getting longer. Yet commuting accounts for only 18 percent of person trips; even more travel is discretionary. More students drive to and from schools. More economies depend on tourism to survive and encourage vacationers to drive distances to visit. Many such economies have shifted from serving local residents with downtown businesses near residential areas, to serving them with outlying big-box discount stores, so more people drive more miles to errands. Shopping and errands make up nearly half of all car trips; social and recreational trips account for a quarter of them. Overall, each single-family household generates ten vehicle trips a day, planning guidelines estimate.[6]

The level of fuel used for all this driving is up, too. By 1997, U.S. highway fuel use had increased to over 150 billion gallons per year, up from 127 billion ten years earlier. Nearly 28 percent of energy used in the U.S. goes to transportation, and of that, 76 percent goes to cars, trucks, and motorcycles — about 21 percent of all energy the country uses. In 1998, increasing use of gasoline helped push the percentage of net oil imports to over half of what's consumed in the U.S; transportation used 11.5 million barrels of oil a day, but the U.S. produced only 6.2 million barrels. Oil imports continue to creep up, as domestic production drops and gas guzzlers like SUVs become an increasing percentage of the vehicle fleet.[7]

Cars also consume expanding amounts of time. On average, we spend over an hour a day in the car and, in places like Los Angeles, perhaps double that. In many cities, much of that time is spent in traffic jams; drivers can encounter congestion at any time of day, not just during rush hour. From 1982 to 1996, time lost to congestion delays tripled in major U.S. cities. Time spent driving to work has grown from 18 to 21 minutes on average. And in addition to the time we spend driving, there is the time we spend taking care of our cars, adding up to a loss of the time we supposedly save by using them.[8]

A Quick (and Sometimes Dirty) Scrapbook of Our Affair with the Car

Page Five[9]

1973 Arab oil embargo causes oil shortages, price increases, long gas lines, and short tempers.

1974 About 300,000 auto workers laid off during this and the following year as demand for large cars drops due to the oil crisis.

1979 Second oil shortage hits; consumers buy more small cars.

1981 U.S. auto production bottoms out; massive layoffs of auto workers in Michigan.

1982 Athens (Greece) institutes restrictions on downtown driving in an attempt to control air pollution damaging both human health and stonework on the city's ancient monuments.

1989 Michael Moore releases his film "Roger and Me" lampooning GM CEO Roger Smith and exposing the severe degradation of Flint, Michigan, resulting from auto company layoffs.

Exxon Valdez spills 11 million gallons of oil in Prince William Sound, Alaska.

1991 First so-called "War for Oil" starts in the Persian Gulf.

1996 Auto companies organize 100-year anniversary celebrations. At a British car anniversary bash in Coventry, a woman stages a protest by taking off her coat to reveal she is wearing nothing but an anti-car slogan.

1998 Net oil imports climb to over 50 percent of U.S. oil supply; light trucks, SUVs, and minivans make up about 50 percent of new vehicle sales.

Global temperature reaches highest level ever.

U.S. passes biggest highway bill ever.

These numbers paint an overwhelming portrait of growing U.S. car-dependency. Perhaps even more alarming: when it comes to cars, the rest of the world apparently wants to be just like the U.S. In other countries, car addiction hasn't reached the U.S. stage, but some places are getting closer. As of 1991, Canadians had twice as much transit service as the U.S. in denser, more walkable and cyclable cities, and drove only a little over half as much per person: 4,130 miles (6,645 kilometers) per year compared to 6,933 miles (11,155 kilometers) for Americans.[10] But since 1991, Canadians have slid south. "Low-density suburban sprawl," notes transportation analyst John Pucher, "is on the increase around virtually every Canadian city." Feeding this trend, the Province of Ontario has cut transit subsidies and prohibited local governments from financing transit with dedicated taxes, even as it has subsidized several new road projects. Canadian transit ridership fell 13 percent from 1990 to 1996; one of few places to buck this trend was Vancouver, which chose to invest more in transit, increased service by 20 percent, and saw ridership go up as a result.[11]

Even in Europe, car use has increased; passenger-kilometers in private cars went up two percent a year through the 1990s as other ground transport stayed level. Western Europe's new car registrations rose 4.8 percent in 1997. Road lengths affected by congestion went up about 50 percent in France from 1988 to 1995. British workers went from driving for half their commutes in the 1970s to over two-thirds by the mid-1990s, and the length of the British commute went up 50 percent during that time as well.[12]

The most phenomenal growth in car sales and driving, though, has occurred in developing countries. In Latin America, the car population has grown exponentially as yearly auto sales climbed from 2.2 million in 1994 to an estimated three million by 2000.[13] In areas of Asia, road traffic went up 30 percent from 1993 to 1998. Before Thailand's economy slumped in 1997, Bangkok was adding 300 new cars a day to roads already so gridlocked drivers had started carrying portable toilets as automotive accessories.[14] At the end of 1996, there were over eleven million motor vehicles in China, nearly double the number there'd been five years earlier. As of 1998, China had more than 100 car producers capable of turning out a total of over three million cars a year.[15] In Eastern Europe and the former Soviet bloc, the 1989 Berlin Wall collapse was followed by an explosion in car numbers in the 1990s. In Moscow, cars increased 84 percent from 1990 to 1994. Private car ownership rose 45 percent in Prague and 100 percent in Warsaw during the same time. These increases have brought epic traffic jams, road rudeness, and air pollution along with them.[16]

Around the globe, then, the quantity of cars, their size, distances driven, fuel used, and time spent behind the wheel are all growing. Whether we like driving or not, in many places we're tied into an overwhelming monogamy with the car. In North America in particular, and increasingly in the rest of the world, we have a drive-in, drive-up, drive-thru, and drive-by society.

Foreshadowing the Future

Perhaps the biggest questions about how our automotive marriage might affect the future are raised by burgeoning global car sales. Auto companies have been expanding factories and markets worldwide, and skyrocketing car sales in developing countries are forecast to continue. Effects on land use, global climate, pollution levels, resource supplies, and economic equity could be dramatic.

Auto producers are already huge, routinely dominating lists of the world's biggest firms. In 1999, GM, DaimlerChrysler, and Ford ranked as the world's three largest corporations on *Fortune* magazine's Global 500 list. The three had combined global revenues in 1998 of $460 billion.[17] In developed countries, ten percent of jobs relate to autos.[18] Globally, auto producers employed ten million people in 1997 and were the world's biggest manufacturing business; GM is the world's biggest single manufacturer. Although the industry ended the 1990s with a glut of capacity, carmakers have continued building new plants in eastern Europe, Asia, and Latin America.[19] Environmental laws governing these factories are often more lax than those in western Europe and North America, and with swelling and overwhelmingly young populations, demographics of these regions offer potentially huge markets for cars. The number of cars per person is still low in these places relative to "mature" markets like North America or western Europe. In 1996, for instance, Thailand had one car for every 38 people; in China, it was one for every 260 people.[20] Compare that to the U.S. ratio of one motor vehicle for every 1.7 people, and you'll see why former GM boss Alfred P. Sloan once wrote of the prospects for worldwide auto sales: "It is easy for Americans to forget how undeveloped this market is. Its potential appears to be almost limitless."[21] There are still over a billion Chinese without cars, and it would take hundreds of millions of car sales just to get China's car ownership rates on a par with Thailand's. In comparison, late-1990s auto sales were at about 15 million a year in the U.S. (hitting a record 16.9 million in 1999), and at just over 50 million a year worldwide.[22]

> *"The American dream of a car — or two or three of them — in every garage is beginning to look like a nightmare for our planet."*
>
> GUS SPETH, IN STEVE NADIS AND JAMES MACKENZIE, *CAR TROUBLE*

As in the automotive courtship's early days, car sales today get global help from media and government. Exports of American TV shows and movies, for instance, portray American lifestyles, which tend to glamorize cars and driving as the pinnacle of cool. Agencies like the World Bank have often favored road-building over rail or other transport. The love affair is also promoted globally by countries using auto production as an economic development tool. Korea and Brazil in particular have entered auto manufacturing. China has its own car plants, and has pursued joint ventures with automakers from Europe and North America, as has India. At the same time, some Third World governments have discarded, even outlawed, non-motorized vehicles. China, India, Indonesia, and Vietnam have restricted pedicabs, rickshaws, and bicycles on some urban streets, or have removed bike lanes to make room for cars. The Chinese government has also taken steps to encourage car ownership, easing restrictions on auto purchases and lowering prices on Chinese-made cars. These policies help wealthier citizens, but

deprive many in the lower classes of both transportation and jobs, worsening divisions between haves and have-nots.[23]

Cultural, political, and economic pressures to buy cars are thus spreading. The developed world has modeled a car-based economy, the developing world wants to follow that model, and much government policy and business practice supports or encourages that. With industry representatives still seeing limitless prospects for global sales, cars are poised to conquer world markets. An auto business that views its growth as limitless, though, conflicts directly with a world bumping up against apparent limits. Swelling auto populations have troubling implications for, at least, global air quality, food production, petroleum consumption, and climate change.

Many vehicles sold in places like China and India still lack up-to-date emissions controls, or use dirty or outdated technology. In 1999, as a World Resources Institute study documented health-threatening air pollution levels in large cities in China, Chinese cars only met U.S. standards for 1970 when U.S. pollution was peaking. Atmospheric chemist Scott Elliott analyzed the pollution levels that would result if 400 million Chinese own cars by 2050, as could happen if car ownership continues rising in Asia. Ozone would blow east to Japan and Korea, blanketing those areas with as much air pollution as in a Los Angeles smog alert, and some of this could reach North America. This number of cars in China would also boost global CO_2 emissions by 30 percent. Not long after Elliott completed these calculations, U.S. west coast air monitoring stations began detecting air pollutants blown over from China. So even as California attempts to clean its air with some of the world's most stringent vehicle emissions standards, its smog could get worse — coming from

China. The Chinese have begun to develop and use cleaner fuels; Beijing and other cities have banned or called for a phase-out of leaded gasoline, and the government wants to increase the number of natural gas and propane vehicles. China is also testing electric vehicles. But newspapers quoted one government official lamenting the lack of funds for at least some of these programs.[24]

If global sales of cars continue growing, we can also expect increased land lost to sprawl and pavement. China, for instance, is funding a lot of road-building, and as a result is losing valuable farmland and exacerbating urban sprawl. By 2000, says at least one estimate, China will have less arable land per capita than all other populous countries except Bangladesh and Egypt. At the same time, ozone pollution from industrial fossil fuel burning is already high enough to hurt Chinese crops; increased emissions from cars could further cut crop yields. Compounding population growth problems, this farmland loss will help push China past the limits of its ability to feed itself, says Worldwatch Institute, and further strain world food supplies.[25]

Growing car sales will also push us closer to oil supply limits, wherever those limits may be. An increasing number of geologists believe they loom uncomfortably near. Forecasts of when oil extraction might peak range from 2000 to around 2040, but many cluster in the 21st century's first two decades. International oil geologists Colin Campbell and Jean Laherrére, associated with Petroconsultants of Geneva, expect world oil extraction to peak by 2010, then start dropping. While a peak in extraction doesn't mean all oil wells will run dry, it does mean that cheap oil will run out. After the peak, the amount of oil available is expected to drop each succeeding year. If at the same time global oil consumption continues rising — it's gone from 3.2 to 3.5 billion tons a year in the 1990s — or even stays level, oil prices will rise. Already, production outside OPEC may have peaked, which means that by 2009, the proportion of oil coming from Middle East countries will grow to 50 percent of world supply. This could bring greater price increases or even the risk of politically inspired oil shocks, since some of the countries with the biggest reserves (Saudi Arabia, Iraq, Iran, and Kuwait) have ambivalent attitudes toward big western oil consumers like the U.S.[26] David Lewis, business historian at the University of Michigan, believes another oil crisis is possible. "In some ways we haven't learned a thing," he says. "Look what will happen to the auto companies if the price goes up and there's a shortage. Trucks — pickups, SUVs, vans — will take a big hit, and that's where the money is."[27] If car use and car-dependency continue growing around the world, 21st century oil shortages have the potential to bring much wider economic dislocations.

Not only might we have more trouble finding fuel to put into gasoline tanks, we might also have increasing problems with the greenhouse gases coming out of them. Rising global oil consumption will both move us closer to oil supply limits and raise CO_2 emissions at a time when most policy makers and climate scientists believe we should be emitting much less. At the Earth Summit in 1992, 132 countries approved the Framework Convention on Climate Change calling for a cut in CO_2 emissions but, by 1997, those emissions had gone up. At the Kyoto climate change summit in 1997, countries again agreed to cuts; industrial nations set targets to reduce CO_2 emissions to 5.2 percent below 1990 levels by 2008-2012.[28] But some scientists have suggested we may need cuts far greater — as much as 70 percent below 1990 levels — to stabilize climate. And instead, as the American Wind Energy Association points out, until at least the late 1990s we have been "sailing serenely on in the opposite direction."[29] If current automotive trends continue, we could see an expanding auto industry emphasizing sales of more and bigger cars around the world. Will we be — or are we already — fiddling around in sport utility vehicles while the planet burns?

"With all their speed forward they [automobiles] may be a step backward in civilisation."

BOOTH TARKINGTON,
THE MAGNIFICENT AMBERSONS

Spreading smog, food production losses, pressure on oil supplies, climate change, and probably other complications, too: as these prospects loom ahead, our automotive marriage continues to be intensified by government policies, land use decisions, advertising, and ongoing promotion of cars by a mainstream media for which the auto industry is a big source of revenue, if not the biggest. After a courtship that's included its share of wrong turns and manipulated decisions, we've reached a dependency on cars that's destructive to health and free choice. At the same time, the problems with this marriage could push us to the break-up point. While for some the relationship continues to be a love affair, for others, the union is well past the honeymoon stage.

PART 2

GROUNDS FOR DIVORCE: WHY OUR AUTOMOTIVE MARRIAGE IS ON THE ROCKS

*"Our transportation is a tangle ... As we enter a new century,
our vaunted mobility is, in fact, obstructed by a car culture in which
every attempt to move is fraught with wasted motion, wasted time,
wasted surroundings, wasted money ... both the quality of mobility
and the quality of life have diminished."*

JANE HOLTZ KAY, *ASPHALT NATION*

"It may be time for humans to retire the car before it retires us."

MARK HERTSGAARD, *EARTH ODYSSEY*

"PERSONAL USE OF CARS AND LIGHT TRUCKS is the single most damaging consumer behavior," write Michael Brower and Warren Leon in *The Consumer's Guide to Effective Environmental Choices*.[1] Driving topped their list of environmentally harmful consumer activities — even without considering accidental oil spills or vehicle disposal — and makes far more difference to planetary health than, for instance, whether you choose paper or plastic at the store. And environmental ills only begin the inventory of our irreconcilable differences with the car. The next five chapters examine some of the symptoms of lovesickness caused by our automotive marriage. In plot terms, this part is the conflict before the resolution; the happy ending comes in Part 3.

CHAPTER 6

Smoke Gets in Our Eyes:
The Damage Done to Air

*"Even the strictest air quality regulations cannot resolve
the conflict between nature and the car."*

THE FINANCIAL TIMES, 18 MARCH 1992

IN THE 1940S, LOS ANGELES BEGAN HAVING TROUBLE with a brown haze that burned people's throats and blocked views of mountains just a few miles away. Puzzled authorities started searching for a cause. Did the smog come from garbage incineration? Industrial use of coal, perhaps? In 1950, biochemist A.J. Haagen-Smit deciphered smog's chemistry and fingered the main culprit: auto emissions.[1] Car and oil interests protested, calling Haagen-Smit's discovery "unproved speculation." In 1954, the Automobile Manufacturers Association sent a delegation west to discuss the problem. At a dinner welcoming them to Southern California, the delegation's leader stuffed paper into a fruit can to simulate an incinerator, then set it on fire. As smoke curled up to the ceiling, he announced to L.A. officials: "That's where your smog is coming from!"[2]

Industry assertions notwithstanding, the volume of science condemning car exhaust as an air pollutant has grown since Haagen-Smit's discovery. With the various ways cars damage the atmosphere, it's easy to see why they're so often identified as the biggest single desecrators of air quality worldwide.[3]

Out of the Tailpipe, Into Our Lungs: Direct Emissions from Cars

Since Haagen-Smit's discovery, we've worked hard to clean up tailpipe emissions. So is the air getting cleaner? Well, yes and no. Individual cars in many countries are cleaner than in 1970, before introduction of emissions controls like catalytic converters. But increases in numbers of cars and miles driven have offset much of the gain. In the U.S., Canada, and Europe, though there has been a "modest reduction" in automotive emissions, cars remain a top source of regulated pollutants.[4] Meanwhile, in other countries, the exploding quantity of motor vehicles includes many that use dirty two-stroke engines or leaded gas, with correspondingly high emissions. In Russia, dangerously high emissions come from swarms of new low-quality cars using low-grade fuels; in India, cities like Delhi have seen the number of diesel buses, auto-rickshaws, and cars swell more than six-fold since 1980, generating air pollution so thick it's contributed to traffic crashes and raised benzene levels to 20 times that of Europe's safe limit.[5]

This pollution starts as all the fiery little explosions inside internal-combustion engine cylinders send "smoke" out tailpipes as carbon dioxide (CO_2), carbon monoxide (CO), volatile organic compounds (VOCs), oxides of nitrogen (NO_x) such as nitrogen dioxide (NO_2), particulate matter, and a few other components, including the leftovers of gasoline additives. Colder engines generate more emissions, so short car trips generate the most pollution per distance traveled. Catalytic converters basically let pollutants pass through for the first few miles, since they must warm to about 700 degrees Fahrenheit to function efficiently. So, for instance, half the VOCs emitted by a 20-mile car trip exit the tailpipe in the first three or four miles. If the engine is cold enough, some gasoline will even blow out the tailpipe as a liquid. Pollutant amounts also vary with engine and fuel type; gasoline engines send more VOCs into the air, for example, while diesel engines emit more particulate matter. Once emitted, some pollutants react in the atmosphere to form others. Ground-level ozone, for instance, forms when VOCs react with NO_x in the presence of sunlight and heat; this is what's accounted for much of southern California's smog.

Lida Grant remembers a hot and smoggy summer day when her work as a landscape architect took her partway up the west slope of the San Gabriel Mountains, east of Los Angeles. "You could taste the air," she recalls. Her eyes itched, her throat felt scratchy. Lida is fit and in good health, but as she walked up a steep driveway at a job site, she suddenly felt short of breath, and then so dizzy she had to stop and put her head down before continuing. When she returned to her office and reported this mishap, the secretary informed her that a third-stage smog alert had been declared that day. "You had a smog attack," she told Lida.

Lida's itchy eyes, scratchy throat, and shortness of breath may indeed have been caused by ground-level ozone. Even at levels that meet legal limits, ozone exposure can produce these symptoms as well as headaches, nausea, and coughing. It's particularly dangerous for the elderly, children, and asthmatics. Among other things, it can increase asthmatics' susceptibility to allergens, and studies show that hospital admissions for asthma and other respiratory distress shoot up when ground-level ozone increases. Repeated exposure to ozone can permanently damage lung tissue. Ozone affects plant life, too, weakening trees so they succumb easily to stresses like drought or insects, turning their leaves or needles a mottled yellow and then brown before they drop off. In farm fields, ozone can cut yields by ten to 25 percent, and causes $5 billion to $10 billion in damage to U.S. crops each year. Cars are top emitters of ozone's precursors.[6]

"Motor vehicle use in OECD countries is now generally recognized as the source of more air pollution than any other single human activity."

ORGANIZATION FOR ECONOMIC COOPERATION AND DEVELOPMENT (OECD) WEBSITE, 1999

Oxides of nitrogen and volatile organic compounds not only form ozone after coming out of tailpipes, they have impacts of their own, as do other pollutants of concern generated by driving.

🚗 *Oxides of nitrogen (NO_x)* can irritate the lungs, increase susceptibility to respiratory illness, and may cause emphysema. NO_x emissions contribute as well to the nitrogen deposition that can cause overgrowth of algae and deplete oxygen in bodies of water. NO_x emissions also lead to the formation of acid rain by converting into nitric acid in the atmosphere. It's this formation of nitric acid that makes an average car's yearly NO_x emissions high enough over time to dissolve a 20-pound steel cannonball. Highway vehicles remain the number one source of U.S. NO_x pollution; they generate more than half the NO_x pollution in OECD countries, and about a third of NO_x pollution in both the U.S. and Canada.[7]

🚗 *Volatile organic compounds (VOCs)* exuded by cars are sometimes neurotoxic or carcinogenic. Benzene, for example, can lead to leukemia even after exposures to low levels (one to 30 ppm) and is also linked to chromosomal damage and various other potentially fatal blood diseases. Most unleaded gasoline contains about five percent benzene, and auto emissions account for 45 percent of airborne benzene in the U.S. Polycyclic aromatic hydrocarbons or PAHs — another type of VOC spewed by cars — account for half of the air-pollution-caused cancer in California. Highway vehicles generate around 40 percent of VOC emissions in OECD countries; in 1997, they accounted for 27 percent of total VOC emissions in the U.S. and were the number two source of VOCs (the top source was industry; solvents and paints used in car manufacturing contribute significantly to these industry emissions). [8]

🚗 *Carbon monoxide (CO)*, the component that makes auto exhaust so deadly in closed spaces, is colorless, odorless, and tends to gather near its source; highest levels are generally found along roads with heavy traffic and at intersections. Motor vehicles remain the number one source of CO pollution in many countries. By binding with hemoglobin, CO prevents oxygen from getting to the brain, the heart, and other tissues. Exposure to CO at levels of 600 parts per million by volume (ppmv) can kill a person in ten hours or less. An hour's exposure to levels near 55 ppmv — typical in rush hour traffic — can impair time perception, vision, dexterity, and mental acuity, and research indicates CO pollution contributes significantly to misjudgments leading to crashes. The headache you get after spending too much time on a congested freeway may be due to CO, and it presents a particular danger for those with heart disease or angina.[9]

🚗 *Particulate matter* comes from tailpipes as well as from road dust and consists of tiny particles of smoke, soot, and dust, plus smaller particles that form in the atmosphere from gaseous emissions like No_x and VOCs. In the 1990s, the EPA estimated that particulate pollution killed 60,000 people a year in U.S. cities, a higher toll than from gun use or car crashes. The smallest particulates are most troublesome for health. Particles smaller than ten microns in diameter, or PM-10, can travel deep into the lungs, increasing asthma and causing other respiratory problems and diseases.

Even smaller particles, PM-2.5 (smaller than 2.5 microns), can go deeper in the lungs and enter the bloodstream. Some particulates carry toxins like heavy metals or other pollutants with them. Diesel engines have historically been big particulate producers: a diesel without emissions controls can produce up to 30 times the particulates produced by a similarly uncontrolled gasoline engine. All cars contribute to particulate loads by generating dust from car parts and road surfaces. Every tire on a car in use loses about a pound a year of rubber dust into the air, soil, and water. When cartoonist Andy Singer lived within 100 yards of a freeway interchange, he watched this kind of black tire dust accumulate on his windowsills. Clutches and brake linings also shed particulate matter. Including road dust, driving generated over 41 percent of 1996 U.S. PM-10 emissions.[10]

Lead remains an emissions problem in many of the world's countries. As of 1999, the World Bank listed only 36 countries that had completed total phase-outs of leaded gasoline (the U.S. and Canada among them; Great Britain's phase-out was expected in 2000), even though benefits of taking the lead out are major, technical obstacles are easy to surmount, and taxation creating a five to ten percent cost difference favoring unleaded gasoline helps consumers adjust to it easily. Some developing countries still use gasoline with "alarmingly large" lead levels, says the World Bank. In many cities worldwide, vehicle exhaust accounts for as much as 90 percent of atmospheric lead emissions.[11] Even low lead levels can harm children. Neurological problems caused by lead plague youngsters in such car-choked municipalities as Bangkok, Jakarta, and Mexico City. Seven of ten Mexico City newborns had blood lead levels higher than World Health Organization norms, said one study. "The implications to the Mexican society, that an entire generation of children will be intellectually stunted, is truly staggering," stated chemist Manuel Guerra.[12] In addition to lowering IQs, lead can cause learning disabilities, reduced attention spans, impaired growth, hearing loss, behavior problems, anemia, nerve damage, and paralysis. Even in countries that have phased lead out, roads and road dust, parking lots, and playgrounds remain contaminated by lead fallout, leaving children, the most vulnerable to lead's ill effects, the most likely to be exposed to the highest levels.

Methyl tertiary butyl ether (MTBE) gives a good example of the way attempted solutions for car problems often create new problems. Used mainly after 1992 and in the U.S. to reduce carbon monoxide pollution, some evidence indicates MTBE may actually increase other pollutants, and its vapors may harm health. In addition, MTBE has contaminated water supplies in several locations. In Maine, one car with a leaky fuel tank contaminated the entire water supply of a school; in Santa Monica, California, at least 80 percent of city wells became polluted with MTBE, forcing the city to import drinking water. MTBE is very soluble in water, does not biodegrade, and may be a carcinogen. People smelling or drinking MTBE-contaminated water detect its foul odor and bad taste and react with dizziness, rashes, swelling, diarrhea, respiratory problems, and nausea. As of 1998, most oxygenated gasoline contained MTBE, and that meant it was in about a third of the U.S. gasoline supply. By 1999, widespread efforts had been mounted to phase it out. The cleanup of MTBE-contaminated water supplies is expected to cost millions at least.[13]

- ***Methylcyclopentadienyl manganese tricarbonyl (MMT)*** is an octane-enhancing fuel additive manufactured by the Ethyl Corporation — the same company that brought us tetraethyl lead. While Ethyl claims that MMT (marketed as "HiTEC(R) 3000") is "environmentally beneficial" because it reduces NO_X and CO emissions, others express hesitation. When eaten in trace quantities, manganese is an important nutrient. But when breathed, manganese may cause nerve, brain, and lung damage, including Parkinson's-like symptoms, as well as impairing hand-eye coordination and slowing reaction time. Few studies have explored potential effects of low-level, long-term exposure — the kind we might all get with widespread use of MMT in gasoline — but there is evidence that exposure to airborne manganese may bring on hyperactive, aggressive, or criminal behavior. The U.S. EPA estimated that only a small percentage (.02 percent) of the U.S. gasoline supply contained MMT as of 1998, but refiners and suppliers aren't required to disclose which gasoline it's in. Canada permitted MMT use beginning in 1978; 20 years later, when the Canadian government attempted to ban the use of MMT due to health concerns, the Ethyl Corporation threatened to sue, calling this a violation of the North American Free Trade Agreement (NAFTA). Backed into a corner by the provisions of NAFTA, Canada caved in and rolled back the ban, paying Ethyl $20 million for lost revenues and court costs. The U.S. EPA also attempted an MMT ban, but was challenged in court by Ethyl and lost. Organizations like Physicians for Social Responsibility have continued to call for an MMT ban despite these court decisions.[14]

> *"It is insane to treat cars as a universal necessity for daily transportation. We will choke to death!"*
>
> JEAN-FRANCIS HELD, IN MARK HERTSGAARD, *EARTH ODYSSEY*

Fumes and Smokestacks: The Car's Indirect Emissions

Evaporative emissions from cars and gas stations: Cars can pollute even when they're not running. Evaporative emissions radiate from fuel left in hot engines after cars are turned off. This "hot soak" can occur on warm days even if cars haven't been turned on.[15] Filling gas tanks also generates evaporative emissions and exposes us to carcinogens. Warning labels have cautioned California motorists about gas stations since the passage of Proposition 65, the state's Safe Drinking Water and Toxic Enforcement Act of 1986. While these labels are non-specific, not necessarily indicative of exposure levels, and so ubiquitous that few pay much attention to them, their language is pretty scary:

Chemicals known to the State to cause cancer, birth defects, or other reproductive harm are found in gasoline, crude oil, and many other petroleum products and their vapors, or result from their use ... [and] are found in and around gasoline stations, refineries, chemical plants, and other facilities that produce, handle, transport, store, or sell crude oil and petroleum and chemical products ....[16]

Depending on the blend, gasoline may contain as many as 225 different compounds of varying toxicities, which evaporate into the air especially if you use a gas hose without a vapor recapture barrier. Topping off your gas tank allows fumes to escape and, even if you don't spill gasoline in the process, it may leak as you drive and the fuel in your over-filled tank heats and expands. Gasoline and crude oil distribution releases toxic and smog-producing vapors as tank trucks or rail cars load and unload, and there can be vapor leaks from pumps, valves, and other equipment in which fuel is stored or transferred.[17]

Idling

It's a myth that cars need a lengthy warm-up before being driven, yet many drivers persist in idling cars to warm them up, or keep them idling while stopped for long periods. This idling habit worsens emissions. In Canada, cities like Toronto and Montreal have passed laws that limit idling to no more than three minutes. Any more than ten seconds of idling uses more fuel than shutting off and restarting the engine. Excessive idling is not only bad for the air, it can be bad for the car. Operating at idling temperatures can leave soot deposits and generate corrosive sulfuric acid in an engine. Cars are best warmed up by starting out slowly when driving, which will cut engine warm-up times in half and save fuel.[18]

Emissions from factories: Car factories typically show up on lists of top air polluters. Making cars involves processes (like metal fabricating) and materials (paints and solvents, for example) that emit a variety of pollutants. Altogether the auto industry sends thousands of tons of CO, NO_x (including nitrogen dioxide), particulate matter, and sulfur dioxide (SO_2) into the air each year. But the industry's biggest air emissions come in the form of VOCs like toluene, xylene, and methyl ethyl ketone. These contribute to formation of ozone or other pollutants and can damage vital organs like lungs, kidneys, and the liver as well as the nervous system. Some such VOCs are known or probable carcinogens. In 1993, each of the ten most polluting U.S. auto plants or parts facilities released over a million pounds of toxins, mostly into the air. Car and car-part makers released 79 million pounds of at least 73 different toxic chemicals that year, of which nearly 78 million pounds went into the air.[19]

Emissions from refineries: Another big contributor to air pollution is the oil refining industry. Petroleum refining in the U.S., for example, accounts for more total SO_2 and VOC emissions than any other single industry. Oil refineries typically emit a long list of toxins and can create health problems for nearby residents. Gasoline accounts for 43 percent of petroleum refinery output; in addition, refineries produce diesel fuel, asphalt, road oil, and feedstocks for plastics and other materials used in cars. Altogether at least half the output from petroleum refineries goes straight to supporting motor vehicle transportation. The U.S. petroleum refining industry released over 68 million pounds of pollutants in 1996. Of those releases, 76 percent went into the air. Significant quantities of ammonia, SO_2, and VOCs like benzene, toluene, xylene, propylene, and methyl ethyl ketone enter the air from refinery discharges.[20]

In-the-car pollution: Your exposure to some air pollutants and toxic compounds might be two to ten times higher inside cars than outside, according to 1999 data. A two-year study in California found that concentrations of carbon monoxide, benzene, MTBE, and other harmful compounds are higher inside cars than at roadside monitoring stations. Commuters driving during rush hour get the highest exposures, often from pollutants emitted by vehicles ahead of them. If you use a carpool lane, pollutant levels inside your car stay lower.[21] Part of a car's interior pollution can come from off-gassing by synthetic chemicals used in car upholstery and components. "When you get into your new car and you smell that synthetic leather, maybe you are breathing [an endocrine disrupter]," says Dr. Ana Soto of Tufts University Medical School.[22] Endocrine disrupters mimic hormones in living tissues and may be responsible for deformities and developmental problems in wildlife and humans, including increased endometriosis in women and sperm count declines in men.

> *"We're playing Russian roulette with the climate and no one knows what lies in the chamber of the gun."*
>
> TIM NAISH, NEW ZEALAND GEOLOGICAL AND NUCLEAR SCIENCE INSTITUTE

Cars and Climate Change

By adding to the greenhouse gases that alter climate, car emissions have helped pull us into a major experiment with the weather and so far the results don't look good.

- Atmospheric concentrations of CO_2, the main greenhouse gas implicated in global warming, are higher than they've been in 160,000 years, and they're rising. At nearly 367 ppmv in 1999, they're 30 percent higher than the 280 ppmv level that had held steady for several thousand years before the Industrial Revolution.[23]

- Global average surface temperature increased by about 0.7 degrees Celsius from 1900 to 1998, a significant increase considering that global average temperatures during ice ages differ by only 5 or 6 degrees from the warm periods between them. Seven of the globe's ten warmest years have been recorded since 1990.[24]

- The incidence of extreme weather events has gone up 28% since 1975. Weather-related damages played a key role in raising 1990s insurance costs to 15 times what they were in the 1960s. "A further advance in man-made climate change will almost inevitably bring us increasingly extreme natural events and consequently increasingly large catastrophic losses," said one insurance company representative in announcing that 1998 natural disasters cost insurers over $90 billion worldwide.[25]

- Sea levels, which have gone up since the last ice age, may now be rising faster. With levels up ten to 25 centimeters in the 100 years ending in 1995, small island nations report losing ground: salt water intrusion has forced abandonment of farm fields on some islands and some low, uninhabited islets used for marine navigation have recently disappeared under water.[26]

- Ranges of disease-carrying mosquitoes have spread, carrying malaria, dengue fever, and other illnesses into new areas.[27]

- Temperature changes have affected the range and survival of some plant and animal species. Several bird and butterfly species have relocated in North America and in Europe, in an apparent response to temperature shifts. Bleaching from higher sea temperatures killed or damaged 80 percent of corals in parts of the Indian Ocean in 1998, including some protected marine parks, and could negatively affect a variety of species that depend on coral for food and habitat.[28]

- Spring comes earlier, fall starts later, and the growing season in many parts of the world, including Alaska and northern Canada, has become longer and warmer. Farmers are plowing up more of the Arctic tundra to grow crops, and permafrost is melting, releasing more CO_2 as it does.[29]

- Arctic ice is thinning; Antarctic ice shelves are breaking up faster; glaciers have shrunk worldwide; and ice fields in Glacier National Park may disappear completely by 2030.[30]

These changes are consistent with computer model projections of global warming's effects, and evidence continues to accumulate that human activities like driving contribute to them. Models project even more change for the future if we don't curb emissions of greenhouse gases, and some scientists believe these changes could come quickly. Sea levels could continue to rise, flooding lowland coastal areas and making them more vulnerable to storm damage. Extreme weather events and natural disasters could continue to increase as could vector-borne diseases. Farming could suffer as warmer temperatures dry out soils and cause more frequent droughts in some areas. Warmer temperatures could worsen air quality problems. Warming-induced hydrological changes could affect forests, rangelands, and aquatic ecosystems, shifting ideal ranges for species faster than they can adapt and leading to local extinctions. The crash of golden toad populations in tropical cloud forests, linked to climate change and a shift in range, is one such species loss that's already taken place; combined with habitat destruction, such changes could have far-reaching negative effects on biodiversity. If melting ice sends masses of fresh water into the ocean, salt-concentration-dependent ocean currents that have warmed Europe for centuries could shut down, plunging northern Europe into deep cold. And certain effects of global warming may create positive feedback loops, accelerating accumulation of CO_2 in the atmosphere even further.[31]

No one knows for sure what will happen as atmospheric chemistry and the climate continue to shift. We do know, though, that driving cars adds to the conditions that are likely driving these changes. In a year, a typical North American car will add close to five tons of CO_2 to the atmosphere. Cars account for an estimated 15 to 25 percent of CO_2 emissions around the globe, 25 percent of U.S. CO_2 emissions, and over 30 percent of Canada's CO_2 emissions. That additional carbon in turn influences global temperatures and local weather patterns in ways we've only begun to understand, and in the U.S., vehicles are the fastest-growing source of greenhouse gases.[32] Cars also contribute to the increase in greenhouse gases by leaking refrigerants from car air conditioners and emitting methane and nitrous oxide from tailpipes. Automotive carbon monoxide emissions have indirect effects that increase greenhouse gas levels still further. Cars may contribute to climate change as well, by encouraging the conversion of green spaces to asphalt-dominated sprawl, thus creating urban heat islands and displacing trees that absorb CO_2 and cool surface temperatures.[33] As atmospheric scientist James Hansen

> *"The biggest single technology causing greenhouse emissions is the automobile, and it is the hardest for nations to recognize as the culprit."*
>
> PETER NEWMAN, INSTITUTE FOR SUSTAINABILITY AND TECHNOLOGY POLICY, MURDOCH UNIVERSITY, PERTH

remarked in 1995, "The climate system is being pushed hard enough that change will become obvious to the man in the street in the next decade."[34] The more we drive, the more we risk pushing the climate.

Cars and the Ozone Hole

Up through model year 1995, auto air conditioners used the refrigerant Freon®, also known as CFC-12, one of the more potent of the ozone-depleting chlorofluorocarbons (CFCs). CFCs were also used to blow foam for car seating. Containing fifteen times the amount of CFCs as are in a household refrigerator, car air conditioners had, by the early 1990s, caused an estimated one-fifth of stratospheric ozone destruction.[35] Unlike ground-level ozone, which can harm us and which we'd like to reduce, we'd like to keep stratospheric ozone so it can continue to protect us from getting too much dangerous UV radiation from the sun. Unfortunately, cars have helped shift the balance in the wrong direction.

There is some good news: the 1987 signing of the Montreal Protocol and later additions to that agreement have led to a phase-out of ozone-depleting CFCs. Air conditioners in cars made in the U.S., Canada, and Europe now use substitutes which have less impact on ozone — mainly a hydrofluorocarbon (HFC) known as HFC-134a. But there is also bad news: HFC-134a is a potent greenhouse gas, up to 3,400 times more effective at trapping heat in the atmosphere as CO_2. Just a few years after the Montreal Protocol encouraged their use, the Kyoto Protocol named HFCs as one of six chemical classes of greenhouse gases whose use must be reduced. The other bad news is that CFCs themselves will still be with us for a while: they persist in the atmosphere, they're still used in older cars, and exceptions in the Montreal Protocol allow some developing countries to produce them until 2010.

Cars produced before 1996 that still have CFC-charged air conditioners carry most of the CFCs still in use in the U.S., perhaps the world. Many of those CFCs will end up in the atmosphere, since air conditioners often leak and CFCs aren't always completely captured when air conditioners are repaired or cars are junked. From the time they escape, CFC molecules can take anywhere from one to 15 years to drift up to the stratospheric ozone layer, and another 150 years to break down. Meanwhile they continue reacting with and destroying ozone.[36]

Converting a car's air conditioner to an alternative refrigerant can cost anywhere from $100 to $800 or more. In North America, that's spurred development of a CFC black market. The CFCs are produced legally in China, Mexico, India, or Russia but then are shipped illegally into the U.S. and other developed countries, where unscrupulous repair shops offer CFC recharges to motorists wanting to avoid the conversion expense. In terms of contraband smuggled into Miami in 1994 and 1995, CFCs were second in value only to cocaine, though enforcement efforts have since reduced the illegal CFC trade. From 1993 to early 1999, U.S. Customs seized over two million pounds of illegal CFCs worth an estimated $32 million.[37]

Though there are signs the ozone layer may begin to heal, ozone destruction is still occurring at both poles, and corresponding increases in ultraviolet-B radiation have been detected at the Earth's surface in places like Alaska and New Zealand.[38] Recent research indicates climate change, too, may harm the ozone layer, especially in the Arctic. As the troposphere warms, the stratosphere above it may cool, and cooler stratospheric temperatures catalyze more destruction of ozone. A 1998 Environment Canada report predicted more serious thinning of Arctic ozone due to this greenhouse gas link.[39] Cars can thus contribute to ozone destruction in two ways, both by releasing CFCs and by emitting greenhouse gases.

Cars and Acid Rain

When SO_2 or NO_x meet water droplets in the air, they form sulfuric and nitric acids respectively, making acid rain. Though acid rain has historically been blamed mostly on SO_2 emissions from utilities and industry, smokestack controls on utilities in particular reduced SO_2 levels significantly in the 1990s, while NO_x levels remained about the same. Now, nitric acid formed by NO_x emissions — about 30 percent of which come from tailpipes in the U.S. — is increasingly showing up as acid rain's main component. Cars contribute to acid rain in two ways. First, vehicles rank as the top emitters of acid-rain-forming NO_x in both the U.S. and Canada. Second, cars account for a big portion of industrially caused acid rain since much SO_2 and industrially produced NO_x in North America comes from industries, including metal ore smelters, that feed vehicle manufacture.[42]

Acid rain has contributed to widespread damage in forests of the northeastern U.S. and eastern Canada, as well as in Scandinavia and continental Europe. It damages leaf surfaces and changes soil chemistry, creating nutrient deficiencies in plants. Acid rain weakens red spruce in North American forests, and may weaken sugar maples and other tree species, by affecting a tree's ability to utilize calcium,

How Cars Rain on Your Weekend Parade

It's not just your imagination: it does rain more on weekends, and car commutes are the likely cause. As ozone and carbon monoxide pollution accumulates, rising to peak levels late in the week, so does rainfall, says a 1998 study by Arizona State University climatologists Randall Cerveny and Robert Balling Jr. Cerveny and Balling found a seven-day cycle corresponding to the work week in pollution levels along North America's eastern seaboard. They theorize that as this pollution rises through the work week, it has a cloud-seeding effect, providing aerosol particles around which rain drops form. The resulting clouds rise into position for rain about the time the weekend hits, making Saturdays 22 percent rainier than Mondays, when both pollution and rainfall levels again drop. The researchers say this weekend increase in rain may happen anywhere downwind of a major pollution source.[40]

Work done by environmental engineering professor Kurt Paterson of Michigan Technological University uncovered a similar seven-day cycle in particulate levels near Michigan's Mackinac Bridge. Paterson's team found a weekly rise in fine particulates that correlates with weekend and holiday traffic over the bridge. Particulates drop at other times of the week, when there is less bridge traffic.[41]

an important component of leaf and needle cells. It can cut crop yields as well. Major damage has been done to lakes and streams by acid rain, since aquatic life is very sensitive to acid levels in water. It's rendered some lakes in New York's Adirondack Mountains lifeless. In combination, ozone and acid rain — a one-two punch from automotive pollution — can devastate forests much more than either one alone. Forests near Los Angeles and in Europe's Rhine Valley have particularly suffered from this mixture. Some auto-pollution-damaged forests near Los Angeles lost half their pines in the 1970s. Acid precipitation also accelerates the decay of roads and bridges, affects human health by leaching lead into the water supply from older pipes, increases our exposure to other heavy metals such as mercury, and eats away at stone monuments and buildings. Classical remains of Greek culture in Athens, pyramids in Egypt, ancient Mayan inscriptions in Mexico, and irreplaceable statues and building facades in Italy are among the artistic and archeological treasures that have been damaged by acidic rain, fog, and vapors in smog. "Kiss Michelangelo good-bye," laments professor of atmospheric sciences Richard Turco, in writing about the problem.[43]

> "The car [is] not only tainting the present but devouring the past and threatening the future."
>
> MARK HERTSGAARD, *EARTH ODYSSEY*

Summing Up the Effects of Auto Air Pollution

Emissions of pollutants and greenhouse gases from tailpipes, auto plants, and oil refineries add up to a lot of damage to health and the environment. Not to be forgotten, wildlife suffer many of the same effects from air pollution as do people. And when it comes to human health, air pollution hurts the health of four to five billion of us every year, say agencies like the World Health Organization and the World Bank. Much of that pollution comes from cars. Many effects of air pollution on human health are chronic and insidious. Some tests show that breathing car exhaust or smog can be as bad for health as smoking. UCLA researchers studying smog's health effects found that non-smokers living in smoggy Glendora scored the same on certain respiratory health tests as chronic smokers from cleaner Lancaster. Some southern California residents are routinely exposed to car-created carcinogens at levels up to 5,000 times higher than considered safe by the EPA. Asthma went up nearly 50 percent worldwide from 1980 to 1989; though the cause of this rise is uncertain, asthma can be worsened by smog. In the U.S., the asthma death rate is three times what it was 20 years ago. Forty percent of asthma cases occur in children, though they make up just 25 percent of the population. A 1995 American Lung Association report found over 12 million U.S. children of 13 and under lived in areas regularly violating ozone standards, putting them at greater risk for asthma and other breathing disorders.[44]

Car fume components can contribute to heart disease, too. Besides the heart-damaging effects of carbon monoxide, particulate matter also generates cardiovascular illness. A 1998 Scottish study found that particulate pollution from automobiles inflames the lungs, in turn affecting blood clotting and increasing risks of heart attack and stroke. Professor Bill MacNee, who led the study, estimated that particulates may cause 8,000 such deaths a year in British cities. "It appears the lung cannot cope with handling lots of very small particles," MacNee told the BBC.[45]

Car emissions can cause cancer in several ways. The U.S. EPA has estimated that 55 percent of cancers attributed to air pollution are caused by car and truck emissions. Studies in Seattle and Switzerland have found cancer rates along busy roads to be two to nine times higher than those on quieter streets. Exposure to auto exhaust components can cause cancer: benzo(a)pyrene, for instance, creates cancer-promoting free radicals in breast cells, and nitrogen dioxide causes some cancers to spread faster in animals. Diesel emissions, which contain over 40 different hazardous substances including arsenic, benzene, formaldehyde and PAHs, have been fingered as at least "probable" carcinogens by several agencies. The risk of lung cancer increases 20 to 70 percent with high diesel exhaust exposure. Cars also likely contribute to increased skin cancer rates, as every one percent drop in stratospheric ozone could mean up to 20,000 more cases of skin cancer. New U.S. skin cancer cases jumped from 10,000 in 1975 to 40,000 in 1996, and deaths have more than doubled.[46]

"What You Can Do [about global warming]: ... Forget the sport utility vehicle ...."

TIME MAGAZINE, 24 AUGUST 1998

It's been estimated that one-third to one-half the U.S. population lives in areas with air pollution levels that are, by government standards, harmful. Worldwide, automobiles remain the biggest single contributor to the air pollution violating World Health Organization standards in all 20 of the planet's biggest cities. Even in places where air quality meets legal standards, says the *New England Journal of Medicine*, air pollution may raise death rates from lung cancer and heart disease.[47] Being married to the car is a lot like being married to a smoker and breathing second-hand smoke. The car has us in a literal choke-hold — reason enough to sue for divorce.

CHAPTER 7

Cleaning Up After the Car: Oil Spills and Other Environmental Messes

"It wasn't his driving that caused the Alaskan oil spill. It was yours."

1989 GREENPEACE AD PICTURING THE CAPTAIN OF THE EXXON VALDEZ

UNTIL THE LATE 19TH CENTURY, gasoline — a byproduct of kerosene manufacture — was considered a waste and a nuisance. Dangerous due to its volatility and hard to get rid of, it was often (and frequently at night) dumped in rivers and streams, killing fish and infuriating anglers. When use of gasoline as fuel for internal combustion engines began, this direct stream-dumping diminished. But as cheap gasoline has helped car use to grow, the corresponding increase in use of petroleum has led to much greater water pollution problems.

The sloppy car spills petroleum products everywhere, dripping oil and gasoline on land and, via its supply lines, spewing crude oil at sea. Not only that, but anyone who has ever seen an auto salvage yard or a major tire pile knows that the car leaves behind literal mountains of other wastes as well. We are forever having to clean up after the car.

Oil Spills, Big and Little, Accidental and On-Purpose

As driving and oil consumption burgeoned in the 1960s, so did the amount of oil extracted, shipped — and spilled. Spills from offshore drilling rigs and tankers turned seabirds and marine mammals into stark poster children for the environmental movement beginning in the late 1960s. A 1967 spill from the supertanker Torrey Canyon off the coast of England became the first massive marine pollution incident and shocked the world into realizing oil transport was far from foolproof. The ship unleashed 35 million gallons of crude, killing an estimated 25,000 birds and fouling both French and British beaches.[1]

With each succeeding spill since then, emergency procedures and international laws governing oil pollution have become stronger. But a lot of oil still gets spilled or leaked on its way from the well to the fuel tank and, says the U.S. Interagency Coordinating Committee on Oil Pollution Research (ICCOPR), the risk of catastrophic spills remains high. Worldwide, the reported amount of oil spilled ranged from a few million gallons up to a few hundred million gallons each year since 1978. The number of small spills (under 100,000 gallons) has grown worldwide and, as of the mid-1990s, totaled around ten million gallons yearly. Large spills (over ten million gallons) continue, too, at a rate of one to three a year worldwide. In the U.S., an average of 8,100 oil spills — over 22 a day — are reported annually. About half of that spilled oil comes from vessels like tankers or barges; the rest comes from other parts of the oil production and transportation system, like pipelines, refining and storage facilities, and tanker trucks or train cars. "It is important to recognize," says the ICCOPR, "that potentially damaging discharges of crude oil or petroleum products can and do occur at every point in this system."[2]

Drilling for oil generates a proportionately small number of spills but large amounts of waste. Drilling's biggest waste product is "produced water:" briny, sometimes toxic, sometimes even radioactive water pumped out of wells along with oil. Produced water contains oil remnants and has often been dumped into lakes, streams, or open waste pits. These pits in particular, filled with oily water or the sludge left over after the water percolates away, become death traps for wildlife and especially birds who mistake them for lakes. Such pits drown or poison as many as two million birds a year just in the U.S. Under offshore oil rigs, other waste products — piles of contaminated sediments, metals, lubricants, and other drilling debris — have been found to leach harmful levels of toxins like arsenic and lead into surrounding ocean water.[3]

As oil drilling has increased in developing countries, so too have complaints about spills, environmental damage, and threats to health. In Papua New Guinea, indigenous peoples near one oil field have complained of effects on fish and game despite the oil company's efforts to make the development "sustainable." In Colombia, oil wells have been repeatedly closed due to violations of health and sanitary codes. In Nigeria, conflicts between oil companies and ethnic groups such as

"It's a mixed blessing."

the Ogoni have stemmed from years of oil drilling and charges that it's destroyed mangrove swamps, forests, fish, wildlife, and fresh water sources.[4]

Oil tankers spilled about three million gallons for each 42 billion gallons (one billion barrels) delivered worldwide from 1980 to 1995. The biggest tanker spill in history happened in 1983 when the Castillo de Bellver caught fire off South Africa's coast and gushed 78.5 million gallons of crude into the ocean.[5] The numbers tell little about what makes such spills so damaging and deadly. As spills leave marine mammals and birds blackened with oil, their fur and feathers are flattened and no longer insulate against the cold. Even if they can clean themselves, they become poisoned by toxins in the crude. If they survive, they may suffer immune system, behavioral, or reproductive damage for years.

> *"The beach wasn't cleaned so much as rebuilt, left scrubbed and sterile. And still it held oil."*
>
> MARYBETH HOLLEMAN, VISITING SLEEPY BAY BEACH IN PRINCE WILLIAM SOUND, EIGHT YEARS AFTER THE VALDEZ SPILL

The 1989 grounding of the Exxon Valdez near Alaska's Prince William Sound spilled close to 11 million gallons of crude oil. The biggest spill in U.S. or Canadian waters, it became one of the more highly publicized and studied spills in part because it fouled such a previously pristine area. Coating 1,300 miles of shoreline, it killed hundreds of harbor seals, thousands of sea otters, and hundreds of thousands of birds like marbled murrelets, harlequin ducks, and bald eagles. By six years later, none of the populations of these species in Prince William Sound had recovered. By ten years later, only one species — the bald eagle — was considered recovered, and residual oil and asphalt could still be found in parts of the Sound. The area's herring population has crashed, affecting the entire food chain. The spill also contaminated beaches and devastated hunting and fishing grounds, decimating the subsistence lifestyle of local native Alaskans. Clean-up and response costs totaled over $2 billion, not including restoration, and some clean-up techniques added to the damage. For instance, high-pressure water spray used to clean oil-covered beaches disrupted contaminated mussel beds still further; ten years later, mussels were another species that had yet to recover from the spill.[6]

Routine discharges of oily waste from tanker holds and ballast tanks still add significant but unknown amounts of oil to marine environments, perhaps even more oil than is spilled accidentally. Not all ports worldwide have waste holding tanks that allow proper disposal of oily waste water from ships. And even where such facilities exist, it's often cheaper and easier, with chances of getting caught slight, to discharge oily wastes into the ocean illegally. The U.S. National Academy of Sciences has estimated that only about a quarter of ocean oil pollution from shipping is spilled accidentally.

Deliberate discharges have been killing as many as 100,000 seabirds each year off Newfoundland, and an Australian study has documented that ongoing illegal dumping of oily wastes from ships is harming birds and wildlife in Australian waters. In the mid-1990s, researchers noticed high numbers of rare penguins dying at the Philip Island Nature Park in Victoria. The penguins, who can range as far as

200 miles from their home colonies in search of food, washed up on beaches smothered in oil — sometimes crude, sometimes refined petroleum products. By essentially fingerprinting the deadly oils, researchers determined they had to have been discharged illegally, and the high number of penguin deaths suggested that this continues to be a widespread practice. In reporting this finding, the researchers pleaded for better enforcement of shipping waste disposal laws.[7]

Pipeline and tank farm spills accounted for 79 percent of the worst oil spills in 1990; tankers accounted for only about 14 percent, and the remainder spewed from other sources (barges, trains, trucks, etc.). A significant percentage of refineries, tank farms (oil storage facilities consisting of numerous large aboveground tanks), and pipelines have leaked large plumes of oil or gasoline into the soil and groundwater. Industry analysts estimate that at some facilities perhaps 70 percent of aboveground tanks leak. In the early 1990s, a 3.8 million gallon underground pool of leaded gasoline, apparently leaked from a nearby refinery, was discovered under Hartford, Illinois; it contaminated groundwater and caused explosions and fires. Near Port Everglades, Florida, a tank farm and port terminal left an underground plume of petroleum products eight feet thick in places. Similar spills have been documented thousands of times in the U.S., and occur worldwide. From 1982 to 1989, the U.S. General Accounting Office estimated somewhere between 2,000 and 3,000 spills

Oil Spill News

Only the biggest oil accidents attract our attention with headlines, but spills happen constantly. Here are a few of the incidents reported during an approximate four-week period while I was working on this chapter:

- January 15, 1999 (Reuters): A huge diesel oil spill floating along the Danube River stretched to 35 miles (55 km) long and 330 yards (300 meters) wide before breaking into smaller patches. Officials concerned about safety at a Bulgarian nuclear power plant installed barriers to keep the oil from being pumped into the plant's cooling system.[8]

- January 19, 1999 (Reuters): Alaskan officials blamed a slow leak from a small pipeline hole for a significant spill of crude oil into the Kenai National Wildlife Refuge. The leak developed due to corrosion in the aging pipeline, officials said.[9]

- January 28, 1999 (Environmental News Network): U.S. Coast Guard officials said thousands of tar balls drifting toward Puerto Rican beaches likely came from an illegal discharge from an oil tanker. The tar balls began washing up on San Juan beaches at the height of the tourist season.[10]

- February 9, 1999 (USA Today): A cargo ship that ran aground about 150 yards off the coast of Oregon began leaking fuel. Oil-covered birds were found and officials worried the spill could affect the habitat of the threatened Western snowy plover.[11]

occurred from aboveground storage tanks. A 1991 court affidavit called it "likely that contamination of soil and/or groundwater due to leaks of aboveground tanks could be found at most if not all" bulk petroleum facilities in the U.S.[12]

Pipelines, too, spill oil both on land and at sea. From 1984 to 1993, nearly all significant spills from offshore oil operations came from pipelines. Oil spills from U.S. pipelines occurred at least once a day in the 1980s. And since 1993, the Environmental Defense Fund has testified, pipeline spills have actually increased, in spite of calls for safety improvements. Recent years have seen major spills from South America to Siberia, where in the early 1990s a pipeline lost enough oil to create a lake of crude seven miles long, four miles wide and six feet deep.[13]

Disposal of used motor oil sends more oil into the water each year than even the largest tanker spill. Worldwide, about 37 percent of ocean oil pollution is washed out to sea from land. Many car owners who change their own oil (in North America, about half do) dispose of it improperly, pouring it down the drain, on the ground, or into the regular trash. In the U.S., this puts about a quarter of used motor oil in the wrong place every year. In 1994, for instance, the EPA estimated that about 23 percent of the used motor oil collected (161 million out of 714 million gallons) was dumped improperly. This oil gets into the water supply along with the toxic heavy metals (lead, arsenic, copper, cadmium) and other substances that end up in oil after it's used in a car engine. Just one gallon (four quarts) of oil can disperse into and contaminate about a million gallons of water. Three-quarters of used motor oil is reused or "recycled" in the U.S., often as fuel for space heaters, asphalt plants, diesel engines or boilers, but because it contains lead and other heavy metals this "recycling" may create toxic air pollution. In the U.S., in fact, the burning of used motor oil for fuel may be the largest industrial source of airborne lead.[14]

LUST, and plenty of it, has been generated by the love affair with the car. In this case, we're talking about leaking underground storage tanks at gas stations, originally dubbed LUSTs by acronym-happy bureaucrats charged with figuring out how to clean up and replace the hundreds of thousands of them in the U.S. alone. As of December 1998, the U.S. began requiring double-walled fiberglass tanks for underground gasoline storage, rather than the old single-walled steel tanks.

"Not only our tankers fail; the whole system is a leaky vessel."

JANE HOLTZ KAY, *ASPHALT NATION*

While this may solve many (though not all) of these problems, the leaked gasoline left by corroded tanks and loose pipe fittings will continue to pose a clean-up task. "Once [water] is contaminated [with gasoline], you can never really rely on it again as being a pure source," says Lois Epstein of the Environmental Defense Fund.[15]

Across the U.S., the EPA has confirmed close to 400,000 leaks from underground gasoline storage tanks. More than a million tanks have been removed from service or replaced since the EPA began regulating and tracking the LUST problem. About 900,000 underground storage tanks are still active in the U.S.[16] LUSTs across North America have contaminated soil and groundwater, caused sewer explosions, and generated fumes that have forced abandonment of numerous homes and at least one shopping center. It's likely that leaking underground storage tanks are a problem in other places worldwide, and could become more so as vehicle use increases in developing countries.

Cars, Roads, and Non-Point-Source Water Pollution

Cars leave lots of little things behind on the road: bits of tire rubber, oil, gasoline, brake lining fibers, heavy metals, and other automotive debris. When it rains and water flows off roads and parking lots into storm drains and then into lakes and streams, it takes with it all this effluent cars have left behind. All these contaminants are non-point-source pollutants; they come not from a single specific location like a smokestack or an outflow pipe but instead from widespread small sources. It's a big problem, and cars account for a big percentage of non-point-source water pollution. In the U.S., says one estimate, petroleum products washed off pavement every year, along with oil dumped into storm drains, send 15 times more oil into the ocean than did the Exxon Valdez.[17] In rural areas, polluted runoff percolates through soil, leaving contaminants there. Studies have documented higher heavy metal concentrations in plants and waterways near roadsides, likely from tire particles containing lead oxide and other metal additives.[18] Cars can muddy and otherwise contaminate water in a few other ways as well.

- *Soil erosion from roads* inflicts major damage on streams, rivers, and lakes. Construction of a divided highway can generate up to 3,000 tons of sediment per mile. Through its life, a road continues to cause soil erosion, especially if it's unpaved. Increased sedimentation from roads can smother spawning beds and rob streams of food and oxygen, killing fish. "If the fishing public was adequately informed of the negative effects of roads on fisheries," writes conservation biologist Reed Noss, "perhaps all but the laziest would demand that most roads on public lands be closed and revegetated."[19]

- *De-icing with road salt* causes serious saline pollution, contaminating groundwater, killing trees, and changing the mix of species along roadsides. Use of road salt may quintuple the chloride concentrations in water bodies near cities, stimulating growth of algae. Road salt may also contain cyanide-based rust inhibitors, making it especially toxic to fish. The ten million or so tons of road salt used annually in the U.S. also contaminate wells and corrode structures like underground utility cables, steel bridges, and roads and cars themselves. Altogether, environmental and infrastructure damage from road salt costs over $5 billion a year.[20]

- *Road-side herbicide spraying* is a widespread highway maintenance practice that also contributes toxins to non-point-source runoff. Altogether, highway department use of herbicides amounts to nearly ten percent of all herbicides sold in the U.S.[21]

🚗 *Anti-freeze and other car fluids* enter the environment from cars, too. Anti-freeze, made of propylene glycol or ethylene glycol, is toxic before it's used; once used, it becomes more toxic because it has absorbed heavy metals and other poisons from the car's cooling system. In 1992 one of the first California condors to be released into the wild was found dead after drinking from a puddle of spilled anti-freeze. Thousands of family pets — an estimated 10,000 U.S. dogs yearly — and unknown numbers of wildlife succumb from drinking sweet-tasting anti-freeze that ends up in driveway or streetside puddles.[22]

Cars and Point-Source Water Pollution

Cars contribute to point-source water pollution — the pollution that comes out of factories in outflow pipes — via mining, metal smelting, auto manufacturing, and petroleum refining. These industries may send more toxins into the air, but also end up on lists of major water polluters. Half the birth-defect-causing chemicals discharged in Michigan from 1990 to 1994 went into a single waterway, and nearly all were discharged by a single auto company plant.[23] In 1988, nearly 16 pounds of reportable toxic substances were released into the environment for every U.S. car produced, a total of over 160 million pounds. Since then, carmakers have cut toxic releases but, as of 1997, still generated 6.23 pounds of reportable toxics, including 2.1 pounds of persistent toxins for every vehicle made: a combined total of almost 60 million pounds.[24] Many of these toxins get into water either directly or via atmospheric deposition.

More water pollutants get discharged by industries that feed materials to cars. Steel mills discharged more than 20 million pounds of toxins directly into U.S. surface waters in 1996, and steel for cars accounted for 15 percent of that.[25] Petroleum refining sent over ten million pounds of toxins into surface waters the same year. Pollution from plants and refineries in other countries is not always as thoroughly tracked, but is likely to be equivalent to what's found in U.S. factories, if not worse.

Even if these industries didn't pollute at all, cars would still impact water supplies. The manufacture of one car uses about 120,000 gallons (450,000 liters) of water. And we use a lot of water to maintain cars, too. As many as 40 to 150 gallons (150 to 570 liters) are used to wash a single car, when washed at home; commercial car washes use from nine to 60 gallons (34 to 230 liters) per wash, depending on the type of equipment used. Car washing can also pollute, with soap and detergents that add phosphates and nitrogen to water and, sometimes, with hazardous compounds used in car-washing products.[26]

When the Love Affair Ends at the Landfill

Automotive scrapping and recycling is about a five-billion-dollar-per-year industry in the U.S. Over 90 percent of scrapped U.S. cars, around nine million of them yearly, go through a recycling process that salvages about 11 million tons of steel and 800,000 tons of nonferrous metals (e.g., aluminum and copper) for re-use. But cars still send plenty of waste to landfills. By the time a car leaves the assembly line, its manufacture — including extraction and transport of the raw materials that go into it — has generated 29 tons of solid waste and 1,207 million cubic yards of air emissions. Manufacture of lead-acid batteries, for instance, consumes over 80 percent of lead used in the U.S. and the mines and smelters supplying this also emit lead into the air. More than 33 percent of a car's environmental costs are incurred in its manufacture; 60 percent come from the actual driving of the car; and seven percent come from disposal.[27]

"It is very difficult to dispose of cars in ways that do not cause further problems."

THE WATERSHED SENTINEL, DECEMBER 1992 / JANUARY 1993

In North America, the typical car gained weight over the 1990s, using more materials and generating even more potential for pollution and solid waste. By 1997, a typical car contained over 3,200 pounds of steel, iron, plastics, aluminum, glass, rubber, fluids, lubricants, lead, zinc, platinum, copper, and other miscellaneous materials. A typical new car contains about 5,000 parts and a growing number of these are plastic, which can be more difficult to recycle than metal and generate significant pollution when the plastics themselves are first produced.[28]

When a car is junked, scrappers strip it of reusable parts, flatten what's left, and send it to a shredder. Shredding a car to retrieve metals requires large electric motors that use a great deal of energy — another consideration in a car's lifetime energy costs. It's also dangerous; fires or explosions from the shredding of gas tanks and other closed containers are common. With shredding, nearly all scrap metal from cars gets recycled, but some still ends up in landfills, including three to four percent of leaded steel used in cars. As the shredder sorts out recyclable metals, it leaves behind a few hundred tangled pounds of residue, a mix of fibers, plastic, glass, rubber, wiring, and other minor components called "floss" or "fluff" or, more technically, "automobile shredder residue" (ASR). By weight, scrapped cars generate about 500 pounds of fluff for every ton of recyclable metals salvaged. This residue, perhaps as much as nine million metric tons a year of it in the U.S., heads to the landfill.[29]

Among the hazardous products coming out of old cars are CFCs from air conditioners, gas and oil left in the engine, radioactive materials from catalytic converters, lead and sulfuric acid from batteries (though most, but not all, lead-acid batteries get recycled), and heavy metals in fluids and switches. Scrappers are supposed to remove hazardous substances before cars are shredded, but that doesn't always happen. Fluff generally ends up containing high levels of heavy metals like zinc, cadmium, chromium, and lead; especially the latter three tend to leach into the environment. Some testing of fluff has also found PCBs and mercury. From the 1960s to the 1990s in North American cars, mercury switches were used widely for small lights, such as those in trunks and glove compartments. A 1995 Minnesota study found that about a third of junked cars still had one or more mercury switches in them as they sat in salvage yards waiting to be shredded. Shredding such a car releases the mercury into the environment; the amount of mercury in just one switch — about a gram — is enough to trigger a fish-consumption advisory in a 20-acre lake in Minnesota. When that state determined that about 86,000 mercury switches went through its auto salvage yards each year, they labeled the finding "cause for alarm."[30]

Old tires, too, create major disposal problems. Officials estimate there are about 800 million scrap tires stockpiled around the U.S., and many more worldwide. Every year in North America we throw out over 260 million tires, more than one tire per year per car. If your household has owned two cars for 20 years, your personal tire pile would contain 40 tires (where would you put them?). Most U.S. states won't accept tires at landfills, because tires trap gases inside and tend to "float" or work their way to the tops of dumps. While a reportedly growing proportion of used tires get "recovered," mostly to be burned as fuel, U.S. tire piles still grow by an estimated 60 to 70 million tires each year.[31]

Once in stockpiles, tires pose a fire hazard. They're composed of very combustible materials — primarily oil and rubber, with a few heavy metals thrown in — and also trap oxygen which will feed a fire once started. From 1971 to 1992, 176 tire fires were reported in the U.S. One that broke out in 1983 in Winchester, Virginia, burned an estimated seven million tires, took nine months to burn itself out, fouled

Cars and Recycling

Cars already contain some recycled materials. Recycled tin cans get recast into auto parts; some bumpers use recycled materials; and much aluminum and steel used in cars is recycled stock. Ninety-seven percent of U.S. lead-acid batteries are recycled, as is a growing proportion of tires.[32] Efforts to make cars more completely recycled and recyclable have been strong especially in Europe, where "end-of-life" vehicle directives would remove hazardous materials from cars and make manufacturers responsible for recycling most, if not all, vehicle materials. Still, there's a long way to go before cars stop generating waste. The sheer number of parts and materials used to produce cars can make recycling them difficult. Cars can contain up to 60 different plastics, most not easy to separate or re-use. Auto glass, for instance, is a layered blend of glass and plastic that makes windshields shatterproof but also not easily recyclable.

And recycling isn't necessarily harmless. Recycling plastic, for one, can create hazards. A Hamilton, Ontario, facility's stockpile of defective PVC auto parts waiting for recycling caught fire in July 1997; 400 metric tons of them burned for four days, releasing dioxins, furans, and other harmful compounds. Toxic ash from the fire settled throughout the city, prompting warnings that residents shouldn't let children play on lawns or eat garden vegetables for fear of dioxin exposure.[33] Metal recycling, too, can cause problems. Near a Los Angeles metal recycler which processes mostly old cars and trucks, residents have reported that "little metal granules push up through the skin rashes of neighborhood children."[34] While better safeguards might mitigate such dangers, their existence also argues for using another point of the reduce-reuse-recycle waste control triangle: *reducing* the use of these materials by reducing our driving.

the air in four states, and resulted in heavy metal pollution in the runoff of water used to combat the fire. In 1999, lightning ignited California's largest tire pile — seven million tires — and the 300-foot flames could be seen for 20 miles. Tire fires are difficult to quench, and firefighters expected this pile to burn for a year, sending five million pounds of contaminants into the air. Stockpiled tires also pose a health hazard. Used tires hold water at any angle and so breed mosquitoes, promoting the spread of mosquito-borne diseases. Asian Tiger mosquitoes (which spread encephalitis and dengue fever) first came to the U.S. in a shipload of used tires from Japan. And burning used tires for energy has proved controversial. While advocates of the practice assert that burning tires for fuel is cleaner than burning coal, critics note that because coal-burning isn't all that clean, this comparison doesn't impose a very high standard, and that tire-burning still generates pollutants like benzene, toluene, methylene chloride, PCBs, dioxins, and furans. Other recycling attempts include using ground tires in asphalt mixes for road repair, using old tires in new ones, and making products like shoes, floor tiles, handbags, and even houses out of old tires. But these recycling avenues use only a small percentage of the tires discarded each year.[35]

Cleaning Up after the Car: A Job That's Never Done

As much as we clean up after it, the messy car keeps adding to the mess it leaves behind. It's a persistent, toxic mess, hard to dispose of and damaging to health and the environment as long as it stays. The more we cater to the car, the harder it gets. Road-building and sprawl, for instance, worsen water pollution both by paving and destroying wetlands that filter out pollution, and by spreading pollution into more places. Oil spills, massive die-offs of birds and wildlife, contaminated drinking water wells, sediment-filled streams, and acid lakes are all reminders of ways the car's abuses range well beyond air pollution. Our list of grounds for divorce has grown longer, but we're not done yet. There are more.

CHAPTER 8

The Little Bad Habits
That Drive Us Crazy:
Miscellaneous Drawbacks
of Living with Cars

*"Owning a car brings joy twice in an owner's life — when it is bought
and when it is sold. In between there is only torture."*

RUSSIAN FOLK WISDOM

MAYBE YOU'VE HAD PROBLEMATIC CARS IN YOUR LIFE. Before my first car divorce, at least three passed through mine. There was the Dodge camper-van whose engine caught fire and left the interior coated with black soot. There was the Renault LeCar with a mystery problem that reduced its gas mileage to about half of what it should have been. There was the blue Volkswagen bug whose air-cooled motor failed so often we ended up changing engines on the side of the road the way most people change tires. From the time a car is purchased until it falls apart, not only the need for repairs but also bad habits like congestion, noise, and parking problems add to our levels of stress and annoyance. As cars subject both drivers and non-drivers to their little bad habits, being married to them — as individuals and as a society — can leave us less than happy.

Purchases, Repairs, Recalls, and Rip-offs

Our relationship with any particular car often starts with trepidation at the auto mall. Methods used by unscrupulous car dealers, especially in the 1940s and 50s, have often left potential customers feeling like a car purchase is akin to getting teeth pulled. Some dealers have used tactics like the high-pressure sales "blitz"; the "bait and switch" (luring customers with bargains, then manipulating them into worse deals); the "bush" (getting customers to sign conditional sales contracts, then upping the price); and the "highball" (having customers commit to new car purchases, then reneging on verbal promises of high trade-in values). Recent regulations have reduced sales shenanigans, but studies show some car buyers still encounter intimidating environments, complicated price negotiations, and broken promises when car shopping. Most years since surveys began in 1992, U.S. consumer agencies have received more complaints about auto sales than about any other business or service.[1]

Assuming a buyer gets through the purchase process, he or she leaves the dealership with a product more likely to bring consumer headaches than any other on the market. Even when one buys a top-quality car, chances are slim for getting one without a single flaw. In the first three months after purchasing new 1998 model cars, owners reported 176 problems, on average, for every 100 vehicles sold. And millions of cars a year end up getting recalled to fix some defect. In 1996, more than 17 million vehicles in the U.S. — more than the number of new cars sold that year — were recalled in 265 separate actions. Between 1966 and 1996, the U.S. averaged around 200 recall actions involving over six million vehicles yearly.[2]

> *"Finding a mechanic who is both reliable and affordable is only slightly easier than finding a parking place downtown on a Saturday night."*
>
> JOEL MAKOWER, *THE GREEN COMMUTER*

Auto repairs, like sales, almost always rank among the top three businesses generating the most U.S. consumer complaints. One study found that auto body shops gave proper repairs to only 29 percent of cars, another that 40 percent of car repair charges are fraudulent or unnecessary. In 1987, *Reader's Digest* sent a car expert with a simple repair problem on an undercover trip to U.S. auto shops and found that 56 percent of mechanics consulted either did unneeded repairs or charged for work they hadn't done. Ten years later, when an expert repeated the test, only a third of repair shops were able to fix his simple problem.[3]

"Is this a good time to bring up a car problem?"

The problem of car theft also haunts owners. The first auto theft took place in Paris in 1896 and soon inspired theft-prevention devices. Early methods to foil car thieves included Bosco's Collapsible Driver, a life-size inflatable rubber doll "so life-like and terrifying," ads claimed, "that nobody a foot away can tell it isn't a real live man." Cars continue to be major targets for theft and vandalism. Although U.S. car thefts declined in the 1990s, still one in every 153 U.S. cars was stolen in 1997. Only 14 percent of car thieves are apprehended.[4]

Fat and Backaches

Cars allow us to avoid exercise, saving work in the short run but impoverishing our health in the process. As *Prevention* magazine's Mark Bricklin has put it, "The modern sedentary lifestyle is a kind of toxic intervention ... very much like a slow infection that gradually creates discomfort, disability, and, finally, disease ... The leading edge of that intervention was the automobile."[5] The "convenience" of cars reinforces our addiction to them; the less we leave them, the less we are able to, as the sedentary lifestyles cars support allow our muscles and our motivation to atrophy. Distances considered walkable have shrunk tremendously since the car literally swept us off our feet.

Aesthetics

Cars have an unfortunate tendency to uglify our surroundings. This may be a matter of opinion, but it's an opinion shared by many: the sprawl and the strip-mall architecture that have emerged as a result of car dependence are considered visually unappealing by most people, notes planner Anton Nelessen based on responses to his Visual Preference Surveys™.

The motels, fast-food chains, neon, and huge parking lots that characterize roadside development influence visual environments because businesses need to catch the attention of fast-moving drivers. Details of building design that delight walkers in a city serve no purpose for so-called thirty-mile-per-hour architecture, where a business might just as well be, and increasingly is, in a big square box with an equally big sign. Sometimes the attention-grabbing artifacts of auto culture can be quaint or amusing, as in hot dog stands shaped like hot dogs or ice cream stores shaped like a cone. More often, though, they contribute to what James Howard Kunstler calls the geography of nowhere: cheap buildings without character surrounded by asphalt, leaving a place looking like it could be anywhere. Highway billboards create another aesthetic scar. Another 5,000 to 15,000 get added each year to the already half a million billboards along U.S. federally funded highways. Yet another aesthetic problem is that of abandoned cars. In the U.S., about a million old cars a year are left sitting like metallic roadkill along roadsides or on private property.[6]

One day I attended a slide presentation on the effect cars have had on the landscape. The man sitting next to me had earlier confessed he was a car nut, but as an image of a congested road lined with neon came to the screen, he muttered: "Yuck!" Moral: Even people who love cars admit that their artifacts are, at least at times, ugly.

Sitting in one position for long periods isn't recommended by back experts but may be required when driving; other forms of transport allow greater freedom of movement. Even if one sits in a comfortable, well-supported position in a car, sitting for too long strains the body. And many people sitting in a car may not be sitting well. More often than being ergonomically designed, car seats are fashioned to be comfortable for 8.5 minutes, the average time a customer sits in a seat when selecting a new car.[7] The Occupational Safety and Health Administration (OSHA) lists driving as a contributor to job-related repetitive motion injuries. Occupational drivers like salespeople or truck drivers can also suffer skeletal and muscular damage from driving's constant low-level vibrations.[8]

Then there's the fat problem. In the U.S., about 55 percent of adults are overweight. That's darn close to the number that don't get exercise. "Currently, more than 60 percent of American adults are not regularly active," report the U.S. Centers for Disease Control and Prevention. This contributes not just to obesity but also to heart disease, diabetes, colon cancer, and other diseases.[9] Cars help this happen by providing a sedentary substitute for physical propulsion. By driving on short trips, we lose opportunities to control our girth and to stay healthy by being active.

Noise

Pioneer traffic engineer William Phelps Eno, concerned about automotive noise, got Paris to ban the use of car horns downtown in 1912. The move was apparently too little, too late for writer Marcel Proust who, that same year, had his Paris study lined with cork to block the sounds of traffic. One wonders what either of them would think of Europe today, where 80 million people suffer daily from "unacceptable levels of continuous outdoor transport noise." Greece ranked as Europe's noisiest country in 1996; in car-choked Athens, 60 percent of residents routinely suffer noise levels of 75 decibels (dB) or higher. Seventy percent of Germans are continuously disturbed by road noise. About 65 percent of Europeans regularly experience noise above 55 decibels (dB), the level around which stress reactions begin and sleep is disturbed. About 20 percent live with 65 dB or more, the level increasing hypertension and heart attack risk. Ten million endure noise levels of 75 dB or above, entering the range of risk for hearing loss. About 90 percent of this noise is caused by traffic, recognized as the main source of noise pollution worldwide.[10]

On the logarithmic decibel scale, every increase of ten indicates a doubling in sound intensity; that is, 70 dB is twice as loud as 60. Busy roads may generate 70 to 85 dB of noise, depending on traffic type, speed, road surface, and other factors. At 66 to 68 dB, over half the population affected by traffic din becomes "highly annoyed" by it, and that percentage goes up as the noise does. The World Health Organization suggests that daytime noise levels not exceed 65 dB, yet as of 1997 at least 124 million people in developed countries were routinely exposed to louder road noise.[11]

Many of us hear traffic noise so constantly we no longer pay conscious attention. Yet noise still affects us, even if we're unaware of it. Perceived instinctually as a threat, noise incites our fight-or-flight response: increasing stress hormone levels, blood pressure, blood fats, digestive disturbances, heart rate, and muscle tension. It affects sleep quantity and quality, hinders learning and language development in children, contributes to poor concentration and job performance, hampers memory, and increases depression, irritability, and argumentative behavior. A 1998 European study demonstrated that big city noise, most of it from traffic, increases heart disease and ulcers. Some researchers also believe there's a link between relentless noise and criminal violence. Traffic noise can literally drive us crazy, and some studies show higher death rates in people exposed to chronic high noise levels like those from a humming freeway. "People's lives are being shortened," says UCLA acoustics professor William Meecham.[12]

Noise pollution affects wildlife, too, altering behavior and interfering with reproduction. As highways roar through natural areas, they confuse birds which rely heavily on hearing songs for courtship and to recognize territory. The British Ecological Society discovered in 1995 that birds living near British motorways had actually lost the ability to sing mating and territorial songs properly: exposed to so much traffic noise, they sang off-key, could not attract mates, and were unable to reproduce. Traffic noise also detracts from outdoor recreation and from day-to-day living. One Maryland family reported trouble hearing their doorbell and TV during rush hour on a nearby state highway; another woman gave up using her porch when traffic became too loud for conversation. As road noise goes up, property values often go down; the aggregate loss of property value in French cities due to road noise amounted to $20 billion as of 1995.[13]

Car noise comes not only from engines, exhaust systems, brakes, horns, stereos, and alarms. A significant amount is aerodynamic, from air whooshing past and through the car; then there is also rolling noise, from tires on pavement. Wider tires (like those used on SUVs) make more noise. As a car's speed goes up, so does its noise level, making high-speed highways the noisiest. So, when we vote for higher speed limits, we also vote for more traffic noise and relatively more stress. Highway departments have spent millions on sound walls even though they've been controversial, blocking views or reflecting sound into some areas as they keep it out of others. All types of car noise have been such a problem in Cairo that the Egyptian government has banned horn honking in certain zones and at certain times. Car alarms may be the most annoying noise of all, with some as loud as 127 dB. As Beijing's car population grew, car alarms started going off mistakenly over a million times a day, said one report, until the city passed a law restricting them.[14]

Perhaps the main problem is a general disregard for the importance of quiet, paired with a general propensity in auto-dependent societies to accommodate the car at almost any cost. This tendency seems well-exemplified by a situation in Arlington, Texas, where city officials wanted to build a road next to a Carmelite monastery and needed three acres of monastery land to make the road six lanes instead of four as originally planned. The Carmelite nuns were willing to sell the city the land they wanted, but not without a promise of sound walls to preserve the quiet needed for their place of worship. Sound walls would be too expensive, said the city, and in May 1998, they filed eminent domain proceedings so they could build the road to their desired width. Ultimately a compromise was reached, but the monastery will likely still sacrifice at least some of its serenity for the sake of faster car trips across town.[15]

Congestion and Parking Problems

Sometimes finding parking seems to take longer than a trip itself. San Francisco drivers say it's standard to circle a block three times before finding a space. That space may be metered; the world has somewhere between four and six million parking meters, and they're generally hungry. If we park in a commercial lot, we'll also pay: just in the U.S., parking is a $28-billion-a-year industry. If we park in a free spot, we still have the worry of something happening to the car while we're gone, or of finding it again, sometimes a challenge at malls, stadiums, or airports. Not infrequently, cars are mistakenly reported stolen because their owners can't find them in large lots. If we leave the car too long or in the wrong place, we may return to find a parking ticket on the windshield, a clamp or boot on the tire, or nothing, if the car has been towed. This generally initiates a whole new hassle. We can challenge the ticket, or we can pay it — in North America we pay billions each year in parking fines. Annually in New York City, police hand out about nine million parking tickets, bringing in $350 million. An estimated 30 to 40 percent of all tickets issued are for parking violations.[16]

Congestion, too, is a top complaint in North American cities. As the 20th century closed, about two-thirds of U.S. city leaders worried about traffic congestion: it's costly, it's hard to solve, it makes citizens unhappy, and it's getting worse. In 68 U.S. cities studied by the Texas Transportation Institute, the cost of congestion totaled $72 billion in 1997, $755 per driver on average. In over half those cities, the time drivers spent stuck in traffic had gone up at least 350 percent since 1982. In Los Angeles, each driver lost an average $1,370 and 82 hours a year to congestion delays, more than two work weeks. The problem affects smaller cities, too, taking up more than 40 hours per year per driver in 24 U.S. cities of various sizes in 1997. All this congestion wasted 6.6 billion gallons of fuel that year, over 100 gallons per driver on average in the most congested cities, and more than twice the amount lost to congestion 15 years earlier. Congestion also increases crash rates, insurance rates, and economic losses, draining away as much as two percent of GNP by some estimates.[17]

"Americans will put up with anything provided it doesn't block traffic."

DAN RATHER

Gridlock is a problem around the world. It's turned Bangkok into something very close to a 24-hour-a-day parking lot; only between two and four a.m. is there generally any let-up in traffic. Cities like Kuala Lumpur, Sao Paulo, and Mexico City have also become reknowned for traffic congestion. In Holland, the average 1996 workday generated at least 50 traffic jams of 2 kilometers or more. In Britain, drivers lose 1.5 billion hours a year to congestion. And if you think congestion's bad now, consider this: forecasts show worldwide traffic volumes doubling from 1990 to 2020, then doubling again by 2050.[18]

Congestion creates stress because we don't like being in situations we can't control. Several studies have linked time spent in congestion to increases in frustration, irritability, anxiety, blood pressure, heart rate, and cardiac irregularities, as well as to higher employee turnover and use of sick days. Gridlock and long commutes exert the most stress on women who drive alone, reports researcher Raymond Novaco, who's also found that congestion and commute stress "spill over" to increase tensions during evenings at home.[19]

Widening roads in an attempt to solve congestion can ultimately make it worse in several ways that include by increasing noise and air pollution. Widening one road can create bottlenecks on others; additional road space also stimulates latent demand, encouraging more people to drive. Added road capacity may also foster development and population growth in the area served by the road, resulting in even more driving. A study of 12 British road-building projects intended to ease congestion found that traffic volumes instead soared after the new roads went in. Studies by the OECD have similarly shown that adding roads to urban areas "has generally failed to ease congestion, and serves only to generate additional traffic." Even if it worked, widening roads to eliminate congestion would be prohibitively expensive. The Oregon Environmental Council figures it would take an extra $12 billion in the next 20 years just to keep Portland's congestion at current levels, costing every person in the metropolitan area an extra $8,000 in taxes.[20]

It's no surprise then, that even with all we spend on roads, congestion has steadily been getting worse. Travel delays per driver nearly tripled between 1982 and 1997, and most experts think congestion will continue to increase. Transportation analyst Deborah Gordon has estimated that "by 2005 the average commuter from one suburb of a metropolitan area to another suburb could spend up to five times as long in traffic as in 1990. This could mean moving at five miles per hour over a ten-mile trip" — slower than the average bicycle, not much faster than a pedestrian. For all our technological advances we are often not moving much faster, and sometimes move more slowly, than we did before cars took over. In 1961, the *New York Times* noted that "Motor trucks [in New York] average less than six miles per hour in traffic, as against 11 miles per hour for horse drawn vehicles in 1911." In the early 1990s, when Portugal's Socialist Party decided to demonstrate Lisbon's congestion increases, they organized a race between a Ferrari and a burro, suburb to downtown along a congested two-kilometer route. The burro won with four minutes to spare.[21]

Automotive Aggression and Road Rage

In 1997, a driver's ed teacher in Durham, North Carolina, gave his students a lesson in road rage. Incensed after a man in another car cut them off, the teacher ordered the student driving to give chase, jumped out when they caught up with the offender at a stoplight, yelled obscenities at him, and punched him through his car window. Not long after the teacher darted back into the driver's ed car and ordered his student to take off, they were pulled over for speeding. The teacher was suspended and later resigned. In 1996, a Massachusetts driver got impatient and plowed through a crowd of New Year's celebrants; he injured 21 people and was charged with attempted murder. In 1998, road rage traveled into an Atlanta fast-food drive-through lane when a customer who had waited too long in the line of idling cars exchanged rude words with the cashier and they began throwing full drink cups at each other.[22]

> *"Almost everyone becomes kind of emotionally crazy behind the wheel."*
>
> DR. LEON JAMES,
> TRAFFIC PSYCHOLOGY PROFESSOR

As awareness of incidents like these has grown, so has use of the phrase "road rage." First uttered in England in 1988, it's since been addressed as a problem by automobile associations and transport departments in several countries. Despite some controversy over whether and how much road rage has increased, there's little argument that awareness of it has gone way up. In the 1990s, getting into a car went from being perceived as a secure extension of home life to something more like a dangerous liaison. We added not only road rage but also carjackings and drive-by shootings to the highway vocabulary (the latest car crime is "crash and rob," where thieves smash cars into stores to gain entrance and steal goods). Now, nearly 49,000 carjackings are attempted in the U.S. each year, most within five miles of the victim's home; over half are successful and, in about a third, someone gets hurt. Even more widespread is aggressive driving, characterized by speeding, tailgating, running red lights, and general recklessness. It leads to road rage when impatience escalates to angry yelling, rude gestures, or attacks. Aggressive driving may cause as many as two-thirds of U.S. highway deaths per year, costing $24 billion annually.[23]

The AAA Foundation for Traffic Safety warns that "every driver on the highway is armed with a weapon more deadly and dangerous than any firearm: a motor vehicle." Raging drivers use cars as battering rams, sometimes even bashing police who try to apprehend them. Guns and cars are road ragers' two favorite weapons, each used in a little over a third of reported incidents. While women account for only about four percent of road rage incidents, more than half the female road ragers use their cars as weapons.[24]

Studies by Louis Mizell for AAA show road rage increasing by about seven percent a year in the U.S., up 51 percent from 1990 to 1995. Road rage has caused an average of at least 1,500 deaths or injuries a year in the U.S. since 1990, says Mizell. Out of 12,828 road rage deaths and injuries he studied, 94 affected children under 15. Since many road rage incidents go unreported, AAA officials believe this is "only the small tip of a very large iceberg." Mizell points out that reasons for road violence are amazingly trivial, like "He cut me off," "She was driving too slowly," or "They kept tailgating me." "She kept crossing lanes without signaling," said one violent motorist. "Maybe I overreacted but it taught her a lesson." Claimed a driver who pulled a gun: "I never would have shot him if he hadn't rear-ended me."[25]

Sliding into the driver's seat is all it may take to turn "otherwise charming people into scowling, quick-tempered road warriors," says Raymond Novaco, who's studied roadway violence since 1985. Driving brings out aggressive behaviors in us, predisposing us to aggressive driving and road rage by putting us in a state of heightened stimulation, requiring heightened responses and triggering loss of inhibitions.[26] Cars by their nature give us a false sense of protection and anonymity, allowing us to forget about common courtesy.

A 1995 British study explains how human territoriality, too, feeds freeway fury. We all have a personal territory as a defense mechanism; anyone entering that space is a potential aggressor. In a car, our territory expands to include not only the vehicle but enough space around it to give us time to fend off a potential attack. This is probably why tailgating is so often seen as aggressive; 62 percent of Britons in the study had experienced it, making it the most common source of road rage. "Many drivers admit to having chased after a driver ... often pressing him by moving to within inches of his rear bumper," says the study. "This is comparable to the manner in which a defending animal will chase an attacker out of its territory."[27]

Why Is There No Pedestrian Rage?

A 1996 British study asked the above question and came up with these answers:

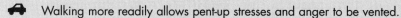 Walking more readily allows pent-up stresses and anger to be vented.

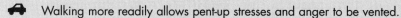 Driving allows stress and tension to accumulate without an outlet.

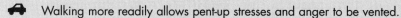 Vehicle congestion is more common than pedestrian congestion (though both do exist).

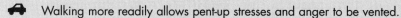 Rules of the road place more restrictions on a driver's movements anyway.

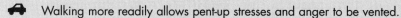 Driving requires more heightened attention than walking, as well as a higher burden of responsibility and tension in order to avoid serious accidents.

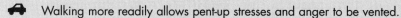 Most drivers have an inflated view of their driving skill, which feeds their ego and self-esteem, and they may feel protective or defensive about it. We don't have the same ego investment in walking.

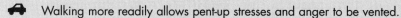 The car straddles a boundary between personal space, where people set their own standards and do what they want, and public space, where behavior is governed by societal rules. When walking, we're clearly in public space and behave accordingly.

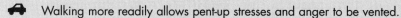 It is easy to express good will and/or to apologize when walking, and we're more likely to do so when our contact is immediate. But in a car, not only are we less likely to be courteous, we can't be. Other drivers are more likely to assume that a specific action is aggressive since in cars we're isolated and can't communicate directly with others.[28]

The driving environment is rife with stimuli that encourage aggressive behavior. The National Highway Traffic Safety Administration (NHTSA) attributes road rage to longer commutes, more congestion, and more rushed and stressful lives. The more miles you drive, the more likely you are to be an aggressive driver. Noise intensifies aggressive responses and, in traffic jams, engine noise and car stereos can ratchet up frustration. Heat also feeds aggression, studies show.[29]

One survey found that two-thirds of British drivers admitted to driving aggressively. In the Greater Toronto Area, 27 percent of drivers surveyed scored three on a road rage scale from one to four, where four equals "maniac." A NHTSA survey found about two-thirds of U.S. drivers fear unsafe driving by others; the same percentage admitted to driving unsafely themselves. Depending on the region, between 24 and 41 percent of U.S. children under 16 have seen other drivers make obscene gestures, say their parents. Such actions tell children that highway hostility is normal, helping to produce whole new generations of road ragers. "Once they enter a car, children notice that all of a sudden the rules have changed," says researcher Leon James. As much as parents might model courtesy face-to-face, if that erodes when they're in the driver's seat, children learn a behavioral double standard.[30]

One potential solution to rage on roads emerges from a 1999 report showing that poor provision of alternatives to driving can feed road rage. This study by the Surface Transportation Policy Project (STPP) found that the number of deaths related to road rage rises where people have fewer transportation choices, and decreases in areas which have more alternatives to cars, such as transit and bike paths. While STPP's findings point to a pleasant solution to road violence, from South Africa comes a more dystopian response. As of 1998, car owners there could purchase an automotive accessory called the "Blaster" which, on demand, throws out fireballs as tall as a person on both sides of a vehicle. Designed to prevent carjackings and other attacks, the Blaster's flame can cause severe burns and reportedly blind a person. It will not, however, damage a car's paint.[31]

Social Isolation and Inequities

At a dinner party one night we were talking about people's sense of community. "I always feel the greatest sense of community right after a blizzard," said one guest. "When the snow stops, people come out of their houses, but for a while no one can drive anywhere. Everyone walks to nearby stores, stopping to talk with neighbors on the way. The streets are white and clean and quiet except for the sounds of conversation and children playing. We might get a half-day of feeling a connection to people around us, then the snowplows come, people jump in their cars again and zoom off, encased in metal and only waving from behind glass. Often they don't even do that." In that dinner conversation, we realized immediately what felt good about the community after a blizzard: the absence of cars, which physically isolate us from one another. When separated by cars, we lose opportunities for the chance encounters with friends and neighbors through which relationships blossom and grow. As they draw us to distant points for work and social life, cars also allow us to avoid looking closely at our immediate surroundings. We can zip by cracked sidewalks or garbage in gutters, removing ourselves from unpleasantness, rather than taking responsibility for local problems. We lose touch with our neighborhoods. It's too easy to get in a car and leave.

In car-dependent countries, the lament about loss of community has become more frequent. Cars feed this as they take over public space, cutting social contact. A study by Donald Appleyard shows that as vehicle trips on a given street go up, interaction between neighbors and their sense of community goes down.[32] Our evolution into geographic disconnectedness has reached its apex along the Interstate Highway System. Far from linking the various geographic and cultural milieus of North America, interstate highways allow us to bypass them altogether. On the interstate, mobility is the purpose of life and amenities exist only to serve that purpose — amenities that have become identical everywhere and give no clue as to a traveler's whereabouts. That disconnectedness extends into the heart of neighborhoods, right up to the front door (if we can find it) which has faded to near oblivion beside the expansive garages with which modern homes greet visitors.

We enter the world from these fortress-like garages, whose doors operate like inverted drawbridges, cranked shut by invisible operators behind the ramparts of steel-walled sport utility vehicles. Cars allow us to isolate ourselves within our own social strata and to have no physical contact with people at other levels. This leads inevitably to a lack of understanding, alienation, and mistrust of those who are different. Instead of providing direct contact and the opportunity for everyday kindnesses, the car erodes social bonds. "With increased use of automobiles," writes Kenneth Jackson, "the life of the sidewalk and the front yard has largely disappeared, and the social intercourse that used to be the main characteristic of urban life has vanished."[33] After 100 years of driving, we've replaced common courtesy with road rage.

Because marriage to the car encourages homes and workplaces to sprawl, it limits opportunities to move around without using cars, making travel harder for people who can't or don't want to drive. The young and elderly in particular become marginalized, losing independence and self-sufficiency in car-dependent areas. Teenagers get trapped in suburbs, lamenting that there's "nothing to do." This in turn traps parents — especially women — into the role of chauffeur and "soccer mom." Everyone in the family looks hungrily ahead to the day the oldest teen turns 16 and can drive him- or herself. But having been dependent for so long on a parent for mobility, 16-year-olds may be less prepared to handle driving than if they developed independence gradually by walking, biking, or taking transit on their own. Children lose opportunities to develop independence and responsibility when they must wait to be driven everywhere they go.

At the other end of the age spectrum, older people who may be losing reflexes or visual acuity needed for safe driving cling stubbornly to cars and licenses, since driving has become so closely tied to independence. A society married to the car has left them little choice. Cars don't allow older people to be independent with safety.

This growing segment of the population needs another means of transport, like transit, to maintain independence, self-esteem, and mobility. Sixty percent of rural U.S. elderly don't have driver's licenses, and at least half live in places not served by public transport. Responding to policies that perpetuate this poor service, Gray Panthers have accused the U.S. government of handicapping the elderly with an "accessibility disadvantage" by pouring money into highways at the expense of transit.[34]

In between young and elderly are broad groups of people who arguably shouldn't drive and sometimes can't get licenses, such as those with medical conditions like diabetes or epilepsy who may be vulnerable to sudden attacks or seizures, or those taking medications that make driving inadvisable. But a society married to the car marginalizes these people, too. It's not fair to treat people with disabilities or illnesses like second-class citizens, nor is it fair to them or others to expect them to drive. But in a society married to the car, that's what we do, with the result that many people who shouldn't or don't want to drive end up doing so.

Marriage to the car also isolates the poor. Even in the car-saturated U.S., more than a quarter of households below the poverty level don't own cars.[35] Jobs may be located far from where the poor can afford to live, putting them at a disadvantage or forcing them to take long, convoluted transit commutes to jobs. And as public funds go disproportionately to highway building, government ends up supporting an inadvertent apartheid. Road-building tends to help car owners, wealthier and disproportionately white, and hurts inner city minority transit users, sacrificing their mobility on the altar of highway construction and in effect imprisoning them in cities. The Cypress Freeway reconstruction in Oakland, California, is one example of a subsidy that helped the wealthy and hurt the poor. Used mostly by wealthier suburban commuters, the freeway cut through a predominantly black neighborhood which suffers its noise and fumes on an ongoing basis. Meanwhile, the poor pay more: "road-impacted neighborhoods" tend to have higher insurance rates.[36] And the poor and people of color pay more from disproportionate exposure to cars' pollutants since major roadways, transport depots, and exhaust sources are too often located in their communities.

In 1965, John Rae pointed out: "American life is organized predominantly on the basis of the universal availability of motor transportation."[37] But "motor transportation," here a synonym for car travel, was not universally available in 1965, even in America, nor is it now. No matter how many cars travel our roads, there will always be people for whom car travel is not an easy or independent option. Exclusive reliance on cars induces dependence in a much larger segment of the population than does a mix of transport options.

Worldwide, marriage to the car perpetuates not only isolation but also social strife. Major wars for oil, such as the 1991 Gulf War, are only the most visible aspects of that discord. There is also a multiple-theater guerrilla war over oil taking place in several spots where oil is extracted. In Nigeria, conflicts over oil reached a tragic crescendo, creating a major international human rights incident, when the government executed literary hero Ken Saro-Wiwa and others for demanding fair treatment of the Ogoni people and compensation for oil pollution of their lands. Other Nigerian peoples are embroiled in oil conflicts, and the group Human Rights Watch issued a report in 1999 stating that oil companies share responsibility with the Nigerian government for human rights abuses in Nigerian oil territories. In response to oil-related protests, the report said, numbers of people have been beaten, detained, or killed.[38]

In South America, human rights groups have long lists of atrocities they say have been committed near oil fields, sometimes, allegedly, by army brigades funded by oil companies. Oil facilities routinely get blown up by guerrillas in Colombia. One 375 mile (600 km) pipeline from Caño Limon to the Caribbean coast has been bombed or mined close to 500 times since it was built in 1986, spilling 1.5 million barrels of oil. Not far away, oil companies want to develop a new oil field in the territory of the indigenous U'wa tribe. But the U'wa, who believe that oil is the blood of Mother Earth and that extracting it will kill the Mother, have threatened mass suicide if any drilling takes place. Even if they were not to follow through on their pledge, oil development would threaten their culture. The U'wa expect they would die in guerrilla warfare that would likely follow oil development into their territory, as it has followed oil development in other South American locations.[39]

> *"One of the greatest ironies of the twentieth century is that around the globe, vast amounts of such priceless things as land, petroleum, and clean air have been relinquished for motorization — and yet most people in the world will never own an automobile."*
>
> MARCIA LOWE, *THE BICYCLE: VEHICLE FOR A SMALL PLANET*

Oil companies have been accused of unduly influencing governments in developing countries.[40] Whether or not the accusations are valid, the needs of oil companies wanting to maintain profits and productivity often conflict with the needs of surrounding lands and peoples and put added pressure on developing country governments already struggling under the weight of other problems. The demand for oil, so much of which goes to feed the car, intensifies if not generates such conflicts. In effect, as a result, people die so we can buy more gasoline.

The Car as Time-Guzzler

With all these problems, we might ask whether our relationship with the car is going anywhere. Well, maybe not anywhere quickly. In an oft-quoted passage, Ivan Illich figures that the average American male driver — fully ensconced in the affair with the car, caring for it, maintaining it, working to earn money to buy things for it, and otherwise showering it with attention — ends up traveling more slowly than a typical cyclist, and not much faster than a pedestrian:

> The typical American male devotes more than 1,600 hours a year to his car. He sits in it while it goes and while it is idling. He parks it and searches for it. He earns the money to put down on it and to meet the monthly installments. He works to pay for fuel, tolls, insurance, taxes, and traffic

tickets. He spends four out of his 16 waking hours on the road or gathering his resources for it. And this figure does not take into account the time consumed by other activities dictated by transport: time spent in hospitals, traffic courts, and garages; time spent watching automobile commercials or attending consumer education meetings to improve the quality of the next buy. The model American puts in 1,600 hours to get 7,500 miles; less than five miles per hour.[41]

This calculation by Illich is just one more measure of the way our bondage to cars detracts from any freedom automobility may impart. In balance, cars tie us down by making us responsible for annoyances we might not otherwise encounter, like car repairs or parking tickets. Even the basic minutiae of keeping the car fueled and operational — things like watching the gas gauge, not locking the keys in the car, and turning the lights off so the battery won't die — take thought and energy. And at the social strife end of the spectrum, the infringements on freedom that take place as we perpetuate driving culture can be life-threatening. Altogether, the many "little" drawbacks to driving add up to that much more reason for frustration with our four-wheeled flame.

CHAPTER 9

Not a Cheap Date:
The Real Cost of Cars

*"The costs of getting around on four wheels are becoming clear to
everyone who takes an honest look."*

GUS SPETH, IN JAMES MACKENZIE ET AL, *THE GOING RATE: WHAT IT REALLY COSTS TO DRIVE*

D ANIEL EGAN, A BICYCLE AND PEDESTRIAN PLANNER from Toronto, remembers when his
younger brother wanted to buy a car. "Flush $50 down the toilet every week,"
advised their father, "and if you can get used to that, buy the car."[1] Egan's father
was right. Our automotive affair has led us away from the good old-fashioned value
of thrift and into sending money down the drain. Marriage to the car makes our wallets thinner not only as we buy our steel sweetheart fuel and repairs, but also as we
pay in indirect and hidden ways to keep the romance alive. Most of these hidden
costs are paid by all of us whether we drive or not. That's a big reason why cars
seem cheaper than they really are and why they sometimes seem cheaper than other
forms of transportation. Really, though, money issues with the car — as in so many
other relationships — give us more grounds for a break-up.

Costs Drivers Pay

Economists classify costs as internal (those paid by the user) or external (those
imposed on someone else). The most obvious internal costs imposed by cars are
those drivers pay straight from their pockets. The American Automobile
Association's 1999 figures show that buying a new car and driving it 15,000 miles a
year for four years costs an average $7,050 annually in the U.S. That's $19.31 a day,
47 cents a mile. At that rate, Daniel Egan's brother would have to flush about $135
(U.S.) a week down the toilet to get used to owning a car. This average doesn't
include costs for more expensive sport utility vehicles and mini-vans, a growing segment of the passenger vehicle fleet. A typical 1999 SUV driven 15,000 miles a year
for four years costs $8,072 yearly and nearly 54 cents a mile.[2] Used cars, of course,
cost less, but their prices have risen faster than those of new cars. The average price
of used cars from dealerships rose to $12,100 in 1997, nearly doubling from ten years
earlier.[3]

Cars' direct internal costs consume about 15 to 20 percent of household budgets in the U.S. and Canada.[4] In Canada, auto-related sales accounted for 35% of
1997 retail sales, more than any other retail category.[5] The average U.S. household
spent about $6,200 out-of-pocket on private vehicles, new and used, in 1998,
which works out to something over $3,000 per vehicle out of pocket.[6] Every year,

the average U.S. household spends more than a sixth of its budget on cars, more than on food and second only to housing; poor households spend twice that proportion. Since the 1930s, car dependency has helped to at least triple the proportion of personal expenditures going to transportation.[7] In comparison, households in developed countries with better transit spend less. European households, for instance, spend only seven percent of their budgets on transport.[8]

Another way to gauge driving's cost is with the amount of work time it takes to pay for a car. If a median U.S. family buys an average new car, they'll need to work about six months to cover the purchase price. If this family owns two new cars and replaces them every three years (nearly 40 percent of U.S. new-car buyers

© Andy Singer.

replace their vehicles at least this often), they will truly be driving to work and working to drive: a full year of every three will be spent working to pay for car purchases. This family will devote even more of its work time to paying for the cars' other costs. Financing cars adds another budgetary burden. In 1996, outstanding U.S. car loans totaled $390.3 billion, about a third of all consumer debt. The average monthly new car payment was over $400 a month. Then there's insurance, for which U.S. car owners paid a net $29 billion in 1996, and which runs $870 a year, on average, for full coverage; registration and license fees, costing about $200 to $250 a year per car in the U.S. in the late 1990s; and the cost of depreciation, as the value of the vehicle drains away over time.

Based on AAA figures, each of our median family's average new cars will cost them $14.96 a day whether they're driven or not, and over 60 percent of that is depreciation.[9]

Economists call that $14.96 a day a fixed cost: it stays the same no matter how much the car is used. Cars also have variable costs, which go up with more driving and down with less. Also known as operating costs, these start with the cost of gasoline and oil, the main expense we associate with driving but actually a small component of what we pay, overall, to drive. While driving an average 1999 car runs 47 cents a mile out of pocket, gasoline and oil consume less than six cents a mile of that. Repairs and maintenance average about $700 to $800 a year, 5.0 cents a mile, and increase with the age of a car.[10] We also pay out of pocket for tolls, parking, and garaging, all of which vary with location.

In other countries out-of-pocket costs for cars are similar or higher. In Canada in 1999, for instance, it cost Cdn$9,011 to own and drive a typical new car 24,000 kilometers, or about 15,000 miles, a year (ranging from $8,600 for a subcompact to $15,000 for a full-size car). Average ownership costs run about Cdn$5,854 a year, including insurance (averaging $1,199), license and registration ($128), depreciation ($3,814), and loan interest ($713).[11]

These out-of-pocket costs for driving are widely perceived as lower than they really are, in part because drivers often consider only operating or variable costs, and neglect ownership or fixed costs. "Motorists typically perceive less than half of their total costs when making trip decisions," writes transportation analyst Todd Litman. And operating costs account for only about 13 percent of overall driving costs, both internal and external. This selective perception is aided by the way we currently price cars and driving, putting most costs up front: generally more than three-quarters of cars' monetary costs are fixed, paid when we own a car whether we drive it or not. Even though our total costs climb as we drive more, it may seem cheaper because we spread the fixed costs out and pay less per unit of driving. As Alan James points out, though, even operating costs of cars are often high compared to

---

Voices of Experience

The best testimonial to the costliness of cars may come from car-free and car-lite folks, who invariably delight in how much money they save by not owning cars. They may rent cars or take taxis in addition to bikes, buses, and trains, but they still save loads over what it costs to own a car.

John Schneider, a business leader in Cincinnati, calls himself "a New Yorker trapped in a Cincinnati body." He decided to forego car ownership in the 1970s, and now, he says, "I just think of all the money I've saved. It's been tremendous." By being car-free, "I've avoided cost and I've gained connection," he adds.

Being car-free at some points in their lives and having no more than one car at others has enabled Steve Clark and his rural Wisconsin family of six "to save money for things in life which we value more: land, travel to Mexico and Cuba, animals." Likewise, by being car-free, says Clevelander Ryan McKenzie, "I save many thousands each year, and use the savings to go on extended international travels."

Daniel Egan notes that in Toronto, his car-free family has paid far less to rent cars and take taxis when walking, biking, or transit hasn't been practical than they'd have to pay to own a car. They now belong to Autoshare, Toronto's car-sharing organization, which has also helped them save. "All the convenience when we need it," writes Egan, "without the hassle." Or the cost. He's used savings from going car-free to pay down his mortgage and adds, "The economic advantage of not owning a car affords our family a better quality of life."

other ground transport. In a study of British driving, James determined that "it is already cheaper in actual journey costs — and potentially half the price or less — for a single car-owning person to travel by train than by car." The true marginal cost of driving in Britain, says James, is 18 to 20 pence per mile, while train fares are generally in the nine to 13 pence a mile range.[12]

Drivers incur non-monetary costs, too; among these are time spent driving, crash risk, and stress. Travel time may cost drivers anywhere from 11 to 34 cents per vehicle mile, estimates Todd Litman. Crashes have non-monetary costs like pain, suffering, and lost quality of life which some studies value at hundreds of billions of dollars a year.[13] Stress, too, has vast non-monetary impacts, in addition to the monetary costs it imposes in such forms as higher medical bills.

Hidden Gifts for the Car: External Costs

The car also imposes costs by using up non-financial resources like clean air, clean water, and quiet. These external costs are dissociated from driving, often hidden, and frequently neglected. Every dollar spent on operating a car imposes $2.70 in external costs, says one estimate.[14] Other studies arrive at different numbers. While economists disagree about the size of external costs, many have done studies showing ways drivers don't cover all of them. Businesses, consumers, and taxpayers pick up the rest; in other words, cars are subsidized. For example, metro New York motorists fall $1.7 billion short of paying for roads and driver services; income, sales, business, and property taxes make up the difference. Minneapolis drivers pay less than half the cost of city-funded road and driving-related projects; the rest comes mainly from property taxes. In New York towns outside New York City, property and other general taxes provide about 80 percent of funding for roads and cars.[15] Studies by Canada's National Transportation Act Review Commission found subsidies to the car in 1990-91 that amounted to about seven times the investment in public transit.[16]

Automobiles are subsidized by many national, state, provincial, and local governments — and that means by all of us. Rather than being shaped by unfettered supply and demand, decisions about cars and driving are influenced by laws, tax codes, and government budgets that often favor automobile use. Allocations for roads that dwarf those for mass transit, tax laws favoring sprawl development, write-offs for oil exploration, and company cars all subsidize driving. Because we pay for them in the form of these subsidies, driving's true costs are hidden and supply-demand signals get distorted: prices lower than true costs generate higher demand for driving, foster inefficiencies like time lost in congestion, and create inequities between motorists and non-motorists. A suburban car commuter, for example, pays only 20 to 25 percent of the true cost of driving in and out of the central city at rush hour, while an inner city resident taking transit pays 80 percent of the true cost. "The American consumer, in deciding between private and mass transportation," wrote *Fortune* magazine in the early 1960s, "has for years and years been presented with a market heavily rigged in favor of using his own car in city traffic."[17]

"Your tax dollars at work": The road construction and maintenance heralded by those signs may represent one of the biggest single subsidies for cars. "Road building has been the most expensive activity pursued by most American states in this century," writes historian Clay McShane. U.S. Federal Highway Administration figures show that state and local road spending almost always exceeds highway user-tax revenues in all 50 states of the U.S. The rest of the money for road building comes from property taxes, general fund appropriations, bonds, and "other." Figures from one government study indicate that auto taxes and fees cover only 70 percent of estimated total roadway costs. Researcher Douglass Lee calculates that U.S. tax-payers contribute over $41 billion a year to cover the road costs that drivers don't.[18] In Canada, vehicle license and fuel tax revenues pay for only around 56 percent of highway costs; over Cdn$5 billion a year come from income taxes.[19]

Such highway spending is often perpetuated by an extrapolated forecast method of transportation planning. Planners may examine a few years' transport trends, assume they will continue without change, then calculate how many new roads will be needed for this assumed traffic growth. When the roads are built, the new road space taps latent driving demand and the projected traffic growth becomes a self-fulfilling prophecy. Then planners repeat the process, projecting future traffic growth based on the growth of preceding years which was, in part, fueled by road building. But since infrastructure availability shapes and influences people's trans-portation decisions, and transportation decisions are price-sensitive, subsidized building or widening of roads to handle some future level of anticipated traffic or to reduce congestion makes little economic sense. Consider this analogy from Terry Moore and Paul Thorsnes:

> No rational concert promoter would decide how big to build a stadium based on the number of people who would come to see the Grateful Dead if the tickets were free. But that is often how transportation planners decide highway capacity: they estimate how many trips would be made on an unpriced facility, then try to build a facility big enough to accommodate that number of trips.[20]

The way new roads are financed can also add to over-building. In the U.S., for instance, federal cost-sharing that contributes 90 percent of the cost of new road construction, but nothing for repairs, shifts the focus of state and local highway departments to laying new asphalt and neglecting the old.

Highway engineers figure the construction costs of a basic two-lane highway at about a million dollars a mile. But since that doesn't include land purchases, bridges, or interchanges, all of which can add major sums to road-building budgets, highway construction costs go up from there.[21] Some of the more expensive freeways have included

> the Los Angeles Century Freeway — $127 million a mile or $2.2 billion total for 17.3 miles that took 30 years to build and displaced 21,000 people;[22]

🚗 the Cypress Structure rebuild, in Oakland, California — $1 billion for 2.2 miles of freeway, plus interchanges, to replace an earthquake-shattered roadway that had been built in 1959 for $4 million;[23]

🚗 the Big Dig, or Boston's Central Artery — at $11 billion and counting, it became, as of 1998, the most expensive surface transportation project ever in the U.S.;[24]

🚗 Corridor H in West Virginia — over a billion dollars proposed with millions spent even before any construction had begun.[25]

In fiscal year 1995, U.S. national, state, and local governments spent almost $80 billion on highways, out of $129.3 billion spent on transportation overall.[26] From 1999 to 2005, the U.S. plans to spend about $175 billion on roads. A 1998 study showed that Cdn$17.4 billion was needed to fix Canada's 15,500 miles (25,000 km) of provincial and interprovincial highways, despite the fact that Cdn$11 billion have already been spent since 1988 in an attempt to do just that. Meanwhile, by some measures Canadian road conditions have actually worsened.[27] The more we spend on cars, the more they want; roads become a black hole for money. And road-building costs communities even more because once land is paved for roads, it is no longer taxed. The U.S. road system has removed about 66,000 square miles of land — and counting — from tax rolls. That land under roads has an annualized value of $75 billion, one study has estimated — another high-cost gift to the car.[28]

Road services cost a bundle, too. Marriage to the car vastly increases the amount we spend on policing roadways to make them safe for cars and to keep us all safe from cars' effects. Great Britain spends about $1.6 billion annually on road safety.[29] U.S. traffic management accounts for an estimated 40 to 70 percent of the work of state and local law enforcement departments; these services, plus auto-related emergency-response and fire-fighting, some medical costs, parking enforcement, accident and auto theft investigations, and street cleaning cost about $68 billion a year more than any user fees paid by motorists.[30] Every time a lane-mile is added to a road, that cost goes up by about $5,000 a year on an ongoing basis.[31] Policing the world is another task required by marriage to the car, as the U.S. especially, but other countries as well, use military force to keep petroleum shipments flowing. Cheap oil is "essential to the American way of life," said U.S. president George Bush in 1990, as he defended the deployment of troops in the Gulf War.[32] The Cato Institute calculated in 1991 that the U.S. was spending $50 billion a year on military defense of Middle East oil.[33]

Fuel production and clean-up are also subsidized. Accelerated depreciation, depletion allowances, expensing of intangible drilling costs, and other favors to oil producers keep gasoline prices artificially low. The U.S. government has also eliminated royalties on federal drilling leases for deep-water drilling, essentially giving away oil deposits on some federally owned areas of the Gulf of Mexico at an estimated long-term cost to taxpayers of $400 million.[34] Analysis by the Union of Concerned Scientists has shown that while other industries pay an average 18 percent in U.S.

income taxes, the oil industry pays only 11 percent.[35] Researcher Douglass Lee calculates the motor vehicle share of oil-producer subsidies at $32.1 billion a year.[36] When it comes to clean-up, the U.S. government has, since 1990, maintained a billion-dollar trust fund, supported by oil import taxes, to clean up oil spills where responsibility wasn't otherwise assigned. But this fund has not covered all spill clean-up costs. Friends of the Earth estimates that oil pollution, health and property damage, and related clean-up costs the U.S. about $10 billion yearly.[37]

Free parking is not so free. Storage space for cars adds to their costs; building a parking space in a garage structure costs $7,000 to $20,000 per space.[38] Estimates of the number of spaces we give each car range from three to eight: one at home, one at work, and the other one to six in fractional-use spaces at stores, restaurants, offices, and other establishments.[39] There were about 110 million parking spaces in the U.S. as of early 1999.[40] About 95 percent of U.S. commuters get free parking, and 99 percent of non-commute trips end in a free parking space. That's a perk with a market value often around $1,800 a year. Employers who give parking spaces to workers provide 300 square feet per car, including aisles and access, which is often more than the office space allocated to many workers.[41]

"Free" parking gets paid for by everyone who owns a business, works, rents, or buys things, whether they drive or not. When employers provide free parking to workers, it eats into their ability to pay higher salaries, or into profits, or both. When retailers provide free parking, they pass the costs on to customers in higher prices. When apartments provide free parking, it raises rents; space for parking also raises home prices. Building codes requiring just one parking space per house raise construction costs by 18 percent. Parking can add $600 a year to the cost of a house and ten percent to the cost of an apartment. In Canada, the costs have been estimated at Cdn$746 per house and Cdn$743 per apartment.[42] And most parking spaces sit empty about 80 percent of the time.[43] This underlines the huge waste parking lots represent. The external cost of off-street parking at homes, businesses, and parking structures, figures economist Mark Delucchi, totals $75 to $233 billion a year in the U.S. That is $414 to $1,232 per vehicle per year and 3.3 to 9.7 cents per vehicle mile.[44]

> *"This apparent affordability of driving is actually sleight-of-hand."*
> TODD LITMAN, *ALTERNATIVES JOURNAL*, WINTER 1998

Congestion costs may total as much as $168 billion a year in the U.S. Of that, an estimated $100 billion may be attributed to productivity losses as we lose eight billion hours stuck in traffic on interstates and other major roads. Congestion also may add an estimated $24 to $40 billion yearly to the cost of goods. In the 68 cities studied by the Texas Transportation Institute, drivers lost billions of hours stuck in traffic in 1998, which cost $72 billion and wasted more than six billion gallons of fuel. Traffic congestion costs the German economy over $110 billion a year, says one study. In Bangkok, congestion costs at least $3 to $4 million per day in wasted fuel and lost production.[45]

Medical and other costs due to crashes drain public and private coffers. Public costs include emergency services, medical costs paid through general health insurance, productivity losses, vocational rehabilitation, and more. Various estimates place the costs of U.S. traffic crashes at $150 billion to $363 billion per year; most such estimates include medical expenses, administrative expenses, property damage, costs to employers, and wage and productivity losses.[46] These estimates may understate crash costs since many crashes involving pedestrians and bicyclists are downplayed or go unrecorded. Also, these estimates don't consider costs of reduced mobility and security to non-drivers. In developing countries, the Red Cross figures the economic cost of motor vehicle crashes, including medical expenses, property damage, and lost work years, is $53 billion a year. Just in India, the bill for road crashes comes to about $3 billion a year.[47]

Pollution costs from cars amount to at least $54.2 billion a year and perhaps as much as $232.4 billion, according to Mark Delucchi. Pollution from motor vehicles incurs costs as it sickens people and shortens lives, damages crops, cuts visibility, damages materials, adds greenhouse gases to the atmosphere, pollutes water, and cuts property values due to noise. In a 1995 study, Delucchi tallied the external pollution costs of motor vehicles as follows:[48]

Air pollution:

Mortality and morbidity	$ 42.1 to 181.7 billion
Damage to crops	$ 2.0 to 3.0 billion
Loss of visibility	$ 3.0 to 10.0 billion
Damages to materials	$ 1.0 to 4.0 billion
Contributions to global warming	$ 2.5 to 22.2 billion

Water pollution:

Leaking tanks	$ 0.1 to 1.5 billion
Oil spills	$ 2.0 to 5.0 billion

Noise pollution:

	$ 1.5 to 5.0 billion
TOTAL	$ 54.2 to 232.4 billion

Sprawl fostered by cars carries a high price tag in several ways. Banks and businesses have begun to recognize that sprawl hurts local economies. A 1995 Bank of America report called sprawl financially unsound, and Atlanta companies acknowledged how sprawl hurts their bottom lines when that city topped U.S. sprawl charts in 1998. Sprawl swallows 2.5 times more land than planned development. Sprawling land use forces us to drive more miles and to spend more time traveling. While people living in city centers drive an average 8,000 miles a year, "inner" suburb dwellers average 15,000 miles per year and people from "fringe" suburbs average 30,000 miles a year. A road system consumes the equivalent of four or more car spaces for every car it serves; people on foot, on the other hand, require only ten square feet to move down a street. As it uses this space, generates urban "heat islands," cuts into greenbelts, increases air pollution, increases flood severity, interferes with social interaction, and fosters expansion of roads and parking lots into barriers for non-drivers, sprawl costs us again and again.[49]

By forcing communities to spread farther across the landscape, the estimated 15 to 50 percent of city land consumed by cars compels more building of infrastructure — roads, water pipes, utility lines, sewers — per household and per person. A typical suburban home requires four times the infrastructure of a duplex. Sprawl also raises the cost of services by requiring school buses, transit, emergency vehicles, snowplows, garbage trucks, and delivery vehicles to travel farther; all this puts upward pressure on service costs and property taxes. Depending on location, sprawl can add $12,000 to $48,000 to the cost of new suburban homes. Sprawl fosters development of outlying discount stores and malls, which drain downtown business coffers and tax rolls. And housing developments that come in with sprawl generally don't pay their way in property taxes. One review of over 700 studies found that sprawling growth often resulted in financial losses to

> *"If drivers had to pay by the mile until the whole bill were covered, sliding behind the wheel would lead to even more sticker shock than a visit to the neighborhood car dealership."*
>
> GUS SPETH, IN JAMES MACKENZIE ET AL, *THE GOING RATE: WHAT IT REALLY COSTS TO DRIVE*

rural communities. A 1994 study by the City of San Jose, California, showed that continued sprawl development would leave the city with yearly deficits of $4.5 million, since the new taxes generated would not cover the costs of the services required. Boulder, Colorado, found it could save about $3,000 per acre per year by preserving land as open space instead of allowing sprawl development.[50]

Car-generated sprawl costs society its best farmland, indirectly causing conversion of anywhere from one to five acres out of farming for every acre actually developed.[51] That raises food prices, in part because as sprawl pushes farm fields to more remote locations, crops have to travel farther to get to market. Half the price of lettuce sold on the East Coast goes into paying to ship it from California. Farmers now get ten cents or less of every dollar consumers spend on food; much of the remainder covers transport and distribution costs. On average, food gets shipped 1,400 miles from production site to dinner plate.[52]

Few transportation studies have calculated the cost of habitat loss that contributes to species extinction as cars and sprawl encroach on wildlands. But some studies have determined a value for biodiversity, and it is this biodiversity that's lost when habitat and species disappear. The estimated dollar value of the benefits to humans from preservation of biodiversity and habitat ranges from $3 trillion to $33 trillion per year; compare this to the total world economy of $26 trillion yearly.[53] These benefits include things like raw material for medicines, food products, soil formation, bioremediation of chemical wastes, recycling of organic wastes, nitrogen fixation, and carbon dioxide absorption. Every square mile of habitat we lose to sprawl costs us an average $50,000 to $550,000 per year in lost biodiversity benefits.[54] And that doesn't count the psychological and aesthetic losses or the reduced quality of life resulting from the replacement of greenspace by asphalt, or the intangible spiritual loss when a species disappears forever.

Other costs mount as well; when tallying the ways cars cost us, it's hard to be all-inclusive. Damage to buildings and utilities from motor-vehicle-caused vibrations probably costs $6.6 billion a year in the U.S. and likely more in countries where such vibrations force expensive restoration of irreplaceable antiquities.[55] Disposal of car bodies, tires, and batteries impose additional costs, estimated at $4.2 billion a year in the U.S.[56] Health care costs go up due to the stress and sedentary lifestyles fostered by car commuting. Also on the list is the cost of social isolation and alienation induced by a car-dominated landscape. And, though this is highly subjective, there is an external aesthetic cost to cluttering the visual landscape with cars and their artifacts.

The Grand Total

Several North American studies in the 1990s attempted to quantify either the total costs of driving or driving's external costs. For example, World Resources Institute estimated that the U.S. spends nearly $300 billion per year on the car (that's about $1,500 per vehicle), above and beyond out-of-pocket costs paid directly by drivers. Peter Miller and John Moffet figured cars cost somewhere between $380 and $660 billion a year. Mark Delucchi calculated the external cost of cars at 79 cents to $1.20 per vehicle mile and as much as $9,927 to $15,053 per car per year. A study by Brian Ketcham and Charles Komanoff calculated external costs of roadway transport at $729 billion a year, and the overall costs of driving at $1.544 trillion in the U.S. — about $7,700 per car per year. Todd Litman figures that driving's total costs range from 84 cents to $1.30 per mile in the U.S. That's the equivalent of over $2 trillion a year.[57]

Various economic analysts, then, tell us that hundreds of billions, even trillions, of dollars get pumped into our love affair with the car. Even half that level of spending could buy a lot of trains and alternative-fuel buses, and still leave plenty of money for sidewalks and bike paths. Recall that on a per-car basis, even considering cheaper used cars, U.S. consumers spend an average of over $3,000 per year per car out of pocket.[58] At the high end of the scale, a new large car or SUV driven 20,000 miles will cost close to $10,000 a year. Adding these internal monetary costs to external costs based on various studies, we get a range of figures that put the true grand total at somewhere between $5,000 and $25,000 per car per year. All things considered, then, each car on the road may represent about $15,000 a year, give or take, of various costs and losses — the equivalent of about $290 a week down the toilet for Daniel Egan's brother, and more if he wants to buy a new SUV.

In other developed countries, per car costs fall in this range as well, and external costs of cars are likewise significant. In Canada, says one study, external costs average Cdn$3,000 per car per year.[59] A study of the external costs of motoring in the U.K. estimated that they totaled £14.16 billion a year, about £590 per car.[60] A 1991 study found that even in Germany, where gas taxes are relatively high, cars imposed external costs of about 6,000 DM per year, 60,000 DM over the 10-year life of the car. The study noted that 6,000 DM per year would also pay for an annual public transport pass, 15,000 miles a year of first class train fares, and a good bicycle every five years. Gas taxes, said the study, would have to rise to 5.50 DM per liter ($14.72/U.S. gallon) to fully cover these costs.[61] Similarly, Brian Ketcham and Charles Komanoff's study found that gas taxes of $17 per gallon would be needed to cover the full costs of driving in New York City.[62]

Ketcham and Komanoff also point out that drug abuse has been condemned for costing the U.S. at least $300 billion a year in health, crime, productivity, and other social costs. Numbers like this have been used to justify a multi-billion dollar U.S. "war on drugs." Meanwhile, their analysis indicates that non-motorists alone lose close to $300 billion a year due to the external costs of motor vehicle use. "The social, environmental, and fiscal costs of auto and truck traffic not borne directly by motorists are in the same league as the costs of drug abuse and addiction," they note.[63]

Again demonstrating the broader costs of spending on cars and roads, Australian researchers have found that the more a community spends on roads, the worse its economy, while the more it spends on transit, the better. "Strategies that build freeways and add to sprawl are draining the economy of cities," writes Peter Newman, describing his 1998 study with Jeff Kenworthy for the World Bank. Newman and Kenworthy's study compared sustainable, rail-based transportation with road transport and found that cities with the most roads and highest car dependence spend the most on transportation per kilometer and have the lowest economic efficiency in their transportation systems. Looking at the gross regional product (GRP) for metropolitan areas around the world, the study found that auto-dependent North American and Australian cities pay a higher percentage of their GRP for transportation than do more transit-friendly cities in Europe and Asia. Even within North America and Australia, cities with more transit and fewer cars and roads end up spending less for transportation overall. Echoing these results, transport analyst Walter Hook argues that Japan is more competitive economically, because the Japanese walk and cycle more, paying only nine percent of their GNP for transport compared to the 15 to 18 percent paid in the U.S. Other studies and figures cast doubt on the idea that road-building generates economic benefits. In the U.S., the rate of return on highway expenditures has declined to below that of private investments since the 1980s.[64]

In exchange for the money we lavish on them, cars may provide us with a certain amount of comfort and convenience. But taking an honest look shows we pay a high price, and having the true cost of driving hidden keeps us paying it despite the many downsides to our marriage with cars. This raises the question: how much would we continue to drive if we knew the true price, and if we had more choice about whether to pay it? Todd Litman gives one answer. Around half our driving is excess, he writes, generated by market distortions that underprice driving, reduce travel choices, and foster sprawl. And underpriced driving actually increases transportation costs overall. Litman estimates that with certain reforms to include more of the costs of driving in the actual price, motor vehicle travel in North America might drop by 40 to 60 percent — and society would save money.[65]

How much does your driving cost?

You can estimate your cost of driving with this worksheet. It helps you determine your out-of-pocket costs, then adds your non-monetary costs, and finally allows you to estimate and add external costs to get a grand total.

Distance (miles or km) you drive per year   _____
     X

Mpg or km/l your car gets   _____
     =

Fuel (gallons or liters) used per year   _____

Yearly cost of car purchase (monthly payments x 12
OR purchase price divided by years owned)   _____
     +

Annual depreciation (ten percent of purchase price)   _____
     +

Yearly insurance premium   _____
     +

Annual license and registration fees   _____
     +

Yearly emissions test cost (where applicable)   _____
     =

Fixed cost of your car   _____ (A)

Fuel costs (fuel used per year above x cost per gallon or liter)   _____
     +

Cost of oil and oil changes   _____
     +

Tires (including snow tires if applicable)   _____
     +

Repairs and maintenance (other than oil and tires)   _____
     +

Out-of pocket parking costs (meters, lots, etc.)   _____
     +

Bridge and road tolls   _____
     +

Tickets and fines   _____
     +

Car washes   _____
     =

Operating cost   _____ (B)

Other costs (e.g., misc. accessories, books-on-tape, car alarm,
car stereo, lumbar support cushion, car phone, etc.) per year   _____ (C)

Your total yearly monetary driving cost [(A) + (B) + (C)]   _____
     ÷

Distance you drive per year   _____
     =

Your monetary cost per mile or km to drive   _____

To consider costs of your travel time, figure the number of hours you spend driving in a year and multiply that by half your hourly wage. Then divide that by the distance you drive annually to get a time cost per distance. You also incur a crash risk cost. Todd Litman estimates this at about five cents per mile (about five cents Cdn per km).[66] You can multiply this by your yearly distance to get a total yearly crash risk cost.

Finally, to make a rough estimate of the external costs you impose when you drive, start by estimating the distance you drive per year in rural conditions; in cities and suburbs when it's not rush hour; and in rush hour traffic. Add 20 cents per mile (18 cents Cdn per km) for rural driving; 33 cents per mile (30 cents Cdn per km) for suburban and city driving in off-peak hours; and 59 cents per mile (54 cents Cdn per km) for driving in cities and suburbs during rush hour.[67]

Distance driven/year in rural conditions x $0.20 or Cdn$0.18 _____
+
Distance driven/year in cities or suburbs in
non-rush hr, x $0.33 or Cdn$0.30 _____
+
Distance driven/year in cities or suburbs in
rush hr, x $0.59 or Cdn$0.54 _____
=
Yearly external cost of your driving _____
÷
Distance you drive per year _____
=
External cost of your driving per mile or kilometer _____

	Yearly	Per mile or km
Your monetary cost to drive	_____	_____
+		
Time travel cost	_____	_____
+		
Crash risk cost	_____	0.05
=		
Your total internal cost to drive	_____	_____
+		
External cost of your driving	_____	_____
=		
The overall cost of your driving GRAND TOTAL	_____	_____

CHAPTER 10

The Greatest Cost:
The Toll from Car Crashes

*"The automobile laconically runs down pedestrians. It gnaws into the
side of a barn or else, grinning, it flies down a slope. It can't be blamed
for anything. Its conscience is ... clear ... It only fulfills its destiny:
It is destined to wipe out the world."*

ILYA EHRENBURG, *THE LIFE OF THE AUTOMOBILE* (1929)

THE DAY AFTER DIANA, PRINCESS OF WALES, died in a horrific car crash in Paris, net-work TV stations broadcast little other than coverage of the wreck. Reports showed a grim scene: a badly mangled car, emergency workers clustered around it, flashing lights, and worried faces. As I watched one such report, the scene cut to a low-ground shot of a fast-moving vehicle, asphalt rushing underneath at high speed. The scene cut again, this time to an overhead shot of the car as it cornered abrupt-ly. At first I mistook this for some sort of news reel re-enactment of events leading up to the crash. But as a low, breathy voice broke in with words like "performance" and "efficiency," I realized it was a car ad. The speed we were witnessing, purport-ed the ad, was a *good* thing.

Even as marriage to the car leaves us battered and bruised, few question the appropriateness of producing vehicles capable of traveling at deadly and illegal speeds, let alone the advertisements exalting this capability. Diana joined at least half a million others killed in car crashes that year worldwide.[1] A significant per-centage of these victims died as young as she, or younger. We've become so accus-tomed to the broken bones, paralysis, and tragic deaths from such car wrecks that we've come to accept them as normal. Yet cars kill at a rate that's anywhere from seven to nearly 100 times as high as that of other forms of transportation.[2] And they're a bigger killer than war: more than twice as many people have died since 1900 in U.S. car collisions as have been killed in all the wars in U.S. history. It is a heavy toll from a conflict largely overlooked: the war waged on us by the car.

Grim Numbers

In 1955, 82 people died in a multiple-car racing crash in Le Mans. In 1965, two trucks rammed into a crowd in Togo and killed 125 bystanders. In 1996, 300 cars piled up on a foggy Italian highway, injuring hundreds and killing eleven. These tragedies made headlines but, even more devastating, are crash deaths that don't — those that take place routinely and claim another life every single minute of every single day around the world. Automobiles have killed over 30 million people in crashes since their debut more than a century ago. They now steal the lives of over 500,000 people worldwide each year (that's a conservative estimate: some place the death toll at a million each year). They injure an incredible 15 million more, adding an injury every two seconds to the death per minute caused by cars. In the space of every 60-second car ad, 31 more lives are directly shattered by the pain, disfigurement, and loss of auto wrecks; countless more people, friends and family of victims, have their lives irrevocably changed.[3]

As of 1990, car crashes ranked as the world's ninth-leading cause of death, but they're climbing the list. The International Federation of Red Cross and Red

"Highways, and not wars, have become the largest arenas of violence in the world."

JULIAN PETTIFER AND NIGEL TURNER, *AUTOMANIA*

Crescent Societies (IFRC) predicts that by 2020 they'll be the third biggest killer. And they'll mostly affect developing countries where, as motor vehicle numbers have shot up, the rate of car crash deaths has also risen rapidly. Already, more people between five and 44 die in car crashes in the Third World than are killed by any single disease; over 70 percent of global road fatalities now occur in Third World countries. Most developing countries suffer 40 or more deaths a year per 10,000 vehicles. Ethiopia suffers 191.6 deaths per 10,000 vehicles, while in Australia and Japan the rate is only 1.9 — 100 times less. New Delhi averaged 3.1 traffic deaths a day in 1998's first half; three-fourths of victims were motorcyclists, bicyclists, or pedestrians. The yearly cost of crashes in developing countries — more than US$53 billion — is a financial loss that about equals and cancels out the amount these countries receive in international aid.[4]

In developed countries, vehicle death rates are lower — generally under five deaths per 10,000 registered vehicles per year — but absolute numbers are still high. Safety improvements and drunk driving crackdowns have dropped death rates per unit of car travel but, as with pollution, vast increases in car miles traveled have kept absolute numbers of deaths in countries like the U.S. about level. Car crashes still cause close to half of what are classified as accidental deaths in the U.S. (the U.S. National Highway Transportation Safety Administration [NHTSA] has switched from calling them "accidents" to calling them "crashes," but some statistics compilations still use the old term). Most years, the number killed on U.S. roads is comparable to the number of U.S. soldiers who died fighting in Vietnam.[5]

Like wars, car crashes kill younger people disproportionately. In the U.S., car crashes are the leading killer of children and young adults aged one to 24, and they cause more than 40 percent of deaths among 16 to 20 year olds. As of 1995, they were the number one killer of girls and women under 34. These early deaths result in the loss of 688 years of life per 100,000 people, which is greater than the loss of life caused by suicide or murder. Worldwide, vehicle crashes are the largest single cause of death for men aged 15 to 44. And many victims of cars are innocent non-drivers, like the California seventh-grader run over on her walk to school by a motorist allegedly blinded momentarily by sunlight. Cars kill one U.S. pedestrian every 96 minutes — over 5,000 deaths a year. They seriously injure or permanently maim another 80,000 pedestrians annually. Often those killed are children playing, like the two run over when a Texas woman attempting to pass a driver's test stepped on the gas instead of the brake and jumped a curb. Older people, too, are more vulnerable to cars; based on 1994 to 1997 data, New York City pedestrians 65 and older are over twice as likely to be killed by a car as they are to be murdered.[6]

The U.S. car crash toll has ranged mostly between 40,000 and 55,000 a year since 1962. In 1998, U.S. car wrecks killed 41,200 people and left 2,200,000 more with disabling injuries; more than 18 million vehicles got into crashes causing property damage or non-disabling injuries only. Altogether, over 21 million vehicles crashed during the year; that was more than one out of every ten registered vehicles.[7] Every 13 minutes, there's another motor vehicle death in the U.S. and, every 14 seconds, another injury.[8] In Canada, car crash death rates are only slightly lower than in the U.S. While there were 2.15 U.S. traffic fatalities per 10,000 registered vehicles in 1995, in Canada the rate was 2.01. Between 3,000 and 4,000 Canadians die each year on the country's roads.[9] The European Union tallies about the same number of car crash fatalities each year as the U.S.; in 1995, there were 45,000. Car crashes send one in three Europeans to the hospital at some point in their lives. In Britain, road safety efforts cut the number of accidents in half from 1965 to 1994. But in the process, children, pedestrians, and cyclists abandoned many roads to exclusive use by motor vehicles, sacrificing these zones to the car.[10]

In his book *How We Die*, physician Sherwin B. Nuland explains that car crash trauma can kill us immediately, usually due to massive damage to the brain, spinal cord, heart, or major blood vessels. Over half of all traumatic deaths are immediate. That's what happened to a 22-year-old Missouri woman just out of college, who braked to avoid a sudden rear-end collision and went over a highway median; the first oncoming car to hit hers ejected her out onto the road and the next ran over and killed her.[11] Or car crashes can cause what's called "early death," within a few hours of the trauma, usually the result of injuries to the head, lungs, or abdominal organs that cause heavy blood loss or interfere with breathing or other body functions. That's what happened to Princess Diana. If neither immediate or early death occurs, crash victims can still succumb to death days or weeks after a crash, surviving the initial blood loss or head trauma but succumbing to complications or infections from internal injuries.[12] Finally, survivors of car crashes may have multiple, disabling injuries for which recovery takes months or even years. Car crashes, for instance, are the biggest single cause of disabling injuries to the back and the brain.[13]

"If anyone walking along the sidewalk were to make deafening noises, spew poisonous gas into innocent faces, and threaten people with a deadly weapon, they would be arrested. Yet a few feet away, on the public roadway, it is considered normal behavior."

STEVE STOLLMAN, NEW YORK CITY
CYCLING/PEDESTRIAN ADVOCATE

Car crashes take a psychological toll as well. The American Psychological Association recognizes at least two disorders resulting from car crashes: post-traumatic stress disorder (PTSD) and acute stress disorder (ASD). Anywhere from 23 to 98 percent of crash survivors may suffer from PTSD, which may last a month or more. And some develop symptoms of ASD — dissociative amnesia, emotional numbness, and a dazed state — lasting two days to four weeks.[14] At any given time, then, over a million people worldwide may be in a post-shock daze because of car crashes.[15]

Even the more conservative estimate of the world's yearly car crash fatalities works out to a daily death rate roughly equivalent to five jumbo jet crashes every day. If 500,000 people per year worldwide died in airplane crashes or, if 500,000 people per year worldwide died in train wrecks, we'd very likely have major investigations of these incidents and possibly even abandon the technologies as unsafe. So why don't we do this with cars?

Forgotten Casualties: The Non-Human World

The Humane Society estimates that around a million wild animals die on U.S. roads every day. Some are common species like white-tailed deer, squirrels, skunks, or chipmunks; some are endangered, like Florida panthers and American crocodiles, and being edged closer to extinction in part by cars. "The car is today's predator," says Pinkerton Academy instructor Brewster Bartlett, also known as Dr. Splatt. Bartlett's students began to quantify road carnage in 1993 for a statistics and environmental education project. The program now includes international participants who enter roadkill data via the Internet.[16] Analysis of the data shows that, depending on road type, conditions, and season, there is on average one roadkill every three miles every week on North American roads.[17] Amphibians and reptiles in particular have had populations decimated near busy roads.

Bill Ruediger, an endangered species biologist for the U.S. Forest Service, believes roadkill is a big factor in the population declines he's noticed in protected species. "Real-life killing and hurting of animals goes on every day of the year on our roads," he says. "They're all being creamed." Likewise, until Parks Canada mitigated the problem with wildlife over- and under-passes, Banff residents called a Bow River Valley section of the Trans-Canada Highway the "meatmaker" because of all the elk, deer, and other animals killed there by cars.[18]

When cars destroy the homes of animals and plants, they take an additional toll. "The most devastating environmental crisis of the turn of the millennium, second only to global warming, is the destruction of wild and rural habitat — and the automobile is the main culprit in that rout," writes Jim Armstrong.[19] Researchers have found not only that habitat loss is the single biggest threat to biodiversity, but also that infrastructure development like road-building ranks as one of the top causes of habitat loss. Road construction in particular presents a threat to 38 percent of endangered or threatened amphibian species and 15 percent of all such listed species. Land development — i.e., sprawl — harms the habitat of 35 percent of federally listed species in the U.S., and off-road driving harms 13 percent.[20]

Roads form asphalt, gravel, or dirt barriers that chop the natural landscape into fragments. Because some plant and animal species can't or don't cross roads, they're unable to feed or reproduce as effectively in road-fragmented areas and may even die out in locations. Such areas are thus unable to support as much biological diversity as expansive unroaded wilderness. Roads also help introduce non-native species into wild areas, allowing them to take over disturbed areas like roadsides and to choke out native plants. They allow vehicle emissions into previously pristine areas, contaminating both air and water and posing a further challenge to species survival. It's little wonder that Horace Albright, National Park Service director in the 1930s, advised: "Oppose with all your strength and power all proposals to penetrate your wilderness regions with motorways." Or that U.S. Interior Secretary Bruce Babbitt declared in the 1990s: "Roads are the enemies of the national parks."[21]

> *"Is homicide by automobile so much less culpable than homicide with a gun?"*
>
> LIFE MAGAZINE, 1906, QUOTED IN JULIAN PETTIFER AND NIGEL TURNER, *AUTOMANIA*

Suburban Safety?

Parents seeking safer havens for their families often move them from inner cities to the suburbs. But recent reports show that a move like this can instead increase danger, and that cars are the reason.

In *The Car and the City*, a 1996 report by Northwest Environment Watch, Alan Durning writes that "people often flee crime-ridden cities for the perceived safety of the suburbs — only to increase the risks they expose themselves to." The report notes that while per capita crime rates actually vary little between different types of Seattle neighborhoods and there is no association between density and crime rates, the risk of injury in a car crash quadruples for suburban residents over what it is for city dwellers — mainly because the suburbanites have to drive more, and drive faster. The report further points out that traffic crashes "kill more northwesterners each year than gunshot wounds or drug abuse do."[22]

The 1998 *Mean Streets* report from the Surface Transportation Policy Project also points a finger at cars and suburbs, as it finds that "sprawling metropolitan areas are the most dangerous for pedestrians." Cars kill pedestrians at the highest rates in such sprawling cities as Orlando, Tampa, Miami, Phoenix, Houston, Atlanta, and Los Angeles. *Mean Streets* points out that children especially are put at risk in such environments, and are being driven off streets: kids' walking trips declined by more than a third from 1977 to 1995 in the U.S.[23] Children's biking has also dropped — down 60 to 70 percent since the 1970s — as safety concerns have led parents to keep children away from traffic. Yet these more restricted children pay a price in loss of independence, confidence, and physical health, and the added car trips they take increase their risk of death and injury.[24]

Crash Risks

In an attempt to mitigate the problem of car crash deaths and injuries, we've identified several factors that increase crash risks. Every unit increase in a motor vehicle's speed, for instance, means greater risk of injury and death in collisions. Increasing speeds from 55 to 65 m.p.h. increases the likelihood of a fatal crash by ten percent. One German study found that increasing speeds from 25 to 40 m.p.h. tripled the proportion of crashes into pedestrians resulting in death. In the two years after the U.S. government rescinded its 55 m.p.h. limit in 1995, vehicle death rates went up about 15 percent in states which had raised their limits, but remained steady in states that hadn't.[25]

Inattention and in-car distractions make autos more deadly as well. About 20 percent of U.S. drivers admit to having nodded off behind the wheel; sleepy drivers cause five percent of fatal crashes. The growing use of mobile office equipment, especially car phones, also takes driver attention away from the road. By using car phones, motorists more than quadruple their chances of crashing, and the use of such electronic devices in cars is on the increase.[26]

Poor vehicle design can also increase risk. Because the design and integrity of a vehicle's passenger compartment influence safety more than size, some small cars get higher safety ratings than bigger ones. Safety design in some larger vehicles (SUVs, for instance) has been regulated differently and sometimes less stringently than in smaller passenger cars. SUVs also have a higher rollover rate, more than twice as high as average vehicles and dangerous enough that NHTSA has proposed special "High Risk of Rollover" warning labels for them. In addition, their size and design mean SUVs, vans, and light trucks pose a greater threat of death and injury to pedestrians, cyclists, and passengers in other vehicles.

Alcohol is well-known for increasing risk on the roads. In 1997, an estimated 39 percent of U.S. traffic deaths involved alcohol. Slightly over a million U.S. residents are injured each year in drunk driving crashes.[27] In Canada, the percentage of fatalities is similar (40 percent).[28] Still, most crashes don't involve alcohol. Even if we eliminated all drunk driving (certainly a worthy goal), there would still be thousands of highway deaths each year. Sober drivers kill nearly all the pedestrians and cyclists who die in New York City each year, says a 1999 study by the pedestrian rights group Right Of Way (see sidebar). Author Charles Komanoff points out that, sadly, the "focus on drunken driving leaves unaddressed the larger problem of aggressive, violent or otherwise irresponsible driving." This, not alcohol, says the study, accounts for the vast majority of cyclist and pedestrian deaths.[29] Car crashes are the main cause of death for U.S. children from birth to

> *"Walk, do not drive, to buy your Lotto ticket. If you have to drive ten miles to buy a ticket then you're three times more likely to get killed in a car crash on the way than you are to win the jackpot."*
>
> DR. MIKE ORKIN, *CAN YOU WIN?: THE REAL ODDS FOR CASINO GAMBLING, SPORTS BETTING, AND LOTTERIES*

age 14; alcohol is a factor in just over 20 percent of these.[30] That means nearly 80 percent of child crash deaths involve sober driving.

These numbers point us toward an often overlooked risk factor, perhaps the biggest one: the car itself, and the extent of our dependence on it. A society married to the car induces people into driving under less than optimal or safe conditions, including a wide range of states that people find themselves in on a regular basis: fatigued, distracted, preoccupied, tense, or rushed, for instance. Even things like dieting or taking a ubiquitous substance like aspirin have the potential to impair driving ability — and thus threaten lives. Aspirin can induce "mental confusion, dizziness and defects in hearing and vision," as well as impairing attention and color perception.[31] A 1997 USDA study found that dieting slowed reaction time in women by 11 percent (men were not studied). "Even though this change seems small," said study team leader Mary Kretsch, "it might be enough, when you're driving, to cause an accident."[32]

Cars are inherently dangerous, and sometimes it doesn't take much for one to cause a crash. In California, a car killed its 79-year-old owner after the man parked it, walked around behind it, and the vehicle slipped into reverse, backing over him.[33] In 1993, a Pennsylvania car crashed into a garage and injured a woman after the car-owner's dog jumped into the unoccupied vehicle and sent it down an embankment.[34] Human bodies don't mix well with hard, fast-moving objects; as they travel at speeds faster than our physiology can always handle, cars expose us to risks that we can reduce, by adjusting road or vehicle design and driver behavior, but never completely eliminate. Yet because cars are so ubiquitous, we have essentially forgotten that they're dangerous pieces of heavy machinery requiring care and diligence to operate. To ask that we all exercise this attentiveness and caution for the hours each day we drive is to ask a lot; it is no wonder we have so many crashes. Not everyone is cut out to be a heavy machinery operator, and not everyone wants to be one. But in a car-based society providing few alternatives, even people who shouldn't or don't want to be drivers often feel forced into that role.

From "Safety Doesn't Sell" to Cars That Save Lives

In 1955, the *Journal of the American Medical Association* published an editorial calling for safety devices in cars. Around the same time, Cornell University studies documented ways cars killed: by ejecting 25 percent of occupants in collisions, for example, or impaling drivers on steering columns. Ford Motor Company responded in 1956 with a package of safety features it called "Lifeguard Design," including safety latches on doors to reduce the risk of being thrown out of a car, steering wheels that wouldn't impale the driver on impact, and optional seat belts. But when sales of these 1956 models later turned down, Ford dropped its safety features, and industry pundits devised the motto "Safety doesn't sell."[35]

It wasn't long, however, before laws began requiring automakers to pay more attention to safety. In the early 1960s, car crash deaths were high and states began passing laws that required seat belt installation. By 1963, after nearly half of all U.S. states passed laws requiring them, it made the most economic sense for automakers to meet the requirements in all the cars they made, so seat belts (at least in the front seat) became standard. Then in 1965, a young Harvard law graduate named Ralph Nader published *Unsafe at Any Speed*, detailing safety flaws in cars and especially the Chevrolet Corvair. Nader was familiar with the studies by Cornell and others about what happened in the so-called "second collision," the crash of the body and vehicle that comes just after the crash of the vehicle itself; one such study found that in 600 fatal crashes, 84 percent of deaths could have been prevented by improvements in vehicle design.[36]

Nader's whistle-blowing had a big effect on the industry, which attempted to counter his efforts in ways that backfired and probably contributed to passage of the U.S. National Traffic and Motor Vehicle Safety Act of 1966.[37] GM had Nader tailed by private detectives; Nader caught them in the act and sued for invasion of privacy, ending up with $425,000 in an out-of-court settlement. GM was also accused of tampering with a federal witness, since Nader was testifying before Congress about auto safety at the time. The incident forced GM to make a public apology.[38] Since then, auto manufacturers — abetted by regulations — have continued to incorporate safer features into vehicles. However, safety still tends to slide in some models where it's less regulated.

> *"My 17-year-old son was killed one year ago in a collision ... Until it happens to you, you are happy to be part of the conspiracy of silence. And after it has, you are one of the quietly suffering who don't have enough strength left to try to change the world."*
>
> LETTER TO *THE GUARDIAN* (ENGLAND), JANUARY 1988

Safety improvements can be a mixed blessing. Air bags and seat belts have increased numbers of car crash survivors, but air bags can also kill small adults and children. As safety features have decreased deaths, many crash victims who now survive do so with crippling leg and ankle injuries caused by car parts smashing in through passenger footwells.[39] Child safety seats have come under fire, too; they are often used improperly, such that parents think children are safe in them when really they aren't. One Maryland couple, for instance, lost their three-year-old daughter after a collision, despite her being strapped into a safety seat that one dealer mistakenly said was installed correctly.[40] Finally, as safety inside cars improves, safety outside cars may decrease as drivers feel more confident taking risks. "Vehicle safety seems to bring more danger, especially for those already most vulnerable, such as pedestrians or bicycles," says the International Red Cross.[41]

Despite the overwhelming number of deaths and injuries from cars, people still seem confused about how safe they really are, or aren't. Safety themes in auto advertising might perpetuate some of this confusion, as when ads quote drivers grateful for safety features or crash survivors who believe their cars saved their lives. In fact, the people giving those testimonials would likely have been much safer if they'd traveled some other way than by driving. No car is statistically as safe as a plane, a train, a bike, or walking. While car passengers suffered 9.2 deaths per billion passenger miles in 1997 in the U.S., only 0.4 air travelers, 0.1 bus riders, and 0.1 train passengers died per billion passenger miles. While in the U.S. in 1998 there were 15.2 car deaths per 100,000 residents, there were only 2.2 pedestrian deaths and 0.3 bicycle deaths per 100,000 people.[42] There are roughly 70 times as many deaths caused by cars as by trains each year in the U.S. and 500 times as many deaths caused by cars as by rapid transit.[43]

Innocent Victims

Since 1899 when an electric taxi rammed H.H. Bliss, the first U.S. pedestrian killed by a car, drivers have only inconsistently been held responsible for damages done by their vehicles, particularly when their victims have been non-motorists. Too often, society blames these victims, speaking of mishaps where a child runs out and "causes" a car to hit him, or where a cyclist "falls under" the wheels of a truck. One of three pedestrians killed in crashes are "drunk," newspapers reported recently; yet these reports were based on a study that counted as drunk any pedestrians with more than 0.01 percent blood alcohol content after death, eight to ten times lower than legal intoxication limits, and didn't consider biological mechanisms (such as microbial action) that can increase post-mortem blood alcohol levels.[44]

The pedestrian rights group Right Of Way has documented this pattern of blaming victims and absolving drivers in Killed by Automobile, a 1999 study of New York City pedestrian fatalities. Drivers were "at least partly culpable" in 90 percent of the city's 1,000 pedestrian and cyclist deaths between 1994 and 1997, the study found, yet police issued moving violations in only 16 percent of cases studied.[45] Case histories illustrate the study's finding that driver failure to observe traffic laws causes most pedestrian fatalities. Take for instance the infant girl "crushed by a car that vaulted the curb on Broadway ... apparently as the driver rushed toward a parking space." Or the three-year-old holding her mother's hand, run over when a speeding driver trying to make a light veered onto the sidewalk. These case histories demonstrate once again that automobiles are inherently dangerous. As the study points out, "Motor vehicle operators are licensed, their vehicles are registered, and insurance is required of them, precisely because of their potential for harm."[46]

Right Of Way memorializes pedestrian and cyclist crash victims by painting full-size "police-chalk" body outlines onto pavement where they've been struck down, writing names, dates of death, and the words "Killed by Automobile" next to the outline. From December 1996 to March 1999, the group had stenciled 250 of these street memorials around New York City. The stencils remain visible for several months before they fade away.[47]

Is It Worth It?

If it has taken you 20 minutes to read this chapter, another 20 people worldwide have been killed by cars while you've done so, and another 600 have been left injured. In reality, however, the automotive toll is even greater: in addition to the crash deaths and injuries covered in this chapter, there are casualties from wars for oil, human rights abuses in some oil-producing regions, oil spill deaths to marine life, oil waste pit deaths to birds and small mammals, excess deaths due to air pollution — and the list goes on.

We can put safety band-aids on cars, but the fact remains that car-based transport is inherently unsafe. Perhaps the safety improvements we need would better involve reducing our risk by reducing our driving and, instead, using the other means of travel that are so much safer. As Australian transport researcher Peter Newman writes, "There are enormous resources and human energy poured into road safety when by far the biggest gains would be made by shifting to other modes and reducing the overall level of car use."[48]

Cars can be useful but, after detailing their drawbacks, we have to ask: is it really worth all this to be married to them? "Half the world will be involved in an auto-accident / At some time during their lives," writes Heathcote Williams in his prose poem *Autogeddon*, "A humdrum holocaust: / The Third World War nobody bothered to declare."[49] All the driving we do perpetuates this war. Using cars involves so many losses: loss of land to pavement, loss of community, loss of clean air and water, loss of quiet, loss of time, and loss of money in addition to the ongoing tragic loss of life. The more we look at all this loss, the harder it gets to honestly justify marriage to the car as being worth it.

How to Divorce Your Car: Let Me Count the Ways ...

"People say, 'How can you live without a car?'
and I just kind of smile and say, 'Very well!'"

JOHN SCHNEIDER, CINCINNATI BUSINESS LEADER, CAR-FREE SINCE 1973

THE RELATIONSHIP HISTORY has been reviewed; grounds for divorce have been established. Now, how can you actually divorce your car? Part 3 describes numerous ways. Whatever your situation, you should be able to find car divorce techniques in these pages that fit your life and circumstances.

The car-free and car-lite folks quoted here talk about the big quality-of-life advantages of driving less or even living without a car. Although the choice to reduce driving in auto-dependent environments has presented some of them with tradeoffs, most have also experienced definite, and sometimes surprising, benefits from reducing their car use or getting rid of their cars altogether. Those benefits have made the choice worthwhile and nearly all of them would recommend some form of car divorce to their friends. Using alternatives to cars, they've found, can be more healthy, more congenial, more economical, and even more fun.

CHAPTER 11

Just Walk Out! Using Your Feet
Instead of Your Car

*"The longest journey begins with a single step, not with a turn of the
ignition key. That's the best thing about walking, the journey itself."*

EDWARD ABBEY, *THE JOURNEY HOME*

THE HUMAN BODY IS DESIGNED TO WALK. Walking helps our bodies and brains work at
their best, and has sparked some of the world's great thinking. Samuel Taylor
Coleridge began crafting *The Rime of the Ancient Mariner* on a walking tour with fellow poet William Wordsworth. Abraham Lincoln routinely hiked a hill near
Springfield, Illinois, so he could better think. Einstein deduced secrets of the universe as he walked. But for all its value, we don't walk much anymore. Even on trips
under a mile, Californians walk only 15 percent of the time; many Britons consider
anything over a quarter mile as beyond walking distance. Perhaps we avoid walking
because car-encouraged sprawl has made destinations more distant, or because cars
have made some thoroughfares too noisy, smoggy, or frightening. Perhaps, though,
we also avoid it because we've forgotten how good walking can still be.

John Schneider of Cincinnati hasn't forgotten. Schneider became a walking
devotee after graduate school. He sold his car, flew to London, and walked from
there to Paris (helped across the water by a ferry). Walking in Europe shifted his out-
look. "Seeing how European society works, where people do walk a lot, and where
towns are built to the specifications of walkers, got me to think a little differently
about things," he recalls. "When I came back I moved to an area near downtown
Cincinnati and really didn't need a car then. And I just never got around to buying
another one." Not only has he saved money, he's had tremendous freedom. Living
within walking distance of shops, restaurants, theaters, the public library, and many
of his business ventures, he says, "I walk everywhere. I think it's made for a richer
experience. I know our city as most people don't, and never — traveling at 35 miles
an hour — ever figure out."

Walk Out for a Better Life

"Walking is man's best medicine," said Hippocrates, and modern health care
agrees. Alarmed by dropping levels of physical activity — only ten percent of U.S.
adults exercise regularly and inactivity contributes to 250,000 U.S. deaths a year[1] —
agencies like the U.S. Centers for Disease Control and Prevention (CDC) and Health
Canada have stepped up efforts to promote moderate exercise like walking.
Walking, they point out, can help you

126

- **reduce symptoms or slow progression of several diseases:** walking can help alleviate asthma, colon cancer, insomnia, and premenstrual syndrome, to mention only a few;

- **keep off extra weight and tone up:** walking uses more muscles than other types of exercise, stretches ligaments, aids flexibility, and eases muscle aches and pains;

- **reduce blood pressure, cut heart attack risk, and manage cholesterol:** a brisk 20-minute walk can help your heart as much as a 20-minute run, with less chance of injury;

- **fend off adult-onset diabetes:** walking helps regulate blood glucose levels and sometimes reduces the need for medication if you're already diabetic;

- **increase bone density and slow osteoporosis:** walking can sometimes help rebuild osteoporosis-damaged bone and may even strengthen bones more than calcium supplements;

- **tune your immune system:** one study comparing walkers with sedentary people found the walkers called in sick only half as much as the sedentary group;

- **maintain mental ability:** older people who take hour-long walks a few times a week have better reaction times and mental acuity than sedentary peers;

- **reduce stress:** walking dissipates energy and reverses physiological changes — tensed muscles, constricted blood vessels, higher heart rate — brought on by the fight-or-flight mechanism;

- **relieve depression and anxiety and improve mood and self-confidence:** walking releases hormones that aid mental health, leaving you more alert, energized, and upbeat;

- **live longer:** a study of older men found that the more they walked, the later they died.[2]

Walking provides these benefits cheaply: no gym fees, no fancy equipment. It can save money on doctors, too. Brown University estimated the U.S. could cut its $50 billion yearly heart disease bill if all sedentary citizens walked an hour a day.[3] Overall, the money-saving potential of walking rather than driving is huge. You'll pay less for gas, maintenance, and parking and, if you walk enough to get rid of a car, you'll save even more.

Walking also has unbeatable quality-of-life benefits. "Walking helps put me back in touch with nature, back in touch with myself," writes car-free Troy Holter from Montana. "I notice the more subtle aspects of the natural environment, a change of color, delicate sounds, the metamorphosis of light, an ever-changing mosaic of sky and clouds, the feel of air on my skin, my body connecting with itself, critters large and small each caught in the web of their universe — all of which leads me to a deeper appreciation of the world I inhabit."[4] Echoes Ellen Jones of Washington, D.C.: "The natural world has become a large part of our daily lives since we've become car-free. Shedding the armor of the automobile, the whole family is acutely aware of the variations in weather, seasons, and daylight hours ... We talk about the smell of rain, the presence of plant and bird life as part of our experience going to and from school and work."[5]

> *"Walking especially adds to my quality of life, offering exercise, down time, and a unique perspective on the neighborhood and community. Because of my walk to work, exercise is now a daily part of my life, and it's great for relieving stress."*
>
> JILL KRUSE, WASHINGTON, D.C., CAR-FREE

The contrast to most city driving couldn't be greater. "Driving around the District," states an article from the *Washington Post*, "isn't exactly a leisurely cruise down Main Street. More often, it's the complete opposite ... Cursing to oneself as a traffic jam on K Street makes you late for your 9 a.m. meeting downtown. Cursing out loud as you are cut off by another driver in Dupont Circle while attempting to get onto Massachusetts Avenue. Or cursing at an unyielding D.C. parking official over that blindingly pink ticket he or she just shoved onto your windshield." The article adds: "There's a small group of people out there who observe these predicaments, chuckle to themselves, and just walk on by. These Washingtonians don't own an automobile."[6]

How Walking Helps Whole Communities

- *Walking makes communities healthier.* Dan Burden of Walkable Communities Inc. shows his audience two slides side-by-side. One depicts a typical strip-mall intersection, a six-lane stoplit corridor full of asphalt, cars, and neon with few visible people. The second image shows a tree-lined main street, wide sidewalks, a narrow roadway, with throngs of folks on foot, window shopping, lounging at sidewalk cafes, and bumping into friends and neighbors. "Which is the healthier community?" Burden asks. Everyone chooses the second image, and everyone gets it right. The key indicator of a community's health, Burden says, is how many people walk in it. Walkable towns help everyone to a better quality of life, maybe children in particular. One study comparing ten-year-olds in a suburb to those in a small, walkable town showed the town kids ranged farther and more often by themselves, while the suburban kids watched four times as much TV.[7]

- *Walking can restore a sense of community.* In yesteryear's compact, pedestrian-friendly communities, people walked to church and corner stores, and talked with friends on front porches while kids played in streets and alleys. Making communities walker-friendly can bring back that lifestyle. Some builders are doing this in neo-traditional developments, with homes built on smaller lots, closer together, their front porches facing wider sidewalks and narrower streets. And such homes are in demand. One news feature profiled a couple who moved into Middleton Hills, a neo-traditional community near Madison, Wisconsin: "She's a cartographer; he's in computer software. Auto addiction is not in their veins. She works at home and he'll get to his nearby job mostly by bicycle. 'We love the idea of being able to walk down the street to buy our groceries,' [she] says."[8] Walker-friendly developments like these can provide more affordable housing, more open space for farming, wilderness, trails, or recreation, more opportunity for neighbors to interact, and less need for a car. Developers like them, too, since smaller lots cut their land costs.

🐾 *Walking can mean safer communities.* "Berkeley cops leave cars and take to the streets," said a 1992 headline. "Neighborhood foot patrols begin."[9] Why? Because, as one resident put it, a "police department disassociated with the people will lead to incidents like Rodney King." Community policing, aided by putting more police on foot and bikes, helps drop crime rates. But it's not just cops walking that makes places safer — more walkability in general helps. When Waikiki, Hawaii, put bike patrols on one main boulevard, cut its width from six lanes to four, and gave the extra space to pedestrians, crime dropped by at least half and inspired Waikiki to consider another reduction in the size of the boulevard, from four lanes to two.[10]

🐾 *Walking helps your community's environment.* Especially when you walk instead of drive for short trips, you help air quality, since cars pollute more during cold starts and short stretches of driving — those most easily replaced by walking — can do significant damage to the air.[11] As Joel Makower writes, "You may be thinking, 'Will I really harm the earth by driving a few blocks down the street to buy a quart of milk?' The answer is yes." He adds, "If just one out of every ten commuters who now drive to work switched to walking, we'd save 2.4 billion gallons of gas a year and reduce carbon dioxide emissions by 25.4 million tons."[12]

🐾 *Walking helps your community's economy.* Big box discount stores and strip malls along multi-lane roads, icons of 30-mile-per-hour architecture, are built to a scale best viewed from a cruising car. There's just one problem: people don't buy things while traveling 30 miles per hour. Discount stores make up for this, dollar-wise, with aggressive marketing and low prices on cheap goods, putting smaller, locally owned businesses at a disadvantage. Studies show that these small businesses can do better in areas conducive to walking. An evaluation of Boston's Downtown Crossing, for instance, showed that after the district became primarily a pedestrian-only zone in 1978, store purchases went up.[13] And shopping within walking distance can help to keep money in local economies, rather than siphoning it off to the distant headquarters of a national chain.

The Opportunities to Walk

Especially in car-dependent North America, driving even on short trips has become a habit. More than a quarter of U.S. car trips are one mile or less and 13.7 percent are a half mile or less.[14] That's a multitude of opportunities to walk instead of drive. Because U.S. residents take 900 million trips daily by car, there are at least 123 million chances to walk instead of drive every day in the U.S. alone. In North America, the average car makes 2,000 trips a year that are shorter than about two miles (three km) — seven opportunities a day for a potentially easy car divorce![15] The Pedestrian Transportation Program in Portland, Oregon, suggests: "Replace at least one car trip a week with a walk. Encourage family and friends to walk with you." This is a great place to start. Over time, you can ratchet up the number of car trips you replace to two a week, three a week — even up to one a day or more.

"My vicinity affords many good walks; and though for so many years I have walked almost every day, and sometimes for several days together, I have not yet exhausted them. An absolutely new prospect is a great happiness."

H. D. THOREAU

Decide on your walking limit. A half mile takes around ten minutes, a mile around twenty. List places within that distance from home and walk when you go there. Once your own walking routine's in place, you might try another of Portland's suggestions: "Organize a neighborhood walk to show your neighbors how many places are within walking distance."[16]

Walking for transportation can be incorporated into daily routines and it's time-efficient to do so, letting you accomplish two things — travel and exercise — at once. The U.S. CDC says walking for shorter periods a few times a day is as effective as using a longer block of time for exercise. Since our daily lives include so many easily walkable short trips, walking routinely to places you have to go anyway is a great way to get in shape and to stay that way.

Walking to work: "I walk to and from work every day in Manhattan," wrote author Jeannie Ralston when she lived in New York City. "The time I walk is the time I use to warm up for work and then to wind down from it. No one makes me do it. I do it because I like to witness New York waking up and then see it sparkling with glamour as evening approaches and because no matter what goes wrong during the day, I know I've at least done one good thing for myself."[17] After a doctor told him high blood pressure could take years off his life unless he exercised, David Engwicht started walking to work, four miles every day. "I discovered it was not only good for my health," he writes, "it became an invaluable time to relax and think. It fed my creative reservoir."[18] If you live within a mile or two of your workplace, walking to work can be ideal. Walk alone and gather your thoughts or, if you feel like being social and live near people who work with or near you, organize a walk-pool: the farthest person from work can start out walking and pick up co-workers along the way.

Commuter Connections, a service of the Metropolitan Washington (D.C.) Council of Governments, encourages walking as a commute option. "Most walkers commute about two miles one-way to work," the organization reports. It suggests starting with a weekend test commute, walking your route to see how long it takes, and then beginning slowly by walking one or two days a week, working up to hoofing it full-time. To support walking commuters, the agency offers a Guaranteed Ride Home program; walkers (as well as cyclists, transit riders, and ride-share participants) can register and are guaranteed a ride home in the event of a legitimate emergency.

"I walk whenever I can. I walk to work here in New York — it's only about five blocks, but a lot of people would have a car drive them."

TED TURNER, IN E MAGAZINE, JANUARY/FEBRUARY 1999

If you're reluctant to walk in case you'll need a car for errands during the day, try batching errands. Do them on, say, two days a week to free yourself to walk the other three. If you're in a two-car, two-income family, this might help you get rid of the expense of an extra car. You and your spouse or partner can trade off walking to work (or taking transit) and using the car. If a day comes when you both truly need a car, you can rent one or take a taxi and probably still save money.

Walking to school: Contemporary kids get driven more than their predecessors in almost every car-dependent country. In Vancouver, British Columbia, in 1985 one third of all children were driven to school; by 1996, that number had jumped to one half. In the U.S., it's nearly three quarters. In the U.K., nearly a fifth of rush-hour traffic consists of kids being driven to or from school.[19] While in 1971, 80 percent of seven- and eight-year-old children walked to school in the U.K., only nine percent did so by 1990, mainly due to parents' fears of traffic dangers.[20] A typical morning in a double-income, two-kid family finds everyone scrambling to get to school and work. Often working parents pile kids in cars, rush them to school or day-care, then rush to work. If your life fits this mold, you may feel you don't have time to walk your kids to school. But replacing the morning rush with a walk can have benefits that may leave you feeling you don't have time *not* to do so. Here is one mother's experience:

> I found that even when I was working (full-time as well as part-time) I felt less stressed when I was able to walk, rather than drive, my kids to their respective day cares ... It was better for me to fit in that walk at the beginning of the day, because it became more than transport time. It became time I spent with my children many mornings a week exploring the local world and playing word games. In some ways, it was preferable to structure longer walk-to-school periods than to attempt significant quality time at home at the end of the day when I was more tired and they were more cranky.[21]

You can walk your children to school on your own, once a week or month if you can't do it every day, or walking kids to school can be a community endeavor. In Australia, Europe, Japan, and Canada, communities sponsor Safe Routes to

School programs to encourage this. These programs help children find safe avenues for walking or cycling to school, involving students in mapping the routes. They sometimes set up no-idling zones around schools and work with local authorities to add facilities to make routes safer. A Safe Routes to School program in Odense (Denmark) cut pedestrian and bike crashes involving children by 85 percent.[22] Safe Routes to School programs are promoted in the UK by the organization Sustrans and in Canada by Go for Green, which distributes workbooks to help teachers and students create local programs.

Several places have also used an innovative approach for getting kids to school called the Walking School Bus. This operates like a regular school bus, but everyone's on foot. In his book *Reclaiming Our Cities and Towns*, David Engwicht describes how such a "bus" can be organized:

> Parents, police, teachers, and authorities map where each child lives in relation to the school and the safest route for these children to go to and from school. Through local papers and other media outlets, volunteers (including senior citizens) are asked to become Walking Bus Drivers. These "drivers" walk a set route, much like a school bus, collecting children along the route and delivering them safely to school. To increase the profile of the Walking Bus, a coloured line can be painted on the side of the road to indicate where it runs and murals painted on the footpath at the various stops.[23]

Engwicht further suggests that Walking School Buses use designated back-up drivers; a highly visible wagon or trolley to carry packs, bundles, raincoats, and other gear, pushed ahead of the driver so it's the first part of the "bus" to enter the street when crossing; and safety vests, colored hats, or flags worn or carried by participants to further increase visibility.[24]

There are successful Walking School Bus programs in Canada organized under Go for Green's Active and Safe Routes to School program. In the U.S., there is the National Walk Our Children to School Day program promoted by the Partnership for a Walkable America. Kicked off in September 1997, Walk Our Children to School Day is now held annually on the Wednesday of the first full week of October at schools across the country.

Similar programs have sprung up to promote walking year-round. When Los Alamos, New Mexico, P.E. teacher Judy Strittmatter and school nurse Dottie Reilly started the Pinon Elementary Walking Club for students, they got *Walking* magazine's Mark Fenton to help them kick it off. Since then, they've held a Walk-to-School Day every month during the school year — sometimes these are Walk-with-a-Buddy Days, encouraging students to walk together — and have given participating students incentives like serving them breakfast or awarding them free gym time. One thrilled student was chosen to walk to school with an Albuquerque race walker. Most Walk-to-School days get a couple hundred participants; one month, 322 out of 400 staff and students walked to school.

City of Boulder, Colorado

above:
Walking School Buses take various forms: this one in Colorado uses yellow ropes for visibility and safety.

Walking School Bus

Scarborough Mirror, April 1999

left:
Students in Scarborough, Ontario, peer through Walking School Bus windows: their hats indentify them as bus members and increase their visibility.

Walking on errands: Walking can be an easy way to do errands within a mile or two of home. For more distant chores, take transit and walk from a centrally located stop. If you must take a car, try leaving it in a central place and walking to do errands from there. Walk to do errands during your lunch hour; if necessary, pick one errand a day so you'll have time to walk both ways and to eat before returning to work. If time won't allow this, walk when doing weekend errands. Think twice about the time it takes to walk compared to driving. "Maybe it takes twice as long to walk to the dry cleaners as it does to fire up the family car and drive there," writes Ellen Jones, "but what about parking the beast? That's real time, too." You can do what Jones calls a transportation time audit (see sidebar): "Think about the total elapsed time it takes to do your errands and ask yourself, 'How far could I walk in that time?'" The results, she adds, "may surprise you. And guess what — it's more fun to walk!"[25]

> "By walking, I really got to know on some kind of fine-grained level not only a diversity of people but also the town that I lived in."
>
> HANK GOLDSTEIN, FREDERICK, MARYLAND, CAR-LITE

Walking locally: Whatever destinations might be in your neighborhood — church, park, community center, friends, or neighbors — you can walk to them. In some ways, writing this down seems a little silly. Isn't it obvious we can walk to places as

---

Transportation Time Audits

Driving instead of walking may not always save time even on individual trips. If you want to test this for a particular journey, try a transportation time audit. Pick a location you frequent, such as work, the library, or a store, that's a mile or less from your home. Clock how long it takes you to get there from the time you step out the door. If you're driving, this will include things like opening the garage door, unlocking the car, fastening your seat belt, waiting at stop lights or signs along the way, slowing for pedestrians and bicyclists, parking, locking the car, and walking the last leg of the journey. Your trip isn't over until you've entered the door of your destination. If you're walking, you'll step out the door, walk, perhaps stop at a few corners or stoplights, keep walking, and enter your destination.

Time the driving trip first, from door to door, and then next time you go, walk at your regular pace and time that trip. You don't have to follow the same route as you used with a car — for instance, are there footpaths or other walkable shortcuts you can use instead? — as long as you leave from and head to the same set of doors. Under some circumstances, usually depending upon how well-designed and walker-friendly your community is, your walking trip may take you less time than driving. Even if it isn't faster, you may be surprised at how close the timing is. Consider also that this time audit does not include time spent working to pay for a car, or time lost due to lack of exercise and deterioration of health. Even if it takes a few minutes longer to walk, it may not be worth the expense — to your bank account, your health and the planet — to drive.

close as within the same neighborhood? Unfortunately not, especially in car-dependent countries like the U.S. where mind-sets are often stuck in the notion that trip equals car. Sometimes it can be hard to break through an accompanying resistance to walking, but breaking through it can also be a lot of fun.

Once, I was invited by a friend to a potluck dinner. I bicycled 17 miles to meet my friend at his house; from there we planned to head to the potluck, about a half-mile away. Was I surprised when my friend pulled out his car keys! "We're driving from here?!?" I croaked, my 17-mile bike ride fresh in my mind. "Well, yes," he replied, seeming puzzled that I would think of doing anything else. "We have food to carry — this big, hot casserole and a couple bottles of wine. They'd be too awkward to carry if we walked." The weather was good, and we weren't late. The cargo didn't look overwhelming. "I'll carry the stuff," I volunteered. "Let's walk." He looked a bit skeptical, but went along with me. We put the casserole in a box and threw in some potholders. I put the wine in my day pack, picked up the box, and we set off.

We got to the potluck around ten minutes later. "Come on in!" our hostess greeted us. "Did you have trouble parking?" Her short, steep driveway offered little storage space for cars. "We had no trouble at all," said my friend, now pleased we had arrived on foot. "We walked over." Our hostess was a bit taken aback. "Oh," she said. Some of the other guests, overhearing our exchange from inside the door, seemed equally surprised. "You *walked* over?" queried a fellow who also lived less

"I'd like you to meet Frank Russ. He's just arrived on foot."

than a mile away in the same neighborhood. "You're nuts!" But it started a conversation on walking and, we could see, got folks to think. My friend, a bit of an iconoclast, got a kick out of surprising other people, and I hoped our action would plant a few seeds: if we had walked, so could anyone else in the neighborhood.

Walking globally: Next time you take a holiday, consider walking. Really. There are lots of opportunities to do this, ranging from cheap and local to expensive and exotic. On the cheap end, you can take day trips to local trails, or even walk out your door to a hiking trail. The American Hiking Society wants to expand the U.S. trail network until there's a trail within fifteen minutes of everyone's home or workplace. You may already live or work within 15 minutes of a good trail, which might link to others leading across your region or even the country. If your local trails are not within walking distance, you might bike to them, or take transit. Some urban areas like Boston and San Francisco have guides showing which trains and buses stop at trails and parks.

For a walking holiday a bit farther afield, a bus or a train can get you to starting points in many locations and you can walk from there. In the U.S., Amtrak stops at Glacier National Park and shuttles into Yosemite Valley. Canada's VIA Rail has stops at Banff and Jasper in the Canadian Rockies. Across North America, long-distance trails like the Pacific Crest Trail, the West Coast Trail, the Appalachian Trail, the National Scenic Historic Trail, the Bruce Trail, or the Trans Canada Trail afford the opportunity for longer walks. While walking some of these requires athletic prowess, segments of many of them are accessible to the less athletic among us. Some long-distance trails have associations supporting them that provide information to potential visitors. The Bruce Trail Association in Ontario, for example, sells a guidebook with trail maps as well as a guide listing bed and breakfast inns along the trail for people who want to hike without roughing it.

> *"Walking, I can smell flowers in people's gardens. It's great to walk through a neighborhood and smell people cooking."*
>
> MARK PETERSEN, ROANOKE, VIRGINIA, CAR-FREE

In Europe, you can walk from the North Sea in Holland to the French Riviera on the Grande Randonnèe Cinq (GR-5). Walking holidays are big in the U.K., where paths meander through pastoral fields, past historic castles, and over windswept Scottish heaths. In Scandinavia, hiking trails crisscross Swedish farms and Norwegian mountains, and backpackers can hike from hut to hut without having to carry tents or cooking gear. Hut-to-hut trail systems exist in other places, too. New Zealand's Milford Track has such a system, as do other tracks in that country.

Walking Well

Make walking easy: A bit of light equipment can expand your ability to walk. With a daypack and a cloth bag, you can comfortably carry a sack or two of groceries home on foot. A wheeled cart or two-wheeled wire basket can help with this, too. People haul things while walking all the time in airports, where ten-minute walks between gates are not uncommon; this is the same time and distance people often drive in towns. You can borrow an airport tool to make walking easier in town: some luggage carriers can be used to bring home groceries and parcels. A little light equipment can help folks in rural areas move away from car- and truck-dependency, too. At our place, we kid about being a "two-cart family." With two garden carts, one lighter, one more heavy duty, we have moved furniture, mattresses, books, dishes, and firewood up to a mile over a rutted track, on foot.

Walk safely: Since modern society often forces us to walk near heavy machinery (i.e., cars), some caution is wise. "We advise pedestrians to walk assertively and

Reclaiming the Road

When my sisters and I were children, our father, in leading us across a busy street, would assert his rights as a pedestrian by glaring at oncoming traffic and calling out, "Five-Six-Oh-A!" That was the vehicle code section giving pedestrians the right of way in California. He repeated this often enough that we grew up with at least a small sense of righteous indignation at cars that would whiz by, ignoring the state-given rights so clearly important to our dad.

Most states and provinces have pedestrian right-of-way laws like California's former 560(a) (it's since been renumbered), but they are widely ignored by drivers and often unenforced by police. In a study of Las Vegas, for instance, Walkable Communities found that "when encountering pedestrians at marked crossing points, few motorists were observed who slowed or yielded."[26] In some places, groups have mounted frontal challenges to the rampant disregard for walkers' rights. The Willamette Pedestrian Coalition (WPC) has staged a number of "pedestrian actions" to get drivers to obey the laws. Sometimes they simply gather a group together and cross the street repeatedly at a legal crossing point, carrying signs reminding drivers that pedestrians have the right of way. One action used the old Burma-Shave advertising method of doggerel verse on successive signs: WPC members painted one line of verse on each of eight signs and carried them sequentially down and across the street. Sign by sign, motorists read:

> When Mary tried
>
> to cross the road
>
> not a single
>
> driver slowed.
>
> As you hurry
>
> home today,
>
> give pedestrians
>
> the right-of-way.

Whatever the tactics, asserting rights to the road has become an important part of advocating walking. Bit by bit, groups like the Willamette Pedestrian Coalition get the message across: streets are for people, not just for cars.

exercise their legal rights-of-way," says Chris Bradshaw, founder of the advocacy group Ottawalk. "Always use caution because drivers are unpredictable, primarily because they are inattentive, and don't always know or follow the regulations."[27] You can increase walking safety by walking facing traffic on roads without sidewalks, walking whenever possible on streets with low speed limits and traffic levels, and wearing reflective clothing or accessories and carrying lights at night. Walk defensively: watch for drivers who don't watch for you. Request information on the pedestrian laws in your state or province — ask law enforcement agencies to produce a brochure on the topic if they don't have one — and then assert your rights. Even when you have the right of way, drivers may not be aware of this or respect it. You can also carry a big whistle, as Sally Flocks of Pedestrians Educating Drivers on Safety (PEDS) in Atlanta, Georgia, recommends; PEDS has sold whistles to pedestrians in Atlanta and beyond. Sally uses her whistle to catch the ears and eyes of inattentive motorists when her safety is at stake — when a driver doesn't see her in a crosswalk, for example. "Pedestrians need to arm themselves — with whistles," she writes. "They can remind drivers of their presence, letting them know when they break the rules."

Car Walking and Street Walking

If you've ever walked along a sidewalk and found a parked car blocking your way, you'll understand what inspired German activist Michael Hartmann to start car walking. In 1988, frustrated that cars blocked not only his way but also wheelchair-bound people and parents with perambulators, he began walking over cars parked on sidewalks. His action captured the imagination of others frustrated with cars taking over public spaces, and car walking spread. It was a featured action at the 1997 Towards Car-Free Cities Conference in Lyon (France), where a group of activists walked over cars parked on sidewalks and left flyers on the windshields alerting drivers they had done so: "I walked over your car because I didn't want to slide under it!"

Hartmann has posted instructions for car walking on the Internet that basically boil down to stepping up onto one end of the car (but not where the car might dent) and taking a few careful steps across it (along the edge) to the other end, then stepping off. He points out that a German court has ruled it's not illegal to walk across a car if the car is parked on the sidewalk, and if the car walker does not intend to damage the car.[28]

From car walking, Hartmann and fellow Munich activists have moved on to street walking — walking in the middle of streets to force cars to slow to walking speeds. For this, the activists can be fined, but they persist in order to make the points that people take precedence over cars and that streets should be shared. Hartmann has street-walked by himself to slow traffic, as well as organizing groups of street-walkers to more effectively slow cars over broad areas. His goal is to have pedestrian rights respected and to help reshape cities so that whole neighborhoods can be free of cars and children can play on streets.

Great Places to Walk

So many places in the world are great places to walk: compact historic city centers, charming small towns, tree-lined residential neighborhoods, or natural areas, from restored urban streams to wilderness. They're best for walking when kept sacrosanct from motorized intrusion and, fortunately, there are places making efforts to limit motor vehicles. In Europe, cities like Amsterdam and Copenhagen have made themselves more walkable by closing some downtown streets to cars. Many European cities also use *woonerven* (singular: *woonerf*), a Dutch term for traffic-calmed streets where pedestrians have priority and cars are allowed only at slow speeds. In North America, too, the list of walkable communities is growing. *Walking* magazine periodically recognizes U.S. towns that have improved their walkability; their 1998 and 1999 lists included towns like Clayton, California; Boulder, Colorado; Dunedin, Florida; Chicago, Illinois; Portland, Maine; Boston, Massachusetts; Portland, Oregon; Chattanooga, Tennessee; Burlington, Vermont; and Madison, Wisconsin.[29]

One indicator of whether a city is a great place to walk, or at least has that potential, is whether the city has an advocacy group working to improve walking conditions, as do Austin; Seattle; Portland, Oregon; Boston; Atlanta; Philadelphia; New York City; Ottawa; and others. You can also look at whether a city has invested money in making itself walkable. And you can use a do-it-yourself walkability audit, such as the Walkable America Checklist from Partnership for a Walkable America, to see if a community is walker-friendly. Your own town might be a great place to walk that's going unnoticed, just waiting for someone like you to assess the possibilities. Even in sprawling suburbs you can find gems like little-known footpaths from one cul-de-sac to another, or trails forged by neighborhood kids through neglected woodlots. Or you may be lucky enough to live in a place where some streets revert occasionally to pedestrian-only walkways, like some of the residential routes in hilly parts of San Francisco Bay Area communities that become narrow, vine-draped stairways for pedestrians for a block or two at a stretch.

"To be walkable," writes Walkable Communities, Inc., "streets must invite people to be part of the scene. This welcome requires street edges that offer safety from traffic, security from personal harm, convenience ... and an environment that is comfortable."[30] The following questions can help you gauge if your community is walkable, or as walkable as it could be:

- Are there sidewalks, and are they wide? Five feet or more, with three feet clear of obstructions, allows two people to walk side-by-side or a wheelchair to pass. In commercial districts, at least eight feet is recommended.

- Are sidewalks and walkways interconnected and continuous, so you can walk anywhere in town without obstruction or danger from cars? It can be annoying, not to mention unsafe, to have a sidewalk end mid-trip, or to run into blockades like overpass supports leaving no room for walkers.

- Is the traffic calmed? Streets designed with low-turning-radius curves, tee intersections, short blocks, tree canopies and other landscaping, traffic barriers like bollards, and paving variations slow cars and are safer for walkers and cyclists as well as drivers.

➤ Are car travel lanes narrow? Skinny streets are both easier to cross and safer, as they tend to slow car speeds.

➤ Are streets and especially intersections well-lit, safe, and easy to cross? Wider streets can use neckdowns (sidewalk extensions that narrow crossing distances) at corners, as well as islands or medians to narrow crossing distances.

➤ Are there places where cars are limited or prohibited completely? Areas like downtown pedestrian malls, *woonerven* or slow streets, greenways, or non-motorized trails can vastly increase a community's walkability.

➤ Are sidewalks nicely furnished? Well-placed benches, shade trees, flower boxes, recycling bins, lighting, transit shelters, and other street furniture help make the street more inviting, more comfortable, and more convenient for you and other walkers.

➤ Is there good access to transit, with stops conveniently located, well-sheltered from weather, and frequently served? Transit services like these provide an important transport link for walkers.

➤ Does the community have these things especially around schools, hospitals, medical complexes, and retirement homes? Traffic calming is particularly important where walkers may be slower than the average adult.

➤ Is new construction compactly designed to favor walking, with businesses located close to homes and stores fronting sidewalks instead of parking lots? New development will be easier to reach by walking if it's located at in-fill sites (lots within communities) rather than beyond a city's edge.[31]

Advocacy for Walking and Walkable Communities

Cars take over streets and scare off pedestrians in a worsening spiral. If walkers put off by too many cars start driving, the increases in the number of cars can scare away more walkers; if trees are cut, sidewalks removed, and streets widened for these additional cars, the street becomes more unsafe and unwalkable. We end up with communities built for cars instead of people. Facilities for walkers often get thrown in as poor cousins to the roads they accompany, and with their less than ideal designs, it's no wonder when they're little used. A study of Las Vegas roadways, for instance, found several walker-unfriendly design problems typical of auto-dependent communities: signals that force pedestrians to wait too long, then allow too little time to cross; light poles and utility boxes blocking sidewalks; driveways and

"I never knew a man go for an honest day's walk for whatever distance, great or small ... and not have his reward in the repossession of his soul."

GEORGE TREVELYAN, IN AARON SUSSMAN AND RUTH GOODE, *THE MAGIC OF WALKING*

drainage grates in walkways; crosswalks too far apart; inadequate disabled access; no medians on wide boulevards; and unresponsive or inconveniently placed pedestrian push buttons.[32]

We can reverse the process that makes roads this way and take back streets by walking on them, narrowing them, replanting trees. One successful change can lead to another, creating an upward spiral back to more walkability. Several organizations around the world are working to encourage such changes. America WALKs, a coalition of local walking advocacy groups, is one. "Work with your neighbors to reclaim your street and your community," urges America WALKs. "Above all, walk! Walk to the store, walk to work, walk your children to school, walk to visit your friends. Remember, you make a difference with every step you take."[33]

If you live in a place where it's not nice to walk, look first at what you can do to make it better. *Walking* magazine's Mark Fenton tells of seeing an in-line skater sweeping glass off a bike path, improving the trail for himself and the community. Mark takes a bag with him on walks with his child, and picks up litter along the way. Little things like this make a difference and they're easy. With more energy, you can try things like the street reclaiming strategies outlined by David Engwicht (see Chapter 16), or joining with neighbors to close your street for a day or for a party. Most towns have procedures for temporary street closures, and some forward-

About Those Walk Signals

You may have noticed, when crossing some streets, what a long time you have to wait for that magic green WALK command. Often it's a very short time before the signal flashes red again, to DON'T WALK. If you have an intersection like this nearby, ask your local traffic engineer to change the signal's timing to give walkers a longer crossing interval. If the engineer needs coaxing, mention that such a change will make streets safer for drivers and pedestrians alike, both slowing down drivers and giving more time for walkers to get out of the way.

You might go further and ask for signals that respond immediately when the pedestrian button is pushed. Walkable Communities recommends this in school zones, pointing out that "Children are impatient and will not wait long periods of time for signals that do not respond readily."[34] I would expand on that: people in general don't like to wait, and anyone walking shouldn't have to. This is like affirmative action for walkers and other non-motorists; drivers already have plenty of advantages on roadways without making walkers wait. If you're walking and not driving, you're helping the whole community and should be treated accordingly.

Here's the kind of second-by-second timing that could be used everywhere for pedestrian push buttons. Second number one: the pedestrian pushes the button. Second two: the light for cross-traffic turns yellow. Seconds three and four: the light is still yellow. Second five: the light for cross-traffic turns red. Second six: the light for the pedestrian turns green. It's a small change that can make a big difference in how walkable a community feels.

thinking jurisdictions even encourage this. In places, non-motorists have closed streets without going through channels. The Reclaim the Streets movement started in Britain when protesters tired of car-clogged roads used minor auto wrecks to shut streets, then filled the blocked lanes with parties. The movement has gone global, with worldwide Reclaim the Streets days taking back public space with a variety of events.

Next look at what kind of community or local government support you need to improve walking conditions. It can help if government has expressed policy support for walking. Communities might do this by following Portland, Oregon's lead and adopting a Pedestrian Master Plan along with a Pedestrian Design Guide. A Pedestrian Plan can set goals and objectives for improving walkability, list specific pedestrian enhancement projects, and identify funding sources for improvements. Portland's plan also classifies streets and neighborhoods by levels of pedestrian use, as Pedestrian Districts, City Walkways, Local Service Walkways, and Off-Street Paths. As of 1999, the city had 16 designated Pedestrian Districts which are compact, walkable areas with good transit where pedestrians get priority.

In the U.K., a National Walking Strategy was prepared (though not immediately adopted) in 1998, and British cities and towns have been developing their own local walking strategies. Guidelines from Staffordshire University's Centre for Alternative and Sustainable Transport (CAST) suggest that such strategies begin with policy statements like, "We will prioritize the needs of pedestrians in transport and land use proposals and improve facilities for pedestrians to promote more and safer walking." Walking strategies, says CAST, can include a variety of objectives such as these examples:

- Establish a Walking Forum, where citizens can suggest walkability improvements.
- Emphasize the Safe Routes to School campaign
- Increase walking's share of trips under one mile to 25% / 50% in five / ten years.
- Have major employers adopt walking commuter programs within two years.
- Review walking links to parks and open spaces as the basis for establishing a local interconnected non-motorized trail network.[35]

Most of all, says CAST, it's important for walking strategy formulators to "think walking." CAST runs training days to teach local officials in the U.K. about walking strategy potential. They also recognize that walking can catalyze community regeneration, since a good walking environment is a good economic environment.

Whether or not such policy support is in place, you can take action to improve walking conditions. "Create a group!" recommends Sally Flocks of Atlanta's PEDS. "You're much better off complaining as an organization. Squeaky wheels get grease, but they get greased a lot quicker if they squeak in unison." She also points out that "neighborhoods already are advocacy groups for pedestrians; the things that a neighborhood wants are often what pedestrians need." Needs of senior citizens and pedestrians coincide, too, since so many seniors are walkers and, as Dorothea Hass of WalkBoston points out, "Senior groups have tons of well-organized, articulate, feisty members. They got a walk light put in here in my community after a pedestrian tragedy — they went to work on that and just didn't let up." So hold a neighborhood meeting — invite all age groups — to identify and list places that discourage walking, as well as walkway improvements you'd like. Write these up and give them to whoever's responsible for street design and maintenance in your community: road commission, planning department, public works, etc. Give copies to elected officials. Back up your requests by demonstrating the need for better walking facilities: you might start with an estimate of the number of people in your neighborhood or community who aren't licensed drivers or car owners, including children, the disabled, elderly, poor, and others (likely a larger segment of your local population than you'd expect). Add any information you may have about people who'd walk more if conditions were improved. Draw on Health Canada, the U.S. CDC, or your local, state, or provincial health department to help back up your requests, given their growing concerns about physical inactivity and its impacts on health.

Traffic engineers generally have a mandate to respond to safety concerns, so it helps to frame your requests in this context. Refer to the walkability questions in the previous section and ask for things your community needs to be more walkable. Also ask for:

- a buffer between you (the walker) and the car, possibly in the form of planter boxes, bollards, or even a bike lane;
- walkways on median strips, combined with well-marked mid-block crossings;
- traffic signals set so pedestrians have more time to cross streets;
- embedded flashing crosswalk warning lights that outline the crosswalk and light up when it is in use, to increase driver awareness and to cut pedestrian death rates;
- repair of hazards like broken traffic control devices, broken glass, or other obstructions in walkways, sidewalk potholes, etc. as well as clearing of sidewalks in areas with snowy winters;
- enforcement of laws requiring drivers to yield to pedestrians.

Finally, ask for more of the street, if not the whole thing. On streets where car lanes are wide and sidewalks narrow, ask for wider sidewalks and narrower lanes. Vehicle travel lane widths of nine to ten feet on local streets and 11 feet on boulevards and parkways should be plenty; those widths are accepted by the U.S. Federal Highway Administration. Some jurisdictions claim they need more space for emergency vehicles such as fire trucks, but communities like Portland, Oregon, have specifically studied this problem and found that fire trucks had adequate access on narrower streets.[36] You can also ask for permanent conversion of lanes from car use to sidewalks and/or bike lanes. A growing number of communities are making these conversions.

You can go farther and organize programs to promote walkability on an ongoing basis. Start a local walking advocacy group. In the U.S., America WALKs can help; in Canada, Ottawalk is a good model. In the U.S., bring the Department of Transportation's Pedestrian Safety Roadshow to town by hosting a seminar to help identify your community's walkability problems and potential solutions, and get help starting a pedestrian safety program. Arrange for your local public access cable TV channel to show "Perils for Pedestrians," a monthly half-hour show that features pedestrian issues and often highlights innovative solutions to walkability problems. Get your city or town to start a Pedestrian Transportation Program like the one in Portland, Oregon. Established partly by efforts of local pedestrian advocates, it builds walkway improvements, works with other city departments to make sure they consider walking, eliminates barriers to walking, promotes walking's benefits to the public, and teaches pedestrian safety.[37] If you have children, encourage their schools to teach pedestrian safety and to promote walking. Consider organizing a Walking School Bus program for the school or district or participating in National Walk Our Children to School Day. However else you may choose to advocate more walkability, you'll be advocating in the best way possible as you take the first step — just walk out!

> *"On balance, I can recommend walking with passion. It is an altogether delectable addiction."*
>
> COLIN FLETCHER, *THE COMPLETE WALKER*

CHAPTER 12

You'll Look Sweet upon the Seat: Bicycles for Transportation

"Daisy, Daisy, give me your answer, do!
... you'll look sweet upon the seat of a bicycle built for two!"

HARRY DACRE, LYRICS FROM THE SONG "DAISY BELL" (1892)

Bᴇɴ Sᴡᴇᴛs, ᴀ Los Aɴɢᴇʟᴇs ᴘʜᴏᴛᴏɢʀᴀᴘʜᴇʀ, doesn't have time to exercise. Instead, he bikes to jobs and on errands within 20 miles. "I have the choice of taking the car or a bicycle," he writes, "but find bicycling more efficient and rewarding ... It is pumping steadily toward a place to do a task that gives me the feeling of productivity I crave ... almost a state of physical and mental meditation." He can travel across town at predictable speeds regardless of congestion, carrying camera gear, spare clothes and books in pannier bags on his front and rear wheels. "I refuse offers of a ride home for me and my bicycle, even from a long distance," he adds. "Time and again, the bicycle gives passage to a place, health to a body, and self-sufficiency to its pilot."[1]

Millions of people shared this kind of enthusiasm during the bicycle's first heyday in the late 19th century and, today, though cars dominate much more road space, millions of people still do. There are, in fact, over a billion bicycles in the world and more bikes are produced each year than cars. There have also been upsurges in bike advocacy and increasing improvements in bike facilities. There's a positive feedback loop here for those who want to bike rather than drive: better biking conditions make it easier to bike more often and, by biking more often, we can inspire more improvements in bicycling conditions. That's the kind of upward spiral that can make bicycling better for everyone and cut car dependency.

Why You'll Want to Go by Bike

Bicycling has the same kind of health, economic, quality-of-life, and community benefits as walking.

> 🚴 *Bicycling can save your life and your health.* "The proof that people enjoy cycling to keep fit," notes Marcia Lowe, "is in the popularity of stationary exercise bikes; the irony, however, is that so many people drive to a health club to ride them."[2] Like walking, regular cycling can increase life expectancy and help prevent heart disease, hypertension, obesity, diabetes, stroke, arthritis, and other illnesses. Because it builds muscle strength, balance, and endurance, cycling can also protect against injury and disability. And it produces endorphins that mitigate pain and depression. As Tom

Davies has put it, "I did not need an expensive psychiatrist to tell me why I was depressed since, after a brisk [bike] ride, I was depressed no more."[3]

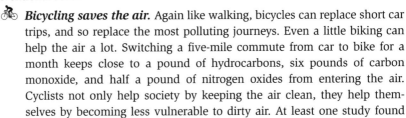 *Bicycling saves money.* If a car is never a cheap date, at least a bicycle can be one. You can find good used bikes for less than $100 in many places. On one trip back to my old home town in northern California, I needed a way to visit friends and wanted it to be car-free. I checked the paper my first morning there, found a bike advertised for $50, walked two miles to the owner's place along a creekside trail, and got a nature hike with my bike-shopping errand. The bike was in good shape, with a rack and wire baskets that could carry luggage. I bought it, spent about $25 more on accessories like a light and lock (I had a helmet with me), and got a week's transportation for $75 and some muscle power. Bike maintenance costs, too, are minimal, even if you don't do your own repairs, and bicycling can save you big money on car costs. Bike commuters in China can cover all their travel costs with a one-time $100 investment in a bike and under $25/year for maintenance. While only ten percent of the world's people can afford a car, it's been estimated that 80 percent have enough to buy a bicycle.[4]

> "One day, returning to Alabama by bike, I stopped to wash my clothes in Roanoke, Virginia. Two fellows were also doing laundry. They admired my courage and physical fitness, and one of them said, 'I'd like to do something like that, if I were as young as you are.' 'How old are you?' I asked. He said, 'forty-three.' I said, 'I'm almost fifty-one' ... I never lift weights, I never condition my abs, I never stretch, I never diet, I seldom see a doctor, I just walk and ride my bike ... Cycling keeps me lean, fit, healthy, and happy. I know that my own move back to the bike was the best decision I ever made."
>
> Ken Kifer, Ken Kifer's Bike Pages, <www.kenkifer.com/bikepages>

Bikes can help whole cities save money, too. They make more efficient use of roads, and building bike facilities costs less than infrastructure for cars. While a single mile of urban interstate highway might cost $100 million, the same amount can build 1,000 miles of bike paths. Even entire countries have saved money with bicycles. When the government of Ghana realized that years of motorization had failed to give it a transport system that met people's basic mobility needs, it switched to bikes. It now promotes production and use of bicycle trailers and builds roads for lighter non-motorized vehicles at a cost that's only about eight percent of building a conventional road.[5]

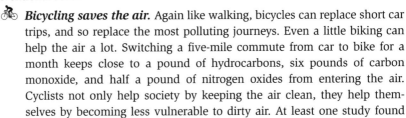 *Bicycling saves the air.* Again like walking, bicycles can replace short car trips, and so replace the most polluting journeys. Even a little biking can help the air a lot. Switching a five-mile commute from car to bike for a month keeps close to a pound of hydrocarbons, six pounds of carbon monoxide, and half a pound of nitrogen oxides from entering the air. Cyclists not only help society by keeping the air clean, they help themselves by becoming less vulnerable to dirty air. At least one study found

that cyclists end up with less pollution in their blood than drivers. A physician interpreting this study's data speculated that "the cyclists' more active respiratory systems did a better job of expelling the pollutants than did the relatively sedentary systems of the people sitting passively in their cars."[6]

🚲 ***Bicycling saves energy.*** Every transit commuter who bikes to the station instead of driving saves an average 150 gallons of gasoline a year. Every car commuter who switches to biking and transit can save 400 gallons of gas a year, on average. And bicycling is the most energy-efficient form of travel, using less energy per passenger mile than any other mode. While walking a mile uses 100 calories, bicycling a mile uses only 35. As Marcia Lowe points out, "In the rush to run engines on gasoline substitutes such as corn-based ethanol, decision makers have overlooked a technology that converts food directly into fuel. A cyclist can ride three-and-a-half miles on the calories found in an ear of corn — without any distilling or refining." [7]

"Car-freedom has given me a great gift: a love affair with my bicycle ...

Cycling keeps me looking young and feeling energetic and connected to the earth. I could never go back to the noose of a car."

ANGELA BISCHOFF, TORONTO, CAR-FREE

🚲 ***Bicycling saves time.*** The average speed of a commuting car (22 miles per hour) isn't much faster than a cyclist's usual ten to 20. That means door-to-door travel times for bikes and cars may be only a few minutes different. Phil Hammerslough of Vermont describes a day when he and his wife left at the same time for the three-mile trip to the business where they both work. He cycled, taking a standard route and stopping for lights, while she drove and took shortcuts. "I arrived less than a minute after her," writes Phil. "She was quite shocked." Bicycles' more efficient use of space makes it harder to get stuck in traffic on them and means they can sometimes travel more quickly than a car, particularly during city rush hours where traffic may slow to five m.p.h. (eight km/h). Studies in some eastern U.S. cities found that bicycles often get their riders to work in less time than cars would.[8]

🚲 ***Bicycling saves land.*** "The family car consumes about three times more space than the average family home," writes David Engwicht. But bicycles require much less space. At least eight bicycles can be parked in the space required for just one car. Bicycles encourage more compact communities, require less asphalt, and save land for other uses. As Lester Brown writes: "It is in the interest of societies everywhere to foster the use of bicycles ... Not only will this help save crop land, but this technology can greatly increase human mobility without destabilizing climate ... the land-saving, climate-stabilizing nature of bicycles will further tip the scales in their favor, and away from automobiles."[9]

Free Bikes

They are pink, yellow, green, white, even checkered, and they are free. They are the "Rainbow of Free Bikes," as the International Bicycle Fund calls them, and they are in cities around the world. Operated by community groups or local governments, free bike programs have sprung up in Copenhagen (Denmark); Sandnes, Lillehamer, and Hamar (Norway); Denver and Boulder, Colorado; Olympia, Washington; Portland, Oregon; Fresno, California; Missoula, Montana; Jasper, Alberta; Ashland, Wisconsin; and probably a few more places by the time you read this. Most of these programs operate by collecting donations of old bikes, refurbishing them, painting them all the same distinctive color or pattern, and leaving them out for free use within a specified area.

The Copenhagen program, started by a community group and now run by the municipality, is a good example of the European approach to free bikes. Copenhagen has a fleet of over 1,000 free bikes. Uniquely designed for easy identification, the bikes fit into special stands which release them upon deposit of a coin equivalent in value to about three U.S. dollars. Users can keep the bikes an unlimited time as long as they stay within Copenhagen's inner city. When they return the bike to one of the special stands, their money is returned. Revenue from advertising on the bikes helps support the program.

The Many Uses of Bicycles

People who go car-lite or car-free often report that a bike is one of their most valuable mobility aids. As a transport tool, writes Wisconsin teacher Steve Clark, "my bicycle gets an A-plus. By using it to meet my daily needs, especially in unconventional ways (like towing a canoe, bringing home an eight-foot Christmas tree, taking the family to church in our pedal car), I'm having a lot of fun proving its practicality." Australian postal workers deliver mail on bikes. Central American health workers bike to visit rural patients. In Asia, bikes and rickshaws carry freight from farm animals to furniture. Still, bikes are underused relative to their potential, especially in North America. As of 1990, less than one percent of U.S. trips were made by bike. Yet on an average U.S. day, two-thirds of people's trips are five miles or less, and 49 percent are three miles or less, all "within reasonable bicycling distance," as *The National Bicycling and Walking Study* notes. Similar proportions hold in other car-dependent countries. Half of Canadians' car trips are three miles (five kilometers) or less; a third are a mile and a quarter (two kilometers) or less. In the U.K., about three quarters of work commutes are five miles (eight kilometers) or less.[10] Especially considering how many trips are this short, bicycles can easily be used much more than they are now, for a wide variety of purposes.

Commuting: In the U.S., about half a million people commute by bike. In places like Holland, Hungary, and Denmark, half the work force commutes on bikes. All those European cyclists who ride to work in skirts and suits show that bike commuting does not require spandex. A relaxed commute of a few miles will get your blood pumping, but you needn't work up a sweat. For longer commutes, it does help to take sweating into consideration. For many bike commuters, sponging down, drying off, and changing does the trick; some places provide showers to encourage employees to bike to work. One California company has not only given bike commuters access to showers, it has provided lockers to store a week's worth of office clothes. The company has also loaned test bikes to employees for up to 90 days, letting them buy the loaners at a discount; given out safety accessories (reflective vest, helmet, mirror, and nite-lite) to any worker committing to bike to the office at least three days a week; provided emergency pick-ups to cyclists with flats; provided lockers for bicycle parking; and cooked free pancakes for everyone who cycled on Bike to Work Day. Companies like this one have figured out that bike commuters benefit themselves and the business by staying healthier and getting to work more alert and happy.

> "After a year or so of driving, I realised how pointless it was in urban Glasgow, so one day I decided to take the bike to work. I can still remember that wonderful feeling of freedom as I set off with my medical bag strapped to the rear carrier. I haven't used a car in my work since, and that first ride to work was 13 years ago."
>
> DR. COLIN GUTHRIE, GLASGOW (SCOTLAND), CAR-FREE

Errands: The less-than-a-mile-long trip to the convenience store, the quick run by the library to drop off books, the jaunt to school for a PTA meeting — these can all be done on a bike. Using a bike encouraged me to cut down on errands by batching them into fewer trips, using the phone, planning more, and buying less. Then cargo-carrying equipment made my remaining errands much easier. I started out using a rack, often carrying groceries in cloth bags secured to the rack with bungie cords, plus a daypack for delicate squishable things like avocados or tomatoes (extracting a ripe avocado from under a misplaced bungie cord isn't pretty). I've also used wire baskets or panniers. But for sheer convenience with errands, bike trailers are great. You can stow stuff in a bike trailer just as you might toss things into the back seat or trunk of a car, and it's amazing how much some trailers carry.

Steve Clark of Wisconsin has a custom-built trailer sturdy enough to haul a canoe behind his bike. When not hitched to the bike, it converts to a garden cart. Jim Gregory and Joan Stein's Bikes at Work trailers can carry up to 300 pounds (136 kg); they've hauled lumber, furniture, recyclables, and even other bicycles. By hitching two trailers together they can haul up to 600 pounds (272 kg) behind one bike. Cheyanne and Randy Gore take their pets to the vet in bike trailers; the dogs go into animal carriers first, and the carriers fit in the trailers. Greg Siple and his wife have used bike trailers to carry cargo and to take their son with them on errands around Missoula, Montana. As their son outgrew the trailer, they got a tandem which gave him the more "grown-up" role of helping to pedal to their destinations (you can also get a detachable extra frame, wheels, and seat that can turn a regular bike into a tandem for kids). Trailers costing up to a few hundred dollars and carrying one or two

Bikes transport almost anything! Steve Clark's daughter Suzy takes over hauling the canoe on a family camping trip (right).

Steve Clark

Spenser Villwoek

Jim Gregory hauls about 500 pounds of recyclables in winter (left).

kids and up to a few hundred pounds per bike are available from a variety of companies. If you're handy, you can build your own trailer using inexpensive materials.

Fun, recreation, and vacations: One year, I suggested to a friend that we go to a Christmas party on our bikes. He thought I was crazy. We were both dressed in nice slacks and might mess up our clothes, he argued; we had wine to carry and, besides, it was dark out. How could we possibly bicycle? Well, I suggested, we could tie our pant legs for the ride over. I offered to carry the wine in my pack. This was December, but it was also California, and the streets and weather were dry. We had lights and red tail-flashers for our bikes, would be traveling on well-lit streets, and the party was only about two miles away. Finally I talked him into it. We ended up having a safe, pleasant bicycle trip. We didn't get sweaty, our helmets didn't muss our hair, our clothes stayed clean and neat and, pink-cheeked and glowing by the time we arrived, we had a darn good time at the party.

The point of this little story is that there are many ways besides the obvious ones to use a bicycle for recreation. You can bicycle *to* fun as well as *for* fun. Parties, picnics, the county fair, softball games — those are all good times to load the family up on their bicycles and to pedal together to the event. Many of us also

The Romp family's bicycle-built-for-four plus trailer carried them from Vermont to Alaska.

Billy Romp

live within a few miles of recreational trails or bike paths and can bike to those places straight from home. If you want to cycle somewhere farther away, consider taking public transportation to get there, if you live in a place where buses and trains allow bikes to board.

Bicycles are also good for long distance vacations — ask the Romp family. Billy and Patti Romp put their family of five on a bicycle built for four, plus a trailer for the youngest, and they cycled together across North America for their summer 1999 vacation. Traveling 5,500 miles from Vermont to Alaska, they had such a rewarding adventure they're thinking of taking a future trip around the world on a five-seat bike. Bicycle touring is booming, "a gold mine," writes John Luton, "without the poisonous tailings."[11] Vermont now earns more from bicycle tourism than from maple syrup. Cycle tourists report bike-friendly conditions in locations like the Oregon Coast Bike Route, Quebec's La Route Verte, New York's Lake Champlain area, and more. The non-profit Adventure Cycling Association offers trips, maps, and other assistance with bicycle touring, and a number of touring companies offer organized cycling trips to destinations around the world.

Freight and deliveries: When a beverage company in San Salvador ran a six-month trial of bicycle trailer deliveries, the young vendor loved riding the mountainbike with trailer; he distributed as many 24-bottle cases in a month as could two people and a five-ton truck. The experiment inspired the company to switch to specially built tricycles at a significant savings; the tricycles cost ten times less per month to operate. The largest industrial bakery in Bogota (Colombia) switched from using 200 trucks to 800 cargo tricycles for its daily bread deliveries to 22,000 customers, and cut its distribution costs considerably. Bicycles are an integral part of business for a large number of self-employed Third World entrepreneurs. In Tanzania, independent dealers sell newspapers by bike; in Sri Lanka, they cycle hot lunches to factory workers; and in India, three-wheeled cargo tricycles deliver bread, soft drinks, and dry cleaning to shops and homes. Heavy-duty tricycles carry a lot of freight especially in Asia. Trishaws in Bangladesh haul more tonnage than all motor vehicles combined.[12]

Bicycles carry cargo in Europe and North America, too. In the U.K., the Royal Mail now uses specially designed recumbent bicycles with trailers that can carry up to about 550 pounds (250 kilograms) of letters.[13] Bike messengers have become a mainstay in major western cities. Bicycle freight services operate in several cities, including Berkeley, California, where Pedal Express uses delivery bikes with waterproof cargo containers holding up to 220 pounds (100 kilograms): they deliver bakery items, documents, and other items often just as quickly as motorized vehicles can negotiate city streets. In Victoria, British Columbia, BikeCartAge offers similar services, advertising: "Is there anything we can't deliver by bicycle? Not much!"[14] The service has even helped people move. In Ames, Iowa, Bikes at Work picks up recyclables and delivers groceries, newspapers, travel tickets, and other items. In Santa Cruz, California, landscapers with Terra Nova Ecological Landscaping bike to jobs hauling special trailers carrying push mowers, brooms, rakes, and other gardening tools. Another area business, Santa Cruz Farms, uses bikes with heavy-duty trailers to cart organic produce to farmers' markets.

Corner groceries in Montreal deliver by bike, even through that city's snowy winters. At times, notes one report, because "bikes can sneak by traffic snarls and snow banks, they can be more reliable than cars in bad weather." Some New York City pizzerias use bikes to make deliveries more quickly and effectively than by car. Toronto customers get meals on wheels delivered by bike. Specialty products peddlers like ice cream and popcorn vendors, window washers, and florists use bike deliveries. One enterprising Canadian promotes safe sex in Toronto by selling condoms from a three-wheeled "Condom Cart;" using a bike gives him a competitive advantage, writes the Community Bicycle Network, because "bikes are a good way to go where the action is."[15] And should the condoms fail, ABC Diaper Service of Toronto provides a complete daily diaper delivery service by bicycle, offering diapers made with unbleached cotton and washing them with environmentally safe products.

Law enforcement: From a handful at the beginning of the 1990s, the number of police bike patrols has mushroomed. By 1999, over 2,000 North American police departments used bicycle patrol units as a low-cost, pollution-free, community-friendly, and effective means of making streets safer. The U.S. Secret Service even patrols the White House grounds with bicycles. Cities that have started bike patrols have found them to be good public relations tools — they are popular with and respected by citizens. The bike patrol in Vancouver, B.C., grew from employing eight officers in 1990 to 65 by 1996, largely due to this popularity.[16]

"Riding a bike allows a police officer to become part of the street environment rather than watching as a spectator, as do officers enclosed in patrol cars," according to Sergeant Rob Rothwell, one of Vancouver's bike cops. "Bicycles are able to go a lot of places cars can't," adds Robin Miller, who once managed the Baltimore-based International Police Mountain Bike Association. Another Vancouver bike cop once cycled through a hotel lobby chasing a thief. Increased stealth and maneuverability give bicycles a policing advantage over cars in many settings. Seattle,

Washington, expanded its bike patrol after it found that using bikes helped to increase arrest rates.[17] Bike patrols can save money, too. A bike, accessories, and clothing for one officer might run around $1,200, compared to the $28,000 cost of a squad car.

Taxi service: Cycle rickshaws have long been a passenger transport mainstay in Asia but, by the 1990s, increasing modernization was making them more scarce in places. In North America and Europe, though, pedicab services have multiplied. One great service can be found in Ghent (Belgium), where CITYgogo uses yellow taxi quadricycles to transport tourists and shoppers around town. They also provide a goods pick-up and delivery service for shoppers, who can take a pedicab to stores, buy items, and then not have to carry them as they continue shopping. In North America, you can catch a pedicab in places like Santa Barbara, California; Green Bay, Wisconsin; New York City; Victoria, B.C.; and more. Main Street Pedicabs of Denver, Colorado, sells pedicabs, provides pedicab services in downtown Denver, and lists some additional pedicab services on its website.

Bikes for All Reasons

Just as there are many ways to use bikes, there are many different types of bikes and pedal vehicles designed for those different uses. Open Road's *Encycleopedia*, an annual compendium of innovative pedal vehicles, lists portable bicycles, folders, recumbents, cargo bikes, and family bikes as well as city bikes, racing bikes, accessories, and trailers. Youth workers at Eugene, Oregon's Center for Appropriate Transport build a range of human-powered vehicles designed by Jan VanderTuin, from folding bikes to cargo carriers. George Bliss of New York City has designed a variety of pedal vehicles including dumptrikes for recyclables and bikes with converted chaise longues as sidecars. Brian Campbell of California has built 14 house bikes, sturdy pedal vehicles with a camper-like insulated sleeper box in back; his largest model sleeps four.[18]

Folding bicycles are a good two-wheeled tool for folks who want to pedal to transit. Car-free firefighter Richard Hoye of Bethesda, Maryland, got a folding bike so he could get to fire stations in different neighborhoods without a car. "The folding bike allowed me to get to most any fire station," he says, by cycling two or three miles to a transit stop, taking a few seconds to fold the bike and get on a train or bus, then unfolding it at the other end of his transit ride to cycle the rest of the way. "It's catching on that bicycling and taking folding bikes on transit and getting out of the car is cool," he says. "This is not a sacrifice, this is an expression of a higher quality of life."

Large tricycles can work well for older riders and for families. David and Carolyn McHale of Bedfordshire (England) began using trikes for transport when their sons were toddlers. "A solo tricycle with two child seats between the rear wheels allowed one of us to transport both children," they write. "We were amazed to find that we could cover many miles quite comfortably with the boys in back." As their sons grew, the family graduated to tandem trikes. "The tandem tricycle is

Electric Bikes

"I'm the first kid on my block to have an electric bike," jokes 20-something Ryan McKenzie of Cleveland, Ohio. "You squeeze a little trigger on your handle bar and then, zip, away you go at 20 miles an hour. I've gone up to 15 or 20 miles on the thing. And it's a blast! It's fun! It's more fun than driving." Electric bikes can be especially helpful if, for instance, you want to ride a bike but don't feel young or athletic enough to pump around your hilly neighborhood. Several companies now sell electric bikes, including ZAP Motors in Sebastopol, California, which also sells small electric motors you can attach to a bike you already own: flip a switch and the motor kicks in, using friction to turn the rear wheel and to give your bike an assist.

Most electric bike batteries have a range of between ten and 20 miles (16 and 32 km) between recharges. But since you can still pedal the bike without the motor running, you won't get stuck if your battery runs low. The motor works mainly as backup, to help you through challenging places, to help pull trailers loaded with kids or groceries, or to take over if you get tired.

so unusual that cars give us a wide berth, and we've never had a safety problem," they note. The stability of the tricycle allows children to clamber on without help from an adult. "'Mum's Taxi Service' consists of a tandem tricycle with a trailer bike, so I can transport children and shopping at the same time," writes Carolyn McHale.[19]

Cargo bikes are used mainly by pedal-freight businesses in North America, but there are also cargo bikes designed for use by private individuals. Christiania bikes, most often seen in Denmark and Holland, are a good example. A product of the alternative Christiania community in Copenhagen, Christiania bikes are really trikes with one wheel in back behind the seat, and two wheels in front straddled by a cargo box. In Montana, Lightfoot Cycles builds utility trikes with cargo containers behind the rider. Trikes like these reportedly do well in snow and ice, and can be useful for older riders and others wanting more stability.

Trailer-mounted solar photovoltaic panels help power Debbie Hubsmith's solar electric bike. Designed by Jeff Rodgers of Off the Grid Systems.

The Human-Powered Vehicle Association (HPVA) supports innovation in pedal-powered vehicle development with technical reports and races that give HPV builders a proving ground. As of 1998, a Varna vehicle designed by Georgi Georgiev of British Columbia held the World Hour Record, after racer Sam

Debbie Hubsmith, an environmental educator in northern California, uses a solar photovoltaic panel and two batteries fitted to a bike trailer to power her electric bike. The trailer still has space enough to haul stuff which, for Debbie, has often been 50 pounds of educational materials she carts to classroom presentations on sustainable transportation. The electric motor helps her get those heavy supplies up hills. The solar panel can fully recharge the batteries in a day and, says Debbie, "even when I'm inside a classroom, there's enough ambient light to get a charge. And the kids love it! They are fascinated by how the solar panels work and they appreciate that it's an environmentally clean form of transportation." Along the same lines, at least one company has begun selling electric bike solar charging stations, bike lockers with built-in photovoltaic panels that allow electric bikes to be securely parked and recharged by the sun simultaneously.

Whittington propelled it over 79 kilometers (about 50 miles) in one hour. Vehicles like these can reach 70 to 80 miles per hour in sprints. Georgiev also builds HPVs that are "pedaled" by hand for paraplegic athletes and riders; other manufacturers build hand-pedaled vehicles for disabled riders, too. Though there aren't human-powered vehicle shops in every town yet, the vehicles do exist, and people who use them often find they open new horizons. Open Road's *Encycleopedia* and the Internet are good starting points when looking for a specialized pedal vehicle.

Make Bicycling a Breeze

Modern methods of city-building and development patterns that cater to cars can make life harder for cyclists. On the other hand, by now many communities even in car-dependent countries at least give lip service to better bicycling. In the U.S., every state has a Bicycle and Pedestrian Coordinator, and funding for bicycle projects increased through the 1990s. In New York State, for example, this resulted in over 1,000 new miles of on-road bicycle routes as well as hundreds of miles of new rail trails.[20]

But don't wait for new bike facilities. There's plenty you can do on your own to make bicycling a breeze. If you're not a regular cyclist, dust off your old bike, or rent one, and take some

"We have given the startup push to be car-free, and all I can say is: it was worth it! I wish that more people could experience what we have from riding our bicycles."

PAUL BUTTEMER, BRITISH COLUMBIA, CAR-LITE

test rides. Decide how far you can realistically and comfortably travel on a bike. Then get out a map of your community and draw a circle around your home with a radius of whatever distance you've chosen. Which places you visit — school, work, shops, friends, library, etc. — are inside the circle? List these, then any time

Bicycles for Learning and Social Change

For years, Bikes Not Bombs has collected old bikes and shipped them as economic aid to Central America and the Caribbean, packaged with bike mechanics training for the recipients; in 1995, they joined with other organizations to use bikes for social change in the U.S. as well. Youth Cycle and Recycle in Philadelphia, Free Ride Zone in Seattle, the Bicycle Action Project in Indianapolis, and others offer Earn-a-Bike programs where at-risk youth are awarded a bike for successful completion of bike mechanics courses that also teach work habits and communication skills. Eugene, Oregon's Center for Appropriate Transport (CAT) offers teens bike mechanics labs, bike rack design, construction, sales experience, and an apprenticeship program in which they learn to build a range of human-powered vehicles.

These organizations are all part of a growing Youth Bicycle Education Network (YBEN) that uses bicycles as the centerpiece for achieving broader social goals. The bicycle, says CAT founder Jan VanderTuin, is a "common sense, outrageously simple approach" and "an elegant solution" not only for transportation but also for community-building and education.[21] YBEN programs give youth important job skills as they produce earth-friendly, beneficial products.

As of 1999, close to 50 community bike programs across North America belonged to YBEN. Some programs operate as storefronts, selling bikes built or recycled in student workshops.

you want to go to one of these places, don't think car, think bike. If your circle includes destinations within three miles of your home, like the post office, library, and your favorite bakery, equip your bike to carry postal parcels, books, and baguettes. The first few times you cycle, expect to notice ways you may need to adjust your bike or riding methods. Let the experience tell you what you need to do to make it easier. Do you need a more comfortable seat, or a different route? Make those changes; don't let initial drawbacks keep you from continuing to bike. Get a bit of basic information about bike facilities in your area.

- Is there a bike map for your area, and how can you get one? Is there a charge? Will they mail it and save you a trip? Ask first at the local parks and recreation and/or public works departments.
- Do local trains or buses take bikes on board? Call the local transit authority.
- Where are the local bike repair shops? Some enlightened places show these on bike maps; otherwise check the Yellow Pages.

If you're pulling a bicycle out of storage, it's worthwhile to get a bike shop to tune it up for you before you do a lot of riding. Outfit your bike with a good lock, tire pump, tool kit, tire patch kit, headlights, tail lights, and water bottle cage. Keep a stash of stuff you regularly carry with you on your bike, like water bottle, food, sunblock, sunglasses, rain jacket or poncho, in one place by the door, ready to go with minimum effort. Carry valuables in a pack or pouch that can easily be removed from the bike when you lock and leave it. Comfortable clothes are important, too. You don't need spandex to bike; just wear clothes in which you can move easily and that won't catch in the chain or spokes.

Others are offered through public schools. Recycle-A-Bike in New York City, for example, established a bike mechanics and environmental education program at intermediate schools and has produced a manual to help others start youth bicycle education ventures.

As they increase participants' skills, bike education programs increase self-esteem and help prevent involvement in crime. And they get more bicycles to places where they're needed, like developing countries and low-income neighborhoods. Some of these programs also supply the wheels for community free-bikes programs. Sean Godfrey, a graduate of the St. Louis BicycleWORKS Earn-A-Bike program, says the experience gave him a sense of direction and a way, through cycling, to connect with the larger community. It also helped him win a scholarship at Northland College in Ashland, Wisconsin, where he helps manage the Sunshine Community Bike Project which has provided free yellow bikes for Northland students and Ashland community members to ride between campus and town. BicycleWORKS, says Sean, "helped me to think more of other people first, to always keep in mind the less fortunate." He adds, "In a world in which many kids are made to feel unimportant ... this program offers a sense of accomplishment and gives many a higher self-esteem."[22]

To deal with weather, one method is the Buttemer family's approach. Paul, Amalia, and their four children keep their one car licensed only six months of each year during the rainy winters in Comox, British Columbia. Over summer, the family goes car-free. "The most vocal proponents of cycling in our family are the two oldest children!" writes Paul. "They really blast us when we get lazy and use the car." It's also possible to cycle year-round in all kinds of weather. Books, papers, and wallets can be the biggest casualties from riding in rain; I carry a few extra plastic bags in which to wrap those things if I'm traveling in wet weather. To keep yourself warm and dry, you can outfit yourself for rain or snow the same way you might for any outdoor sport. Jim Gregory and Joan Stein, who ride year-round in sun, rain, and snow, have found that slip-on rubber boots over sneakers work best to keep their feet dry, and they use neoprene gloves for their hands. In winter, they use studded tires on their bikes. They've made their own using car studs or sheet-metal screws, and a good thick tire liner to keep the studs or screws from puncturing their tubes. "With these studded tires, we get better traction on ice than if we're walking," says Joan. You can also purchase snow tires manufactured for bikes.

There are risks to cycling, as there are to any form of transport, but less than 1,000 people die in bike accidents each year in the U.S., 40 to 50 times less than the number who die each year in cars. Fewer than two percent of traffic fatalities involve cyclists.[23] Collisions with cars are the biggest cause of cyclist deaths, causing a little over 90 percent of bike fatalities. On the other hand, "operator error" (riding at night without lights, for instance, or riding against the traffic flow instead of with it) contributes to an estimated 50 percent to 70 percent of all bicycle crashes.[24] This means there are several things you can do to increase your cycling safety.

Educate yourself. Get a good cycling book (*Effective Cycling* by John Forester, for instance, or *Urban Bikers' Tricks and Tips* by Dave Glowacz), read bicycling magazines, join a bicycling club, or take a course like Can-Bike in Canada or Effective Cycling in the U.S. Learn the laws of your area.

 Wear a helmet. Many of the nearly 1,000 U.S. bicyclists killed in crashes each year die of head injuries. A considerable share of these could be prevented by riders wearing bicycle helmets. Make sure the helmet fits properly: it should be snug and level on your head and shouldn't slide or shift.

 Use lights and reflectors. Car-bike collisions occur disproportionately at night. Whether you intend to ride at night or not (there's always the possibility you may need to), equip your bike with the best headlight you can afford and make sure it always works. Add a tail-light (the red ones that flash on and off work well) along with reflectors on your bike, and reflective clothing on yourself. Reflective clothing increases your visibility during the day, too.

 Ride with traffic, not against it. The safest way to bike, and the legal way, is to travel with the flow of traffic. Traveling against the flow confuses motorists and other cyclists, and can result in crashes.

Finally, remember this conclusion from a British Medical Association study: "The benefits in terms of life-years gained from the increased physical activity of bicycling far outweigh any possible negative effects in life-years lost from injuries or fatalities."[25] You can minimize your chances of being hurt, and maximize benefits to your health, by riding a bike and riding it safely.

Great Places to Bike

"In my opinion, there's a direct relationship between the quality of cycling and the quality of life," writes J.C. McCullah. "Some of our most livable cities — Seattle, Eugene, Madison, and Palo Alto — are also the best cycling cities. The bicycle can be an instrument of change."[26] In Davis, California, 25 percent of the population commute to work by bike. Ten percent of all trips, and 25 percent of trips during peak hours, are made by foot or bike in central Toronto. Residents of Groningen (Holland) make more than half their trips between home and work by bike. While only about three percent of North America's vehicular traffic is by bicycle, in Japan it's 27 percent.[27] What makes the difference in these places? A few features get mentioned repeatedly in descriptions of the best burgs for biking:[28]

> *"Now that I'm used to living without a car, I have an incredibly convenient life. I couldn't do it without a bike."*
>
> DAVE SNYDER, EXECUTIVE DIRECTOR, SAN FRANCISCO BICYCLE COALITION, CAR-FREE

 A good quantity of well-mapped, well-signed, interlinked, and safe bike routes, whether they be striped lanes, dedicated paths, or quiet roads.

🚲 Good bicycle parking with plenty of conveniently located bike racks, bike lockers, and attended bike lots for secure long-term parking.

🚲 A local bus and/or train system that allows bikes to board.

🚲 At least some streets where cars are restricted or slowed in favor of non-motorized travel.

🚲 Respect for cyclists in the form of citizen support, government backing of bike programs, or both.

🚲 Shops, homes, workplaces, and other destinations located in a compact area, without much sprawl.

Good weather may help, too, but bad weather doesn't necessarily stop a place from being good for cycling. In North America, the cities of Madison, Montreal, and Toronto have consistently high cycling levels despite snowy weather. Rain doesn't stop Seattle, Portland, or Vancouver, B.C., from being recognized for good biking. University towns often have good facilities for cyclists, as do places with active cycling advocacy groups, bicycle advisory committees, and/or paid bicycle coordinators. In North America, some of the best cities for biking are listed periodically by *Bicycling* magazine. Examples from recent lists include

🚲 *Chicago, Illinois,* which reportedly has more bike racks than any other U.S. city, and the very active Chicagoland Bicycle Federation which lobbies for better biking conditions and hosts workshops, a hot line, and library to help cyclists.

🚲 *Denver, Colorado,* whose trail system includes a "bicycle expressway," the 12-mile Cherry Creek Trail, with underpasses allowing 1,000 bike commuters a day to skim below city streets non-stop.

🚲 *Madison, Wisconsin,* where over 21 percent of the University of Wisconsin community commutes by bike, and ten percent of all trips are made by bike, even in winter.

🚲 *Palo Alto, California,* where the bikeway system includes lit bike paths, bicycle bridges, and a two-mile bicycle boulevard; city employees get seven cents a mile to ride bikes on business, and private workers get paid, too; Alza Corporation, for one, pays workers $1 each day they bike in.

🚲 *Portland, Oregon,* with a Yellow Bike free bikes program; "Bike Central" stations offering supervised parking, showers, and changing rooms for bike commuters; buses and trains that take bikes; some blue-paved bike lanes; and a 140-mile loop trail circling the city, connecting with over 30 parks.

🚲 *Toronto, Ontario,* where a dynamic community of cyclists, including the Song Cycles choir on bikes, creates a hub for innovative bike programs: bike racks or lockers at subway stations; a supervised indoor bike-parking lot, Pedal'N'Park; bike-friendly businesses; and lots of cycling events and conferences.[29]

Countries that are great places for bikes include Germany, where investment in bike facilities over the past several years has greatly increased bicycle use, and Japan, where bicycle use is ten times that in the U.S. and where there are bicycle parking towers in which bikes are parked by crane. Here are some other examples:

🚲 **Holland** has invested in an extensive system of cycleways and bike parking. In Dutch cities, cyclists have special bridges and underpasses, can ride against traffic on some one-way streets, get to leave intersections first after a red light, and get priority over cars in any traffic-calmed residential *woonerf*. There are bicycle facilities at transit stations throughout the country. In some Dutch towns, bicycles are used for more than half the trips people take.[30]

🚲 **Denmark** has cycle lanes alongside 75 percent of its major roads, and the Danish, like the Dutch, use bikes extensively.[31] Copenhagen has what may be the world's premier free-bikes program, and one of the city's most famous landmarks is a weather vane depicting a woman riding a bike. Denmark's Queen makes a point of cycling and, in a recent political race, a comedian who ran a mock campaign for a seat in the Danish Parliament promised cyclists, "If I win, the wind will always be at your back." He won the election.

🚲 **Cuba** turned to bicycling when the Soviet Union's collapse left it without a ready source of oil. In the subsequent three years, Cuban travel shifted from 15 percent by car and 85 percent by bus or foot, to five percent by car, 30 percent by bus, and 65 percent by bicycle. The number of bikes in Havana rose tenfold; oil consumption dropped by more than half. Many Havana streets have been closed to cars; some have been planted with trees and

---

Reaching a Critical Mass

"Bicycles become the dominant vehicle!" one headline declares. "Bicyclists own the road," trumpets another. These reports describe Critical Mass bike rides, monthly massings of enough bicyclists to fill the roads as they ride. The rides make two main statements: bicyclists deserve better treatment, and biking can be sheer, unadulterated fun.

In San Francisco, where Critical Mass started in September 1992, riders gather as if by magic every fourth Friday at 5:30 p.m. at Justin Herman Plaza despite the fact that no one organizes the ride. The crowd swells with cyclists until, with an organic surge of movement, everyone takes off and takes over downtown streets, weaving around each other in exhilarated camaraderie. "It's like this weird euphoria that is indescribable," says Chris Carlsson, one of the San Francisco Critical Mass originators. "It's like a rolling party."

Critical Mass aims to "end bicycle invisibility, reclaim public space, and put forth a vision that cities are pretty car-choked and need not be," comments Donald Francis, a Mass rider. During rides, bicycle invisibility ends at every intersection as stopped cars watch cyclists stream by. Drivers show mixed reactions: some smile and give a thumbs

converted to car-free parkways. Some informal counts have found Cuban bikes carrying more passengers per vehicle than the typical U.S. car.[32]

🚲 **China,** where decades ago the government chose bikes for transport because they moved more people more cheaply than anything else, still has over 300 million bicycles and is the world's largest bicycle manufacturer. Cities commonly have five- or six-lane bicycle avenues, guarded parking lots for bikes, and repair shops or sidewalk bike mechanics in most neighborhoods. In Tianjin, traffic monitors once counted over 50,000 bicycles passing through an intersection in one hour. As China's economy shifts and more Chinese get cars, it remains to be seen whether bikes will hold their own.

Advocating Better Bicycle Facilities

"Perhaps the greatest potential for change lies with the individual cyclist," writes Marcia Lowe. "Pressing employers and local authorities to provide cycling facilities — and simply using bicycles whenever possible — can have a great impact."[33] Advocate better bicycle facilities first by biking. Just seeing someone else on a bike can open people's eyes to cycling's possibilities and practicalities, especially if the bike is unique or shows the variety of things that can be done on two wheels. People frequently ask me about my bike trailer when I pedal it into town, and my spouse catches eyes with his recumbent bike. Seeing such things can open more minds to biking and ultimately help to get better consideration of bikes in political decisions. Let business, civic, and political leaders know that you cycle, and encourage bike-friendly planning and more support for bikes. Find out who makes decisions about building bicycle facilities in your community and contact them. Let the road commission or public works department know if you spot dangerous potholes along

up, others appear helplessly annoyed or angry at the extra wait. A few receive flyers which read:

> We're sorry! Gridlock is more and more common these days ... it'll probably go on getting worse, unless we do something ... We know you aren't responsible for the organization of our cities around motorized traffic, and if we have contributed to your delay, we're sorry! ... Critical Mass isn't blocking traffic — we ARE traffic. We're sorry you're not already out here on your bicycle riding with us! But we heartily invite you to join us next time. Remember, every day is a good bicycling day!

Critical Mass rides now take place regularly in cities worldwide. The character of rides varies by location; some try to be completely legal, but others do things like running red lights to keep the bicycling mass together. Some cyclists consider it controversial, but others point out it's helped improve cycling conditions in places. San Francisco's rides, for instance, have helped win better bicycling programs by showing city government that there is, in fact, a critical mass of bicyclists deserving better treatment.

roadsides or broken glass in bike lanes. Call the planning department, public works, or the bicycle advisor if you have an idea for improving cycling, like a good place for a bike path or a spot where better lane striping may be needed. Among the things you might ask for are:

- a good bicycle map, if your community doesn't already have one; the best maps show dedicated bicycle paths, bike lanes, and bike routes along with streets *not* recommended for biking, and include basic biking information like local bike laws, major bike parking locations, bike repair shop locations, and bike group/agency contact information;

- interconnections to link up any dead-ends in the system of bike routes and lanes;

- secure and weather-protected bike parking, such as racks under overhangs or bike lockers at transit stops or in parking garages. Let store owners know you come by bike and, if they have a good bike rack close to the door, thank them for it. If they don't, tell them how much a good bike rack would encourage you to keep coming back;

- sensors at traffic lights that will trip signals for cyclists, or even signals especially for cyclists, as are used in various places in Europe;

- bike lanes distinguished by red or blue pavement. This is a technique widely used in European countries like Denmark and Holland;

- showers at major transit stations, as are found in many airports and at workplaces;

- bike racks on buses, space for bikes on trains, and bike lockers at transit stations.

Many of the same advocacy ideas outlined in Chapter 11 on walking work for biking, too. And opportunities abound to get more involved in bicycle advocacy, especially through the many excellent local and regional bike advocacy groups that exist around North America and in other parts of the world. These groups — examples include the San Francisco Bicycle Coalition, Chicagoland Bicycle Federation, and Montreal's Le Monde à Bicyclette — have played pivotal roles in advancing bicycling in their communities. Getting involved in educational efforts helps advocate biking, too. You can organize a Bike to Work day or week; one nifty guide to doing this is the booklet "How to Organize a Bike Week Event" in the B.E.S.T. Advocacy Toolkit (see "Selected Resources"). Bike safety workshops can also help, since safety fears are one big barrier to biking. Work with local law enforcement, schools, or bike clubs, or get help from national organizations. In the U.S., the League of American Bicyclists (LAB) is the main national group serving cyclists with advocacy and education. Among its many programs and services, LAB can help you locate a local or regional advocacy group; it also sells a

> *"When I see an adult on a bicycle, I do not despair for the future of the human race."*
>
> H. G. WELLS

Bike Month Organizer Kit that lists key contacts and contains ideas for promoting Bike Month (every May in the U.S.). In Canada, most bicycling advocacy groups operate at a local or provincial level. Critical Mass rides constitute another form of advocacy (see sidebar). Along with these larger efforts, it's still important to do little things to help biking become an everyday occurrence, by helping to make your community more inviting for bicycling. And again, the best way to advocate better bike facilities is to use your bike. With more than a billion bikes in the world, chances are you already have a bike of your own: dust it off and start to use it! You *will* look sweet upon that seat.

SINGER

© Andy Singer

Let Someone Else Take You for a Ride: Transit and Other Forms of Shared Transportation

"Where the systems perform well, riding on public transportation can be a luxury. People lucky enough to leave their cars in the garage and avoid gruesome traffic tie-ups ... may very well be gaining something — such as time on a train to read the newspaper or take a nap."

STEVE NADIS AND JAMES MACKENZIE, *CAR TROUBLE*

JENISE DOTY AND HER CAR-FREE FAMILY OF FIVE took their longest vacation by train, a 7,000-mile trip from Minnesota to Guadalajara and back, and loved it. Daniel Egan's children delight in riding Toronto's streetcars and subway system. When David and Jane Henshaw of Somerset (England) used trains on their way to house- and pet-sitting jobs around the U.K., they would "sometimes unwind with a Guinness on the train home!" they write. "Try doing that on the motorway." Ryan McKenzie lives five minutes from a bus stop in Cleveland, where buses come so frequently he rarely checks schedules. His travel time, he writes, "is of much higher quality than when I used to drive ... you get so much more peace of mind when you can simply sit back and let someone else get you there. Now that's freedom to me!"[1]

All these people have experienced first-hand the many benefits that shared transportation has over the one-person, one-vehicle pattern that characterizes monogamy with the car. While transit is not as low-impact as walking or cycling, it offers a range of options for traveling faster, farther, and at greater efficiencies than if driving a car alone. Buses, trains, car-sharing, carpools — whatever form it takes, shared transportation can give a big assist to car-free or car-lite living, in ways that are often cheap, convenient, safe, and even fun.

The Many Benefits of Shared Transportation

Worldwide, transit plays a huge role in moving the human race. Despite automotive inroads, it's still true that fewer than ten percent of the planet's people own cars. That makes buses and trains transport mainstays for most of the globe. In India, bus trips account for about 40 percent of urban journeys. In Moscow, over 85 percent of motorized trips are on transit. Even in car-dependent countries like the U.S., millions of people ride transit. About 35 million U.S. citizens use transit on a regular basis, including ten million who use it every work day. In transit-rich cities like New York and Chicago, transit carries up to 70 to 90 percent of travelers into and out of central business districts.[2] All this travel has a range of advantages over using cars.

🚐 *Transit cuts congestion, pollution, and energy use.* During World War II, when saving energy meant survival, governments encouraged use of transit and carpools as a way to conserve. "Fill those empty seats!" exhorted Uncle Sam posters. "Car sharing is a 'MUST'!" Transit's energy-saving potential is indeed high. In general, transit uses fewer British thermal units (BTUs, a measure of energy) per passenger mile than do cars and light trucks. While a single-occupant car uses over 5,000 BTUs per passenger-mile, a train car carrying 19 people uses about 2,300 and a bus carrying the same number only about 1,000. Transit can also cut emissions. Going by bus instead of by car cuts nitrogen oxide pollution by 25 percent, carbon monoxide by 80 percent, and hydrocarbons by 90 percent per passenger mile. Taking rail cuts nitrogen oxide by 77 percent and carbon monoxide and hydrocarbons by more than 99 percent. While some transit may be more polluting — diesel buses, for example, emit high levels of particulate matter — growing numbers of cleaner transit vehicles are far better. Buses powered by compressed natural gas (CNG), for instance, produce almost no particulate pollution. And putting more trains and buses in congested urban corridors cuts traffic and increases travel speeds for both transit riders and motorists. One full 40-foot bus will take 58 cars off the road; a six-car rail train can take 900 cars off the road, which would otherwise clog 68 city blocks at 15 m.p.h. As a slogan for British Columbia's transit agency says, "Relieve Clogged Arteries, Go Transit."[3]

🚐 *Transit saves land.* Unlike freeways, which disperse development as sprawl, transit — especially rail — encourages compact development. This also saves money and energy and cuts pollution, since less sprawl requires less infrastructure. Where cities introduce rail, "an immediate process of urban consolidation begins," write Australian transport experts Peter Newman and Jeff Kenworthy.[4] After Vancouver's Skytrain was built, for instance, new development began to cluster around several stations. At New Westminster, about 14 miles (22 kilometers) from downtown Vancouver, new housing and commercial space joined an older town center and rebuilt public market to revitalize the station area. Development also clustered around the Metrotown station, which has a center with hotel, theaters, apartments, and shops linked to the station with a raised pedestrian concourse.

> *"The bottom line is this: investment in public transportation makes dollars, and it makes sense. The benefits to motorists, to businesses, to transit riders, and to ... society as a whole far outweigh the costs."*
>
> CAMPAIGN FOR EFFICIENT PASSENGER TRANSPORTATION

🚐 *Transit helps jobs and the economy.* One study estimates a $3 to $3.50 increase in business revenues for every dollar invested in transit. A study by Bates College economist David Aschauer showed that transit investments improve productivity possibly twice as much as road building. Aschauer's conclusion: "Public transportation spending carries more potential to stimulate long-run economic growth than does highway spending." Labor-intensive transit creates local jobs, and more of them. Spending a billion dollars on transit creates 7,000 more jobs than spending a billion on roads. And by providing low-cost access to jobs, transit has been an important part of helping people transition from welfare to work. For instance, the suburban communities of Deerfield and Northbrook, Illinois, have used transit vans that shuttle between a commuter rail station and local businesses, transporting workers from Chicago's inner city who would otherwise have no access to suburban jobs.[5]

🚐 *Transit saves money.* Transit users spend from about $200 to $2,000 a year for travel, much less than the usual cost of a car.[6] It's possible to compare fuel costs to transit fares and not see much difference, but that ignores the fixed costs of driving. With fixed costs included, transit often comes out cheaper, and can even cost less than out-of-pocket driving expenses alone. The 120-mile round trip I used to take from Santa Rosa to San Francisco cost $8.80 on the bus; driving cost about $5 for gas, $2 for the bridge toll, and anywhere from $2 to $16 for parking. That's a minimum of $9 out-of-pocket, likely more. Depreciation and other ownership expenses would raise the car trip's cost to at least $21; that $8.80 bus fare looks better all the time. Trains, too, can save money. Especially on shorter trips, Amtrak fares are often comparable to out-of-pocket driving costs and cheaper than flying (see sidebar).

🚐 *Transit saves time, hassle — and lives.* Leaving the driving to someone else might mean a longer trip overall, but you can spend the time doing something else: reading, writing a letter, catching up on work, having quality time with your kids. Sometimes, too, transit can be faster than driving by car. In 1993, Santa Barbara's Metropolitan Transit District established an express bus route between Isla Vista (near the University of California) and Santa Barbara City College. The bus trip takes 30 minutes, reportedly less than driving. As word got out, the number of people taking this bus increased by 255% in two years. Using transit also frees you from responsibility for a car at either end of your journey. This means no time wasted hunting for parking, no concerns about feeding meters or getting parking tickets. Using transit can also mean traveling in a less tense, more serene atmosphere. Especially on trains, you can get up and move around as much as you want, a feature especially appreciated by children. And according to the National Safety Council, transit is one of the safest ways to travel. Where the average death rate per 100 million passenger miles is about 0.95 for autos, it drops to 0.04 for trains and 0.01 for buses.[7]

🚌 *Transit restores community and equity.* Transit can help restore community by bringing people out of metal-box isolation and into more contact with one another. Transit gives a wider range of people safe, independent mobility, helping integrate young, old, poor, disabled, and other non-drivers more fully into community life. Without transit, such people fall through the cracks. Instead of fostering road rage, using transit encourages common courtesy. And because of the way transit influences land use, it can help communities be more cohesive by nature of their compactness. Shared transportation is also the most equitable way a society can provide mobility to people, regardless of income, age, and ability. This equity can be cost-effective in unexpected ways. When Orange County, California, looked at cutting transit vans for seniors, an analysis showed that without the vans, many elderly users might be forced into nursing homes at an annual public cost of $35,000 per person. The vans allowed many of these people to stay in their own homes.[8]

> *"By taking public transportation, I have a better sense of what other people's lives are like, and feel part of a bigger community."*
>
> SALLY FLOCKS, ATLANTA, GEORGIA, CAR-LITE

Leaving the Driving (or Car Ownership) to Someone Else

Lift aside the vague and bureaucratic word "transit" and you'll find myriad ways in which you can let someone else take you for a ride. The list below includes various shared transportation possibilities. Some are standard forms of transit. Others are variations on the car which, in some car-dependent locations, may be the best choices available. These generally leave the car ownership to someone else even if sometimes you have to do the driving. If you're among those who live close to a transit stop — even in the U.S., over half the population lives within two miles of one — using transit should be relatively easy and can be a major aid to car divorce. No matter where you live, it's likely that at least one or two of these options are available to you, and possibly more.

> *"'Our family used to see the country on the superhighways,' says one [Amtrak] tourist. "But they're not so super anymore, are they?"*
>
> STEPHEN GODDARD, *GETTING THERE*

Long-distance trains: "In my many travels I've been comfortable and I've been uncomfortable, and comfortable is better ... that's why I take the train," writes Jim Loomis, author of *All Aboard! The Complete North American Train Travel Guide*. "For long-distance travel, the train is the only civilized option left for us." Truly, there's nothing like treating yourself to a sleeping berth for a long train ride and kicking back to watch the miles, moonrises, and mountains glide by out your window. Positive media reviews and rising riderships point to a growing recognition of the pleasure of long-distance train travel. In the U.S., Amtrak carries over 20 million passengers a year and serves over 500 cities (some with bus connections); VIA Rail serves over 400 cities in Canada and the two systems interconnect in a few spots.[9] Intercity trains in Europe are extensive and widely used. In North America, you're more likely to find good intercity train connections in populated areas like the northeast corridor of the U.S., the Great Lakes area of Canada, and along the west coast.

High-speed rail: Used for years already on intercity routes in Europe and Japan, high-speed trains typically travel at speeds from 125 to 185 m.p.h. (200 to 300 km/h). Trains like the Swedish X2000 "tilt train," which tilts into turns for smooth, high-speed cornering, have persuaded airline passengers to switch to rail; half the passengers on the Stockholm to Goteburg X2000 high-speed "tilt train" route used

---

Faster Than Flying: Short-Hop Trains

If we own cars, we often don't think of taking a bus or train, and it doesn't occur to us that the bus or train might be cheaper or sometimes even faster. In August of 1997, the *Wall Street Journal* ran a story called "Even When It's Quicker to Travel by Train, Many Fly," pointing out a similar selective perception pattern with trains and planes. Many people fly from "force of habit," the story said, while others seem unaware that train services exist. Examining a handful of "short hops" (pairs of major cities less than 200 miles apart), reporter Susan Carey found train fares much cheaper than flying — in one case as low as only a tenth of the plane fare — and train travel times to be comparable to flying times, if not less when check-in and driving times to airports were considered.

The Chicago-Milwaukee run is a prime example. It takes only an hour and a half to travel between these cities by train, and an hour longer to fly — even though the flight itself takes only 18 minutes. "By the time a Chicagoan starting out downtown actually steps onto the plane at that city's O'Hare Airport," wrote Carey, "the Amtrak train he could have caught a couple of blocks from his office is pulling into downtown Milwaukee."[10] Carey focused on comparing trains to planes, but the comparison can be extended to cars as well. The chart below adds distances, car travel times, and costs to Carey's data for three short hops.[11] The train is the cheapest option for all these trips, and the fastest for two of them.

	Distance	Train	Car	Plane
San Diego-LA	124 miles	2:30 hours $13	2:24 $25-62	2:30 $110-204
Chicago-Milwaukee	90 miles	1:30 hours $19	1:50 $18-45	2:30 $68-372
New York-Albany	156 miles	2:30 hours $32.50	3:12 $32-78	3:30 $88-428

to fly.[12] In North America, Amtrak's high-speed Acela trains were scheduled to start regular service in the Northeast corridor in 2000, traveling at speeds of up to 150 m.p.h.

Local and regional rail: Taking Portland's MAX light rail to work is "a lot less wear and tear" and "actually gives me more productive time" than driving, says one attorney who's a regular rider. That's a frequent theme from commuters and others who use any of a range of local and regional rail transit systems. These include underground trains like the New York subway and the Paris Metro; light rail systems like MAX or the MetroLink in St. Louis, Missouri; electric heavy rail like the BART system in the San Francisco Bay Area; as well as cable cars, people movers, and other transit on tracks. A good local or regional rail transit system often plays a key role in turning an urban area into a world-class city.

Intercity buses: "I can't think of any time that's more wasted than driving between cities," says Ryan McKenzie. "If I can hop on a Greyhound and sleep, meet somebody I never would have met, just stare out the window, read, relax, I'd much rather do that and I don't have to worry about the car breaking down or getting into an accident or getting sore from having to sit in one position." Intercity buses provide important services between cities, especially where trains no longer run. Long-distance buses are a mainstay throughout the developing world, and many European countries have intercity buses whose schedules coordinate tightly with trains.

Local buses: "For seeing neighborhoods, there's nothing like the bus," says Nancy DenDooven, who's written a book about touring Portland, Oregon's neighborhoods via the local bus system. Various kinds of buses make up most of the local transit systems available around the world. In some Ontario communities, local transit systems, school buses, and other transport services have teamed up to provide better mobility for both students and the community at large. One community made use of a schoolbus return run to give seniors and grandchildren rides to a nursing home for visits. Another used school buses to expand evening and weekend transit routes. In yet

> *"I ride the bus in Los Angeles ... this confession, I've found, can stop conversations cold."*
>
> STEVE LOPEZ, *TIME* MAGAZINE, 31 AUGUST 1998

another, a transit system and school district shared buses between commute runs during morning and evening rush hours, and between school runs at other times. Many buses now carry bikes as well (more about this in Chapter 17).

Jitneys, shuttles, and demand response services: Shuttles are increasingly used as inexpensive, flexible ways to expand transit's range in suburbs. In Portland, MAX light rail uses taxi shuttles which meet trains at stations and take passengers to their final destinations. Free and low-fare jitneys (cars or vans that operate as demand warrants on mostly fixed routes without fixed schedules or stops) can be an inexpensive way to fill transportation gaps, too. Examples include the kind of jitney service offered by the Alliance for Downtown New York between downtown Manhattan and the Hoboken and Staten Island ferries. Demand response services, also called paratransit, often serve the elderly or disabled. Often using small or medium-sized vans, they provide door-to-door service in response to a phone call. Increasingly, services like this use computers and "smart" systems to track riders and routes, increasing efficiency. One demand response service, Taxibus in Rimouski, Quebec, uses taxicabs to serve scheduled stops; passengers reserve rides at least an hour ahead (without reservations, schedules are canceled) and pay a low, set fee for the economical service.[13]

Ferries: David Levy used to drive to work across a congested bridge in Norfolk, Virginia; when he started bicycling and using a ferry to cross the river, he cut his commute time in half and saved himself plenty of frustration. "The whole commute was less than 15 minutes," he says. "I arrived at the office in a good mood — which I never had before — and felt fresh when I got home." In places like San Francisco, Boston, New York, Seattle, Toronto, Vancouver, and Hong Kong, ferries carry thousands of commuters. When the 1989 Loma Prieta earthquake collapsed a section of the San Francisco-Oakland Bay Bridge, ferries picked up the slack, even returning to service on some routes that had been abandoned decades earlier.

"The Reg"

When Debbie Hubsmith started catching the morning bus out of semi-rural San Geronimo Valley in northern California, she noticed the same cars would pass her every day as she waited at the stop. That gave her an idea: why not start a rideshare program? She liked riding the bus, but there was only one a day at 7 a.m. — clearly, the area needed more options.

Debbie and other area citizens started GO GERONIMO, which in turn started The Ride Registry. Nicknamed "The Reg" (its companion is "The Skedge," a more conventional rideshare program using a bulletin board and web-posted computer files to match riders), it's a registry for safe drivers and safe riders. Local folks sign up and go through a background check with the Marin County Sheriff to make sure they don't have criminal records or bad driving histories. If they pass, they're issued a laminated photo-ID card that identifies them as part of the program.

After that, no scheduling is necessary. "Reg" members in need of a ride simply stand at the side of the road and hold up their laminated card. This identifies them to driving members of the program as someone who wants a ride, and as someone who's safe to pick up. In turn, drivers show their cards to potential riders to identify themselves as a safe lift. Drivers generally take riders at least as far as a better-served bus stop or regional bus terminal with access to a wide array of buses throughout the day.

As of summer 1999, "The Reg" had about 400 members. People enjoy using it, and not just for transportation. "One of the things we hadn't thought about was how much fun it is to connect with people you've never met before in your town," says Hubsmith. "So there's a social component, too."

Carpools and ride sharing: Carpooling can be as simple as making the sharing of rides a common courtesy and a habit, or it can be systematically arranged by computer. In Quebec and Ontario, Montreal-based Allo Stop connects drivers and passengers heading out of town; the company registers members, arranges driver-passenger meeting places, determines per-trip fees and, for safety, makes sure at least two passengers ride with any given driver.[14] In Marin County, California, GO GERONIMO's Ride Registry offers large, laminated ID cards to foster safe ridesharing without the need for scheduling (see sidebar). And commuter services in many metropolitan areas offer computerized ridesharing match lists that can help people find or form carpools. Carpools can use the same car and driver for every trip, with riders paying the driver a share of costs, or carpool members can take turns providing the car and driving. Ride boards are a great example of a simple, low-cost ridesharing service that's easy for any community: divide a centrally-located bulletin board into two sections for rides offered and rides wanted, subdivide each of those into sections for one-time rides and ongoing rides, then leave cards, pencils, and tacks out; people post ride and contact information, and match up. Businesses have encouraged carpools with techniques like preferential parking, either saving the best spots for carpoolers, or charging parking fees to those who don't carpool, or both. When a company in Woodland Hills, California, started charging non-carpoolers $30 a month for parking, the employees formed about 200 carpools virtually overnight.[15]

Holding up a photo ID laminate gets rides for members of "The Reg" in San Geronimo Valley, California.

Peter Oppenheimer.

Vanpools: The 3M Company started the first corporate-sponsored vanpool program in the U.S. in the early 1970s. "We started a vanpool with 12 passengers and we've had a full van ever since," said one vanpool driver at a 3M subsidiary. "The van saves people a lot of hassle." It saves money, too. "Most vanpoolers pay a fraction of what it would cost to drive their own vehicles," says Laurel Severson of 3M's Commute-A-Van program. 3M purchases and maintains the vans and gives vanpools preferential parking. Employees serve as vanpool drivers and coordinators, and riders pay a fee as a payroll deduction. The company benefits from reduced demand for parking and more efficient land use at its facilities. The program had about 100 seven- and twelve-passenger vans as of 1999 and it pays for itself. Similarly, about 60 of 850 employees at Stamford, Connecticut-based Clairol pay just $28 a month to commute to work in four vans supplied by the company. Some rental car companies have subsidiaries that help businesses and individuals organize vanpools: Enterprise Vanpool, for instance, and VPSI Inc. of Budget Rent-A-Car. Individuals can set up their own vanpools by having a designated driver lease a van and then charging passengers a low monthly fee.[16]

Station cars: Parked at transit stations and used by transit passengers to get from the station to home and back, or to work and back, station cars are being tested as a way to help extend the reach of transit. As of early 1998, about 100 U.S. commuters were using station cars in test programs around the country, and such trial programs continue.[17] In some station car trials, electric cars have been used, in others natural gas or gasoline cars; and most often, the cars get used by multiple drivers on any given day. In different trials, different systems have been tested, but generally transit riders who want to use a station car do so by either reserving it or checking it out of a parking area with a smart card, then driving it to their next destination. Once they return it to a station (either the original pick-up site or another participating site), it's available for the next user. Station cars are helpful in situations like reverse commutes, for instance, where people can take transit to suburbs but their actual job sites may be a long way from the closest transit station. The BART system in northern California has used electric station cars with a range of up to 70 miles and a top speed of 65 m.p.h.; they get their users to the station in the morning, get plugged in to recharge at special parking spaces, then get their users home again at night, where they can again be plugged in for a recharge.

Car-sharing: "Car-sharing perfectly meets our needs for an alternative to a second car," says Loree Devery of Portland, Oregon. "It's so much more expensive to own and maintain a second car when we only really need it once or twice a month." With car-sharing, you get cleanly out from under the burden of owning a car. Car-sharing participants belonging to a co-op, association, or service that owns a number of cars, sign up to use a car when they need one. Car-sharing can also be done on a small-scale neighborhood basis, as encouraged in the book *The Car Club Kit*. See the related sidebars and "Selected Resources" for more information on car-sharing; it has the potential to be a doorway out of excessive car ownership in auto-addicted areas.

Car rentals: "We rent cars when we need them," writes car-free Ellen Jones of Chevy Chase, D.C. "The joy of not owning a car is that we can rent exactly the type of vehicle we need when we need it: subcompact, full-size sedan, van, or the occasional convertible ... We keep a mental list of trips to do while we're renting a vehicle. For example, while our bicycle trailer can handle most loads to and from Strosneider's Hardware, the occasional broken storm window has to wait for repair until the next time we have a rental vehicle."[18] In places where car-sharing is not yet available, car-rentals can provide a safety valve for car-free living in a car-dependent world. Perhaps as the car-sharing idea spreads, more car rental agencies will offer rentals by the hour. If you decide to use rental cars in place of owning a car, ask for rentals by the hour and see what happens.

Car-Sharing Gains Ground

Car-sharing started in Europe and has grown there to include over 100,000 participants. Already popular in Switzerland, Germany, Austria, and Holland, European car-sharing programs continue to grow. And in North America, where some form of the service is now offered in most major Canadian cities and services are starting up or are being planned in several U.S. locations including Chicago, San Francisco, and Seattle, car-sharing is gaining ground and making many members very happy. "I really enjoy the convenience," said one member, who sold her car when she joined the Victoria Car Share Co-op in British Columbia. As of January 2000, 188 of the 514 members of Vancouver's Co-operative Auto Network (CAN) had gotten rid of their cars after joining the group and, said CAN founder Tracey Axxelson, "They're feeling liberated."

Car-sharing works in part because it charges members only when they drive and thus saves them money. A study by CarSharing Portland, the first U.S. car-sharing service, showed members saved an average $154 per month. Other studies show car-sharing decreases distances driven by as much as 50 to 70 percent, thus benefiting society by reducing congestion, pollution, and infrastructure costs. It's estimated that one car-sharing car can replace four owned cars, decreasing the need for parking lots. One Lufthansa Airlines car-share program for employees at two German airports reportedly saved the company over $20 million by displacing the need for additional parking structures.[19]

Once car-sharing programs get big enough, they can provide a variety of vehicles. In Portland's program, members have access both to passenger cars — including a new electric-gas hybrid — and pickup trucks. Berlin's Stattauto has some electric cars, recharged using solar panels.[20] Mobility CarSharing Switzerland, in partnership with other transport services, offers passes giving members discounts on transit, taxis, and long-term car rentals as well as share-vehicles ranging from convertibles to vans. Car-sharing members thus can access a wider range of mobility choices for far less money than if they owned cars.

Taxis: After I sold my car in the early 1990s, taxis became my travel means of last resort. I'd use one if I got into the central bus terminal late at night and didn't have my bike to get me the rest of the 17 miles home, or if I had more luggage than I wanted to carry under my own steam. I ended up using taxis once or twice a month, and they were expensive because my taxi trips were long ones, but I still saved hundreds of dollars since I wasn't paying car insurance, registration, etc. If you're a soccer parent, taxis can help you take a break from having to cart your child to and from activities. In some places, businesses with names like KidMobile, Kids Kab, and Kids Taxi have sprung up specifically for this purpose. For a few dollars a ride, the businesses provide safe rides for children, with extras like having the driver meet parents before the child uses the service. Older children might take regular taxis in a group, which may be cheaper than having several different parents go in several different sport utility vehicles to pick them up.

Car-Sharing in Ten (Mostly) Easy Steps

1. Decide if you're a good candidate for car-sharing. If you own a car that's not needed for a daily commute and that's driven less than 8,000 to 10,000 miles (12,000 to 16,000 km) yearly, you'd likely save money if you car-shared and sold that car.

2. Find a car-sharing program, or start one (see "Selected Resources" under "Shared Transportation" for more information).

3. Fill out an application. Some organizations charge a small application fee ($10 to $30). They check your credit and, for insurance purposes, your driving record before admitting you as a member.

4. Pay a one-time refundable deposit, usually $300 to $500. Get a key, smart card, membership card, and/or number that will give you access to program cars.

5. Call in advance to reserve a car for the time period you want, specifying pick-up and ending time (the earlier you call, the more likely you'll get the car you want).

6. Walk, bike, or take transit to the car you've reserved. Car-sharing programs leave cars parked at various fixed locations around town, often close to transit stops.

7. Use your key, card, or number to access either a lockbox holding the car key or the car itself. Drive away.

8. If you need a fuel refill while you've got the car, save the receipt; most programs cover fuel costs in time and distance fees and will reimburse you for filling up or will provide a fleet gas card.

9. Return the car to its parking space when you're done, but no later than the ending time of your reservation. Some programs track your time and mileage with onboard computers, while others ask you to fill out a receipt or call in when the car's returned.

10. Pay a monthly bill that includes an administrative fee (usually $10 to $20) plus time and distance fees for your actual car use, often at around $2/hour and $0.40/mile. No fuss, no muss: insurance, maintenance, etc. are covered by the car-sharing program.

Delivery services: Let someone else take your stuff for a ride — consider making purchases by phone and getting goods delivered. It makes more sense for a delivery van to drop things off while traveling a regular route than for you to make a special trip. This is an especially good option if the delivery vehicle uses alternative fuel; UPS, for example, has converted a number of its delivery vans to compressed natural gas in the U.S. and to propane in Canada. Federal Express, too, has a clean fuels program, operating vehicles in the Los Angeles area on a range of alternative fuels, including CNG and electricity.[21] Better yet, if you have access to a bicycle delivery service, hire them to take your stuff for a ride.

How and Where to Find Good Transit

If you live in Curitiba (Brazil), you have access to what may be one of the world's best bus systems. In Curitiba, though many residents can afford cars, they prefer the bus. Three quarters of Curitiban commuters take the bus — well over a million a day — even though Curitiba's rate of car ownership is the second highest in Brazil.

Innovative boarding tubes help make it quick and easy to use Curitiba's buses.

Due to its bus system, the city as a whole uses 25 percent less fuel than other Brazilian cities of comparable size, and ranks among the cleanest in air quality.

Curitiba's system works well in part because it's designed to function like a subway, but without the expensive underground infrastructure. Buses get prime road space, using exclusive lanes that cars can't enter. They zip between pick-up points organized more like subway stations than like traditional bus stops. Large tube-shaped boarding structures make trips faster since passengers pay at a turnstile to enter the tube, then are ready to board the bus quickly when it arrives. The system also integrates bicycle paths and pedestrian areas with bus routes. Bus ridership in Curitiba, at about 700 million trips per year in 1995, has been growing about ten percent a year. More than a quarter of these bus passengers are former car drivers. As authors of a *Scientific American* article about Curitiba point out, "Whereas intensive road-building programs elsewhere have led paradoxically to even more congestion, Curitiba's slighting of the needs of private motorized traffic has generated less use of cars and has reduced pollution." And like urban transit systems in most of Brazil's state capitals, the system in Curitiba is profitable. Curitiba has provided this system to its people for an initial cost of less than five percent what a subway might cost.[22]

Curitiba is a great example of what's possible in transit, but even if you don't live there, there are hundreds of places you can access good systems. Many European cities are known for good transit. While transit lags behind in North America, there are communities with decent systems, and a rail revival has increased the number of new rail transit systems in places like Los Angeles, Dallas,

> *"The bus added to my feeling of empowerment, as well as my 'no-car' savings. I remember sitting on a Plaza bench thinking, 'I could even take this bus to enroll in a summer course at Oxford!' — and so I did!"*
>
> THE LATE ESTELLE PAGE OF SONOMA, CALIFORNIA, WHEN SHE WAS CAR-FREE

St. Louis, and Salt Lake City. Transit is easier to find in cities with intermodal hubs, major stations that serve both long-distance and local transport. Washington, D.C.'s restored Union Station, for instance, full of shops and restaurants, is also an intermodal hub where you can catch Amtrak or the D.C. Metro. Restored Union Stations in Chicago, Philadelphia, Baltimore, and Worcester, Massachusetts, offer similar combinations of shops, eateries, Amtrak, and local transit. In Toronto, the Union Station downtown opens above ground to the heart of the city and below ground to Toronto's underground path system.

To function best, transit seems to need some sort of permanently embedded backbone, like a rail line or a guided busway, whose route can't be easily changed. Knowing that line will be there provides security and certainty to others wanting to invest in a neighborhood, and is better assurance for economic vitality. Regularly scheduled transit also works best in more compact communities with at least eight households per acre. Good transit:

- runs frequently, at least every ten minutes during high-use hours, and connects seamlessly with other scheduled services;
- is user-friendly, with good, easy-to-read signage, maps, and/or digital displays showing when the next train or bus will be arriving;
- has comfortable stops and stations providing safety and weather protection for passengers, and good access for the disabled;
- takes people where they want to go, at times when they want to be there.

Sometimes you have to search a bit to learn what transit services are available in an area, and allow enough time — at least a month — to learn by experience how they can work for you. Start by checking with the local government, transit agency, chamber of commerce, the Internet (websites are increasingly a prime source of transit information), or public library to find answers to these questions:

- What local transit operation(s) serve your area?
- Where is the closest local bus stop to your house? Find out not only the closest stop, but also route numbers for buses that stop there, and get schedules for those routes. Ask where you can get a route map for the whole system.
- Does the local bus connect to a longer-distance service like Greyhound, Amtrak, or VIA Rail?
- How might your kids take transit to and from school, if they're not using a school bus? Or to and from the public library or the soccer field? Give them the project of finding out.
- What routes might you take to reach places you regularly go: work, shopping, entertainment, etc.?
- Is your area served by a jitney or demand response service, and do you qualify to use it? Paratransit will come right to your door, but is often restricted to seniors and the disabled.

🚌 Does transit in your area offer incentive programs, such as discount ticket books for frequent riders?

🚌 What is the closest long-distance bus stop to your home, and does the bus go places you like to visit? Call Greyhound or check the yellow pages under bus transportation.

🚌 What's your closest long-distance train station? Check with Amtrak in the U.S. or VIA Rail in Canada.

Advocating Better Transit

In places where transit is poor or service cuts are threatened, asking for changes can make a big difference. In 1993, for instance, New York City's Straphangers Campaign stopped a fare increase and saved nearly $10 billion for subway and transit system repairs, in part by using "negative ribbon cuttings." Campaigners who organized these events tied black ribbons together, rather than cutting them, to symbolically close subway stations and show what might happen if fares were raised and funds

---

Transit Tips

"Using transit is easy, but it is different than driving," says the *California Transit Guide*.[23] If you've never used transit before, a few tips can help, since little things like reading bus schedules can be tricky for the uninitiated.

🚌 Sometimes schedules use funny symbols to indicate when a bus or train does not provide service, like on Sundays or holidays. Read timetables carefully to catch these exceptions.

🚌 Bus schedules don't always list every stop, but instead may list times for main stops, called time points. If you want to board between time points, be at the stop no later than the time listed for the previous time point.

🚌 Buses and trains may not stop automatically at minor stops. If you want to board from such a location, you may need to flag down the driver. Some rural or small town buses will let you flag down a bus between stops. Some may also swing a short way off regular routes to pick up and let people off. If you're unfamiliar with a service, ask about boarding and disembarking procedures.

🚌 To ease trips that involve more than one bus or train, write connection times down on a pocket-sized index card for quick reference. Take along a book, writing project, or handwork like knitting.

🚌 Allow a bit of extra time for reaching your destination. By far the majority of the buses and trains I've taken have been on time, but delays do happen.

🚌 Transit phone operators, drivers, and conductors can be a great help, so ask them questions. Drivers will often let you know when your stop is coming up, if you ask.

🚌 Live near a well-served stop or station. This can vastly expand the places you can reach by public transport.

slashed.[24] They garnered enough public support to get politicians' attention, and helped get results when the Straphangers Campaign asked for better treatment of transit and its users.

If you want to step into the role of a transit advocate, it helps to know what you've got. If you haven't used a system much, use it more and learn it. If the system is good, tell your friends and encourage more use of whatever system exists. Organize a social event that uses the bus or train, or go out to lunch somewhere near a stop or station and take a friend along. If it's a bad experience, tell your local politicians and work on them to change things. Using the system and knowing what it's like can also help you more easily see where it needs improving. Think, too, about how transit might be expanded in your area, especially by building on existing resources. Find out, for instance, where rail rights-of-way are and who if anyone is using them. In some communities, new rail transit systems have been built using old abandoned tracks, or by routing along former rail corridors. Learn about and draw on the experiences of other communities. National organizations and conferences like RailVolution, an annual gathering that highlights transit innovations, can help you link to and learn about these.

Find out the comment procedures for your local transit authority and use them. If you're a frequent transit user, your knowledge and opinions can help system administrators and decision-makers. Letting them know what you think also lets them know that the system really does have users, and that those users care about their decisions. Add your voice to any local transportation advocacy group that may exist in your area; check with the library to find one. Public works or transit departments should know about such groups, too; if there's a local group working actively on transit issues, the transit department should be hearing from them.

> "To walk or take transit is a public act which makes the street a safer component of community. To drive is a private act which turns the street into a utility."
>
> PETER CALTHORPE,
> THE NEXT AMERICAN METROPOLIS

Advocate better service not just for yourself but for the one-third of people who don't or can't drive. Chances are you'll be among those yourself at some point, whether you choose to be or not. Think broadly about what groups might want to advocate better transit. Senior citizens groups (Gray Panthers and others), disability rights activists, student groups, environmental groups, and transit workers' unions all have an interest in seeing better transit. Many chapters of the League of Women Voters also work actively on transportation issues. National groups can give you a link to transit issues in other communities and keep you informed about the bigger picture. In the U.S., for instance, the National Association of Railroad Passengers follows Congressional decisions about Amtrak and lobbies for service improvements, reporting to members in monthly newsletters.

One of the best proposals I've seen for advocating transit is the idea of requiring public officials (usually elected officials) to ride it at least once or twice a week. The rationale behind this parallels the common requirement that local officials live in the jurisdiction where they work, so they'll know the area and its facilities well enough to make good decisions about them. Suggest this in your own community. Also consider asking your local politicians and transit providers for some specific features that will improve transit service. Here are a few good things to ask for:

- Upgraded stops and shelters that provide weather protection and safe, comfortable seating.
- Low-floor buses — they're more comfortable and faster to board, and they can often accommodate wheelchairs and bikes more readily.
- Bike racks on buses, space in train and subway cars for bikes, and rules that allow bikes to be carried on to buses, subways, and trains.
- Computerized information systems to give passengers real-time information about bus and train schedules and delays.
- Dedicated bus lanes and priority signalization that will give transit preferential rights-of-way, improving performance and reducing operating costs.
- Good discounts on monthly and yearly transit passes, with special deals for commuters, students, and attendees at special events.
- More intermodal hubs for better links between buses, trains, ferries, and other travel modes; these can also be community centers, with services, businesses, bike rental and parking, daycare centers, etc.
- Smaller buses on low-density suburban routes.

Familiarize yourself with funding sources for transit and suggest a few to your local service provider if they're not getting good transit funding already. The Surface Transportation Policy Project can help U.S. advocates learn about current transit funding possibilities. And don't let highway boosters talk you out of transit funds. As various transportation experts point out, it is in motorists' self-interest to pay for transit, since it's a cost-efficient way of reducing gridlock. Remind local, state/provincial, and national governments of the importance of investing in transit and of the fact that investments in transit pay back. Finally, the most important way you can advocate transit is to use it yourself. More people riding transit can help encourage more transit — and that means more opportunity to let someone else take you for a ride.

CHAPTER 14

On the Rebound: Alternative Fuels

*"Don't fool yourself: There's no such thing as
an environmentally responsible car."*

JOEL MAKOWER, *THE GREEN COMMUTER*

YOU'VE PROBABLY SEEN IT HAPPEN: a person leaves one relationship, just to get into another — on the rebound. This new flame looks better at first, but later turns out to have the same old problems and maybe some fresh ones. It's not just with people that we dash into new entanglements without enough regard for possible problems. There's a rebound risk with cars, too, and that's getting noticed by a few folks who know about the car's future.

I got the feeling Amory Lovins had noticed this when I heard him speak at a 1996 transportation conference. Energy expert Lovins, cofounder of Rocky Mountain Institute, looks at the automotive future and sees Hypercars™, aerodynamic vehicles made of strong, light composites and powered by super-efficient, usually hybrid electric/internal-combustion engines. The synergy of these combined features can increase efficiency and reduce pollutants by an astounding factor of ten. But even as he promotes these cleaner cars, Lovins points out that they "can buy time, but can't solve the transportation problem." Their high efficiencies could induce more driving, making problems like sprawl and congestion worse, if they become too common before we make other transport reforms. It's both good news and bad news, Lovins told us in 1996, that vehicles like Hypercars™ "are happening more quickly than you think." He added: "We need to have clean cars but then not use them very much. Whether we're ready for this or not, it's coming right at us."

Rushing into the Next Love Affair

Since 1996, there has indeed been movement toward alternatively fueled vehicles. Signs of a shift away from internal combustion have mounted as automakers have made increasing investments in alternatives, especially hybrid cars and fuel cells. In 1998, GM chairman John F. Smith Jr. forecast a "slow phase-off" of internal combustion within 30 years and told the *Wall Street Journal:* "It is prudent for us to be working very hard on alternative technology."[1] Trend-setting California has seen electric and compressed natural gas (CNG) vehicles become more common, and has a growing number of electric, CNG, propane, methanol, and ethanol refueling stations. Utilities and delivery companies have increased their use of alternative fuels. The Sacramento Municipal Utility District (SMUD) not only uses electric cars in its fleet, it loans them to customers for trials and has installed electric vehicle recharging stations widely in California and other states. Southern

California Edison also has a large fleet of electric cars and trucks. The U.S. Postal Service now owns over 10,000 vehicles that run on either CNG or electricity. Several hundred New York taxis now use CNG, as do a growing number of taxis in Third World cities like Cairo. And these are just a few examples.

In the late 1990s, unveilings of new electric, hybrid, CNG, and fuel cell cars accelerated. Major auto companies made so many announcements of cleaner-fuel models and prototypes at the 1998 Detroit Auto Show that reporters wrote it up as a "green" event (carmakers were, however, still touting gas-guzzling SUVs as their biggest sellers). The 1999 show likewise featured several alternatively fueled models. Later that year, DaimlerChrysler unveiled a hydrogen-fuel-cell car in California, predicting it would go on sale by 2004, and other carmakers announced hybrids: Honda introduced its two-door, two-seat Insight, with ultra-low emissions, fuel efficiency of 70 m.p.g. (30 km/liter), and a late-1999 release date, and Toyota announced that its four-door, five-seat, 60 m.p.g. (26 km/liter) Prius, first released in Japan in 1997, would hit U.S. markets by mid-2000.

> *"Carmakers aren't eternally married to internal combustion ... the speed with which it's abandoned, given something better, may astound some observers."*
>
> JIM MOTAVALLI, *FORWARD DRIVE: THE RACE TO BUILD "CLEAN" CARS FOR THE FUTURE*

This rash of activity was in part fostered by government programs of the early 1990s, in part by intensified concerns about climate change after treaty negotiations in Kyoto at the end of 1997. In 1990, California's Air Resources Board passed a Zero Emission Vehicle (ZEV) mandate which initially required two percent of all vehicles sold by major automakers in California to be ZEVs (i.e., electric) starting in 1998. About the same time, the city of Los Angeles approved a ten-point initiative to promote electric car use. Although intense pressure from carmakers later delayed adoption of the statewide ZEV mandate until 2003, it made a big contribution to jump-starting alternative vehicle development. The Clinton-Gore administration announced a Partnership for a New Generation of Vehicles in 1993, a government-industry initiative with the goal of completing, by 2004, production prototypes for affordable, low-pollution cars getting up to 80 m.p.g. By 1998, the U.S. government owned over 34,000 alternatively fueled vehicles (AFVs), and by 1999 had committed to buying AFVs for at least 75 percent of new vehicle purchases. Other national and local governments, too, have programs fostering alternative fuels.[2]

Most major automakers now market AFVs, though some are sold or leased only in limited areas. Automakers in both North America and Europe have reported initially sluggish sales of electric cars in particular, but new developments in AFV technology have continued coming. Better battery packs have extended ranges of electric cars somewhat, and an increase in natural gas refueling stations have made CNG vehicles more practical. As sales of cleaner cars increase, it remains to be seen how many people will hear the caveats issued by Amory Lovins and others and realize that emissions are not the only issues troubling our love affair with the car. While alternative fuels may cut tailpipe emissions and increase energy efficiency, they don't reduce or eliminate:

- 🚗 pollution generated by car manufacture and disposal;

- 🚗 auto-induced sprawl or the need for land-consuming parking lots;

- 🚗 animal roadkills, or the decrease in biodiversity caused by habitat-fragmenting roads;

- 🚗 human death and injury from cars (as car critics point out, the first U.S. auto fatality involved an electric car);

- 🚗 congestion, since single-occupant electric or hydrogen vehicles will clog roads just as quickly and waste just as much time as gasoline vehicles;

- 🚗 lung-damaging particulate matter from road and tire dust;

- 🚗 the social costs incurred when a freeway cuts a community in half, or the resulting loss of community when towns are built more for cars than for people;

- 🚗 the second-class status of children, the elderly, and the disabled who cannot get around as well if mass transit remains impoverished as we subsidize private cars;

- 🚗 damage to health as cars encourage sedentary lifestyles;

- 🚗 road rage.

Widespread conversion to the next new fuel technology is not a panacea and does not eliminate the need for judiciousness with using cars. That said, there is a constructive role for alternative fuels in a healthy transportation system. To whatever extent we continue using motorized vehicles, we'd make a positive step in powering those vehicles as cleanly as possible. The biggest benefits for healthy transportation, however, still come from reducing trips, walking or biking, and taking transit whenever possible. In conjunction with such reductions, cleaner fuels can be useful for public transport, car-sharing, rental cars, taxis, and vehicles used by the disabled. It makes sense to use them in utility and delivery fleets, when jobs require travel beyond the cargo-bike range. And for the moment, for people living in extremely car-dependent areas, they can offer a better option than gasoline-powered internal combustion. In fact, with the alternatives now available, there are few good reasons to continue using gasoline-powered internal combustion vehicles for any purpose in the long run.

> *"Even if all existing cars were to become nonpolluting vehicles overnight, enormous problems would remain in terms of congestion and the dislocation of social and family life."*
>
> MARK DERR, *ATLANTIC MONTHLY*, JANUARY 1995

Looking for Ms. or Mr. Right-Fuel

Two main problems have catalyzed the search for alternatives to gasoline-powered internal combustion cars: 1) concerns about the long-term availability of non-renewable and politically costly petroleum-based fuels; and 2) concerns about air pollution and climate change resulting from using them. To cut our petroleum use, we've tried two approaches: using fuels that replace gasoline or diesel in internal combustion engines, and using systems of propulsion that replace internal combustion altogether. This section describes the former, the next section the latter.

Studies show that emissions from alternative fuels vary depending both on conditions of use and on production methods. Methanol produced from biomass, for example, has the potential to reduce greenhouse gas emissions if the biomass is produced without fossil-fuel-derived inputs. Methanol made from coal, however, emits 60 percent more greenhouse gases than gasoline when used in passenger cars and up to twice as much more when used in heavy-duty vehicles.[3] This variability makes it hard to say with certainty whether one fuel is cleaner than another. Despite such comparison difficulties, here's a quick run-down of the main fuels considered as potential improvements on gasoline and diesel in internal-combustion cars.

Ethanol/gasohol: Ethanol, or grain alcohol, comes from fermenting and distilling vegetable matter, usually corn, other grains, or high-sugar crops like beets. Ethanol runs a few million vehicles in Brazil, where it's been used on and off for a couple of decades. In North America, ethanol is most often blended with gasoline and sold as gasohol. These blends, usually five to ten percent ethanol, can be used in regular cars without major engine modifications. Gasohol has accounted for about five to eight percent of fuel sold in the United States since 1980. In both Brazil and the U.S., the ethanol fuel industry has been government-subsidized; ethanol production costs more than twice what it costs to make gasoline. The Brazilian program has gotten mixed reviews, in part because growing crops for large-scale ethanol fuel production has displaced both food crops and large areas of Amazonian rainforest. Ethanol's CO_2 emissions vary, and can sometimes be greater than gasoline's. Some research shows gasohol blends reduce carbon monoxide emissions, but increase smog-producing NO_x and VOCs. While ethanol produced from waste biomass might fill a fuel niche with relatively low impact, more widespread conversion of farmland to producing fuel for cars instead of food for people could be an issue if ethanol use increases.[4]

Methanol: Otherwise known as wood alcohol, methanol can be produced from a variety of carbon-based materials: wood, crop residues, and other biomass, as well as natural gas and coal. Most methanol used today is made from natural gas, because that's the cheapest source. As a fuel for internal combustion engines, it's been used most heavily in California, where the state government has a large fleet of methanol cars. Methanol can also be used as a hydrogen source for fuel cell cars. Technical difficulties and corrosiveness make use of pure methanol impractical, so it's usually mixed with gasoline in blends using up to 85 percent methanol. In balance, methanol vehicles produce about as much ozone and CO_2 as regular cars, and fewer toxins overall but more formaldehyde, a probable carcinogen. Methanol does emit fewer particulates and nitrogen oxides but, sometimes, more CO_2 when used in diesel trucks and buses.[5]

LPG (propane): Liquefied petroleum gas or LPG — otherwise known as propane — is the most widely used substitute for gasoline: about four million vehicles worldwide use it. A byproduct of oil and natural gas production, it is non-renewable but burns more cleanly than gasoline. It is also less toxic and poses no water or soil pollution danger since it becomes gaseous when leaked. Burning propane in an internal combustion engine creates less carbon monoxide than gasoline. NO_x emissions, though, are sometimes higher and CO_2 emissions are the same. Cost savings from propane's lower price and the carbon monoxide emissions reductions have made it an attractive option for some uses in the short term. Some UPS delivery vehicles in Canada use propane, as do many taxis in Winnipeg and Vancouver.[6]

Natural gas: For use as a motor fuel, natural gas can either be liquefied or compressed. While safety, technical, and cost problems of liquefied natural gas (LNG) have limited its use mainly to demonstration projects, use of compressed natural gas (CNG) is expanding quickly worldwide. As of 1999, the Natural Gas Vehicle Coalition counted over a million CNG vehicles in use globally, mostly in Europe and Latin America, where Argentina has an estimated 400,000 of them. CNG vehicles, especially buses, are used increasingly in western Europe, Russia, New Zealand, and North America. CNG stations are opening in New Delhi as part of a cleaner fuels program that is also expanding supplies of low-sulfur diesel and lead-free gasoline across India. Several automakers sell CNG vehicles, and the number of CNG fueling stations is increasing across North America. In the San Francisco Bay Area, the CarLink program has used CNG cars in a demonstration car-sharing station-car program. CNG is non-renewable, but current plentiful supplies, low cost, and the fact that it is cleaner than gasoline have encouraged its use; many see it as a transition fuel on the way to hydrogen. Natural gas emits much less carbon monoxide and particulate matter than gasoline, as well as fewer smog-producing VOCs. It decreases greenhouse gas emissions only modestly, though (up to about 20 percent), and cuts nitrogen oxides little if at all.[7]

Biodiesel: Pure biodiesel, non-toxic, biodegradable, and renewable, is made from vegetable and/or animal fats. Often, though, what's called "biodiesel" is really a biodiesel blend containing up to 90 percent petroleum-based diesel fuel. Biodiesel reduces emissions of particulates, carbon monoxide, and reactive hydrocarbons; pure biodiesel eliminates sulfur emissions. It's considered "CO_2 neutral" — i.e., the CO_2 it emits equals the CO_2 absorbed when the oilseed crops used for biodiesel production are grown. Like other biomass fuels, biodiesel is expensive to produce. Government investment has encouraged its use in Europe, and there are a few biodiesel demonstration projects in North America. When the Pan American Games came to Winnipeg in 1999, athletes staying near a training center in Fargo, North Dakota, traveled to events in buses fueled by B20, a blend containing twenty percent biodiesel. Using the fuel required no engine modifications, and the bus drivers noticed the improvement in tailpipe emissions and smell.[8] If you're as enterprising as Kaia and Josh Tickell, you can make your own biodiesel; the Tickells have done this and used it to drive their Veggie Van across North America several times (see sidebar).

The Vegetable Oil Van

"This van gets 1,300 miles per acre," reads the lettering on one van window. "Powered by vegetable oil," reads the other. The Veggie Van, which started as a college project by Kaia and Josh Tickell, runs on biodiesel made from used restaurant oil in the Tickell's own "Green Grease Machine." Its exhaust smells like french fries. Really.

Touring across the United States, the Veggie Van has covered 10,000 miles through 25 states and 20 major cities, towing the Green Grease Machine behind it. This machine makes biodiesel by first straining food matter out of used vegetable oil, then running the oil through a process called transesterification. It's simpler than it sounds: it can be done in a kitchen blender and serves to "crack" oil molecules into smaller units so they'll be easier to handle in modern diesel engines. The only byproduct of the process is glycerin, used to make soap and other products.

Biodiesel reduces emissions by up to 75 percent over petroleum-derived diesel fuel, and can be used either pure or as a blend with standard diesel. The Veggie Van, a Winnebago with a two-liter diesel engine getting 25 miles per gallon (about 11 km/liter), needed no alterations to run on pure biodiesel. "The only thing we changed was the fuel we poured into it," writes Josh Tickell. "But, oh, what a change! We marveled as the exhaust went from a cloud of black, smelly smoke to a clean, french fry-scented puff of air."

The three billion gallon supply of used vegetable oil generated each year in the U.S. could run a lot more Veggie Vans. The Tickells are hoping it will, and have written a book to help that happen: *From the Fryer to the Fuel Tank: The Complete Guide to Using Vegetable Oil as an Alternative Fuel.*

Internal Combustion's Competitors

Internal combustion's predicted demise may mean that, as auto technology shifts, any of the above fuels used to replace gasoline in today's engines could at best play a transitional role. The main questions may be how long this will take, and just how much air pollution, climate change, and finite petroleum supplies will continue giving us incentives to get rid of internal combustion. The descriptions below highlight internal combustion's main competitors as well as a couple of minor ones. Battery electrics and hybrids are already on the market; fuel cells are promised shortly. A couple of these — hybrids and compressed-air cars — do use internal combustion technology, but in such a modified form that they really have different sorts of engines.

Battery-powered electric vehicles: "Why Wait for Detroit?" trumpets the title of one book on electric cars. "Drive An Electric Car Today!" You can indeed drive an electric car today, and you could have driven an electric car on just about any day of the 20th century as well as during the last part of the 19th since some of the first cars built were electric. Even though major carmakers haven't always been interested, a core of enthusiasts has been making their own electric vehicles for some time, and the conveyances they've built cover a range of designs and uses. Today's battery electric cars have the same basic parts as did early electrics: an electric motor and a set of onboard storage batteries that run the motor usually for anywhere from 25 to 150 miles (40 to 240 km) before needing a recharge. Most electric cars also use regenerative braking, which helps recharge the batteries as the brakes are applied. Advantages of electric vehicles include that they have few moving parts and require little maintenance; that there are zero emissions from the tailpipe (there is no tailpipe); that they are quiet; and that their operating costs are lower, though their purchase price can be higher.[9] The biggest barriers to their widespread adoption are their limited range and long battery recharge times (generally four to eight hours). Electric vehicles vary in size from buses and vans down to neighborhood vehicles, street-legal versions of golf carts with seat-belts, windshields, and lights. These are lightweight, low-cost ($5,000 to $8,000), low-speed (25 m.p.h. or less), and short-range vehicles.

The environmental cleanliness of battery electric cars depends on how they're recharged. They can be cleaner if you do what author Noel Perrin did with his electric car, and build an array of solar photovoltaic panels to recharge it. At the other extreme, plugging in where coal is the main power source causes electric cars to generate more of some pollutants — sulfur oxides, particulates, and CO_2 — than gasoline vehicles. Even considering power plant emissions, electric cars reduce the worst tailpipe pollutants — carbon monoxide, volatile organic compounds, and nitrogen oxides — and cut oil consumption.[10] Some people call electric vehicles "nuclear cars" because of the risk that their use might increase electricity demand to the point where more nuclear power plants would be built. One study estimated that U.S. excess electrical capacity could recharge "several tens of millions" of electric cars during low peak hours overnight.[11] But another later study found that widespread conversion to electric cars might, in fact, require upgrading the power grid; the study found that conversion of just ten percent of Florida's cars to electric vehicles would require utility systems to add thousands of transformers to prevent power supply disruptions.[12]

Fuel-cell vehicles: Several pundits predict that fuel cells will replace internal combustion, and some say as many as half the cars out there could be fuel-cell driven by as early as 2020. It may start happening soon: at least six carmakers say they'll have fuel-cell cars on the road by 2003 to 2005, with plans to expand their production and marketing into the 21st century. Even before then, between 2000 and 2003, the California Fuel Cell Partnership, involving fuel cell maker Ballard Power Systems, the State of California, two carmakers, and three oil companies, will put 50 fuel-cell-powered passenger vehicles on California roads, including 20 buses. A handful of fuel-cell buses are already in operation. Fuel cells used for transportation are basically stacks of membranes that serve as templates for a chemical reaction that combines hydrogen and oxygen to produce electricity as fuel is fed to the cells; the process also generates water vapor and heat. The first fuel-cell vehicle was a 1959 tractor, and NASA has used fuel cells extensively in spacecraft. Research has reduced the size and weight of fuel cells so they'll fit in cars; the main technological problem remaining is how to deliver fuel to the cell. Using hydrogen directly requires storage of hydrogen on the vehicle and, as of 1999, the best way to do that had yet to be worked out. Using hydrogen directly would also require construction of hydrogen refueling stations. To get around these problems, engineers have also worked on fuel-cell cars using methanol or gasoline as hydrogen sources. This approach involves extracting hydrogen from these liquid fuels in an onboard reforming system, which cuts the need for new refueling stations but results in vehicles with carbon monoxide and carbon dioxide emissions from the reforming process.[13]

"There's been a sea change, from profound skepticism about fuel cell and hybrid cars to a real commitment."

PETER SCHWARTZ,
GLOBAL BUSINESS NETWORK

The cleanest way currently known to use fuel cells is to fuel them with hydrogen generated from water using solar photovoltaic panels. The process that's envisioned is this: arrays of photovoltaic panels make electricity from sunlight, and that electricity splits water into hydrogen and oxygen. The hydrogen gas is piped to refueling stations, then delivered to fuel-cell cars. In the cars, the hydrogen feeds directly into the fuel cell, generates electricity to run the car, and emits water vapor and heat as waste. With all the work being done on fuel cells, as well as recent solar technology advances, this is a scenario that's getting closer to reality. Still, it's likely that the first fuel-cell cars on the market will use methanol or gasoline as fuel, with onboard reformers to convert it to hydrogen, and these will have some carbon emissions. Whatever system is adopted, most research and development money for alternative vehicles is flowing into fuel cells as the 21st century begins.

Hybrid vehicles: Hybrids combine an electric motor with a small internal combustion engine in an attempt to blend the best of both worlds. Like battery electrics, the hybrid car is not a new idea. Ferdinand Porsche built a hybrid prototype around the turn of the century, as did General Electric; hybrid trucks were produced in Philadelphia from 1910 to 1918; and from 1917 to 1918, a model called the Woods Dual Power coupe was produced in Chicago. Today's hybrids have a longer range than pure electrics and are also highly efficient, traveling at up to 60 to 80 m.p.g. The electric motor and internal combustion engine in a hybrid work together either in series — the engine charges batteries, which in turn power the electric motor, which turns the wheels — or in parallel, where either the engine or the electric motor can propel the vehicle directly. Again like electric cars, most hybrids use regenerative braking. They pollute less than standard vehicles, although some use diesel engines which are problematic for their particulate and NO_x emissions; though the small diesels used in hybrids are cleaner than the smelly, sooty versions in trucks and buses, they're still polluting enough to attract criticism from government agencies and environmental groups. In the 1995-99 Future Car competition, in which university engineering teams designed cars that combined fuel efficiencies approaching 80 m.p.g. with low emissions and consumer comforts, many of the entries were hybrid gasoline-electric vehicles. Hybrids have come to market quickly, first in Europe and Japan and reaching the North American market as of 1999; they're predicted to be widely available within a few years.[14]

Clean-Fuel Transit

Friday nights on Santa Barbara's State Street, it's standing room only on the open air electric shuttle that runs through the lively commercial district. Hydrogen fuel-cell buses on demonstration runs in Vancouver and Chicago have been so popular with Chicagoans that many wait longer to ride them, passing up earlier diesel buses on the same routes. CNG buses have become the alternative fuel bus of choice for California schools and, when Boise, Idaho, converted its bus fleet to CNG, it reduced air pollution by 37 tons a year in the process. Cities and countries around the world have put more clean-fuel buses in service. Latin American and European countries have expanded natural gas bus fleets in particular. As of 1999, about one in five new bus purchases in the U.S. was for alternative fuel vehicles.[15]

Transit systems have found benefits from clean-fuel buses besides cleaner air. An analysis of CNG buses by the Sacramento Regional Transit District and SunLine Transit Agency found they cost 27 to 38 percent less per mile.[16] Transit agencies have generally found propane and natural gas buses easy to maintain, and transit riders seem to like them, too. After State College, Pennsylvania, began converting its bus fleet to CNG, the community's response was "phenomenal," says Hugh Mose, general manager of the region's Centre Area Transportation Authority. "In my 22 years in the transit industry, I have never received more positive comments from bus riders and non-riders alike."[17]

Solar cars: A true solar car uses vehicle-mounted photovoltaic panels as the sole power for an electric motor. You might see electric cars with a few photovoltaic panels on them to extend the range and life of batteries. A car that uses solar panels for this purpose, but gets most of its power from an outside source, is considered "solar-assisted." To date, most true solar cars have been built by college and university teams for demonstration races like North America's Sunrayce or the World Solar Challenge in Australia. To compete effectively, solar cars must be very lightweight (most racing prototypes weigh only a few hundred pounds), have very efficient drive trains, and be extremely aerodynamic; most look like long, flat spaceships on wheels, and often have only three wheels to reduce rolling resistance. Champion solar cars can reach speeds topping 60 m.p.h. (100 km/h), though average speeds for long-distance solar races fall between about 20 and 50 m.p.h. Most solar cars use batteries to store energy, but only a limited number to keep the vehicles' weight down. On cloudy days stored battery power can keep a solar car running, but if clouds persist, the car will slow down and ultimately stop. Some simple solar car designs might be used as neighborhood vehicles.

The SunCoaster, designed by students at Lewis and Clark College, for instance, seats a driver under a roof of solar panels, weighs 220 pounds, and can reach a speed of 19 m.p.h. (30 km/h) on the sun's rays alone. Recent design advances like attaching motors directly to wheels for higher efficiencies could move solar cars closer to practical applications.[18]

Compressed-air cars: Yes, there are even cars that run on air. In 1999, French engine designer Guy Nègre made news when his design for a compressed-air "ZP" taxi was chosen for mass production in Mexico. Mexican officials plan initially to purchase 40,000 compressed-air taxis and ultimately to replace the entire 87,000-vehicle fleet with air cars. The taxis, with specially modified lightweight internal combustion engines, run on compressed air in city conditions, reaching up to about 60 m.p.h. (95 km/h) for about 125 miles (200 km) before needing to be refueled. Compressed-air tanks under the vehicles hold about 80 gallons of air at 300 bars (a measure of pressure) and can be refilled under high pressure in three minutes or, if one uses a small compressor plugged in at home, in about four hours. At higher speeds and for longer distances, the engines can also be fueled by gasoline, methanol, or propane. Nègre's engines, planned for use in fleet vans and pickups as well as in taxis, have a regenerative system that takes in air during braking; the air is ultimately emitted through a carbon filtering system, reportedly purified and cleaner than the air taken in.[19]

Finding Alternative Fuels and Vehicles

The field of alternative fuel vehicles is changing quickly; places to find them will change as that happens. So far the kinds of AFVs most readily available to consumers include:

- electric bicycles (see Chapter 12);
- neighborhood electric vehicles: sold by major golf-cart manufacturers and companies like Bombardier and Global Electric MotorCars, about 400,000 of them were in use as of 1998, mostly in sunbelt cities and retirement communities;
- electric cars, vans, pickups, and SUVs: easiest to find in California, Arizona, and Florida, harder but still possible elsewhere in North America. Models available as of 1999 included GM's EV-1, Chrysler EPIC minivans, Ford Ranger pickups, Toyota's RAV4 SUV, and Solectria's Force sedan and Flash pickup, among others;
- hybrid vehicles: Toyota's Prius and Honda's Insight were the first for sale in North America;
- CNG vehicles: while most car companies offer CNG vehicles to fleet buyers, some may provide CNG vehicles to individual buyers on special orders at specified dealers.

The Internet is a good place to scan what's currently available. Check websites of the various alternative fuel associations — the Natural Gas Vehicle Coalition, for instance, has a "market exchange" on its website that lists new and used natural gas vehicles for sale, and the Electric Vehicle Association of the Americas (EVAA) usually has a few ads offering used EVs of various specifications for sale, often hobbyist-built. Check sites of automakers, including smaller producers like Solectria, and agency sites like the U.S. Department of Energy's Alternative Fuels Data Center website; the California Energy Commission's Alternative Fuel Vehicles page; and WestStart-CALSTART, a joint private-public venture promoting a range of low- and no-emission vehicles. DOE's Fleet Buyer's Guide website is often recommended and includes information on buying clean-fuel vehicles and available tax incentives for both fleet buyers and individuals. For print sources, the American Council for an Energy Efficient Economy offers a yearly consumer guide called the *Green Guide to Cars and Trucks* that lists some models. Another source is Michael Hackleman's *The New Electric Vehicles*, which includes a list of smaller companies that build and sell EVs and components. Fairs and shows that promote alternative energy or vehicles can be places to buy such vehicles, too. We bought a used electric car, for instance, at the Midwest Renewable Energy Fair. Local distributors of fuels like propane and natural gas may be able to help as well.

You can also get a few alternative-fuel vehicles that defy classification. One example is The Twike, a sort of cross between a human-powered vehicle and an electric car. Developed in Switzerland, The Twike seats two in car-like chairs inside an enclosed body — but down in the footwell are pedals for both driver and passenger. It starts up using an electric motor, but then is pedaled by its one or two occupants for most of the trip, essentially an electric vehicle with pedal-power backup. Pedaling extends the vehicle's range and keeps its battery storage and the amount of energy needed for recharging to a

Pedal power helps extend the range of the electric Twike.

minimum. However, the vehicle's just a bit too heavy to be pedaled around once the electricity has run out. Another tricky-to-classify vehicle is the Sparrow, a one-person electric vehicle that registers as a motorcycle but has three wheels, an enclosed body, and goes up to 60 m.p.h. (95 km/h). Billed as "The World's First Personal Transit Module," the Sparrow is marketed specifically as a commute vehicle.

Just as you can build your own house, you can build your own alternative-fuel vehicle. This is most often done by converting an existing internal combustion car to propane, CNG, or electricity. There's a thriving culture of hobbyists who have done this, especially with battery electric vehicles. Converting a car to an electric vehicle involves replacing the engine with an electric motor and a few other components, as well as filling the trunk, hatch, or back seat with batteries, usually lead-acid ones. For people with mechanical and electrical ability, this can be a do-it-yourself job; several instructors teach how-to-convert courses, or you can get a book or kit and teach yourself. The components needed for a conversion cost around $5,000. You'll also need a car; a small, lighter-weight car with a well-kept body but a burned-out engine is ideal.

You can convert an existing vehicle to propane or CNG with kits that replace the fuel storage and delivery system, keeping the car's original internal combustion engine. CNG kits cost $4,000 to $5,000, propane kits around $3,000; they include fuel tanks and lines and a handful of other components to help deliver the fuel to the engine. The disadvantage of converting a car to CNG or propane is finding space for the new fuel tanks which are usually larger than gasoline tanks. Some conversion kits allow you to go "bi-fuel": to maintain the gasoline tanks along with the new fuel tanks and to switch between them.

Practicality of AFVs depends partly on being able to refuel them. You can find some AFV refueling station maps and lists on the Internet. California leads the country in refueling stations; as of 1999, the state had over 1,000 for various fuel types. About 200 of those were electric charging stations, like the one installed near the office of the Union of Concerned Scientists in Berkeley, California, which draws power from renewable energy sources. If you live in an area with a good supply of gasohol refueling stations, you can use gasohol with a regular car, no modifications required. You'll also likely find more AFVs and charging stations in communities that have signed on with the U.S. Department of Energy's Clean Cities Program. The program encourages local agencies to both use AFVs and help establish markets for them. Nearly 80 cities or regions had joined the program by the close of the century; these communities owned and operated over 160,000 AFVs, mainly in fleets, up from 30,000 in 1993 and 120,000 in 1997.[20] Among participants is Denver, Colorado, which bought neighborhood electric vehicles for city employees to use on business; the economical vehicles ($6,200 to purchase, about a penny a mile for the electric "fuel") have quickly become popular. "These vehicles are great for short distance trips to meetings around town," says Ernie Oakes, the Clean Cities manager for the region covering Denver. "There isn't a city around that couldn't be doing this."[21]

If you want to try out an AFV, you can rent one in places. In Europe, it's possible to rent AFVs in many countries. In North America, EV Rentals (for "Environmental Vehicle") operates out of Budget Rent-A-Car locations to rent electric and CNG cars. After opening first at the Los Angeles Airport in 1998, the company expanded to other locations: Sacramento and Ontario, California; Las Vegas; Phoenix; Albuquerque; Denver; Salt Lake City; Columbus, Ohio; and Atlanta, Georgia, either have outlets or are being considered for them. With electric vehicle rentals in particular, customers get a ten-minute briefing on the vehicle, a review of travel plans to make sure they fit the vehicle's capabilities, and free recharging at area charging stations. "Many customers come in with reservations for gasoline cars and we convert them at the counter," says operations manager Terry O'Day. "Then they'll come back after a weekend and say things like, 'Thank you so much. It really made our trip memorable.'"

Avoiding the Rebound: Alternative Fuels in Healthy Transportation

For healthiest transportation, AFVs need to be used in the context of reforming the entire transportation system. That overall reform involves a broad shift from using a car for nearly every trip to, ultimately, walking, cycling, or taking transit for most trips. There are several alternative fuel proponents already acting on this principle.

"Hypercars™ cannot solve the problem of too many people driving too many miles in too many cars; indeed, they could intensify it. Avoiding the constraint du jour requires not only having great cars but also being able to leave them at home most of the time."

AMORY AND HUNTER LOVINS,
ATLANTIC MONTHLY, JANUARY 1995

Actor Ed Begley Jr., for instance, who's done a lot to promote electric vehicles, jumps in his EV1 only when his bike or public transportation won't get him where he wants to go.[22] Michael Hackleman, who's built, lectured on, and written about electric vehicles for years, is now car-free and working on some innovative electric transit ideas.

Some excellent images of healthy transportation come from Richard Register's book *Ecocity Berkeley,* which makes the important point that the built form of a city should allow people access by proximity, so they'll need vehicles less often. The book's sketches show ecocity public spaces filled with walkers and cyclists, but also a few motorized conveyances, mostly solar- and wind-recharged electric carts, delivery vans, and buses. What makes a difference in these sketches is the scale of vehicles (small), the mix of vehicles and people (far more people than vehicles), and the kind of access supported by city design.

These examples point the way to avoiding a rebound relationship with alternative fuel cars. We have the technical capability right now to eliminate and replace gasoline-powered internal combustion cars entirely. But if we leave our marriage to internal combustion cars behind and move — on the rebound — into a union with just as many or more alternative fuel vehicles, we'll still have relationship headaches. If, though, at the same time we make transportation and land use changes that support walking, cycling, and transit, together with changes in our relationships with motor vehicles themselves, we'll make the most of the benefits of cleaner fuels as well as making transportation healthier all around.

CHAPTER 15

Long-Distance Relationships: Telecommunications

"Let your fingers do the walking ... "

YELLOW PAGES MARKETING SLOGAN

"IJUST LOVE WORKING AT HOME SO MUCH," says Amelia Kassel, who left a nine-to-five library job in 1984 to start an information brokerage at her house in the country north of San Francisco. The computer, modem, and phone are the indoor focus of her home-based business; outside is a pastoral scene that is a constant soothing presence. "I love the quiet, the peacefulness, the green that's out my window," she says. "And I hate driving!" Since she started working at home, she doesn't do much of it: her car travel has dropped from 15,000 to about 5,000 miles a year. She loves the feeling, too, of being more productive. "I probably get twice as much done as I did when I worked in the library," she estimates. "Now, I would never go back to work for any organization."

Telephones, e-mail, the Internet, fax machines: the various long-distance access tools allowing Amelia Kassel and others like her to do business from home are shifting how we live, work, communicate, and travel. Human resources managers surveyed in 1999 expected telecommuting to be the number one trend changing the nature of work in coming years. In the U.S., remote work of all kinds is expected to grow about 18 percent a year through 2015. The number of Internet hosts and users worldwide has exploded in the last five years and is expected to about double in the next five. Electronic commerce, remote conferencing, distance learning, and other tele-services are expanding rapidly, too.[1]

Like alternative fuels, the telecommunications boom offers some good news and some bad news. By providing access without requiring mobility, telecommunications can vastly reduce the need for a car. At the same time, though, telecommunications has the potential to encourage more travel — perhaps the same way computers, once touted as tools for a "paperless office," have actually led to more paper use. Whether telecommuting and other forms of remote access end up reducing or expanding travel depends on how we approach the burgeoning opportunities to use them.

Wearing Slippers to Work

Like Amelia Kassel, I work at home. My commute to my home office crosses two rooms and requires no vehicle (unless you count the slippers I often wear to work). Not only can those of us working at home wear whatever we want to the office, we reap other personal benefits from using travel-replacing forms of telecommunications, by:

☎ **saving money** — on fuel, maintenance, depreciation, etc. — by driving less;

☎ **saving time** by avoiding lengthy commutes: workers tend to travel about 75 percent less on days they telecommute;[2]

☎ **eliminating the need for second cars** — or even first cars, in some households;

☎ **avoiding stress:** it takes an hour to recover from a one-way, 30-mile drive to work, say researchers at Florida International University;[3]

☎ **gaining schedule flexibility:** employees like the flexibility of telecommuting so much, studies show, that many would change jobs to do it, and over a third of telecommuters would quit if their employers ended their telecommuting programs.[4]

Using telecommunications can help organizations, too, mainly by saving them money. The U.S. government hopes to have three percent of its employees telecommuting by 2002 and expects to save $150 million a year by doing so. Telecommuting helps employers attract and keep employees, reduces needs for office and parking space, cuts absenteeism, and increases productivity anywhere from ten to 50 percent. Distance learning can save money for schools by letting them provide a wider range of programs with lower staff and travel costs. When replacing travel, telecommunications can help society by cutting congestion, reducing greenhouse gas emissions, and cutting pollution. According to U.S. EPA Administrator Carol Browner, one day of telecommuting by ten percent of the U.S. work force can drop air pollution by almost 13,000 tons. The potential congestion and pollution-cutting benefits of telecommuting have governments promoting the concept throughout Europe and North America.[5]

There are, however, a few caveats. Use of telecommunications does not bring benefits automatically, but only has the potential to bring them. Increases in virtual "travel" also have the potential for negative effects.

☎ Such increases may contribute to sprawl, if more telecommuters choose to live and work in remote locations.

☎ It's possible, say labor unions and feminists, that some telecommuting arrangements can be exploitive, as when employers downsize and replace regular employees with telecommuting independent contractors who receive no benefits.

☎ Expectations of higher productivity from telecommuting employees can lead to a different kind of work stress.

☎ The isolation of working away from an office can be difficult, and the lack of boundaries on work time can worsen workaholism in some people.

Telecommunications can encourage more travel in part by generating economic growth which in turn generates more trips, and by broadening the geographic scope of business and personal relationships, giving people more reasons to travel.[6]

Given its conflicting tendencies, use of telecommunications may bring small declines but probably not big ones in trips taken society-wide, believes telecommunications expert Professor Patricia Mokhtarian of the University of California at Davis. After all, people have noticed that telecommunications could substitute for travel since the 19th century — probably as soon as telegraph wires made the Pony Express obsolete. Various predictions since then have expected travel decreases: in 1914, for instance, *Scientific American* forecast a drop in transit congestion due to telecommunications. Instead, travel and telecommunications have grown simultaneously, tending to complement each other rather than one replacing the other. This big-picture pattern, writes Mokhtarian, shows few signs of changing, despite successes with cutting travel in some specific telecommuting programs.[7] On the other hand, if your intention is to avoid travel and divorce your car, then telecommunications can help you do that.

> *"Just because we're on the information highway doesn't mean we know where we're going."*
>
> PATRICIA MOKHTARIAN

Long-Distance Access without Having to Travel

It's increasingly easy to substitute a phone line and computer for a road and car to "get to" jobs, school, shopping, banking, and even health care. Telemedicine, for instance, can substitute for some (though not all) health-care travel by allowing doctors remote viewing of medical data like x-rays, providing services like telepsychiatry, or offering medical call centers that dispense basic health information. People using call centers often can listen to information from an automated audio health library, or transfer directly to a nurse who listens to their symptoms, then gives advice for self-care, arranges a doctor's appointment, or directs the person to the emergency room, as appropriate. Since it's estimated that perhaps 40 percent of health care consists of information exchange between practitioners and patients, this can save a lot of expense, travel, and waiting room time.[8] Other tele-access strategies have the potential to substitute for even more travel. Below are a few of the primary ways this can happen.

Telework has saved me miles of commuting since I started working from home in 1985. It helped Jan Hazzard skip a 17-mile round trip commute by working from home one day a week when she was office manager for the mayor of Portland, Oregon. Seventeen employees of the Acacia Group, a financial services company near Washington, D.C., saved an average of nearly two hours of commuting time every telework day after their company started a telecommuting program.[9]

Telework gets divided into two main categories: telecommuting, where regular employees work from home one or more days a week; and other remote work, usually by self-employed individuals or people with home-based businesses. Both types can also take place at neighborhood or regional telework centers, satellite offices set up by specific companies in areas where large numbers of their employees live, or by government agencies or independent services that rent spaces short-term or long-term to telecommuters. As of 1999, an estimated 16 million U.S. employees, 11 percent of the civilian work force (over twice the number as in 1992) telecommuted at least occasionally. Another 20 to 40 million were self-employed in home-based businesses, and over twice as many businesses were being started in homes as in offices or storefronts. Canada's telework force numbered about a million in 1999. The Gartner Group, information technology consultants, predicts that over 137 million workers worldwide will be telecommuting in some fashion by 2003.[10]

"Having my office at home is a feature that greatly reduces the need to drive."

SALLY FLOCKS, ATLANTA, GEORGIA, CAR-LITE

Telecommuting doesn't work for everyone, but for many, hesitations fall away once its advantages are experienced. For instance, despite employees' fears to the contrary, consultant Joanne Pratt reports, teleworkers get more promotions than their in-office colleagues, and a 1997 survey of teleworkers found 60 percent of them felt it had positively affected their careers.[11] Marty Gallanter, a writer who provides services to people and businesses in New York from his home in Tyler, Minnesota, said at first his clients were hesitant when he moved from the Big Apple to the backwoods. But then, he says, "They realized that I could respond to them more quickly than someone who had to take a taxi across town."[12]

Computer, information, and service industry jobs as well as certain desk jobs lend themselves to telecommuting, at least on a part-time basis. Among major employers who've begun telecommuting programs are Allstate Insurance, Apple

---

Is Telecommuting for You?

Based on June Langhoff's "Aptitude Test" in *The Telecommuter's Advisor*, you're telecommuting material if:

- you have a job in which you spend much of your time working alone, and you're comfortable with that;
- you're goal-oriented, well-organized, a self-starter, and work well with minimum supervision;
- you're able to focus on tasks and can effectively control distractions;
- you're a good and efficient communicator, both in writing and on the phone;
- the social aspects of hanging out in a workplace aren't a high priority for you;
- you have a location at or near home — either a home office or a telework center — from which you can work;
- you don't need or can replicate the support systems (secretary, assistant, major machinery like photocopiers, reference materials) available at an office.[14]

Computer, Federal Express, Levi-Strauss, McGraw Hill, Patagonia, Pacific Bell, Union Pacific, and Xerox.[13] Many state and local governments, provincial governments in Canada, and national government departments have telework programs, too. Top occupations for home-based businesses include consulting, business and computer services, sales, graphic arts, and writing. And these have a high rate of success; 85 percent of home-based businesses are still going three years after they've started. Once you've had a taste of the independence they provide, it's hard to go back to a regular job, and the telecommunications tools developed over the last two decades have added to that independence. When I started working from home in 1985, I had a phone, computer, printer, and post office box, but no fax, copier, e-mail, or Internet access. Since then, each time I've added one of these tools to my home office, my need to travel for work has dropped another notch.

Telemeetings: When thunderstorms kept Minnesota governor Jesse Ventura from flying to the 1999 Reform Party conference to speak, he hooked up by telephone and spoke anyway. Executive Bill Holtz has replaced miles of travel with 30 cent-per-minute video meetings from the basement of his Philadelphia home, where the videoconferencing equipment he's installed gives him visual contact with staff and customers worldwide. The Canadian Association for Distance Education holds annual conferences that alternate every other year between face-to-face meetings and virtual events, with audio and video sites set up throughout Canada.[15]

RUBES ®   **By Leigh Rubin**

7-10 Creators Syndicate, Inc. © 1995 Leigh Rubin!

By permission of Leigh Rubin and Creators Syndicate.

Telecommuters

Though past predictions of videophones in every home haven't materialized, teleconferences and videoconferences have become an everyday reality for workplaces. Their convenience as well as cost and travel savings can be significant. A one-hour teleconference for 12 people might cost around $200, whereas travel costs to bring those dozen to an in-person meeting could reach $6,000. Remote conferences range from the simple — three-way calling or a small conference call — to the more elaborate: for example, videoconferences with satellite hook-ups to high-tech conferencing centers worldwide. Teleconferencing and videoconferencing can be combined with other remote access services, such as displaying meeting materials on a website.[16] There are now specialized Internet sites providing services like virtual auditoriums with audio, video, and features allowing interaction between speakers and audience members.

I find conference calls a great convenience — once someone arranges them, you just dial the designated phone number at the appointed time, and there you are. Teleconferences can be this way too, I learned, when I participated in one for the first time in June 1999. Collecting more material for this book, I "went to" a Local Government Commission (LGC) teleconference on designing walkable streets. Over a hundred of us called in on a toll-free number, filling the phone line with snippets of conversation and background noise from all over the U.S., until the moderators asked us to either use the mute buttons some phones now have or be very quiet so the conference could get underway. Attendees had received a guidebook on designing walkable streets, so we had visuals to follow as featured speaker Dan Burden referenced the guidebook's photographs and elaborated on examples in its pages. The LGC reached a broader audience, saved money, and saved staff time by organizing this as a teleconference instead of an in-person event and, for me, it was great to take part in the two-hour meeting without having to travel.

Teleschool, called "distance learning" or "distance education" by most people, can help you learn without having to commute or relocate. Betsy Kahn is one person who's done this. When she wanted to return to school for a Master's in Library Science, the closest degree program was 40 miles from her Connecticut home down Interstate 95, the "nightmare highway of the East Coast," she says. With that as a disincentive, and with three young sons at home, she nearly abandoned returning to school. Then she found out about the University of Illinois at Urbana-Champaign distance learning program: with one initial two-week session plus a weekend a semester on campus, she could do the rest of the program from home, online. "It gave me a sane way to accomplish my goal without having to strain my family life," she says. Even with a few long-distance trips, she adds, "It was so much more convenient than it would have been to commute on I-95."

Many distance learning programs are based around interactive video. The program Betsy attended connects mainly via the Internet. There are synchronous sessions, where everyone logs on and "attends" a lecture or discussion at the same time, listening to instructors on audio and "discussing" in chat rooms via lines of text on computer screens. There is asynchronous discussion using a bulletin board format, where students can log on at their convenience to read and post messages. Sessions are archived so they can be reviewed again at any time. Some aspects of the program seem up close and personal, in a virtual sort of way. Before lectures, says Betsy, students would log on early to chat. "It was kind of like when you meet outside the classroom, where everyone has their cup of coffee and starts talking about the homework and what else is going on in their lives," she says.

The distance learning program saved Betsy two or three commutes a week (40 miles each way) over two academic years, saving time and miles traveled, even considering the trips she took to campus in Illinois. In addition to its use by colleges and universities, distance learning is used increasingly to augment regular grade school programs, to expand programs available to underserved or advanced students, to help homeschoolers, and to reach students in small towns and rural areas. It's also used for in-service training in teaching and other fields.[17]

Tele-errands: When I talk with people about getting around without a car, one of the first things they often ask is: "How do you bring home groceries?" I've done so on foot and by bike, but telecommunications can also bring home the bread. Phoning for groceries and getting them delivered used to be a common service; some stores have started offering it again, and the Internet is helping to bring it back. Online grocery store services like those now operating in major cities are likely to spread rapidly, and provide one more way to get groceries without driving.

Common Internet purchases now include not only food but also computer software and hardware, books, music, clothing — and cars. Fifteen percent of U.S. adults purchased goods on the Internet in 1998, logging on and filling virtual "shopping carts" by pressing a few computer keys, then usually getting the ordered products delivered. Forecasts indicated that over 50 million Americans will use the Internet to buy over $50 billion in goods and services by 2002.[18]

Another way to take care of errands long-distance has been with us much longer than the Internet: the telephone. One study found that if ten to 20 percent of commuting, shopping, and business trips were replaced with phone calls, the biggest pollution savings would come from replacing the shopping trips.[19] Besides cutting pollution, you can eliminate car trips and save your own time and money by using a phone to do one or more of the following:

☎ Call first before shopping to make sure what you're looking for is in stock.

☎ Comparison shop by phone.

☎ Make actual purchases by phone and mail.

☎ Ask for your purchases to be delivered.

"The first step in letting your fingers do the driving," suggests Ellen Jones of Washington, D.C., "is to confirm the availability and price of the product you are seeking over the telephone. This saves an unproductive trip right off the bat. The home run comes when you can persuade the business to ship the product to your home using a credit card to cover the cost of the goods and shipping. Even businesses not accustomed to mail order can get into the swing of this type of customer service over the telephone."[20]

Finding and Creating Opportunities for Tele-Access

Perhaps the most important way to reduce our travel is to get into the habit of considering, each time a trip suggests itself, whether the trip is necessary. Do you have to go to the post office, or can you buy the stamps you need by phone, mail, or Internet? Do you have to pay bills or transfer funds in person, or can you do so by telebanking, via phone or computer? Can you replace a meeting with a conference call? Practice considering such questions and you may find yourself asking for phone numbers, e-mail, or website addresses more often than you ask for travel directions.

If telework appeals to you as a way to cut driving, there are scores of books about telecommuting and working at home that can give you more information. These books give advice about how to seek jobs at firms with telecommuting programs and how to start telecommuting at your current workplace, whether it offers a program or not. As June Langhoff, author of *The Telecommuter's Advisor*, writes: "If your company already allows flexible work options such as telecommuting, it will be relatively easy to convince your supervisor to let you telecommute. The main issues will involve proving your reliability and the appropriateness of your job for distance working."[21] It's harder, she adds, if you're setting out to be the first telecommuter from your workplace — but it can be done. You'll first need to convince your employer that a telecommuting program makes business sense. Langhoff suggests strategies like researching potential cost savings, highlighting company concerns such as parking shortages that could be addressed by telecommuting, and circulating information about telecommuting throughout the company. Her book also includes a sample proposal for a telecommuting program. Before dismissing the idea of trying to get telecommuting started in a company without it, consider that most telework programs begin in response to one employee's request or need, says Commuter Connections in Washington, D.C. Many employers have told Commuter Connections, which offers telework seminars and a Telework Resource Center, that they'll seriously consider telework program proposals from individual employees if those proposals are well-thought-out and show how the organization would benefit.

To take advantage of higher-tech tele-access options, you don't necessarily have to have all the latest equipment at home. If you can walk, bike, or bus to a public or university library, you'll often find public Internet access there. Some telework centers and office support companies rent videoconference set-ups. Kinko's copy centers, for instance, offer videoconferencing rooms at some of their branches. Teleworkers who may need a real office occasionally can use what's now called "hoteling" to book an office by the hour or by the day. Sometimes this is done within companies, sometimes at telework centers. Though the telework centers that have opened over the last decade have had mixed success, they do still exist, particularly in places with air quality and congestion problems, where local governments are working to cut travel and pollution.[22] Many telework centers are government-sponsored, so it may be easiest to find one by contacting regional, state, or provincial agencies that promote telework. These can often be found within departments of energy, air pollution control agencies, or travel demand management offices. Local agencies that promote ridesharing programs can also often direct you to various telecommuting opportunities, including telework centers, if they exist in your area.

Telecommunications and Divorcing Your Car

Like the previous chapter, this is in part a cautionary one. Telecommunications can help reduce travel in the context of a life where reducing travel is a goal, but without that goal, it may increase our travel by car as well as by plane, which is also environmentally destructive. And in using telecommunications as a servant, we have to be careful not to let it master us. As telecommunications tools become faster and more powerful, they can have a tendency to speed everything up: the pace of global commerce, the rate of industrial resource use, and our own pace of life. A way to balance these tendencies is to keep telecommunications use as simple as possible, as much as possible: often a basic phone call is all that's needed to avoid a trip. Be wary, too, of letting telecommunications increase travel in your own life. Otherwise there's a risk of getting pushed away from a lifestyle conducive to car divorce. Patricia Mokhtarian points out a few of the ways that telecommuting can do this: "People might decide to take more excursions to avoid cabin fever at home. Or telecommuters who once carpooled to work might decide to drive alone on the days when they do go into the office ... If telecommuters have a shorter drive to work, new trips for shopping or socializing on their telecommuting days may become more appealing ... Telecommuting could potentially motivate some people to move even farther from work than they live now."[23]

"Work is no longer a place. Work is simply something you do."

JUNE LANGHOFF, *THE TELECOMMUTER'S ADVISOR*

At the same time, Mokhtarian says, "We do know that telecommuters drive less."[24] As of 1997, she estimated that each day, about two percent of the U.S. workforce telecommuted, and that this probably reduced vehicle miles traveled by about one to two percent. That's not enough to counteract an otherwise huge increase in vehicle miles traveled, but it does indicate a potential benefit for individuals. Telecommunications can be used as a tool to aid car divorce — when doing so, remembering the intention of driving less and enjoying life more might be the best way to realize the benefits of tele-access.

CHAPTER 16

Get Support:
Social and Political Strategies for
Ending Car Addiction

"Our lives and landscape have been fashioned to the automobile's dictates
for three-quarters of a century. A rescue movement is in order."

JANE HOLTZ KAY, *ASPHALT NATION*

WHEN I LIVED IN NORTHERN CALIFORNIA, people used to say our county had the highest concentration of therapists per capita in the U.S., possibly the world. The local yellow pages listed all manner of therapists — psychiatrists, psychologists, marriage, family, and child counselors — offering all kinds of therapy — group therapy, art therapy, hypnotherapy, relationship counseling — as well as special treatments for alcoholism, anxiety, workaholism, and even garden-variety depression. All this therapist activity fostered support groups galore. There were twelve-step groups, men's groups, women's groups, groups for the newly married, and groups for the newly unmarried. The community college offered classes like "Couples Communication" and "Choosing a Healthy Relationship." What a great place to get a divorce! Support around every corner.

With divorce from a car, the same principle applies: since every divorcee needs support, the more depth and variety of support for non-automotive mobility a community offers, the easier a car divorce can be. This support sometimes comes from government if elected officials or planners take steps to create supportive environments for non-motorists. We can also get support from businesses and from each other. Many of the ways we can do this — programs and policies described in this chapter — have already been used successfully in places around the world. Think what a great (and supportive!) community could be created if they were all used in one place.

Land Use Support

The link between land use and transportation is a tight one: you can't plan land uses without profoundly affecting transportation, and vice versa. This means that planning communities for people, not for cars, can do a lot to support freedom from car-dependence. Planners can start from the premise that people need access, not just mobility; planning can then create access with proximity instead of asphalt. Clustering parks, shops, schools, churches, jobs, and homes within half a mile of each other, for instance, and putting major destinations near transit stops, makes it

202

easier to travel without driving. Likewise, planning that limits growth supports non-car travel. The measures listed below not only make car-free travel easier, they make communities better places to live in general.

Foster urban villages: In Arabella Park in Munich (Germany), 10,000 people live in garden apartments near businesses, schools, and sports facilities providing 18,000 jobs. Residents can walk to shops and services, take rapid transit to downtown Munich from a centrally located station, or relax in landscaped car-free plazas that give the community a human scale, filling it with social interaction. In Vancouver's False Creek, 10,000 people live in terraced townhomes and apartments set in car-free green spaces overlooking the waterfront. A meandering walking and cycling boulevard links homes with shops, and the area is served by frequent trolley buses.[1] These two examples of what transport experts Peter Newman and Jeff Kenworthy call "urban villages" recreate the intimacies of old-style walking cities. Their "elegant" densities, connections to transit, mix of services close to homes, and good walking and cycling facilities make it easy to live car-free. With extensive greenery and limits on autos, they balance city with nature. They can be fostered with removal of barriers like zoning regulations preventing high densities, or planning documents that encourage their development. Vancouver has fostered urban villages by writing language into its 1995 Livable Region Strategic Plan calling for "complete" communities,

---

The Newman-Kenworthy Strategy to Win Back Cities

Traffic calming, urban villages, and light rail: these three ingredients constitute a cure for car-dependence that transport experts Peter Newman and Jeff Kenworthy believe can win back cities. Newman and Kenworthy based their formula for urban renewal on years of research into the relationship between land use and transport patterns. Their work uncovered "a direct correlation between the extent of car use and a city's overall form and density. In simple terms, the more space devoted to cars ... the more sprawling and energy-wasteful the city." Conversely, they found that cities relying on public transport had higher density and more efficient energy use, and "importantly, these included some of the most economically successful and attractive cities in the world."[2]

Urban villages provide diverse living, working, shopping, and recreation opportunities in a compact area. Traffic calming lets streets stay pleasant and pedestrian-friendly by restraining cars. Light rail provides attractive quality transportation linking urban villages to each other and to large city centers, using a form of energy (electricity) that can ultimately come from renewable sources. Combining the three makes for an integrated walk-, bike- and transit-friendly city that provides a high quality of life with low use of resources.

Newman and Kenworthy detail these concepts (and more) in their 1999 book *Sustainability and Cities: Overcoming Automobile Dependence.* For those who want an earlier, shorter introduction to these ideas, they've also written, together with Les Robinson, a delightful 50-page color-illustrated guide called *Winning Back the Cities.*

where sources of work, goods, and services are located close to homes to reduce travel. Portland, Oregon's 2040 Plan fosters urban villages by concentrating development in a series of walkable regional centers along its transit lines.[3]

Orient development around transit: As Oakland, California's Fruitvale Transit Village takes shape, housing and community services for this multi-ethnic neighborhood are clustering around a BART station that also serves several bus routes. Even before construction of a planned pedestrian plaza, 68 new senior housing units a block from the station are fully occupied and new businesses have opened, reversing the neighborhood's decline.[4] In the nearby Silicon Valley town of Mountain View, a development called The Crossings sits where a failed auto-oriented shopping center once was. Designed by architect Peter Calthorpe, it clusters small houses, condominiums, apartments, and parks near shops and a commuter train station.[5] These transit-oriented developments (TODs) group housing, services, and public places within walking distance — usually a quarter mile — of transit. An important feature of TODs is pedestrian-friendly design (Calthorpe has called them "pedestrian pockets"), allowing people to walk between transit and homes or offices. Local governments can help development orient around transit by encouraging this in planning documents. Toronto has encouraged TODs by allowing developers to build higher-density units the closer they build to transit stations and by using transferable development rights, where landowners farther out can sell development rights to builders of projects near stations.[6]

Zone for a mix of uses: The mix of uses typical of old-style neighborhoods with corner stores and of small-town Main Streets where apartments perch over shops or nestle behind them cuts car use by putting shopping and work close to home. In contrast, suburbs where homes, shopping, and offices are segregated into expressway-bound tracts virtually require driving for most trips. Local governments can change zoning to replace such segregated land uses with a mix. Having stores, homes, and workplaces in the same neighborhood reduces travel distances, counteracts sprawl, and makes walking and bicycling easier. With mixed use, apartments can be put over stores, even in retrofitted malls. Mizner Park in Boca Raton, Florida, for instance, replaced an outdated shopping center and its sea of parking with terrace townhouses over offices, restaurants, and shops, all oriented around a new park. The mix of uses lets residents shop, work, or eat out without having to drive.

Make parking requirements more flexible: In a California city where regulations required 2.2 parking spaces per housing unit, architect Dan Solomon noticed that, in comparison, the General Plan called for 2.8 public library books per thousand residents. That meant a 4,000 unit development he built, averaging 2.7 people per unit, generated the need for only 30 new library books — but 8,800 parking spaces.[7] Inflexible requirements like this reinforce car-dependency, cost money, and distort social priorities. Instead, local governments can give developers options. Several North American cities let developers pay cash in lieu of building parking spaces —

Palo Alto, California, and Calgary, Alberta, are two — and generally use the cash to construct shared public parking for multiple users, allowing fewer spaces to be built in fewer places, saving both public and private money and resulting in more pedestrian-friendly street design. In some places, businesses can reduce parking requirements if they provide bike parking or promote carpools or transit, for instance, by giving employees or customers transit passes.[8] Some cities will reduce parking requirements if an opportunity for shared parking already exists — for example, cutting parking requirements for a church if it's built next to a school that's closed Sunday mornings. In addition, some places use parking maximums, paired with lower minimum parking requirements and on-street parking control; others cap the total number of parking spaces that can be built in an area.

Put boundaries on urban growth: In the 1970s, Oregon passed a law establishing 20-year urban growth boundaries (UGBs) around its cities, outside of which development was not allowed. Since then, more jurisdictions, including several northern California cities, have established UGBs to help curb sprawl. UGBs help limit the area to which public infrastructure — roads, sewers, water, utility lines — must be provided and so save local governments money. By containing growth, they also make travel and transit service easier and more efficient, and can reinforce a community's sense of place and identity. For UGBs to work, governments both inside and outside the boundary — city and county, usually — need to cooperate to control sprawl. Especially when coupled with permanent greenbelts, UGBs can keep development compact and cities livable. While some real estate developers complain that UGBs make land and housing too scarce, others say it reduces risk to know precisely where development will be allowed in the long run.

Favor infill development: Maryland's Smart Growth initiatives direct state funds into projects in already-developed locations, rather than in outlying areas.[9] Colorado, Rhode Island, and other states are pursuing similar policies. Most cities and suburbs have plenty of room for infill development: "granny" units in back yards or over garages, for instance, or additional businesses on abandoned real estate or oversized parking lots. Infill development helps limit sprawl, cuts infrastructure costs, and supports transit, cycling, and walking by keeping communities compact. Local governments can allow such infill by intensifying land use and relaxing density restrictions in city centers and at transit villages. While neighborhood residents sometimes object to the idea of higher densities, many of density's impacts can be contained by restricting parking, since objections to density intensifications like second-unit developments often center around traffic.

Remodel suburbs: Suburbs often turn out to be about the least supportive places to live if we want to divorce our cars. But suburban strip malls can be remodeled into places more like traditional towns. Landscape architect Richard Untermann advocates taking sprawling, miles-long commercial strips along arterials and converting them into a series of walkable Centers. As in transit-oriented developments, these would include a mix of uses — shopping, offices, and housing — in close proximity.[10] To convert an already-built-up arterial to a series of Centers, Untermann offers the following suggestions:

- put Centers at major intersections, about a mile apart;
- make existing shops and residences more accessible by foot and bike, removing barriers like fences or constructing gates as well as increasing and linking sidewalks and walkways;
- increase density within Centers by adding shops and housing on upper levels, or new buildings in parking lots; add shops fronting the street and sidewalk to create a walker-friendly edge;
- redirect parking, as feasible, to the backs and sides of stores; add clear walkways within parking lots, using striping or raised sidewalks or both;
- add sheltered transit stops at main entrances to shops, linked by walkways to the rest of the Center.

Such remodeling, Untermann believes, is cheap compared to accommodating sprawl with new roads and infrastructure. The same financing mechanisms used to build roads can pay for public facilities — sidewalks, bike lanes, transit stops — needed for this kind of remodeling.

Financial Support

Alimony from the car can help support a transition to a car-free or car-lite life. To get that alimony, we can charge for more of the full costs of driving and turn fixed into variable costs that depend on how much a car is driven. These strategies don't increase driving's true cost, but instead shift costs to the proper place — so they're obvious to, and paid directly by, the driver. And they reward people who drive less, placing costs more squarely on those who drive most. Often, linking costs directly to driving saves people money by allowing greater individual control over

---

The Singapore System of Pricing Roads

Not wanting their small island state to be overrun with cars and choked by congestion, Singapore's government began to charge for auto ownership and driving in the early 1970s. The country now boasts the world's leading example of full-cost auto pricing as well as a population that's 70 percent car-free despite high incomes. Singapore's system includes:

- an annual road tax per vehicle, higher for vehicles with large engines;
- a surtax on auto imports, up to 45 percent of a car's value;
- a registration fee of 150 percent of a car's value;
- additional penalties for registering cars over ten years old;
- a vehicle quota system, in which transportation planners set maximum allowable new car ownership levels each month, and potential buyers must bid for Certificates of Entitlement to purchase cars.

"consumption" of driving. For instance, shifting the source of road repair funds from property taxes to weight-distance taxes (see below) could both drop property taxes and allow people to equitably reduce their tax payments by driving less and using lighter vehicles. Below are some useful ways to get the kinds of financial support that can price travel more optimally and encourage car divorce.

Stop miscellaneous subsidies for cars and roads: Government subsidies for oil, cars, and roads place many driving costs on taxpayers in general. Getting cars off this kind of welfare might start with eliminating subsidies to oil companies. In the U.S., for instance, oil companies get taxpayer support from oil depletion allowances, enhanced oil recovery credits, intangible drilling cost deductions, and more. Friends of the Earth estimated these subsidies would total around $10 billion from 1998 to 2002.[11] Eliminating them would put these costs back in the marketplace, improving the competitiveness of renewable fuels and non-motorized travel.

Charge feebates and rebates when cars are purchased: This basically amounts to a system of high purchase taxes on gas-guzzling larger luxury cars, along with credits on fuel-efficient vehicles, with amounts set to be revenue-neutral; that is, the high taxes on luxury cars would pay for the administration of the program and for the credits to fuel-efficient vehicle buyers, so there would be no net revenue gain. Feebates and rebates can also be used to encourage efficiency-increasing and noise-reducing equipment, such as low-rolling-resistance tires, for instance.

Increase the use of road pricing and tolls: Congestion pricing, analogous to peak pricing on phone bills, gets road users to pay more of driving's full costs: during rush hours, as more people use roads, congestion pricing charges them more to do so. Singapore, with its electronic road pricing system, has developed this approach extensively (see sidebar). Some U.S. spots use congestion pricing; for instance, Lee County, Florida, uses electronic equipment to charge cars half-price tolls during certain off-peak times. Tolls can be added to existing highways and bridges. As of 1999,

That's just to own a car; driving adds more fees. In 1975, Singapore started an Area Licensing Scheme requiring motorists to buy a license to drive into a six-square-kilometer "Restricted Zone" in the central business district. In the late 1990s, this was converted to an Electronic Road-Pricing system. Motorists purchase smart cards for reader units in their cars; sensors at zone entrances debit the cards as cars pass by. Charges change with time of day and levels of congestion. Singaporean motorists also pay a 50 percent gasoline tax, a surcharge on leaded fuel, and high parking fees.

These pricing structures support high transit use: Singaporeans take two-thirds of motorized trips on transit, up from 33 percent before 1975. While car ownership in Singapore has still grown (mostly for status reasons, some believe), the rate has been lower than in other Asian countries.[12]

states like Arkansas, Florida, Pennsylvania, California, and South Carolina had expressed an interest in doing so. Charging entrance fees to cars entering high-pollution areas is another way to price roads. Road pricing revenues can fund transit — another remedy for congestion and pollution.

Shift the road repair burden from property taxes to weight, distance, and environmental fees: When cars are re-registered each year, more of the registration fees can be based on the distance traveled as well as on vehicle weight to reflect the additional wear and tear that heavier, more frequently used automobiles impose on roads. In the same way, environmental fees can be levied against vehicles that create air and noise pollution — the more noise and emissions, the higher the fee. Such fees also help shift the road maintenance burden away from property taxes, placing it more equitably on those who use roads most, and most heavily.

Charge for insurance by the mile or kilometer: With current systems of paying one yearly lump sum for auto insurance, those who drive less end up subsidizing those who drive more. Shifting insurance payments from a lump sum to a per-mile or per-kilometer basis (also called distance-based vehicle insurance) is more equitable and gives a financial incentive for less car travel; also, it makes plain sense since more driving means more crashes. One variation on distance-based insurance is pay-at-the-pump, where part of the insurance cost is added to the per-gallon or per-liter price paid for gasoline. The rest is paid the way most people pay for it now — as an annual or semi-annual fee — and incorporates factors like the driver's record and place of residence.

Charge for parking: There is no such thing as a free parking space. The "free" parking which is provided for about 95 percent of car commutes and 99 percent of non-

---

Major Laws to Help Change Car-dependence

Several national and international laws and policies could make conditions better for divorcing our cars. Whether they actually do so will depend on how they're implemented in the early 21st century. None of them guarantee a turnaround of auto culture; in fact, some have already been labeled too weak. But all offer at least the potential to help rein in car-dependence.

🚗 Kyoto Protocol: The CO_2 emissions reduction targets in this global climate change treaty have countries worldwide looking at ways to reduce CO_2 emissions. Some countries have aimed initiatives for cutting CO_2 at fuel consumption and car use.

🚗 Britain's Transport White Paper: Issued in 1998, this paper calls for British transport policy to emphasize walking, cycling, and transit, with no major road construction schemes. By increasing congestion pricing and parking charges and sending the proceeds to transit, the policy aims to shift ten percent of Britain's drivers out of their cars.[13]

work car-trips amounts to a massive subsidy for driving. To correct this, for starters, employers who offer parking as a benefit can give employees the option of cash instead. Called "cashing out" free parking, this typically reduces car commuting by 15 to 25 percent. Landlords or business parks can charge separately for apartments or offices and parking, renting spaces instead of giving them away with each unit. Businesses with good bicycle commuting or carpooling programs could save money this way, as could renters without cars. Going a little farther, local governments can charge for parking throughout their jurisdictions, and eliminate requirements for businesses to provide free parking. Los Angeles companies which began to charge for parking cut the number of solo drivers by 26 percent in one case, and raised vehicle occupancy by 30 percent in another.[14]

Offer location-efficient mortgages: Urban residents without private vehicles have more buying power for things other than transportation, particularly if they work close to home. Recognizing this, a collection of organizations led by Chicago's Center for Neighborhood Technology introduced the Location Efficient Mortgage (LEM) program in late 1999. The program lets car-free homebuyers qualify for larger loans than they might with standard loan qualification measures. Potential homebuyers can apply a LEM to purchases of townhomes, condominiums, or single family dwellings anywhere in Seattle, Chicago, Los Angeles, or San Francisco. Other cities such as Portland, Oregon, are likely to follow. The more efficient a home's location (the closer to transit, services, and workplaces), the better the possible loan. The LEM can add thousands of dollars of home-buying power, making housing more affordable for car-free urban households.

Provide incentives for walking, cycling, and transit: Beckmann's Bakery in Santa Cruz gives a five-percent discount to anyone arriving by bike; the ten-percent

---

ISTEA and TEA-21: The 1991 U.S. Intermodal Surface Transportation Efficiency Act (ISTEA) made transport decision-making more local, flexible, and citizen-oriented, shifting some spending from roads to transit and non-motorized modes. The 1998 Transportation Equity Act for the 21st Century (TEA-21) retains these features even though the bulk of funding still goes to highways.

U.S. Clean Air Act: With its legal ability to deny federal road-building funds to jurisdictions out of compliance with air quality standards, the Clean Air Act serves as an ultimate cap on sprawl in U.S. cities. Things have to get pretty bad before this provision is used (as it has been in Atlanta, Georgia), but it does give communities an extra incentive to make walking, biking, and transit use easier.

Livable Communities Initiative: This proposal would fund sprawl-busting strategies like community-centered development, transit, and greenbelts around communities. Related initiatives by states could help, too, such as statewide "smart growth" laws in Maryland, Rhode Island, and Colorado that limit road subsidies and other infrastructure investments outside designated areas.

discount they also give to senior citizens means that seniors who bike to the bakery get a whopping 15 percent off. Restaurants in downtown Allentown, Pennsylvania, give discounts to customers who come on foot.[15] The University of Washington gives free transit passes to students, supporting non-car travel and saving money by avoiding parking construction. In Cincinnati, the Southwest Ohio Regional Transit Authority/Metro cuts bus fares to 50 cents flat systemwide all summer to encourage ridership and cut ozone levels. The flat fare has increased ridership by up to 19 percent on some days, keeping thousands of cars off the road and helping Cincinnati attain compliance with federal ozone standards.[16] Low or even free fares help get more people on transit; along with cutting pollution, this can provide a range of other benefits. When Hasselt (Belgium) decided to provide free transit instead of expanding its road system, the result was an incredible 800 percent increase in transit use; along with construction of more pedestrian and bike paths, this lessened traffic, reduced traffic deaths, increased social activity, attracted business, and even allowed the town to cut taxes.[17] Removing direct disincentives is important, too: laws in some locations (including in Canada, as of late 1999) tax transit benefits such as free bus or train passes from employers.[18] Making transit benefits non-taxable, where they aren't already, will provide more incentive for their use.

Give developers incentives to build compact communities: Developers have a natural tendency to want to build at higher densities, since more compact communities let them sell more housing units with less investment in land. But zoning requirements often won't let developers build higher-density developments, or houses without garages, for instance. Relaxing such requirements can give developers a better incentive to build more affordable and less car-dependent housing. Local governments can assess fees on developers based on how much infrastructure their developments require — mitigation fees, for instance, are used in California and other places. This can be done locally but might better be done on a statewide or even national basis. Tax credits for building in city centers can also help keep communities compact.

Establish a BTU tax and/or raise gasoline taxes: A higher gasoline tax can help compensate for the external costs of cars and support mass transit, which benefits motorists as well as transit users since mass transit can be a cost-effective way to cut gridlock. Transit also provides better transport choices for those who can't afford higher gas taxes. Perhaps the best way to raise gas taxes and do it fairly is to develop transit alternatives first, in anticipation of the increase. First, highway funds can be redirected away from new road-building and into road maintenance and transit; second, higher gas taxes can be phased in over time, raising the tax only a cent or two every few months; and third, the increased gas tax revenues can be used to repair damage done by cars while continuing to fund transit, particularly for low-income and rural

> *"We think the highway system to a large extent has reached the end of its era. The real focus is now trains."*
>
> KEITH KENNEDY, SILICON VALLEY MANUFACTURING GROUP

riders. In addition to raising national gas taxes, we can allow local and regional governments to levy gas and auto use taxes. Quebec, for example, lets cities collect auto user taxes to finance transit. In Montreal, such taxes supply nearly half the revenue for Montreal's Agence Metropolitaine de Transport.[19]

Infrastructure Support

In car-dependent countries, infrastructure spending has gone overwhelmingly to support cars via road-building. To support car divorce, we need to shift that balance. Here are ways to do that.

Freeze construction of new roads and parking lots: In general, we don't need new pavement. Instead, we need to make better use of the pavement we already have. Putting a freeze on building new roads and parking lots is a fiscally sensible and even conservative proposal. Gas taxes and user fees can be used to repair and maintain existing roads, to fund transit, and to repair environmental damage caused by roads and cars. Cutting funds for new roads offers a path away from

"This city is going to hell! That used to be a parking lot."

wasteful pork-barrel projects and helps level the playing field for transit. Outside of developed areas, cutting road funds and placing moratoriums on road building in such places as U.S. National Forests can be a big step in fostering the needed restoration of wildlands.

Put roads on diets: Burcham Road in East Lansing, Michigan, used to be fat. Four lanes wide and full of speeding cars, it frustrated neighbors with noise and safety problems. Then traffic engineer John Matuszak calculated that halving the lanes would still provide enough capacity for the road's traffic, so he put it on a "diet." He trimmed the road to one lane each direction, then added a center turn lane and bike lanes on each side. These changes calmed traffic, cut noise, improved driveway access, and helped walkers and cyclists feel more comfortable. After Burcham Road was successfully slimmed, Matuszak put other East Lansing roads on diets. Other cities — Toronto, Ontario; Kirkland, Washington; and Lewiston, Pennsylvania, among them — have slimmed roads, too.[20] Many road diets drop four-lane arterials to three; some drop four lanes to two. In the process, road space gets re-allocated to walkers and cyclists, making road diets very supportive of those divorcing their cars. The safety improvements benefit motorists, too. A variation on this can be applied to road-widening proposals: instead of widening two-lane roads to four, recommends traffic engineer Walter Kulash, they can in many cases be rebuilt into three-lane "Super-Twos" providing as much capacity but more cheaply and safely. Residential streets as well can become leaner and more economical if allowed to be "skinny." Skinny streets already exist in older neighborhoods, but newer ones have been fattened by hefty minimum width requirements. Dieting in this case consists of changing local standards to decrease minimum widths. Some Oregon communities have dropped width minimums to between 20 and 28 feet from 34 feet. Skinnier streets support walking and cycling by using land more efficiently and cutting distances between places, as well as by reducing car speeds.[21]

Make withdrawals from the asphalt land bank: River Place in Portland, Oregon, a pedestrian and cyclist-oriented mix of apartments, shops, and businesses overlooking the Willamette River, was built in part on a former parking lot.[22] William Warner's Waterplace Park in Providence, Rhode Island, replaced a highway removed from downtown. Roads and parking lots can become housing, new businesses, parks, or gardens, or they can be restored to wild space, depending on the site. Richard Register and Ecocity Builders have depaved and converted parking lots to gardens in various spots near San Francisco Bay. And depaving can be done by any landowner. Richard Hoye tore up his driveway when he went car-free; Jan Lundberg's old driveway is now a vegetable garden.

Add and widen sidewalks and other foot-friendly infrastructure: Local governments can widen sidewalks and narrow travel lanes to create intimate streets. In traditional neighborhoods in Chicago, where sidewalks are provided and buildings are closer together, residents walk for 37 percent of their trips, compared to only three percent in suburban areas.[23] Walkable Communities Inc. further recommends that every home be within a quarter mile (or about half a kilometer) of at least a small area of public space, like a "pocket" park.[24]

Improve bicycle facilities: When Erlangen (Germany) invested in bicycle facilities, bike trips rose from ten to 30 percent of travel in 12 years.[25] A combination of safe roads and an interconnected system of bike routes, lanes, and paths, along with secure and convenient bike parking can go a long way to encourage cycling. And we've got a great infrastructure for bikes out there already, if only there weren't so many cars on it. Local governments can reallocate more of the existing infrastructure to bikes. Some citizen groups have done this themselves by painting their own bike lanes. Edmonton activists, for example, painted a bike lane late at night where one had long been requested but refused by city authorities. Activists have done the same thing in some places in Europe.

> "All you have to do is make it easier to ride a bike than drive a car. People will take it from there."
>
> ELLEN FLETCHER,
> FORMER CITY COUNCIL MEMBER,
> PALO ALTO, CALIFORNIA

Expand, improve, and invest in transit and intercity rail: Curitiba's transit investment has paid off in lower air pollution than in other comparable cities in Brazil, and in enough fare-box revenue to fund public building construction. Portland, Oregon's transit investment has paid off in pollution control and savings on road spending, and helped a vibrant downtown attract hundreds of millions of dollars in private investments.[26] Governments also get congestion control payoffs by investing in transit. Without transit systems in San Francisco, Los Angeles, Chicago, Washington, and New York, over three million additional commuter vehicles might be added altogether to roads in those cities.[27] Without rail transit to and from Manhattan, New York would need 120 new highway lanes and 20 new Brooklyn Bridges to handle the traffic. U.S. taxpayers recover their $15 billion total investment in transit with congestion cost savings alone.[28] Yet the American Public Transportation Association (APTA) has estimated that U.S. transit gets only a one dollar investment for every six dollars in subsidies given to cars.[29] To further benefit from transit, national investments in it can be expanded. In addition, local governments can invest in transit with local taxes and give incentives for private transit services. Converting existing road lanes to dedicated rights-of-way for buses is another way to invest in transit.

Traffic calming islands like these allow bikes through, but stop cars.

Rand Berthaudin, B.E.S.T.

Calm traffic: Traffic calming slows and reduces traffic with a range of techniques. Residential streets are traffic-calmed to form *woonerven* or slow streets in the Netherlands, Germany, and Scandinavia. In the U.K., the government has begun to designate traffic-calmed Home Zones where, as with *woonerven*, streets have lower speed limits, and pedestrians and cyclists have priority over cars. Roundabouts or traffic circles used to calm traffic in Seattle have been so successful there's a waiting list of neighborhoods who want them. Boulder, Colorado, has modified its grid-pattern streets to accommodate walkers and cyclists while limiting through-traffic, with strategic placement of intersection diverters (planted curbs that block intersections to cars but allow bikes and walkers through). Cars still have access to every house in the neighborhood, they just can't speed through it. Other examples of traffic calming devices include neckdowns or chokers (curb extensions that widen sidewalks at intersections) and speed tables (crosswalks raised to sidewalk level, with a gradual ramp up and ramp down to street level on each side, to slow vehicles and allow elderly and disabled to cross streets).[30] Street trees and urban forests can also calm traffic by limiting visual fields, which tends to slow drivers.[31] Traffic calming must be designed with cyclists in mind to avoid blocking cycling routes; poorly designed neckdowns, for instance, can make intersections more dangerous for cyclists.

Reclaim streets: Street reclaiming is what happens when people revert to using streets for their traditional purposes of meeting and exchange, as outdoor living rooms rather than as high-speed hallways. In his book *Street Reclaiming*, David Engwicht points out two ways in which this can happen. The first is psychological reclaiming, where you simply use the street for more non-driving activities — street parties, for instance, or walking kids to school. You can also make physical changes that alter the street's feel without downsizing road space, like hanging banners or adding benches along sidewalks. Psychological reclaiming is usually what Reclaim the Streets actions do, taking over a street for a short time for parties or demonstrations. Physical reclaiming goes one step further and takes road space from cars more permanently, converting it to uses that enhance neighborhood life. Emphasizing that neighborhoods which reclaim their streets must first reduce their driving, Engwicht offers ideas for physical reclaiming like painting a carpet on a portion of the street and furnishing it with chairs to create a community meeting space. Depending on the region, some legal hurdles may need to be jumped to reclaim streets this way and to make the change permanent.

Free cities from cars: Car-free and car-restricted zones can create inviting public spaces like Boston's verdant Southwest Corridor, Boulder's thriving outdoor Pearl Street Mall, or the networks of auto-free streets gracing European cities like Amsterdam and Copenhagen. Closing out cars can make terrific space for people and is often great for business. Several Tokyo shopping districts ban cars on Sundays; when people regain possession of these streets, says one report, an air of carnival prevails.[32] Some U.S. attempts at pedestrian streets have failed, but proper planning can vastly increase their chance of success. "Most European, Asian and

Latin American pedestrian streets are doing just fine," writes planning consultant Patrick Siegman, "and the ones created in the past several decades on most American college campuses are being expanded. A pedestrian zone at Stanford University, for example, has gone from three miles up to five miles closed to private cars." Elements that make a pedestrian street successful, says Siegman, are excellent transit access (such as a transit hub), plenty of housing (like apartments above shops or nearby), intimate proportions (e.g., three- to five-story buildings lining narrow streets), major destinations (for instance, Santa Monica's zoning allows movie theaters on its pedestrian mall, but not elsewhere), cooperative management and promotion, and a solid urban growth boundary around the city.[33] Increasing such car-free streets over time can contribute to vibrant car-free city centers. Some cities, and even countries, in Europe have begun organizing car-free days. When more than 30 French cities declared a car-free day for city centers on September 22, 1998, traffic in Paris dropped 15 percent even though only about four percent of city roads were designated car-free "green streets" for the day.[34] The event was so successful, France repeated it in 1999, and the idea has spread to other European locations.

> "You can't say any longer the car has liberated mankind. In fact, the car has ... strangled ... our urban areas ... increasingly in the cities the car will have to be phased out."
>
> JACK MUNDY, IN JULIAN PETTIFER AND NIGEL TURNER, *AUTOMANIA*

Free parks and natural areas from cars: Asked about pressures on U.S. national parks and the way people are "loving them to death," Interior Secretary Bruce Babbitt said, "The people aren't the problem, it's the cars." Highly visited parks like Yellowstone, Yosemite, and the Grand Canyon have studied ways to reduce car traffic. Perhaps farthest along is Grand Canyon, where a shuttle system has operated since 1974 and a light rail line is planned from Tusayan, outside the park's southern border, to the Canyon's south rim. Once the line is completed, visitors will leave cars at Tusayan (car-free visitors can get to the park via bus, which connects with Amtrak) and take light rail to stops in the park; alternatively fueled shuttles will go from those stops to points along the rim, for those who don't walk or cycle. To reduce motor vehicle and road impacts in a broader range of natural areas, groups like Wildlands Center for Preventing Roads (Wildlands CPR) have led efforts to encourage the removal and revegetation of roads in public wildlands as a means of ecosystem restoration. There are also movements to make urban parks — among the last areas to admit cars in the early 20th century — auto-free again. In New York City, Transportation Alternatives has campaigned to turn Prospect Park and Central Park into car-free havens. There's also been discussion of making San Francisco's Golden Gate Park auto-free.

Group Support

Advocacy groups can help those divorcing their cars in a rainbow of ways. Some, like Toronto's Advocacy for Respect for Cyclists, offer referrals to legal assistance when motorists run roughshod over non-motorists' rights. Others, like Transportation Alternatives in New York City, offer member discounts at participating bike-supportive businesses. A few, like the Bicycle Transportation Alliance in Portland, Oregon, offer services such as lending bike trailers to members. If you get involved in advocating transportation reform, several good general transport reform groups can give you support. Among them are Car Busters Magazine and Resource Center, the Surface Transportation Policy Project in the U.S., Sustrans in the U.K., and B.E.S.T. and Transportation Options in Canada (you'll find more listings in "Selected Resources"). You can also get help from neighborhood groups, which generally support reductions in traffic to improve neighborhood life. Also, you can get help from e-mail listserves such as < CarFree@one.list >, where participants trade car-free travel tips and encouragement. In addition, the group techniques and programs described below focus on helping people live less car-dependent lives.

Transportation demand management agencies and programs: Commuter Connections, formed by the Metropolitan Washington Council of Governments to cut pollution and congestion, helps commuters switch to walking, bicycling, ridesharing, vanpooling, telecommuting, and transit use. The GO Boulder office supports car-free travel options such as walking, cycling, shuttles, and buses. Metropolitan areas across North America have similar transportation demand management (TDM) programs, as do some smaller communities. The San Geronimo Valley Healthy Start Collaborative, in a semi-rural part of Marin County, California, formed GO GERONIMO in 1996. Within three years, it was offering residents help with ridesharing, holding bike repair classes, organizing community bike rides, installing bike racks, and working on establishing a community-based shuttle service. TDM offices have formed on some university campuses; Cornell University, for instance, started a TDM program when campus congestion and parking demand began to overtax streets and parking lots. Along with increasing parking fees, Cornell bought transit passes for employees and discounted parking for carpoolers. The program cut staff and faculty traffic by 26 percent in the first year, and saved over $6 million — mostly in avoided parking facility costs — from 1991 to 1998.[35]

David Engwicht's traffic reduction strategies: In 1994, David Engwicht realized that "car trips are packaging — a 'waste' we produce in getting access to 'products'" and that traffic might be cut the same way recycling has cut trash. Based on that insight, he devised the "5 R's of Traffic Reduction," with three strategies for households and two for neighborhoods or communities:

- **replace** car trips with walking, cycling, and transit;
- **remove** unnecessary trips by batching errands, sharing rides, using the phone, or getting deliveries;
- **reduce** trip lengths by shopping and/or working locally;
- **reuse** saved space by reallocating and reclaiming streets;

- **reciprocate** for mutual benefit with walking buses, car sharing clubs, bike-maintenance clinics, transit passes, and shop-and-work-local incentives.

Engwicht also fashioned a Car Activity Diary to help households cut car use without cutting back on activities. To use the diary, you list car trips taken in a day, then figure how they might be replaced, removed, or reduced — and whether that would be easy, moderately easy, or hard to do. Groups testing the diary in Canada and Australia estimated potential driving reductions at 49 to 80 percent and figured 25 to 30 percent of them would be easy. Engwicht also developed a Traffic Reduction Kit — the kit's first trial helped participants in Brisbane (Australia) reduce car use by 34 percent — and a Traffic Reduction Treaty process in which neighborhoods sign agreements to cut car use and "put less traffic in each other's neighborhood." This both supports less driving and allows neighborhoods to reclaim street space.[36]

Global Action Plan for the Earth (GAP) EcoTeams: GAP EcoTeams help households cut resource use. Each EcoTeam brings four to eight households together for four months to discuss reducing garbage, water and energy use, driving, and overall consumption. Then participants invite neighbors into the program. For a $35 materials fee, each household gets program support materials and a 100-page workbook including action suggestions. Transportation examples include steps for forming a carpool, suggestions for walking and biking instead of driving, and ideas on how to cut driving on vacation. Teams also get before- and after-measurements of their resource use. The roughly 900 teams that formed between 1991 and 1999 reduced their fuel use an average of 15 percent. EcoTeam graduates also save money by cutting driving and resource use, averaging $200 to $400 per household per year. And the support they provide fosters a deeper sense of community among participants. EcoTeam members in Portland taught each other how to keep their bicycles in good condition and how to find local transit schedules on the Internet. EcoTeams have been successful enough at reducing resource use that municipally-funded teams have been started in U.S. cities as diverse as Kansas City, Chattanooga, and Philadelphia.

Auto-Free Orange County's "lifestyle counseling": Jay Laessi and Mark Petersen cofounded an organization to advocate car-free living in one of the world's bastions of car-dependency: Orange County, California. Built around the premise that going car-free can be a high-quality lifestyle choice, Auto-Free Orange County has over 200 members, and it's growing. The group offers a range of services to members, including a kit listing local walking, biking, and transit opportunities; a regular newsletter describing auto-free vacations as well as Orange County neighborhoods that meet the group's nine criteria for supporting auto-free lifestyles (housing, employment, shopping, schools, entertainment, medical services, a gym, parks, and a walker-friendly environment must all be within 20 minutes by bike, bus, or foot); and monthly meetings, for starters. Then there's auto-free "lifestyle counseling," complimentary for every member. In lifestyle counseling sessions, new members are asked a series of questions, such as "Where do you live? Work? Go for entertainment? Social life? Would you like to relocate?" Based on the answers, the counselors determine how feasible it is for members to go car-free, or whether they should choose car-lite instead. Either way, they're advised about ways to lessen car-dependence. So far, about half the participants have been good candidates for a car-free lifestyle. "I'm not into being a martyr. We don't suggest going car-free unless it's easy," says Laessi. "I'd like the auto-free lifestyle to be like a resort vacation." The group also supports car-free travel through its magazine program: members collect donated once-read magazines and place them on buses for riders to read. It's a small way to improve the image and experience of bus rides, and each magazine sports a sticker with contact information for Auto-Free Orange County. Says Laessi: "I wish we could offer drink service and hot towels, but we're not there yet."

A Few Last Words on Support

With any divorce, finding support as you establish a new way of life can show you that you're not alone. It's the same when you divorce your car. The diverse opportunities to get support for a car divorce show that even though our world seems overrun by automobiles, there are groups of people who want to turn that tide. Hooking up with them and pursuing the programs or advocating the policies described in this chapter is bound to make divorce from your car at least a little easier, certainly better supported, and maybe even like a resort vacation.

CHAPTER 17

Play the Field:
The Spice of Transportation Variety

"Carpooling, cycling, transit, telecommuting, vanpooling, walking ...
so many choices! Luckily, there are as many travel alternatives as
there are reasons to make the switch."

GO GREEN CHOICES BROCHURE

"WHICH LIFE WOULD YOU RATHER HAVE?" Mark Fenton asked the crowd at the 1997 Pedestrian Conference of America. "The life of Mark #1 or Mark #2?" Mark #1, he explained — playing the part in his jacket and tie — had two cars in the garage, a job 40 minutes away, and a stress-filled highway commute at least five days a week. His job and commute left him little time to walk or get much physical activity, and he had high blood pressure. Mark #1 then stripped off his tie, jacket, and slacks to reveal gym shorts and a t-shirt underneath, instantly becoming Mark #2. This Mark, in contrast, telecommuted two or three days a week and dressed accordingly, spent time he would have lost to car commutes on walks with his kids, and walked on errands in his pedestrian-friendly community. He commuted by transit the other days, walking an energizing 15 minutes between the transit station and his office. "Which Mark would you rather be?" Fenton asked the crowd. All hands voted for Mark #2. Those present agreed with Fenton's point: the life that incorporates walking and variety in transportation is often of far better quality than one that doesn't. Married to automobiles, we've given up that variety, and trying to get all our transport needs met with cars leads overwhelmingly to dysfunctional transportation. Variety, on the other hand, is the spice of car-free and car-lite life, and that's what this chapter's about.

Combining Travel Techniques

Combining travel modes sometimes takes planning, but once that's done, it can bring a convenience that rivals or surpasses using a car. Here are a few ways that combining techniques can help reduce or replace driving.

Combining walking and transit: Car-free Richard Hoye of Bethesda, Maryland, likes to tell friends, "I can walk to France." He lives in an older, compact part of town less than a mile from a Metro station. He can walk out his door, walk ten or 15 minutes to the station, hop on a train and, within minutes, get to Washington's National Airport to catch a flight to France, or anywhere else for that matter. This combination of walking and transit connects him to the rest of the world, and it can easily connect everyone else living along the Metro line. Even if you're not traveling the world, a good combination of walking and transit can make travel a delight, particularly in walkable cities with good, frequent transit stops. Since the average person will walk no more than about ten minutes to get to transit, frequent spacing of stops is important (though in places where it's not available, the longer walks are great exercise opportunities).[1]

Portland, Oregon's walkable downtown has a major bus mall and several light rail stops at its heart; walkable regional centers in Portland cluster around transit stops. Boston's Southwest Corridor combines a pedestrian-friendly linear park above-ground with transit lines and stations beneath. Combining walking and transit makes these communities more livable. Dorothea Hass says a combination of walking and transit has been her travel mainstay for at least eight years of car-free living in Boston, where over 90 percent of transit passengers get to stops or stations on foot and 70 percent of commuters use this combination to get in and out of downtown.[2] In the transit-rich neighborhoods where her family has lived, "we are not at all unique," she adds. A combination of walking and transit has also helped many of her friends and neighbors to go car-free.

Combining bicycling and transit: This combination can help you cover distances with freedom and flexibility, since with a bike your destination can be beyond walking distance from the transit stop and, if you miss the bus, you can always bike. When I lived in northern California, Sonoma County Transit helped my car-free travel because its buses had bike racks. The racks were easy to use: just lift the bike up about 18 inches into the rack, secure the front wheel, get on the bus, and go. By the second or third time I did this, I could secure the bike in the rack and be on the bus in less than 20 seconds. An increasing number of bus systems now use racks like these. As of 1998, about 20 percent of U.S. transit buses carried bike racks, and the number was growing. In the Seattle area, King County Metro's 1,300 buses carry over 40,000 passengers with bikes each month. Rail transit and subways sometimes take bikes on board, too. When Caltrain added onboard bike racks to some train cars on its passenger line between San Francisco and Silicon Valley, ridership jumped enough to repay the initial investment within six months.[3] Taking bicycles on trains is common in Europe, where in places like Denmark, large bicycle symbols stenciled on train cars show where bicyclists board. Some transit systems require bike users to obtain a permit before boarding with bikes

Sportworks

Bus bike racks like these are a great aid to car divorce; this one holds two bikes at a time.

although, as bikes-on-transit programs have become more common, permit requirements have often been dropped. Check with your local system to see what the
requirements may be.

Good bicycle access to transit stations, bicycle ferry programs, and secure bike
parking — especially bike lockers at stations — also help. In Seattle, the Bicycle
Alliance of Washington encourages more people to bike, in part by helping them get
locker assignments at transit stations. Another option for Seattle area bike-and-rid-
ers: combining cycling with vanpools. As of January 2000, 30 percent of King County
Metro Rideshare's fleet of vanpools — 225 out of 700 vans — had bike racks on
them. If vanpool riders request a bicycle rack, Metro will install one free. Racks can
hold two or four bikes.[4] Folding bikes also make the cycling-transit combination easy
since they can usually be folded quickly and carried easily on to trains or buses. Kent
Peterson combined a folding bike and a vanpool (without a bike rack) to commute
to work in the New York City area. "It worked great," he writes. An entire magazine
is devoted to traveling this way: *A to B*, published in the U.K.

The Bikestations now sprouting near transit stops along the west coast may be
the ultimate aid to combining bicycling and transit. They offer valet bike parking,
bike lockers, showers, changing rooms, restrooms, bike rentals including electric
and folding bikes, repairs, bicycle and transit route information including maps,
cafe refreshments, and more. The first Bikestation to open, in Long Beach,
California, also holds bike safety and maintenance classes and has a trial bike loan-
er program for commuters who want to try the cycling-transit combination.
Building the Long Beach Bikestation cost around $125,000, the equivalent of about
six car spaces in a typical parking garage. Within 18 months of its 1998 opening, it
was parking 1,500 bikes a month, and that number was increasing by ten percent
a month. Similar Bikestations have since opened in Berkeley, Palo Alto, and some
Los Angeles locations.

Combining local with long-distance travel: Combining local with long-distance
travel modes can help make trips car-free from door-to-door. When taking a long-
distance trip by train or plane, we often think of driving for the trip's first leg, but it
doesn't have to be that
way. For instance, inter-
modal train stations in
cities like Toronto,
Chicago, and Washington,
D.C., bring together buses,
subways, and trains, gathering people from local

About 2,000 cyclists a day
bring their bikes on board this
Caltrain line between San
Francisco and Silicon Valley.

Caltrain, CA.

areas and sending them off on long-distance trips, or vice versa. In some locations, walking and bike trails lead to intermodal hubs as well. In Maryland, the 14.5 mile (23.3 km) BWI Trail links communities near the Baltimore Washington International Airport not only with the airport itself but also with an Amtrak station, a light rail station, Patapxco State Park, and the Baltimore and Annapolis Trail.[5] In Worcester, Massachusetts, the rehabilitation of Union Station has linked rail, bus, taxi, and airport shuttle services and has improved bike and walking access to the station area and downtown.[6] And the Washington, D.C., area is just one of several spots in North America that have train service to airports. Others include St. Louis, Chicago, Baltimore, Philadelphia, and Boston. Most North American airports are served by transit buses if they aren't served by rail.

Combining cohousing and car-sharing: In cohousing developments, residents live in their own houses or units but share certain common areas, like gardens, kitchen, dining room, or a meeting/party area. Cohousing aims both to reduce use of materials and to increase a sense of community. Cohousing groups share appliances like lawn-mowers and coffee urns, so why not cars? In fact, at least one cohousing group in North America — Greyrock Cohousing in Fort Collins, Colorado — has begun to discuss starting a formal car-sharing program, and other cohousing groups share cars and rides on an informal basis. Dana Snyder-Grant of New View Cohousing in Acton, Massachusetts, notices that "cohousing makes it natural to share rides — the more spontaneous interaction between people living in our cohousing group makes this easier." Maryann Jones of Southside Park Cohousing reports this as well. "There has never been a time when I have needed a car and one hasn't been forthcoming from other cohousing residents," she writes. "And I have shared my car with others on a regular basis." Robyn Williams of Pinakarri Community in Fremantle (Australia) writes that residents share cars within her cohousing group as well. "At the moment it's nothing more than an informal arrangement at the time of borrowing," she writes, "but as old cars die I hope people won't replace them and that we will use each other's." Just as cohousing groups might incorporate formal car-sharing into their plans, co-neighborhoods (groups of neighbors who decide they want to share more resources among each other) are also a natural for car-sharing.

Combining car-sharing and car rentals with other modes: If you have access to car rental services or a car-sharing organization, you can save a lot of money as well as wear and tear on the planet if you cut your car ownership to one or none, switch to walking and bicycling for more of your trips, then rent or reserve a car for only those times you need it. You can keep a list of "car errands," then rent a car and do them all on one day. You can also rent special-purpose vehicles instead of having to own them, as Warren Leon and Michael Brower point out in *The Consumer's Guide to Effective Environmental Choices.* "Television ads notwithstanding, most of those who own four-wheel drive all-terrain vehicles rarely drive through blinding rainstorms on muddy hillsides," they write. "If you plan on going camping in the outback two or three times a year, consider renting a four-wheel drive vehicle for those few occasions."[7] Using this strategy might also demonstrate that you don't "need" a car as much as you thought. When my parents went from two cars to one, they expected to use rental cars and taxis in place of having a second vehicle. But, says my mother, "we've only had to rent cars once or twice a year, which really surprised us. And in six years, we've never had to use a taxi."

Develop a Transportation Menu

Don't expect to replace a car with just one other means of transport; instead, play the field! If you want to live car-free, the best strategy is usually a combination of strategies. "If you just substitute one mode for another, you're going to fail," says car-free Ryan McKenzie. With a variety of options, though, you can meet a range of travel needs without using a car. For most people, walking works well for trips up to a mile or two, and can give you painless exercise as you travel; bicycling easily fits trips up to five or ten miles, and gives you independence; transit (or some sort of shared transport) works well for longer journeys; and telecommunications will give you access without requiring mobility.

Phil Smith, pedestrian and bicycle coordinator for Missoula, Montana, calls this kind of choice a transportation menu. Instead of assuming that travel means driving, we can look at a menu of choices whenever we plan to go somewhere. One transportation menu par excellence comes from the Kids and Transportation Program of the Greater Portland Council of Governments in Portland, Maine. Their fold-out map "A Kid's Guide to Getting Around Greater Portland" lists ways kids can get around town without needing a parental lift: two local bus services, two shuttle services, two intercity buses, a ferry, walking trails, and trails for bikes, wheelchairs, in-line skates, and skateboards. The map highlights and color-codes trails and transit routes, making it easy to see how kids can cross town without a car. It also shows locations of schools, libraries, museums, parks, bike shops, shopping centers, and

By permission of Kirk Anderson

theaters; lists police and safety phone numbers; and has plenty of answers to the perpetual kid complaint, "There's nothing to do!" It's part of what gets a high proportion of local students to walk to school and may give Portland fewer soccer parents per capita than anywhere in the U.S.

Portland got funding to produce this map from the Maine Department of Transportation. They encourage other communities to follow their example, and can give tips to anyone wanting to pursue a similar project on a city-wide basis. If you don't have funding support, you can develop a simple map like this. Make it a project for your kids, or for the local Boy Scout, Girl Scout, or Boys and Girls Club. Start by getting or making a copy of a basic map of your community. Then make a list of the places kids might want to go — schools, playgrounds, libraries, museums, sports fields, swimming pools, clubhouses, etc. — and mark those locations on the map. Next, find out where the bike trails, walking trails, and bus routes are in your community, especially the ones that lead to these marked locations. Draw those on the map as well, make copies (color ones if appropriate), and you should have a mapped menu that shows your community's non-auto transportation choices. This sort of transportation menu can be a fun project for kids and ultimately can help to free a lot of overburdened parent chauffeurs.

Even if you don't make a map like Portland's, you can develop a written transportation menu that can help you travel car-free. Start by listing your area's existing transport support systems. Are there walking paths, bike trails, transit lines? Is there a rideshare service, or car-sharing? Then figure out where these services are relative to where you are and where you want to go. Find all the transit stops within walking distance of your house, for instance, and list the destinations to which they'll transport you. You can use John Schubert's Circle Game (see sidebar) to help determine what's within walking distance of your home or workplace, and what's within biking distance. Add a list of your own access and mobility tools: bike, bike trailer, telephone, e-mail, etc.

You can expand a transportation menu beyond the transport means covered in this book. Running, kayaking, cross-country skiing, and in-line skating have all been used as transportation and commute methods. Sandra Harting of Toivola, Michigan, a distance runner and university researcher, carpools in the morning, then routinely jogs home from the campus where she works, some 21 miles from her home. She also (literally) runs errands on foot. Kayaking is popular along North America's west coast, with major cities on picturesque bays. Vancouver, Seattle, and San Francisco all have kayak commuters. A few folks now travel on electric scooters with brand names like Zappy, Zip, and Transport, oversized skateboards with steering handles that can zip along at up to 12 miles an hour and travel ten to 20 miles between charges. The scooters have enough range for some commutes and many in-town errands, and can be folded up and taken on transit.

Keep variety in mind as you complete your menu, since the more variety of mobility support you can access, the easier it will be to divorce your car. You might not always need a menu list, but it's a good way to get in the habit of remembering non-car transportation choices. I put mine on my wall where it reminds me of all the options I have for travel and access to things. You can also add to your menu over time if you learn of more ways to travel car-free. Then, when it comes time to use your transportation menu, ask a few key questions:

(?) ***Do I really need to take this trip?*** This is a question made more necessary by the fact that driving can sometimes be a little too habitual. One man who wanted to break his driving habit decided to tape a note to himself on the driver's side door of his car that asked, "Do you really need to take this trip?" Dianne Patrick of Marquette, Michigan, has done something similar with her annual New Year's resolution to use her car less. "Every day I get up and ask myself if I have to use the car, and if the answer is no, it stays in the garage," she says. If you ask: "Is this trip necessary?" and the answer is no, great! You don't have to go anywhere and can do something else instead. If, on the other hand, the answer is yes, move on to the next question.

(?) ***How can I get where I want to go without using a car?*** Your transportation menu, plus the information and suggestions provided throughout Part 3, should give you a variety of ways to answer this question. Still, there may be times when you ask it and come up with no other way to get where you need to go without driving alone in an internal combustion car. It happens, and sometimes it happens more often because our current system caters so much to the car. Then you can ask:

(?) ***What changes would allow me to take this trip without using a car?*** Some of these changes might be collective, getting into the realm of advocacy and the types of policies explored in Chapter 16. Better land use, safer and slower streets, more support for transit, less subsidization of highways, car-free city centers: these can all help us win a collective divorce and move beyond the problems of car-dependency. But you might also be able to respond to this question with individual changes — location and lifestyle choices that you can make on your own.

Location, Location, Location — and Other Lifestyle Factors

What are the top three aids to divorcing your car? The answer may be the same as your realtor's favorite phrase: location, location, location. Location might be the main factor determining how easy it will be for you to divorce your car and how far you can take that divorce. Living in downtown San Francisco, John Holtzclaw doesn't need a car. Living in downtown Boston, Dorothea Hass doesn't need a car. Location helps Michael Rairden, too: living car-free in Montreal, he says, "I never feel marooned by not having a car." Attitude is part of this, too, he believes. He thinks automatically of walking for short trips: "If it's somewhere I can walk to in 15 minutes or less, I just start putting one foot in front of the other and walk there." In each of these locations, people can walk to stores, restaurants, cultural events, and other services nearby. They also have access to good transit services and can therefore easily reach both local and distant destinations. "Proximity, both to work and transit, is very important," says Jill Kruse, who went car-free in 1992 while living in San Francisco. She adds that this location "made the decision to give up my car easy."

Some locations make divorcing a car harder. Even a lot of car-free folks say they don't think car-free living is feasible in a rural or semi-rural area. And there are many places where lack of services makes mobility without a car difficult. Yet there are people who've done it, and in some rural or semi-rural areas, combinations of such things as electric bicycles, working at home, telecommunications, and/or occasional long-distance bus or taxi service might be enough. Steve Clark's household is car-lite in rural Cushing, Wisconsin: he and his wife and four children have one car, and Steve himself doesn't drive. He commutes 13 miles each way to work by bike, even in winter, and gets transport variety from different bikes, bike trailers, and a pedal car. Steve Clark's choices show one way to approach a car divorce if you're in a location that doesn't support car-free transportation very well. There are other things you can do, too, if your location and lifestyle don't seem to mesh with divorcing your car.

> "We shop at neighborhood grocery stores and we get to know the merchants, and if we need to buy something and we find we don't have enough money, they just say, oh, you know, take it and pay me next time."
>
> DOROTHEA HASS,
> BOSTON, MASSACHUSETTS, CAR-FREE

Moving: Our society is a transient one. The average U.S. resident moves 12 times.[8] That's 12 opportunities in a lifetime to choose a less car-dependent place to live. Chances are you'll move some time in the next five or so years. When you do, consider looking for a new location that supports a divorce from your car: close to bus routes or rail lines, close enough to walk or bike to work or shops. If everyone did this the next time they moved, we could dramatically reduce the number of cars and vehicle miles traveled in a very short period of time.

Purchasing a home within walking distance of a train station helped David and Jane Henshaw of Somerset (England) go car-free, even with work as animal sitters that required lots of travel (their other major tool was a pair of folding bicycles).[9] A Boston-area cohousing group made sure to choose a location for their cohousing that was close to commuter rail service.[10] "Whenever I move, I choose a residence where I can get around without a car," says Brian Newman. "Often that requires no sacrifice — the neighborhood that I want to live in turns out to be the place that best fits a car-free lifestyle." In their walkable Washington, D.C., neighborhood, with schools, library, community center, stores, and the Metro all near home, Ellen Jones and her family have been able to live car-free with ease. "During the Blizzard of '96 we were never without bread, milk, or videotapes because we could walk to goods and services," writes Ellen.[11] If you're planning to move, the questions below can help you assess how well a new home or community might support car-free travel.

(?) Can you easily walk, bike, or take transit to work? This is important: even though work trips constitute only 20 percent of our travel, they tend to be the least discretionary — and other travel decisions tend to follow from whether or not we drive to work.

(?) Does your employer, or do other community employers, offer bicycle commuting support, carpooling, vanpooling, and/or telecommuting programs?

(?) What services, stores, schools, and other facilities are within walking distance (whatever that distance may be for you) of your home / your job site?

(?) What's within biking distance, and are the routes near your potential new home comfortably bikable? Also check to see whether bikes are allowed on transit, and ask for a local bike map.

(?) Where's the nearest transit (bus, light rail) stop, and is it within a 15-minute walk from your home? What areas does the transit system cover, and does it reach places you'll want to go, like your job site, schools, shops, medical services, sports stadiums, theaters, libraries, or parks? Check to see also if it links with other transport services, like passenger train stations or airports; if it operates past midnight and/or before 7 a.m.; and if there is a transit map or guide available.

(?) Are there additional services such as long-distance train service, car-sharing, car rentals, paratransit, taxi service, a ride matching service, etc.?

(?) Is the community compact and does it have plans to stay that way? Does it have other features that support car-free travel, like car-free streets or parks or an urban growth boundary?

"My boyfriend sold his car before moving to DC with me ... when I made the suggestion, he admitted that he had never considered it, but the combination of our future circumstances — moving to a city with good transit and horrible parking — and the fact that I've been an advocate of car-free living, enabled him to visualize that it could be done. He's now happily car-free and glad to be without the burden."

JILL KRUSE, WASHINGTON, D.C., CAR-FREE

You can also use the Circle Game (see sidebar) to help you focus on how well a location might support divorcing your car. And find out what sort of support for non-car transport exists in the local government. If there's a bike coordinator, local transit coordinator, or other staff position(s) to support these alternatives, the community is investing in non-auto travel. Look also at what sort of support for non-car transport exists among residents. A bicycle, pedestrian, or transit advocacy group can hold local agencies and elected officials accountable and make sure non-car travel gets real attention and support from government.

Simplifying and slowing down: Ryan McKenzie considers going car-free a core component of what he calls a "lower-mileage lifestyle." Driving less, traveling less, and consuming less come "as a package deal," he says. "I don't think you can be car-free and live exactly as you might if you were a car owner. While this necessarily means that life will be different, it doesn't at all follow that it will be worse. I like

The Circle Game: How to Reduce your Driving

Thanks to John Schubert, who devised the original version of this game when working with an EcoTeam in Bend, Oregon.

1. Find your neighborhood on the map.
2. Place the point of a divider compass on the approximate location of your home.
3. Draw a circle with a two-mile radius with the compass.
4. Now find the places that you regularly visit and circle them or mark them with a highlighter. Include your workplace, bank, grocery store, gym, school, place of worship, movie theaters, parks, the library, and any other place you visit at least once every two weeks.
5. Note how many of these places fall within the circle.
6. Choose one of the places that falls within the circle and commit to walking, biking, or taking transit to it instead of driving every time you go.
7. Every week, every two weeks, or every month (depending on how fast you want to go), commit to walking, biking, or taking transit to another location from within the circle. Continue adding locations until you routinely use alternatives to the auto for getting to every location within a two-mile radius of your home or workplace.

living a low-mileage, low-throughput lifestyle, and making that choice, I think I live more completely, more deeply." A lot of people who live car-lite or car-free echo the sentiment that less driving can lead to a life that's simpler, more relaxed, and less dominated by material goods. Loree Devery, for instance, likes being part of Carsharing Portland instead of owning a second car because "I just don't want one more *thing*, and a car is just another *thing* to have to take care of."

If you long to abandon a fast-paced, high-consumption lifestyle, cutting back on driving can help. By choosing to divorce your car, you step away from the rat race, move at a slower pace. You get more exercise, you have more direct contact with neighbors and people from other walks of life, and you think twice about buying lots of extra stuff when you aren't using a one- or two-ton car to haul it around. Likewise, choosing a more relaxed pace of life can support a car divorce. If it's hard for you to choose a location that reduces your need for a car, think about choosing a lifestyle that will do so. Or do both.

People who go car-lite or car-free tend to be more efficient with errands, and that can help simplify their lives. Sometimes they end up with more time by doing so. "Once you make a decision to do without a car, you begin to prioritize your time differently," writes Steve Clark. "If you are going to make a trip somewhere, it's going to take some effort, so you make sure ahead of time it's something you really want to do, something with real importance or meaning. Too many of us spend 90 percent of our leisure time running here and there, rarely feeling good about it. Consequently, people who don't drive probably have more time to do the things they really want to do."

8. Choose one of the places that falls outside of the two-mile radius, and commit to finding a closer alternative. Example: If your grocery store is outside the two-mile radius, change to a grocery store that is inside the radius.

9. See how many of the places outside a two-mile radius from your home you can replace with an alternative closer to home, ideally within your circle.

10. Experiment with expanding your circle or using concentric circles to determine places within walking distance and biking distance from your home. For example, if you decide to walk to all places within a mile, and bike to all places within four miles, draw circles with those radii on your map and identify all the walkable and bikable destinations within them.

11. When you move, draw a two-mile circle around potential new homes to help you find a new location based on its proximity to services, work, and school.

12. When looking for new services or a new job, use the circle technique to help you find services or jobs closest to your home.

With a lifestyle shift away from driving and toward simpler, more local options, we can also shift dollars away from subsidizing a monogamous relationship with the car to supporting a variety of travel choices. When I think about this I envision, for instance, replacing gasoline stations with true service stations for all manner of traveler, providing services to walkers, cyclists, and transit vehicles. Service stations that sell food already do serve pedestrians and cyclists; add socks, bandaids, and spare tubes for bike tires, and they become multimodal. Shifts like this have already begun in places like the Missouri communities along the 233 mile (375 kilometer) Katy Trail. The trail crosses nine counties along the Missouri River between St. Charles and Sedalia and is used by as many as 300,000 people each year, providing economic sustenance for small towns that have sprouted bed-and-breakfast inns, cafes, and bike rental/repair stations along the trail.

> "Car-freedom helps to move our lives towards simplicity ... We don't have to earn much money so we can focus more on job satisfaction rather than salaries ... And at the end of the day, we're content that our ecological footprint was lighter than if we had been driving."
>
> ANGELA BISCHOFF AND TOOKER GOMBERG, TORONTO, CAR-FREE

Try a Trial Separation

Since divorce can be scary after a long relationship, you might not want to jump into divorce from a car. Ease into it instead with a trial separation. One way to start is by getting rid of a second or third car; those extra cars cost in terms of dollars, health, and quality of life. Use some of the money you save to get a new bike, take transit, and take a taxi or rent a car when absolutely necessary. It's likely you'll still have cash left over. Then work on reducing your use of, and perhaps ultimately selling, the remaining car. Take easy steps first, like walking to the nearest store occasionally. Once you feel comfortable with the easy steps, pick something that might require a little more investment of time or money — for instance, buying and using a transit pass, an electric motor for your bike, a bike trailer, or a folding bike. Look at methods of group support and consider using one of those to help you on your way.

You might want to try your trial separation on a weekend first, when your schedule may be more flexible. Then, again, with careful planning, try it on a week day. Perhaps you can designate a day a week to go car-free. Richard Hoye followed a gradual process like this and ended up car-free. When he started, he says, "I wanted to see if I could take care of all my needs without a car for one full day." First, he did a trial walk to the nearest subway station and located closer bus stops that could take him to the subway in case he had packages to carry. "I went through the experience of learning how to use the buses, and of getting comfortable with the ten- to

A Few Good Places to Live Car-Free in North America

Even in car-dependent North America, there are cities and towns with features that make car divorce relatively easy. Listed below are just a few of those. Most of these places have walkable downtowns, good transit, bicycle-friendly streets or bike paths, and access to long-distance trains, among other things.

- Boston, Massachusetts: auto-free streets and corridors; extensive transit; excellent advocacy support for walking, from WalkBoston; served by Amtrak.

- Boulder, Colorado: urban growth boundary; pedestrian mall downtown; GO Boulder office supports non-car transport; traffic-calmed neighborhoods; excellent bike path network and bike map.

- Chicago, Illinois: good transit; some fuel-cell buses; restored Union Station is an Amtrak hub; great bicycling support; location-efficient mortgages available; city-wide Walking School Bus program.

- Davis, California: growth control measures have kept city relatively compact; extensive support for bicycling; transit that connects to nearby state capital, Sacramento; Amtrak station.

- Eugene, Oregon: Amtrak station; extensive river bike path; support for bicycling; home to several bicycle enterprises, including Burley Trailers, Bike Friday, and the Center for Appropriate Transport.

- Madison, Wisconsin: walkable downtown; miles of multi-use trails and greenways; year-round support for bicycling; good transit connections.

- Montreal, Quebec: excellent transit; compact and transit-oriented land use; excellent bicycling advocacy group, Le Monde à Bicyclette; bicycle cargo delivery and car-sharing available.

15-minute walk," he says. "In the past, I would have driven if I had to go 15 minutes." His one car-free day worked well enough that it soon became one day a week, and then more. "It took me about a year of gradually increasing it from one day a week, to two days, to three," he says, "and finally it was weeks and then months at a time that I had not driven the car."

Plan ahead for your car-free day: get bus or train schedules ready, pump up your bike tires, or just dust off your most comfortable pair of walking shoes. Was this a day on which you'd planned to do errands? Phone the stores you've thought of visiting and see if they deliver. Better to have a delivery service drop goods by on its normal route than for you to make a special trip. If you give yourself permission to use the car in case of emergency, try to make your definition of "emergency" a narrow one. If you find yourself in a real emergency, you'll probably want to call for your community's publicly supported emergency vehicles anyway.

"Once I got rid of my car, I found I had to be creative in getting around, but it wasn't impossible. Even in the suburbs."

HANK GOLDSTEIN,
FREDERICK, MARYLAND, CAR-LITE

- 🚲 New York City: great advocacy groups, such as Transportation Alternatives and Right of Way; high density living; extensive transit; Amtrak station; 60 percent of the population is car-free.

- 🚲 Portland, Oregon: urban growth boundary; transit-oriented development; extensive bus and light rail transit; excellent support for bicycling; active walking advocacy group; car-sharing available.

- 🚲 San Francisco Bay Area: extensive public transit; transit carries bikes; served by Amtrak; areas of transit-oriented development; excellent advocacy groups; bicycle cargo delivery available.

- 🚲 Seattle, Washington: Amtrak station; extensive system of bikeways and multi-use trails; good support from transportation demand management agency of King County.

- 🚲 Toronto, Ontario: excellent transit; compact downtown and transit-oriented land use; excellent support for bicycling; home of world's only choir on bikes.

- 🚲 Vancouver, British Columbia: good transit; transit-oriented developments; good support for bicycling; excellent transport reform advocacy group, B.E.S.T.

- 🚲 Victoria, British Columbia: compact, walkable downtown; bicycle cargo delivery available; excellent transit; good bicycling support.

- 🚲 Washington, D.C.: restored Union Station forms a hub for Amtrak; excellent rail transit system; good support from transportation demand management agency, Commuter Connections.

Nearly every community has emergency vehicles and, short of that, most communities have taxis. "Owning a car for the (hopefully) rare emergency strikes me as just plain silly," writes Kent Peterson. In 13 years of living car-free, he can remember only two emergencies and neither required car ownership to remedy. The requisite trip to the hospital was made in an ambulance one time and a cab the other.

After trying car-free travel for a day, you might want to challenge yourself to go car-free longer. Turn it into a game and see how many days in a row you can live car-free. Be creative in coming up with alternatives. Do you have a friend or family member who's also interested in a car divorce? Try doing some of these things together. Walk, bike, or carpool into town with a neighbor to do some errands. Or walk with a neighbor to the bus or subway to commute to work. Turn shopping trips into social occasions.

"We have walked, biked, or taken public transit everywhere we have gone in the past year with minimal problems. Oh, yeah, it takes a little planning — okay, a lot of planning! — but the benefits are awesome. We were apparently spending so much on vehicles and vehicle-related stuff that since we have been without all of those trappings, we now only work as nurses two days a week.

That is eight days a month compared with 20 to 24 before!"

CHEYANNE AND RANDY GORE,
WASHINGTON STATE, CAR-FREE

How did I feel after my own "trial separation"? I drove again one morning after five months of being car-free and found I had a new attitude about my car. I felt much more aware of its power to destroy. I drove it with a great deal more caution. I felt a detachment from it that I hadn't before. I noticed how much exhaust came out of its tailpipe. I registered how much gas I had to put in it, how much time I had to spend to get and keep it going again. Most of all, though, I remembered my sense of elation at having gone so long without driving even though I lived in such a car-dependent area. When I put the car back in the garage I felt determined to do it again — and that much closer to cutting the umbilical cord and selling my car outright.

One way or another, we can cut the use of cars. Not only can we still live lives of high quality without cars, we often discover lives of higher quality by breaking out of car-dependence. "For the creative spirit, car-free living has a lot of potential," writes Ellen Jones, whose family was car-free for most of the 1990s. "How do we do it? My favorite guidepost is a comment my husband made one evening ... 'All we have to fear is a lack of imagination.'"[12]

CHAPTER 18

Car-Dependent No More:
Ending Auto Dominance

"The pleasure to be derived from cars is so mediocre
compared to the delight of doing away with them."

ANDREW GIMSON, *SPECTATOR* (LONDON), FEBRUARY 1985

B Y FAR THE BEST PART OF WRITING THIS BOOK has been talking with car-free and car-lite folks who've shared their stories. They've often had such fun and gained so much satisfaction from "divorcing" their cars, and their enthusiasm for the process is both infectious and inspiring. Almost invariably, car-free people I've interviewed have relished the benefits they've reaped from the experience — saving money, improving fitness, lowering stress, raising quality of life — and would recommend it to their friends.

Getting rid of their car has been a cause to celebrate for some. "It was a life-affirming decision for us," says Ellen Santasiero of Bend, Oregon. Selling the car after a year of working up to it, says her husband John Schubert, brought "a huge sense of relief." One man who freed himself from car ownership after joining the car-share co-op in Vancouver, British Columbia, celebrated by smashing his old car to pieces. For others, the pleasure of doing away with their cars has come from doors opened and discoveries brought by car-free living. "Being car-free gives me much more freedom and peace of mind," says Debbie Hubsmith. "Living without a car, I live more locally, and experience life at a human rather than a mechanical speed. Living car-free or car-lite lets you smell the flowers, interact with strangers, and realize — deep inside — that we are all so much alike." Robert Silverman of Montreal, too, finds rich, local pleasures in being car-free. "It's a very liberating experience," he writes. "Without a car, one gets to discover what is near and appreciate that more. I discover parks never seen from a car, pretty streets and houses, ethnic neighborhoods, and distinctive architecture ... Gandhi said: 'There is more to life than accelerating its speed.' I agree."

> *"There is absolutely no question that I'd recommend living car-free to my friends. The irony is, however, that many of my friends are already car-free!"*
>
> DOROTHEA HASS, BOSTON, MASSACHUSETTS, CAR-FREE

Reality Check for a Car-Dependent World

Experiences like these show how people who divorce their cars can live better lives as they drive less. But this isn't to say that divorcing your car guarantees instant happiness, or that every instance of traveling car-free will be a breeze. "Living without a car is a joy, but no easy feat," writes car-free John Akre.[1] In fact the barriers to car-free life can make traveling without a car difficult at times. Hank Goldstein tells of walking 80 miles from Baltimore to Wilmington, Maryland with a friend, not long after he first went car-free. "To cross the Susquehanna River, we wanted to walk across the bridge over the Conowingo Dam, because it's very dramatic," he says. "We got to the bridge and were halfway across it when the bridge police came to chase us. We discovered there was no legal way to cross that bridge without a car. We would have had to go 40 miles north to the Appalachian Trail to legally cross the Susquehanna."

This is far from the only place in North America where it's illegal to bike or walk. Laws like this that favor cars are only one of an array of impediments to traveling auto-free. There are also physical impediments: roads without shoulders that scare off all but the most intrepid cyclists, for instance, or barriers on sidewalks blocking walkers. There are service impediments, like transit systems that are poorly supported or infrequently scheduled. There are land use impediments, like the sprawling development that turns trips even between "local" destinations into major travel. There are financial impediments, like the underpricing of driving that leads to perhaps twice as much car travel as people would otherwise choose. There are even cultural impediments, in the form of co-workers or peers who expect you to drive. Barriers like these, in combination with family and work demands, influenced Hank Goldstein, as they have others, to revert to car-lite rather than car-free living. "I don't have a love affair with the car, in fact I hate cars, yet I'm forced in my life to drive," he says. He is working to change things by planning and developing a pedestrian community in West Virginia.

"So many opportunities have been made available to us since we're car-free."

SCOTT SMEDBERG, MINNEAPOLIS, MINNESOTA, CAR-FREE

Until such efforts become more widespread, though, and until more barriers are removed, our car-dependent infrastructure leaves many with limited and difficult choices when it comes to wanting to travel without a car.

Given this car-dependency, even many car-free people — those who don't own cars and mainly use other means of transport — choose to use cars on occasion. But at the opposite extreme, using cars to the exclusion of everything else is what's created so many problems in the first place. The solution is to find a level of car divorce that's comfortable for you. Whether you choose to go car-free or car-lite, use alternatives as much as you can and help make your own world a better and safer place for them. It's true, it's an asphalt jungle out there. But the worst thing you can do is let that scare you away. In a world set up for cars, traveling without one is not always easy — but it's rarely impossible. A few folks who have committed to never setting foot in a car — as has Alan Streater, a physics professor and cycling advocate from Pennsylvania — show that this is true. It might not always be convenient or desirable, but whatever you want to do, wherever you want to go, there is almost always a way to get there without a car.

Visions of Less Auto Dominance

Planners and bureaucrats sometimes lament, "we'll never get people out of their cars." This also gets used as a justification to build more roads, starve transit budgets, and further force our union with the automobile. But lest we get too stuck in this marriage and think nothing will ever change our car-dependence, consider the example of cigarettes. Regulations and attitudes about cigarettes have changed immensely since the U.S. Surgeon General's report condemned them in 1964. Smoking is not gone, and may never be, but it is much reduced and efforts continue to reduce it further. One wonders what might happen if we had a Surgeon General's report on the automobile and on what it does to our health both individually and collectively.

> "Rather than sacrificing convenience, selling our car reduced some of the hassles that car owners take for granted."
>
> DANIEL EGAN, TORONTO, ONTARIO, CAR-FREE

There are striking parallels between smoking and driving. Both are addictions, in that we often keep doing them despite knowing that they hurt us, and despite sometimes preferring not to. Both are reinforced by commercial and government actions (e.g., cigarette and car ads, tobacco farming support payments and road-building subsidies). Both can be hard to give up. As they challenge smokers to quit, organizers of The Great American Smokeout use the slogan: "Don't quit quitting." Driving, too, can hook us to the point where we just keep drifting back to it if there's a car around. Both are sources of second-hand smoke and carbon monoxide; both are especially harmful to children, the elderly, and people with respiratory problems. Anti-smoking activists say it's unfair that second-hand cigarette smoke is "being breathed by people who want clean air." The same can be said of car exhaust. "Most children who live in large cities in the developing world breathe air that is the equivalent of smoking two packs of cigarettes a day," says Devra Lee Davis of the World Resources Institute.[2] A big contributor to this dirty air is second-hand smoke from vehicles.

> "The car, it seems, is nothing less than addictive for human beings. Like cigarettes, cars are a source of seductive pleasure that eventually comes to enslave its users."
>
> MARK HERTSGAARD, EARTH ODYSSEY

The relatively quick shift in attitudes toward smoking over the last few decades shows that a similar shift in attitudes toward driving is at least possible. Are we on the verge of such a shift? When it comes to cars, British transport analyst John Whitelegg believes a critical mass of people now recognize that "the time for change has arrived and that change has to involve a transition from auto-dependency and all that goes with it to lower levels of car use and higher levels of accessibility and environmental quality." While Whitelegg points out that "the existence of such a critical mass ... does not guarantee that this change will take place in the short term," the change has more chance to manifest if it springs from the grassroots.[3] If Whitelegg is correct and there truly is a critical mass of people wanting freedom from car-dependence, small changes such as the many examples in this book — Walking School Buses, bike delivery services, more telecommuters, efforts to limit sprawl — could be, or become, components of a bigger shift.

Let's consider how such a shift could happen and how it might look in a town of, say, 50,000 people. Suppose this town includes a neighborhood group, two active cyclists, a Girl Scout leader looking for troop projects, a parent concerned about the safety of his children walking to school, a senior citizen concerned about her own safety crossing streets, and a couple of employees with parking hassles. You probably know people like these in your own town, and maybe you're one of them. Starting with some simple actions from these people, this town — today a typical car-dependent community — could soon look very different.

Suppose one of the cyclists notices teenagers hanging around the town's street corners, looking for things to do, maybe getting into a little trouble. He knows about the Youth Bicycle Education Network and decides to start a youth bicycle workshop. The workshop cooperates with industrial arts programs at local schools and expands opportunities for the town's teens, many of whom start cycling proudly around town on bikes they've built or repaired themselves. Within a few years, the shop starts a free bikes program, which gets more townspeople cycling. Our other cyclist decides to start a pedal delivery service. She gets Jim Gregory's book *Cycling for Profit*, follows its instructions to start her business, and is soon delivering groceries, meals-on-wheels, and other items by bike. Within a few years and as she adds employees, she adds recycling pick-up and diaper delivery (based on Toronto's ABC Diaper Delivery Service). Both these cyclists make bicycling more visible to the town's business community. When they suggest better bike racks at area businesses, several stores and offices comply and a couple even supply bike lockers. Seeing the bike racks and lockers, another few town residents start biking.

Meanwhile, our concerned parent reads about Safe Routes to School and Walking School Bus programs and decides these look like great ideas. He finds a sympathetic teacher and together, they organize a Walk Our Children to School day. It's a success and kicks off the organization of several Walking School Buses. Soon, groups of children wearing colorful scarves or caps designating their Walking Buses can be seen around town, following volunteer adult leaders who deliver them to local schools. Many of the Walking Bus leaders are retired folks who love spending time with the kids and helping out with community safety. The kids and the bus leaders get healthier, too, since they're all getting regular moderate exercise on the way to school.

The Walking Buses, and a glance at Portland, Maine's travel map for kids, gives our Girl Scout leader an idea: she'll get her troop to create a map like Portland's, showing not only ways kids can get around by foot, bike and bus, but also the safest routes to schools. The Girl Scouts draft a rough map, a local foundation puts up money to produce it, and pretty soon kids are using it to walk, bike, and bus around town. Soccer parents breathe a sigh of relief as their mileage drops accordingly; with less chauffeuring to do, they actually get a little time to themselves.

"Our children are the only kids in their classes whose parents have no car. They love it. It gives them status with their classmates — children seem naturally to understand the health and environmental benefits."

DR. COLIN GUTHRIE,
GLASGOW (SCOTLAND), CAR-FREE

More people are biking and walking, but too many cars still speed on the town's streets, according to our neighborhood group. One of the group's leaders reads David Engwicht's book *Street Reclaiming*, enthuses about the book at a meeting, and the group soon starts a little psychological street reclaiming by hanging banners across the street and setting furniture out in on-street parking spaces along curbs. They notice that traffic slows near these changes; eventually the group paints carpets over a couple of parking spots and leaves furniture out permanently in those locations. These communal outdoor living rooms become favorite hangouts for the neighbors. Other neighborhoods around town take notice and decide to do some street reclaiming of their own.

All this looks good to our senior citizen, but she's still having trouble crossing the street downtown; too many cars zip through ignoring pedestrian rights. After one of her friends is killed in a crosswalk, she contacts pedestrian advocacy groups America WALKS and Right Of Way for advice. Following Right Of Way's lead, she paints a body outline on the street to remind people where her friend was killed, then she and a few other outraged seniors form their own walking advocacy group. They start using whistles to get drivers' attention and organize a sign-carrying action similar to those staged by the Willamette Pedestrian Coalition, to educate drivers about pedestrian rights. The local public works department responds by improving crosswalks and walk lights at a couple of key intersections. Feeling empowered, more seniors start walking, whistles in hand.

About the same time, parking conditions are getting crowded at one of the town's major employers. A couple of workers tired of circling the lot decide, independently, to do something about it. The first writes up and submits a telecommuting proposal to her employer, detailing how much money such a program could save the company. The company agrees to a trial telecommuting program, and enough employees love it that it grows; within a few years about a third of employees are telecommuting at least two days a week. The second employee organizes a vanpool. He leases a compressed natural gas (CNG) van, gets a few other commuters to sign on, and works out a deal with the company for preferential parking. The vanpool riders save money and stress, so pretty soon there are a few more CNG vanpools. Vanpools and telecommuting empty enough of the parking lot that the company sells off a chunk of it for a big chunk of cash. When that spot gets converted to landscaped apartments, some company employees move in and start walking to work.

Within a few years, these changes have more people walking, bicycling, telecommuting, and sharing transportation. So far, the changes have required little government action, but with all this citizen initiative, it's likely the town government would do at least a few things to follow the people's lead. They might, in response to neighborhood group requests, increase traffic calming on residential streets. They might expand their transit system with natural gas buses after seeing the local vanpools' success. They might add bike racks to those buses, or convert some vehicle lanes to bike lanes and sidewalk space for the town's growing number of walkers and cyclists. Suppose there's a long-distance train station downtown; our town's government might get a grant to add a transit hub and something like a Bikestation nearby, which also increases train use. Government action could in turn inspire more citizen action; it's not much of a stretch to imagine a few people starting a car-sharing business, or local banks starting to offer location-efficient mortgages.

All the changes above are based on things that have actually happened in U.S., Canadian, British, or Australian communities. We could go further and suppose our town votes to discourage use of gasoline-powered internal combustion cars within its city limits; essentially, the whole town would divorce its cars. At first glance this may seem a little far-fetched, but it's worth envisioning here because it could in fact be done with existing technology and financial mechanisms, and without any "sacrifice" in quality of life.

The town might start by using money from its road budget to improve walking, bicycling, and transit facilities. It might also support its car divorce with incremental increases in parking fees, or an increase in the local gas tax. It could phase in a road pricing system that would charge cars as soon as they crossed city limits. To keep parked cars from building up just outside the limits, the town could establish an urban growth boundary there and start buying land and development rights for a greenbelt just outside it. Suppose the town also approves a zoning plan to encourage mixed uses and higher densities near transit. It converts suburban malls into village-like neighborhoods by turning some retail space into apartments and town homes and ripping up parking lots for parks, more homes, schools, and libraries. The town also identifies areas that should, over time, be restored to their natural state; no new construction is allowed in those locations. As people and businesses move away from those areas, natural attrition allows buildings to be removed and the land to be restored. Development clusters around transit stops; areas farther from transit are depaved and turned into parks, arboretums, wildlife areas, or community gardens. Ultimately, everyone living in town is within a 15-minute walk of both transit and a park or garden area.

The number of cars and the amount of driving in town had already dropped in response to earlier citizen initiatives; now they drop further in response to fiscal incentives and land use changes. This frees enough street space that the town can close some central streets to cars. At first, a five-block area is closed to cars every Thursday night for a big community market and party: musicians on street corners, outdoor cafes,

"Most of the world does not get around by car, but the car companies are pushing hard to quickly motorize the planet. If they succeed the results will be catastrophic. The only way I can think of that we can say to other countries, "don't make the same mistake we have," is to recognize what we have done and work to get our own cities and countries back onto a sustainable path. And that begins with how we live our own lives."

TOOKER GOMBERG,
TORONTO, ONTARIO, CAR-FREE

and what seems like everyone in town wandering through as local farmers sell produce and businesses host sidewalk sales. The market's so much fun it's soon held twice a week, then the town center becomes permanently car-free, with walking and cycling the main way people travel through it. Pedicabs transport some people who don't walk or bike themselves. Deliveries are made to businesses with cargo bikes. The only motorized vehicles are a few electric wheelchairs.

All these changes mean that most people don't need a car, and a growing number realize they don't want the responsibility of owning one. The car-sharing business in town expands. Its $200 membership fee and hourly charges are cheap compared to what it costs to own a car. Enough people join that the business raises plenty of capital. Taking advantage of fleet purchase discounts, it buys some hybrid vehicles; a few electric cars, trucks and vans; some CNG cars; and some neighborhood electric vehicles to use as transit station cars. It also partners with the town government to open neighborhood-based vehicle-sharing depots near transit stops. These depots serve as pick-up locations for car-sharing, but more important is their role as overall transportation/access centers. They rent and repair a range of bicycles, bike trailers, electric bikes, and pedal-powered work vehicles — employing some of the youth bicycle workshop graduates — in addition to the various alternatively-fueled cars. They also provide tele-access centers with fax machines, computers, Internet access, office space, and carrels for students and telecommuters.

By now many of the town's gas stations have been closed or converted to multimodal travel service stations or other uses, but our town still has a couple of them that mostly fuel cars used for out-of-town trips. These stations now also dispense compressed natural gas; a couple have installed solar photovoltaic panels to produce hydrogen on a small scale for fuel-cell buses the town is starting to add to its transit system. Let's suppose that on any given weekend, one-quarter of the town's people take an out-of-town trip. Of these, half take the bus or train. The other half use cars, with an average of two people per car. That means about 3,000 cars get used, less than one car for every ten people in town. If all of North America reduced its usage to that level, the car fleet would drop from over 200 million to only 30 million. Imagine the sheer amount of land area that could be freed by having so many fewer cars — not to mention reductions in pollution, noise, resource use, and all the other auto impacts that we've come to accept as inevitable. And this could be done in such a way that everyone's travel needs would still be met.

If some of these changes are taking place simultaneously in the rest of the world, transport variety is becoming the norm, and communities are becoming transit-oriented. A growing number of people pick car-sharing over private car ownership, and the cars these programs offer are not gasoline-powered. Many auto workers have other, better jobs, including some with transit and some with car-sharing organizations. People who have left car ownership behind have done so with little net loss of mobility or access, and a big gain in the quality of their lives. Cities have become so pleasant that fewer people feel the need to flee them, taking pressure off wilderness parks and habitat. In response to popular support, governments have essentially stopped building new roads. Money has been re-routed into maintenance of existing key roads; since new road construction has stopped, there is so much money available for repairs that pot-holes have become a thing of the past. A dwindling number of internal combustion vehicles chug along the roadways, paying the full true cost of the privilege as they go. Most of these are rented vehicles, used by their drivers for occasional long-distance trips.

If enough environmentally concerned North Americans responded to the finding that car driving is their most environmentally harmful activity and decided to divorce their cars, going either car-lite or car-free, we might move a long way toward the visions above. A shift like this could make the world look quite different in 20 or 30 years. It could give us a world of compact, convivial communities, with distinct boundaries, surrounded by green space, connected more often by rail. It could contribute to a more relaxed pace of life, clean the air and water, and restore a blessed quietude that has otherwise all but disappeared behind engine noise. We would be healthier, walking and cycling down streets in the shade of trees planted where asphalt used to be. Children and the elderly would feel safer on the streets and have more independence without having to rely on others to drive them places. We'd

> *"We see a lot of positives in not owning a car — we save money, there's less hassle, we don't have to deal with parking problems. All those things are advantages that make us keep doing what we're doing."*
>
> JOAN STEIN, AMES, IOWA, CAR-FREE

have billions of dollars worth of infrastructure that could be reallocated to other uses. Parking lots could be re-striped as basketball or tennis courts, and restaurants could claim roadway space for outdoor cafés. We would save money, and we would save lives. In short, we would gain tremendously. We'd be glad to have divorced our cars — and might even decide divorce was the best thing that could have happened for us.

An all-at-once community-wide car divorce may be unlikely, but the components of such a change are not, nor are the individual actions that could lead up to one. Such individual actions needn't be difficult, and they can be effective. There's no question that institutions have a lot to do with our current state of car-dependence, and there are many government and business practices that need to change. But there are still a lot of things we can do now to help make our own lives, our neighborhoods, and our immediate communities less car-dependent and more livable. And if more people exercise their power of choice, the range of choice will expand. The more we make choices for change individually, the more these choices can build into a collective pressure — a trend, a movement — with the power to shift the whole system. At some point, the personal becomes political, and that point comes quickly in decisions we make about using cars: our personal travel choices can influence transport, fiscal, and land use policies. By divorcing our cars, we can build a constituency of grassroots support for the broader changes we need in our transportation systems, and lead our leaders by example. If we take the initiative to change our own lifestyles, we can also help the institutional change to happen.

There is no one thing that will end auto dominance. Instead, it will take an integrated approach with many small steps, and the most important of those may be yours as you walk your child to school, or walk to a transit stop, or walk to a bike rack to retrieve your bike and pedal away. These steps model possibilities for the people we see, and who see us. We can't wait for Detroit, Washington, Canberra, Brussels, or Ottawa to make the changes for us. Come on your bike, and they'll see the need for bike lanes. Come on foot, and they'll see the need for sidewalks. "Use it or lose it" applies to every alternative to car transport: if we don't use them, they'll fade away — but if we do, they can flourish, and so can we.

SELECTED RESOURCES

* Books, organizations, and other resources marked with an asterisk (*) can help you with the practical aspects of car-free or car-lite living. Unmarked resources mainly provide background information or help with advocacy.

Further Reading

Bank of America, Greenbelt Alliance, California Resources Agency, and Low Income Housing Fund. *Beyond Sprawl: New Patterns of Growth to Fit the New California.* San Francisco: Bank of America et al., 1995.

Berger, Michael. *The Devil Wagon in God's Country: The Automobile and Social Change in Rural America, 1893-1929.* Hamden, Conn.: Archon Books, 1979.

* Bredin, Alice. *The Virtual Office Survival Handbook: What Telecommuters and Entrepreneurs Need to Succeed in Today's Non-Traditional Workplace.* New York: John Wiley & Sons, 1996.

Brower, Michael and Warren Leon. *The Consumer's Guide to Effective Environmental Choices: Practical Advice from the Union of Concerned Scientists.* New York: Three Rivers Press, 1999.

Bullard, Robert D. and Glenn S. Johnson. *Just Transportation: Dismantling Race & Class Barriers to Mobility.* Gabriola Island, B.C.: New Society Publishers, 1997.

Burchell, Robert W. et al. *The Costs of Sprawl — Revisited: Transit Cooperative Research Program Report 39.* Washington, D.C.: National Academy Press, 1998.

Burden, Dan. *Street Design Guidelines for Healthy Neighborhoods.* Sacramento, Calif.: Center for Livable Communities, 1999.

Burger, Joanna. *Oil Spills.* New Brunswick, N.J.: Rutgers University Press, 1997.

Cervero, Robert. *The Transit Metropolis: A Global Inquiry.* Washington D.C.: Island Press, 1998.

Durning, Alan Thein. *The Car and the City: 24 Steps to Safe Streets and Healthy Communities.* Seattle: Northwest Environment Watch, 1996.

* Edwards, Paul and Sarah. *Working from Home: Everything You Need to Know About Living and Working Under the Same Roof.* 5th ed. Los Angeles: J.P. Tarcher, 1999.

Engwicht, David. *Reclaiming Our Cities and Towns: Better Living with Less Traffic.* Gabriola Island, B.C.: New Society Publishers, 1993.

*— *Street Reclaiming: Creating Livable Streets and Vibrant Communities.* Gabriola Island, B.C.: New Society Publishers, 1999. More from Engwicht on street reclaiming at < www.lesstraffic.com > .

Flink, James J. *America Adopts the Automobile, 1895-1910.* Cambridge, Mass.: MIT Press, 1970.

— *The Automobile Age.* Cambridge, Mass.: MIT Press, 1988.

— *The Car Culture.* Cambridge, Mass.: MIT Press, 1975.

Flower, Raymond and Michael Wynn Jones. *100 Years on the Road: A Social History of the Car.* New York: McGraw-Hill Book Company, 1981.

* Forester, John. *Effective Cycling.* 6th ed. Cambridge, Mass.: MIT Press, 1993.

Freund, Peter and George Martin. *The Ecology of the Automobile.* Montreal: Black Rose Books, 1993.

Gelbspan, Ross. *The Heat is On: The High Stakes Battle Over Earth's Threatened Climate.* New York: Addison-Wesley Publishing Company, 1997.

* Gershon, David. *EcoTeam: A Program Empowering Americans to Create Earth-Friendly Lifestyles.* Woodstock, New York: Global Action Plan for the Earth, 1997.

Goddard, Stephen B. *Getting There: The Epic Struggle Between Road and Rail in the American Century.* Chicago: University of Chicago Press, 1996.

Gordon, Deborah. *Steering a New Course: Transportation, Energy, and the Environment.* Washington, D.C.: Island Press, 1991.

Green Scissors Campaign. *Green Scissors: Cutting Wasteful and Environmentally Harmful Spending and Subsidies.* Washington, D.C.: Friends of the Earth, 1996.

Greenpeace. *The Environmental Impacts of the Car.* Seattle: Greenpeace, 1992.

* Gregory, Jim. *Cycling for Profit: How to Make a Living With Your Bike.* San Francisco: Van der Plas Publications, 1999. Available from Bikes at Work Inc. (see Cycling resources, below) and booksellers.

Guillet, Edwin C. *The Story of Canadian Roads.* Toronto: University of Toronto Press, 1966.

* Hackleman, Michael. *The New Electric Vehicles: A Clean and Quiet Revolution.* Ashland, Oreg.: Home Power Publishing, 1996. Available from Michael Hackleman, P.O. Box 327, Willits, CA 95490; < mhackleman@saber.net > .

Hart, Stanley I. and Alvin L. Spivak. *The Elephant in the Bedroom: Automobile Dependence and Denial: Impacts on the Economy and Environment.* Pasadena, Calif.: New Paradigm Books, 1993.

Herman, Michele. *Bicycle Blueprint: A Plan to Bring Bicycling Into the Mainstream In New York City.* New York: Transportation Alternatives, 1993.

Houghton, John. *Global Warming: The Complete Briefing.* New York: Cambridge University Press, 1997.

Illich, Ivan. *Energy and Equity.* New York: Harper and Row, 1974.

International Federation of Red Cross and Red Crescent Societies. *World Disasters Report 1998*. New York: Oxford University Press, 1998.

Jackson, Kenneth T. *Crabgrass Frontier: The Suburbanization of the United States*. New York: Oxford University Press, 1985.

Jacobs, Jane. *The Death and Life of Great American Cities*. London: Jonathan Cape, 1962.

Johnson, Elmer W. *Avoiding the Collision of Cities and Cars*. Cambridge, Mass.: American Academy of Arts and Sciences, 1993.

Kay, Jane Holtz. *Asphalt Nation: How the Automobile Took Over America and How We Can Take it Back*. New York: Crown Publishers, Inc., 1997.

Ketcham, Brian and Charles Komanoff. *Win-Win Transportation: A No-Losers Approach to Financing Transport in New York City and the Region*. New York: Komanoff Energy Associates, 1992.

Komanoff, Charles and Members of Right Of Way. *Killed by Automobile: Death in the Streets in New York City 1994-1997*. New York: Right Of Way, March 1999.

Kunstler, James Howard. *The Geography of Nowhere*. New York: Simon & Schuster, 1993.

* Langhoff, June. *The Telecommuter's Advisor: Real World Solutions for Remote Workers*. Newport, R.I.: Aegis Publishing, 1999.

Liebs, Chester H. *Main Street to Miracle Mile: American Roadside Architecture*. Baltimore: The Johns Hopkins University Press, 1995.

Litman, Todd. *Transportation Cost Analysis: Techniques, Estimates and Implications*. Victoria, B.C.: Victoria Transport Policy Institute. (regular updates)

* Loomis, Jim. *All Aboard! The Complete North American Train Travel Guide*. Rocklin, Calif.: Prima Publishing, 1998.

Lowe, Marcia. *Alternatives to the Automobile: Transport for Livable Cities: Worldwatch Paper 98*. Washington, D.C.: Worldwatch Institute, 1990.

— *The Bicycle: Vehicle for a Small Planet: Worldwatch Paper 90*. Washington, D.C.: Worldwatch Institute, 1989.

MacKenzie, James. *The Keys to the Car: Electric and Hydrogen Vehicles for the 21st Century*. Washington, D.C.: World Resources Institute, 1994.

MacKenzie, James, Roger Dower, and Donald Chen. *The Going Rate: What it Really Costs to Drive*. Washington, D.C.: World Resources Institute, 1993.

* McCrea, S. and R. Minner, eds. *Why Wait for Detroit? Drive an Electric Car Today!* Fort Lauderdale, Fla.: South Florida Electric Auto Association, 1992.

McShane, Clay. *The Automobile: A Chronology of its Antecedents, Development, and Impact*. Westport, Conn.: Greenwood Press, 1997.

— *Down the Asphalt Path: The Automobile and the American City.* New York: Columbia University Press, 1994.

Makower, Joel. *The Green Commuter.* Washington, D.C.: National Press Books, 1992.

Malaspina, Mark et al. *What Works: Air Pollution Solutions.* Washington, D.C.: The Environmental Exchange, May 1992.

Mann, Eric. *L.A.'s Lethal Air: New Strategies for Policy, Organizing, and Action.* Los Angeles: Labor/Community Strategy Center, 1991.

Moffet, John and Peter Miller. *The Price of Mobility: Uncovering the Hidden Costs of Transportation.* New York: Natural Resources Defense Council, 1993.

Motavalli, Jim. *Forward Drive: The Race to Build "Clean" Cars for the Future.* San Francisco: Sierra Club Books, 2000.

Mowbray, A.Q. *Road to Ruin.* Philadelphia: Lippincott, 1969.

Musselman, M.M. *Get a Horse!: The Story of the Automobile in America.* Philadelphia: Lippincott, 1950.

Nader, Ralph. *Unsafe at Any Speed: The Designed-In Dangers of the American Automobile.* New York: Grossman Publishers, 1965.

Nadis, Steve and James J. MacKenzie. *Car Trouble.* Boston: Beacon Press, 1993.

National Safety Council. *Injury Facts.* Itasca, Illinois: National Safety Council. (annual)(continuation of Accident Facts)

Newman, Peter and Jeffrey Kenworthy. *Sustainability and Cities: Overcoming Automobile Dependence.* Washington, D.C.: Island Press, 1999.

Newman, Peter and Jeff Kenworthy with Les Robinson. *Winning Back the Cities.* Leichhardt, New South Wales: Pluto Press Australia/Australian Consumers' Association, 1992.

Noonan, B. and S. H. Cousins. *The Car Club Kit.* Coventry: Car Club Publications, 1998. (To order, write publisher at P.O. Box 1237, Coventry, CV6 3ZB, U.K. or check < www.mobilecube.co.uk/carsharing.htm > .)

Organization for Economic Cooperation and Development. *Roadside Noise Abatement.* Washington, D.C.: OECD Publications and Information Centre, 1995.

Perrin, Noel. *Life with an Electric Car.* San Francisco: Sierra Club Books, 1994.

* Perry, David B. *Bike Cult: The Ultimate Guide to Human-Powered Vehicles.* New York: Four Walls Eight Windows, 1995.

Pettifer, Julian and Nigel Turner. *Automania: Man and the Motor Car.* London: Collins, 1984.

Rae, John. *The American Automobile: A Brief History.* Chicago: University of Chicago Press, 1965.

Register, Richard. *Ecocity Berkeley: Building Cities for a Healthy Future.* Berkeley, Calif.: North Atlantic Books, 1987.

Sachs, Wolfgang. *For Love of the Automobile: Looking Back into the History of Our Desires.* Berkeley: University of California Press, 1992.

St. Clair, David J. *The Motorization of American Cities.* New York: Praeger Publishers, 1986.

* Schneider, Kirk and Philip Capo, eds. *California Transit Guide: A Complete Directory to Public Buses, Trains and Ferries.* Davis, Calif.: California Transit Publications, 1991.

Schneider, Kenneth R. *Autokind vs. Mankind.* New York: W.W. Norton & Company, 1971.

Schneider, Kenneth and Blanche, eds. *The Quotable Car: A Literary Mosaic Highlighting Changing Views of Automobility.* Berkeley: Continuing Education in City, Regional and Environmental Planning, University Extension, University of California, 1973.

* Smale, Tony, Jane Henshaw, Peter Henshaw, and David Henshaw, eds. *Life Beyond Cars.* London: Railway Development Society, [1996].

Smith, Robert A. *A Social History of the Bicycle: Its Early Life and Times in America.* New York: American Heritage Press, 1972.

Sperling, Daniel. *Future Drive: Electric Vehicles and Sustainable Transportation.* Washington, D.C.: Island Press, 1995.

* Sussman, Aaron and Ruth Goode. *The Magic of Walking.* New York: Simon & Schuster, 1980.

Surface Transportation Policy Project. *Aggressive Driving: Are You at Risk?* Washington, D.C.: Surface Transportation Policy Project, 1999.

Surface Transportation Policy Project et al. *Mean Streets 1998: Children at Risk, An Annual Report on Pedestrian Safety and Federal Transportation Spending.* Washington, D.C.: Surface Transportation Policy Project, 1998.

* Taylor, James, Robert Gentile, and Anne McKinnon, eds. *Car-Free in Boston: The Guide to Public Transit in Greater Boston and New England.* Boston: Association for Public Transportation, 2000.

U.S. Environmental Protection Agency. *Indicators of the Environmental Impacts of Transportation: Highway, Rail, Aviation, and Maritime Transport.* Washington, D.C.: U.S. Environmental Protection Agency, October 1996.

U.S. Environmental Protection Agency, Office of Air Quality Planning and Standards. *National Air Pollutant Emission Trends, 1900-1996.* Research Triangle Park, North Carolina: U.S. Environmental Protection Agency, December 1997.

— *National Air Quality and Emissions Trends Report, 1997*. Research Triangle Park, North Carolina: U.S. Environmental Protection Agency, December 1998.

U.S. Environmental Protection Agency, Office of Pollution Prevention and Toxics. *1996 Toxics Release Inventory*. Washington, D.C.: U.S. Environmental Protection Agency, May 1998.

U.S. Federal Highway Administration. *Our Nation's Travel: 1995 NPTS Early Results Report*. Washington, D.C.: U.S. Department of Transportation, September 1997.

U.S. Federal Highway Administration. *The National Bicycling and Walking Study: Transportation Choices for a Changing America*. Washington, D.C.: U.S. Department of Transportation, 1994.

Urban Ecology. *Blueprint for a Sustainable Bay Area*. Oakland, Calif.: Urban Ecology, 1996.

WalkBoston. *Improving Pedestrian Access to Transit: An Advocacy Handbook*. Washington, D.C.: U.S. Department of Transportation, Federal Transit Administration, 1998.

Weyrich, Paul M. and William S. Lind. *Conservatives and Mass Transit: Is It Time for a New Look?* Washington, D.C.: Free Congress Foundation, 1996.

Whitelegg, John. *Critical Mass: Transport, Environment and Society in the Twenty-first Century*. London: Pluto Press, 1997.

Wildlands Center for Preventing Roads. *Road-Ripper's Handbook*. Missoula, Mont.: Wildlands CPR, 1995.

Williams, Heathcote. *Autogeddon*. New York: Arcade Publishing, 1991.

Zielinski, Sue and Gordon Laird, eds. *Beyond the Car: Essays on the Auto Culture*. Toronto: Steel Rail Publishing/Transportation Options, 1995.

Zuckermann, Wolfgang. *End of the Road: The World Car Crisis and How We Can Solve It*. Post Mills, Vt.: Chelsea Green Publishing Company, 1991.

Selected Organizations, Programs, and Other Resources

Below are some key organizations, programs, publications, and online resources mentioned in this book, plus a few more thrown in for good measure. This section includes international, national, and a sampling of regional transportation reform-oriented organizations. Resources marked with an asterisk (*) provide practical tools or pointers to help individuals travel car-free.

For more transportation reform organizations, see the Surface Transportation Policy Project's *Directory of Transportation Reform Resources*. For more cycling organizations, see the League of American Bicyclists' annual *Almanac of Bicycling*. The Sierra Club lists additional web links on transportation and sprawl at < www.sierraclub.org/sprawl/resources/links.asp > .

General

Adbusters / The Media Foundation, 1243 West 7th Avenue, Vancouver, B.C. V6H 1B7 Canada; Tel 604-736-9401 or (US and Canada) 1-800-663-1243; Fax 604-737-6021; E-mail < adbusters@adbusters.org > ; Web < www.adbusters.org > . International creative network of culture jammers who've produced anti-auto ads, among others. Publishes *Adbusters* magazine.

Alliance for a Paving Moratorium / Fossil Fuels Policy Action Institute, P.O. Box 4347, Arcata, CA 95518; Tel 707-826-7775; Fax 707-822-7007; E-mail < alliance@tidepool.com > ; Web < www.tidepool.com/alliance > . Advocates a halt to new paving. Publishes *Auto-Free Times.*

* Association for Commuter Transportation, 1518 K Street NW, Suite 503, Washington, D.C. 20005; Tel 202-393-3497; Fax 202-638-4833; E-mail < acthq@aol.com > ; Web < http://tmi.cob.fsu.edu/act/act.htm > . Supports local and regional transportation demand management agencies. Website includes links to U.S. commuter assistance programs.

* Auto-Free Orange County, P.O. Box 338, Laguna Beach, CA 92652; Tel 714-452-1393; E-mail < autofree_oc@hotmail.com > . Promotes auto-free lifestyles in Orange County, California, and beyond. Range of member services includes Auto-Free Lifestyle Counseling.

* Auto-Free Ottawa, Box 57006, 797 Somerset Street West, Ottawa, Ontario K1R 1A1 Canada; Tel 613-237-1549; E-mail < an588@freenet.carleton.ca > ; Web < www.flora.org/afo/about.html > . Promotes car-free transport in the Ottawa area.

* B.E.S.T. (Better Environmentally Sound Transportation), 822-510 West Hastings Street, Vancouver, B.C. V6B 1L8 Canada; Tel 604-669-2860; Fax 604-669-2869; E-mail < best@best.bc.ca > ; Web < www.best.bc.ca/ > . Promotes appropriate transport in British Columbia; sells the "B.E.S.T. Advocacy Toolkit for Alternative Transportation," runs Vancouver's annual Bike Week, helps workplaces set up trip reduction and bicycle incentive programs, and more.

Campaign on Auto Pollution, International Center for Technology Assessment, 310 D Street NE, Washington, D.C. 20002; Tel 202-547-9359; Fax 202-547-9429; E-mail < cap@icta.org > ; Web < www.icta.org/campaigns/cap/ index.htm > . Coalition which works toward "rehabilitating our dependency on polluting cars." Publishes *Getting There: A Newsletter for the Transportation Activist.*

* Car Busters Magazine and Resource Centre, Kratka 26, 100 00 Praha 10, Czech Republic; Tel 420-2-781-08-49 ; Fax 420-2-781-67-27; E-mail < carbusters@ecn.cz > ; Web < www.antenna.nl/eyfa/cb > . Address for U.S. subscriptions and orders: P.O. Box 10141, Berkeley, CA 94709. Provides resources for the international car-free movement. Publishes *Car Busters* magazine.

Car Free Cities Network, c/o Eurocities, 18 square de Meeus, B-1050 Brussels; Tel (32) 2 552 08 74/75; Fax (32) 2 552 08 89; E-mail < cfc@eurocities.be > ; Web < www.eurocities.cfc > . Founded in 1994; European member cities (70 as of 1999) commit to reducing auto traffic and encouraging sustainable transport.

* CarFree listserve, E-mail < CarFree@one.list > ; Web < www.onelist.com/ community/CarFree > . An e-mail discussion group about car-free living. Participants from around the world (mostly North America and Europe).

Carfree Times, E-mail < postmaster@carfree.com > ; Web < www.carfree.com > ; on-line quarterly newsletter on the effects of automobiles on cities. The newsletter is just one part of the carfree.com website, offering a wealth of information on car-free city design. Website master J.H. Crawford has also written the forthcoming book, *Carfree Cities.*

Center for Livable Communities, Local Government Commission, 1414 K Street, Suite 250, Sacramento, CA 95814-3966; Tel 1-800-290-8202 or 916-448-1198; Fax 916-448-8246; Web < www.lgc.org/clc/ > . Educates local governments about techniques for building more walkable, bikable, and livable communities.

* Center for Neighborhood Technology, 2125 W. North Ave., Chicago, IL 60647; Tel 773-278-4800, ext. 115; Fax 773-278-3840; E-mail < hoeveler@cnt.org > ; Web < www.cnt.org > . Promotes affordable, appropriately scaled ways for city residents to meet basic needs, including transportation; put together the first location-efficient mortgage program in the U.S.

Centre for Alternative and Sustainable Transport (CAST), School of Sciences, Staffordshire University, College Road, Stoke on Trent, ST4 2DE, UK; Tel +44 (0)1782 295771; Fax +44 (0)1782 747167; E-mail < cast@staffs.ac.uk > ; Web < www.staffs.ac.uk/schools/sciences/ geography/CAST/ > . Promotes use of low-impact modes of transport.

The Commons, E-mail < post@ecoplan.org > ; Web < www.ecoplan.org/com_ entry.htm > . Sustainability website maintained by EcoPlan International.

Includes information about car-sharing, car-free days, and a range of other sustainable transport issues.

* Commuter Connections, Metropolitan Washington Council of Governments, 777 North Capitol Street NE, Suite 300, Washington, D.C. 20002-4201; Tel 800-745-RIDE; Fax 202-962-3218; Web < www.commuterconnections.org >. Provides assistance with telework, ridesharing, and non-motorized commutes in the Washington Metropolitan area.

Congress for the New Urbanism, 5 Third Street, Suite 500A, San Francisco, CA 94103; Tel 415-495-2255; Fax 415-495-1731; E-mail < cnuinfo@cnu.org >; Web < www.cnu.org >. Promotes community design favorable for non-car transport. Distributes "Transportation Tech Sheets" on traffic calming, pedestrian paths, and other transport-related urban design topics.

Conservation Law Foundation, 62 Summer Street, Boston, MA 02110; Tel 617-350-0990; Fax 617-350-4030; E-mail < issues@clf.org > or < members@clf.org >; Web < www.clf.org >. Active in transportation issues. Maintains the Transportation for Livable Communities Network website, < www.tlcnet.org >, which includes an active transportation reform e-mail listserve.

* Detour Publications, c/o Transportation Options, 761 Queen St. West, Suite 101, Toronto, Ontario M6J 1G1 Canada; Fax 416-504-0068; E-mail < detour@web.net >; Web < www.web.net/ ~ detour/detour/ >. Distributes and produces sustainable transportation-related publications; their great catalog is now available both on-line and in hard copy format.

Ecocity Builders, 1678 Shattuck Ave., #66, Berkeley, CA 94709; Tel/Fax 510-649-1817; E-mail < ecocity@igc.org >; Web < www.citizen-planners.org/ ecocitybuilders >. Promotes ecologically healthy communities through design, planning, research, community projects, and education. Has sponsored several depaving projects.

* Global Action Plan for the Earth, P.O. Box 428, Woodstock, NY 12498; Tel 914-679-4830; Fax 914-679-4834; E-mail < info@GlobalActionPlan.org >; Web < www.GlobalActionPlan.org >. Organizes neighborhood EcoTeams to help households reduce their use of resources for transportation and more.

* GO Boulder, City of Boulder, 1739 Broadway, 2nd Floor, P.O. Box 791, Boulder, CO 80306; Tel 303-441-3266; Fax 303-441-4271; E-mail < winfreet@ci.boulder.co.us >; Web < http://go.boulder.co.us >. Transportation planning agency for the City of Boulder. Promotes walking, biking, transit, telecommuting.

* GO GERONIMO, P.O. Box 304, San Geronimo, CA 94963; Tel 415-488-8888; Fax 415-488-9398; Web < www.gogeronimo.org >. Has developed innovative ridesharing programs, ride registry with photo ID cards, and bicycle advocacy programs to help community residents travel more sustainably.

* Greenbelt Alliance, 530 Bush Street, Suite 303, San Francisco, CA 94108;
Tel 415-398-3730; Fax 415-398-3730; E-mail < greenbelt@igc.org > ;
Web < www.greenbelt.org > . Good source of information on urban growth
boundaries and city-centered growth; promotes transit; distributes *Transit
Outdoors: The Transit Guide to San Francisco Bay Area Regional Parks*, also at
< www.transitinfo.org/Outdoors/ > .

Institute for Local Self-Reliance, Midwest Office: 1313 Fifth Street SE,
Minneapolis, MN 55414-1546; Tel 612-379-3815; Fax 612-379-3920; National
Office: 2425 18th Street NW, Washington, D.C. 20009-2096; Tel 202-232-4108;
Fax 202-332-0463; Web < www.ilsr.org > . Has published several transportation
reform reports.

Institute for Transportation and Development Policy, 115 W. 30th Street, Suite
1205, New York, NY 10001; Tel 212-629-8001; Fax 212-629-8033; E-mail
< mobility@igc.apc.org > ; Web < www.itdp.org > . Promotes sustainable
transportation internationally.

International Council for Local Environmental Initiatives, City Hall West Tower
16th Floor, Toronto, Ontario M5H 2N2 Canada; Tel 416-392-1462; Fax 416-392-
1478; E-mail < iclei@iclei.org > ; Web < www.iclei.org > . U.S. Cities for
Climate Protection office: 15 Shattuck Square, Suite 215, Berkeley, CA 94704;
Tel 510-540-8843; Fax 510-540-4787; E-mail < iclei_usa@iclei.org > .
Membership organization of local governments and their associations. Works
toward tangible improvements in global environmental conditions through the
cumulative impact of local government initiatives, including local climate
protection and transport reform.

* Kids and Transportation Program, Greater Portland Council of Governments,
233 Oxford Street, Portland, ME 04101; Tel 207-774-9891; Fax 207-774-7149; E-
mail < ehermann@gpcog.eddmaine.org > . Produced the "Kid's Guide to
Getting Around Greater Portland" and provides other resources, including a
classroom activity guide, to foster positive alternative transportation
experiences for children.

Livable Oregon, 621 SW Morrison, Suite 1300, Portland, OR 97205; Tel 503-222-
2182; E-mail < amber@livable.org > ; Web < www.livable.org > . Helps build
livable communities; among its "smart development" fact sheets is an
excellent backgrounder on "Skinny Streets."

National Center for Bicycling and Walking, 1506 21st Street NW, Suite 200,
Washington, D.C., 20036; Tel 202-463-6622; Fax 202-463-6625; E-mail
< bikefed@aol.com > ; Web < www.bikefed.org > . Works with public officials,
health and transportation agencies, and citizens to create more bicycle-friendly
and walkable communities. A project of the Bicycle Federation of America;
publishes newsletters and offers advocacy materials on website.

National Trust for Historic Preservation, 1785 Massachusetts Ave. NW,
Washington, D.C. 20036; Tel 800-944-6847; Fax 202-588-6038; Web
< www.nationaltrust.org > . Among many historic preservation activities, the

Trust works to discourage sprawl; publications include *How Superstore Sprawl Affects Communities (And What Citizens Can Do About It)* and *Smart States, Better Communities.*

Noise Pollution Clearinghouse, P.O. Box 1137, Montpelier VT 05601-1137; Tel 888-200-8332; E-mail < npc@nonoise.org > ; Web < www.nonoise.org/index.htm > . Source for noise pollution news and resources; helps activists working against noise pollution, including transportation noise.

Pedestrian and Bicycle Information Center, University of North Carolina, Highway Safety Research Center, 730 Bolin Creek CB#3430, Chapel Hill, NC 27599; Tel 877-925-5245; Web < www.walkinginfo.org > or < www.bicyclinginfo.org > . Sponsored by U.S. DOT. Operates bicycle and pedestrian clearinghouse; source of federal documents on pedestrian and bicycle planning.

Project for Public Spaces, Inc., 153 Waverly Place, 4th Floor, New York, NY, 10014; Tel 212-620-5660; Fax 212-620-3821; E-mail < pps@pps.org > ; Web < www.pps.org > . Promotes use of transport — walking, biking, transit, and street design — as a tool for enhancing communities.

* Rails-to-Trails Conservancy, 1100 17th Street NW, 10th Floor, Washington, D.C. 20036; Tel 202-331-9696; Fax 202-331-9680; E-mail < rtcmail@transact.org > ; Web < www.railtrails.org > . Helps convert abandoned rail corridors into trails. Website includes a U.S. Trail Info Center.

Reclaim the Streets, P.O. Box 9656, London, UK N4 4JY; Tel 0171-281-4621; E-mail < rts@gn.apc.org > ; Web < www.gn.apc.org > . Organizes road blockades and street parties to advocate walking, cycling, and public transit, and to counteract car culture.

Right Of Way, 305 Broadway, Room 402, New York, NY 10007; Web < www.rightofway.org > . Pedestrian and cyclist rights advocacy organization for New York City. Authors/publishers of *Killed by Automobile: Death in the Streets in New York City, 1994-1997.*

Surface Transportation Policy Project, 1100 17th Street NW, 10th Floor, Washington, D.C. 20036; Tel 202-466-2636; Fax 202-466-2247; E-mail < stpp@transact.org > ; Web < www.transact.org > . Advocates balanced transport policies, produces a wide range of policy reports, and assists local transport reform advocates. Publishes newsletters: *Progress* and *Transfer.*

* Sustrans Information Service, PO Box 21, Bristol, UK BS99 2HA; Tel 0117-929-0888; Fax 0117-915-0124; E-mail < info@sustrans.org.uk > ; Web < www.sustrans.org.uk > . Works on practical projects to reduce car use, including the National Cycle Network and Safe Routes to School.

* Transportation Options, 761 Queen Street West, Suite 101, Toronto, Ontario M6J 1G1 Canada; Tel 416-504-3934; Fax 416-504-0068; Web < www.web.net/ ∼detour > . Promotes sustainable transportation. Held the Second Auto-Free Cities Conference in 1992 and the Moving the Economy

conference in 1998; their published conference proceedings are excellent information sources.

Transport 2000 Canada, 117 Sparks Street, Suite 100, Ottawa, Ontario; mailing address Box/C.P. 858, Station B, Ottawa, Ontario K1P 5P9 Canada; Tel 613-594-3290; Fax 613-594-3271; E-mail < t2000@transport2000.ca > ; Web < www.transport2000.ca/ > . Federation of seven regional organizations representing transit users and promoting healthy transportation.

Transport 2000 UK headquarters: The Impact Centre, 12-18 Hoxton St., London, UK N1 6NG; Tel 0171 613 0743; Fax 0171 613 5280; E-mail < transport2000 @transport2000.demon.co.uk > . Federation of environmental and consumer groups, trade unions, and others concerned with the impacts of transport on the environment and society.

Union of Concerned Scientists, Two Brattle Square, Cambridge, MA 02238; Tel 617-547-5552; Fax 617-864-9405; E-mail < ucs@ucsusa.org > ; Web < www.ucsusa.org > ; Transportation Office, 2397 Shattuck Ave., Suite 203, Berkeley, CA 94704; Tel 510-843-1872; Fax 510-843-3785. Promotes sustainable transport and alternative fuels. Good source of publications.

Urban Ecology, 405 14th Street, Suite 900, Oakland, CA 94612; Tel 510-251-6330; Fax 510-251-2117; E-mail < urbanecology@urbanecology.org > ; Web < www.urbanecology.org > . Works for sustainable cities. Publishes *Urban Ecology.*

Victoria Transport Policy Institute, 1250 Rudlin Street, Victoria, B.C. V8V 3R7 Canada; Tel/Fax 250-360-1560; E-mail < litman@vtpi.org > ; Web < www.vtpi.org > . Wide-ranging source of materials on transport costs and policies. Informative website with many downloadable publications.

Wildlands Center for Preventing Roads, P.O. Box 7516, Missoula, MT 59807; Tel 406-543-9551; E-mail < WildlandsCPR@wildlandscpr.org > ; Web < www.wildrockies.org/WildCPR/ > ; Works to protect and restore wildland ecosystems by preventing and removing roads and limiting motorized recreation. Clearinghouse of information on road impacts. Publishes *The Road RIPorter.*

World Transport Policy & Practice, Eco-Logica Ltd., 53 Derwent Road, Lancaster LA1 3ES UK; Tel + 44 1524 63175; Fax + 44 1524 848340; E-mail (administration) < pascal@gn.apc.org > ; (editorial) < j.whitelegg@ lancaster.ac.uk > . Quarterly journal committed to sustainable transport and to reducing global dependency on cars, trucks, and aircraft; Vol. 5 no. 3 (1999) is a superb, 300-page special issue on car-sharing.

Walking

American Hiking Society, 1422 Fenwick Lane, Silver Spring, MD 20910; Tel 301-565-6704; Fax 301-565-6714; E-mail < info@americanhiking.org > ; Web < www.americanhiking.org > . Has a database of local organizational members, which can direct you to trails in your area. Trails for All Americans initiative aims to provide access to trails that allow anyone to walk from Connecticut to California. Publishes *American Hiker.*

* America WALKs, P.O. Box 29103, Portland, OR 97210; Tel 503-222-1077; Fax 503-228-0289; E-mail < americawalks@hevanet.com > ; Web < www.webwalking.com/amwalks > . National coalition of walking advocacy groups, including WalkBoston, PEDS (Atlanta), Willamette Pedestrian Coalition (Portland, OR), and others. Call, write or check website for complete listings. Helps communities set up local walking advocacy groups.

* Go for Green, 30 Stewart St., P.O. Box 450 — Stn A, Ottawa, Ontario K1N 6N5 Canada; Tel 888-UBACTIV; Fax 613-562-5314; E-mail < info@goforgreen.ca > ; Web < www.goforgreen.ca > . Promotes active living and links transportation, recreation, and environment. Distributes an *Active and Safe Routes to School* video, and *Blazing Trails through the Urban Jungle* Safe Routes to School handbooks for students and teachers.

* Greenest City, 238 Queen Street West, Lower Level, Toronto, Ontario M5V 1Z7 Canada; Tel 416-977-7626. One of the first groups in Canada to develop Walking School Bus and Safe Routes to School programs. Focuses on revitalizing urban life and improving air quality in Toronto.

* Ottawalk, Ottawa, Ontario, Canada; Tel 613-230-4566; E-mail < ottawalk@flora.org > ; Web < www.ottawalk.org > . First metro walking advocacy association in North America and a model for others; works to improve walking conditions in the Ottawa region. Publishes *Ottawalk News*; sponsored "Slidewalks to Sidewalks" program to improve winter walkability; and other programs.

* Partnership for a Walkable America, c/o National Safety Council, 1121 Spring Lake Drive, Itasca, IL 60143; Tel 630-285-1121 (contact Harold Thompson at 1-800-621-7615, ext. 2383 or 630-775-2383 for Walk Our Children to School information); Web < www.nsc.org/walkable.htm > . Promotes better pedestrian safety and access. Provides Walk Our Children to School planning kits; Walkable America Checklist at < www.nsc.org/walk/wkcheck.htm > (printed copies in English and Spanish available from U.S. Dept of Transportation, National Highway Traffic Safety Administration, Office of Communication and Outreach, NTS-21, 400 Seventh Street SW, Washington, D.C. 20590; Fax 202-493-2062) and Resources for a More Walkable World at < www.nsc.org/walk/resources.htm > .

Pedestrian Program, U.S. Department of Transportation, Office of the Secretary, P-15, 400 Seventh Street SW, Washington, D.C. 20590; Tel 202-366-8044; Fax 202-366-7909; E-mail < leverson.boodlal@fhwa.dot.gov > ; Web < www.ota.fhwa.dot.gov/walk/ > . Sponsors Pedestrian Safety Road Show.

Pedestrian Transportation Program/Pedestrian Coordinator, City of Portland, Office of Transportation, 1120 SW 5th Ave, Suite 800, Portland, OR 97204; Tel 503-823-7004; Fax 503-823-7371; E-mail < pedprogram@trans.ci.portland.

or.us > ; Web < www.trans.ci.portland. or.us > . Sells copies of the Portland Pedestrian Master Plan and the Portland Pedestrian Design Guide ($15 each or both documents for $25). The Pedestrian Design Guide is also available on the website.

* Perils For Pedestrians TV, 5305 Bradley Blvd., Bethesda, MD 20814; E-mail < john@pedestrians.org > ; Web < www.pedestrians.org > . John Z. Wetmore, director. Produces monthly cable TV program on pedestrian issues, appearing on public-access cable stations across the U.S. Website lists episode topics and tells you how to arrange for Perils for Pedestrians to be shown on local public access cable channels.

Walkable Communities, Inc., 320 S. Main St., High Springs, FL 32643; Tel 904-454-3304; Web < www.walkable.org > . Directed by Dan Burden, expert on improving community walkability and livability. Burden leads workshops to help communities become more walkable. Website includes photo images of walkable places.

Cycling

* *A to B*, 19 West Park, Castle Cary, Somerset, BA7 7DB, UK Tel/Fax 01963 351649; E-mail < post@a2bmagazine.demon.co.uk > ; Web < www.a2bmagazine.demon.co.uk > . Entertaining small press magazine promoting car-free travel using folding bikes and transit; includes regular consumer reports on folding and electric bikes.

* Adventure Cycling Association, P.O. Box 8303, Missoula, MT 59807; Tel 800-755-2453; E-mail < acabike@adv-cycling.org > ; Web < www.adv-cycling. org > . Offers North American cycle tours; sells books, maps, and guides that can help individuals plan their own long-distance trips. Publishes *Adventure Cyclist* magazine and *The Cyclist's Yellow Pages*.

* Advocacy for Respect for Cyclists, Toronto, Ontario, Canada; Tel 416-504-2918 ext. 1; E-mail < arc.to@poboxes.com > ; Web < www.web.net/ ~ detour/ arc/ > . Lobbies for cyclists' rights, provides legal defense support and information to cyclists, organizes street actions to reclaim road space for cyclists, and generally works against auto-dependence.

* Bicycle Alliance of Washington, P.O. Box 2904, Seattle, WA 98111; Tel 206-224-9252; Fax 206-224-9254; E-mail < bikeinfo@bicyclealliance.org > ; Web < www.bicyclealliance.org > . Works to get more people bicycling, more often, throughout Washington state.

* Bicycle Transportation Alliance, P.O. Box 9072, Portland, OR 97207-9072; Tel 503-226-0676; Fax 503-226-0498; E-mail < info@bta4bikes.org > ; Web < www.bta4bikes.org > . Statewide cycling advocacy organization which runs youth bike safety programs, coordinates bike to work days, rents bike lockers, loans out a bike cargo trailer, and more.

* Bikes At Work, Inc., 216 N. Hazel, Ames, IA 50010; Tel 515-233-6120; Web < www.bikesatwork.com > . Formerly Fresh Aire Delivery Service and Fresh Aire Trailer Works. Manufactures bike utility trailers; operates a recycling pickup service; sells co-owner Jim Gregory's book *Cycling for Profit*. Website includes photos of bikes hauling cargo, sometimes with loads weighing hundreds of pounds.

Bikes Not Bombs, 59 Amory St, #103A, Roxbury, MA 02119; Tel 617-442-0004; E-mail < bnbrox@igc.apc.org > ; Web < www.nemba.org/b_not_b.html > . Operates a Bicycle Recycling and Youth Training Center; among many programs, sends recycled bikes to Central America and has trained Nicaraguan war veterans, disabled people, and others as bike business owners and mechanics.

* Bikestations: Long Beach Bikestation, 105 The Promenade North, Long Beach, CA 90802; 562-436-BIKE(2453); Bikestation Palo Alto, Palo Alto Caltrain Depot, Palo Alto, CA; 650-327-9636; The Bikestation at Berkeley, Berkeley BART Station, 510-549-7433; Web < www.bikestation.org > . Provide valet bicycle parking and other services to encourage bicycle use and link bicycles and transit.

*Canadian Cycling Association, 1600 James Naismith Dr., Gloucester, Ontario K1B 5N4 Canada; Tel 613-748-5629; Fax 613-748-5692; E-mail < general@ canadian-cycling.com > ; Web < www.canadian-cycling.com > . National organization promoting cycling in Canada; offers CAN-BIKE training courses, teaching cycling skills.

* Center for Appropriate Transport, 455 West First Avenue, Eugene, OR 97401-2276; Phone: 541-344-1197; Fax 541-686-1015; E-mail < cat@efn.org > ; Web < www.efn.org/ ~ cat/ > . Promotes community involvement in manufacturing, using, and advocating sustainable transport; houses projects like publicly-funded youth bicycle education; a rideable bicycle museum, with various vehicles for rent or sale; and Human Powered Machines, a work bike, recumbent, and trailer fabrication business.

* Chicagoland Bicycle Federation, 417 S. Dearborn Street, Suite 1000, Chicago, IL 60605-1120; Tel 312-427-3325; Fax 312-427-4907; E-mail < cbf@chibikefed. org > ; Web < www.chibikefed.org > . Vigorous bike advocacy group promoting cycling safety, education, and facilities improvements for the Chicago region.

Community Bicycle Network, 761 Queen St.West, Suite 101, Toronto, ON M6J 1G1 Canada; Tel 416-504-2918; Web < www.web.net/ ~ detour/cbn/ cbn.html > . Supports community-based bike repair and recycling as well as creation of bicycle-related businesses in the Toronto area. Also includes BicycleShare project, Song Cycles choir on bikes, and the Toronto ReCycled Art Society.

* Effective Cycling video, classes, and book. *Effective Cycling* by John Forester (Cambridge: MIT Press, 1993 [6th ed.]) is the book, available at bookstores everywhere. *Effective Cycling* is also the name of the video, available through

the League of American Bicyclists (LAB; see entry below) or Seidler Productions, 191 Pine Lane, Crawfordville, FL 32327; 850-925-6331. Effective Cycling courses are offered through the LAB by certified instructors across the country.

* European Cyclists' Federation, Rue de Londres, 15 (b.3), B-1050 Brussels, Belgium; Tel +32 — 2 512-9827; Fax +32 — 2 51-5224; E-mail < office@ecf.com > ; Web < www.ecf.com > . World's largest cycling advocacy group, with 50 member groups in 29 countries.

Human-Powered Vehicle Association, P.O. Box 1307, San Luis Obispo, CA 93406-1307; Tel 877-333-1029; Fax 310-823-1064; E-mail < office@ihpva.org > ; Web < www.ihpva.org > . Formerly the International Human Powered Vehicle Association. Promotes improvement, innovation, and creativity in design and development of human-powered vehicles.

* ICEBIKE Web Site. < www.enteract.com/ ~ icebike/ > . An on-line compendium of information about winter cycling; includes clothing, equipment, and techniques tips; companion to the ICEBIKE E-mail list (subscribe by sending E-mail to < listserv@listserv.heanet.ie > with the following in the body of the message: < subscribe icebike >).

International Bicycle Fund, 4887 Columbia Drive South, Seattle, WA 98108-1919; Tel/Fax 206-767-0848; E-mail < ibike@ibike.org > ; Web < www.ibike.org > . Promotes sustainable transportation, international exchange, and bicycles in transportation planning and cross-cultural programs.

International Police Mountain Bike Association, 28 E. Ostend St., Baltimore, MD 21230; 410-685-2220; Fax 410-685-2240; E-mail < ipmba@aol.com > ; Web < www.ipmba.org > . Provides training and resources for bike patrols around the world.

* League of American Bicyclists, 1612 K Street NW, Suite 401, Washington, D.C. 20006; Tel 202-822-1333; Fax 202-822-1334; E-mail < bikeleague@ bikeleague.org > ; Web < www.bikeleague.org > . The national membership organization for U.S. cyclists; founded in 1880 as the League of American Wheelmen, it promotes cycling for fun, fitness, and transportation. Publishes *Bicycle USA* magazine and the annual *Almanac of Bicycling*, which includes listings of state and local bike advocacy groups.

* Main Street Pedicabs, 3003 Arapahoe Street, Suite 226, Denver, CO 80205; Tel 303-295 3822; E-mail < pedicab@usa.net > ; Web < www.pedicab. com > . Builds and sells pedicabs; provides pedicab service in Denver; website lists and links to pedicab services in other locations.

Le Monde à Bicyclette, 911 Jean-Talon est, bureau 135, Montréal, Québec H2R 1V5 Canada; Tel 514-270-4884; Fax 514-270-9190; E-mail < lemab@cam.org > ; Web < www.cam.org/ ~ lemab/ > . Bicycle advocacy organization for Montreal.

Network News, P.O. Box 8194, Philadelphia, PA 19101; Tel/Fax 215-222-1253 (to fax, enter *21 on hearing message); E-mail < john-dowlin@usa.net > .

Urbanist John Dowlin distributed this quarterly compilation of news clips about human-powered transportation for 20 years and now has back issues available at $2 per individual issue and $95 for a nearly complete set of the archives. He also edits and distributes the *Cycle & Recycle* annual wall calendar ($10), which celebrates careful use and re-use of bicycles and the world's limited resources.

* Open Road Ltd., The Danesmead Wing, 33 Fulford Cross, York, YO10 4PB UK; Tel +44 1904 654654; Fax +44 1904 654684; E-mail < peter@bcqedit.demon. co.uk >; Web < http://bikeculture.com >. A small company devoted to promoting bicycling worldwide; publishes the *Encycleopedia*, an annual compendium of innovative, practical, commercially available pedal vehicles. Also publishes *Bike Culture Quarterly* and *Bycycle* magazines.

* San Francisco Bicycle Coalition, 1095 Market Street #215, San Francisco, CA 94103; Tel 415-431-BIKE; E-mail < sfbc@sfbike.org >; Web < www.sfbike. org >. Very active bicycle advocacy organization for San Francisco.

* Transportation Alternatives, 115 W 30th Street, #1207, New York, NY 10001-4010; Tel 212-629-8080; E-mail < info@transalt.org >; Web < ww.transalt. org >. Bicycle advocacy organization for New York City; publishes newsletter *Transportation Alternatives.*

* Workbike.org, E-mail < info@workbike.org >; Web < www.workbike.org >. Online source of information about cargo bike delivery services, pedicab services, and makers of trikes, cargo bikes, and pedicabs. Associated with the company Zero which runs a London human-powered delivery service and sells a range of workbikes.

Youth Bicycle Education Network (YBEN), 31 East 52nd Street, Indianapolis, IN 46205; 317-253-3632; Web < www.yben.org >. International organization promoting the bicycle as a vehicle for youth development and community building. Provides affiliated organizations that teach skills and values to youth through bicycles with cooperative development of resources, news and information, research, and evaluation services. Publishes newsletter *Re:Cycle* and a variety of resource manuals and guides.

Shared Transportation

* Allo Stop: 4317, St-Denis, Metro Mont-Royal, Montréal, Québec, Canada; Tel 514-985-3032; 5, Yorkville Ave (Metro Yonge/Bloor), Toronto, Ontario, Canada; Tel 416-975-9305; other locations. E-mail < allostop@mlink.net >; Web < www.allostop.com >. Canadian ride-sharing service with ten offices in Ontario and Quebec.

American Public Transportation Association, 1201 New York Avenue NW, Washington, D.C. 20005; Tel 202-898-4000; Fax 202-898-4049; E-mail < info@apta.com >; Web < www.apta.org >. Membership organization for U.S. transit providers. Produces a Transit Fact Book and a Local Organizing Kit, to assist with advocacy for transit.

* Amtrak, National Railroad Passenger Corporation, Washington Union Station, 60 Massachusetts Ave NE, Washington, D.C. 20002; Tel 800-USA-RAIL; E-mail < service@sales.amtrak.com > ; Web < www.amtrak.com > . Reservations and schedule information for Amtrak passenger train service available via toll-free phone number or web site.

* The CarSharing Network, Web < www.carsharing.net > . Tracks and provides information about car-sharing programs worldwide; links to a wealth of car-sharing information. If your town doesn't have car-sharing and you want to start it, check the resources at < www.autoshare.com/beginners/guide.html > . Also see "Business Planning Study for Car Sharing Mobility Services in Portland, Oregon," developed by Oregon's Bicycle Transportation Alliance and sponsored by the Oregon Department of Environmental Quality. Posted on the web at < www.deq.state.or.us/aq/busplan.htm > .

* CarSharing Portland Inc., 2106 SE Division St. (office), mailing address 1905 NE Clackamas St., Portland, OR 97232-1514; Tel 503-872-9882; Fax 503-239-5058; E-mail < carsharing@carsharing-pdx.com > ; Web < www.carsharing-pdx.com > . First car-sharing service in the U.S. Also offers consulting services to other car-sharing start-ups.

Community Transportation Association of America, 1341 G St. NW, Suite 600, Washington, D.C. 20005; Tel 202-628-1480; Fax 202-737-9197; Transit Hotline 800-527-8279; Web < www.ctaa.org > . Promotes practical community transportation alternatives that fall between private cars and mass transit, including paratransit, rural transit services, and more.

Co-operative Auto Network (CAN), Suite 209, 470 Granville St., Vancouver, B.C. V6C 1V5 Canada; Tel 604-685-1393; Fax 604-685-1353; E-mail < vancan@vcn.bc.ca > ; Web < www.cooperativeauto.net > . Vancouver's car-sharing network, founded in January 1997.

* Enterprise Vanpool, Tel 1-800-VAN4WORK; Web < www.vanpool.com > . A division of Enterprise Rent-A-Car, specializes in providing full-size vans and mini-vans to groups of co-workers for vanpool commuting. Website includes instructions on how to start a vanpool.

* Greyhound Lines, Inc., P.O. Box 660362, Dallas, TX 75266-0362; Tel (877) GO-BY-BUS [(877) 462-9287]; +1 (402) 330-8552 (International areas without toll free access); (800) 752-4841 (Assistance for passengers with disabilities); (800) 345-3109 (TDD); Web < www.greyhound.com > . Provides intercity bus transport throughout North America.

* Mobility CarSharing, Muhlenplatz 10, 6000 Luzern 5, Switzerland; Tel 041-41-419-46-55; Fax 041-41-419-46-99; E-mail < mail@mobility.ch > ; Web < www.mobility.ch > . Private carsharing company that partners with public transit to offer overall mobility packages to customers.

* National Association of Railroad Passengers, 900 Second Street NE, Suite 308, Washington, D.C. 20002; Tel 202-408-8362; Fax 202-408-8287; E-mail

< narp@narprail.org > ; Web < www.narprail.org > . Promotes intercity passenger rail service in U.S. Monthly newsletters provide updates and travelers' advisories about train fare and schedule offers and changes. Website includes "hotline" section, updated weekly.

National Station Car Association, E-mail < stncar@ix.netcom.com > ; Web < www.stncar.com > . Guides development, testing, and commercialization of station cars around North America. Those interested in starting station car demonstration programs in their areas can e-mail the association for more information.

* Railway Development Society, Roman House, 9-10 College Terrace, London E3 5AN UK; Tel +44 (0)20 8981 2992; Fax +44 (0)20 8981 2994; E-mail < Railwatch@argonet.co.uk > ; Web < www.argonet.co.uk/users/railwatch/ > . Volunteer organization that watchdogs rail matters in the U.K. Publishes *Railwatch* magazine.

* Ride boards on the Internet: "Ride Share: The Commuter's Choice" is an Internet ride board, at < http://rideshare.ba.ca/List.asp > ; it's used by people in the Ontario region. Shareride.com < www.shareride.com > is an Internet ride board for the U.S. and Canada. Freewheelers Nationwide Internet Lift-Sharing Service operates in the UK. E-mail < freewheelers@freewheelers. com > ; Web < www.freewheelers.com > .

* Straphangers Campaign, 9 Murray Street, New York, NY 10007; Tel 212-349-6460; Fax 212-349-1366; E-mail < straphangers@nypirg.org > ; Web < www.straphangers.org > . A campaign of the New York Public Interest Research Group (NYPIRG), Straphangers advocates safe, comfortable, reliable, and affordable transit.

* U.K. Public Transport Information (pti); Web < www.pti.org.uk > ; also lists a national phone hotline (0906 55 00 000) for all rail, bus, and coach services in England, Scotland, and Wales. Covers all travel by rail, air, coach, bus, ferry, metro, and tram within the U.K., and between the U.K. and Ireland, plus rail, ferry, and coach travel between the U.K. and mainland Europe.

* VIA Rail Canada, reservations and travel schedules, 800-561-3952 from Canada; 800-561-3949 from U.S.; Web < www.viarail.ca > . Canada's national passenger rail service.

* VPSI Inc., 1220 Rankin Street, Troy, Michigan, 48083; Tel 1-800-VAN-RIDE(826-7433); Fax 248-597-3501; E-mail < info@vpsiinc.com > ; Web < www.vanpoolusa.com > . Provides van leases for vanpoolers; 800 number will direct callers to local offices that can help with getting into vanpools.

Alternative Fuels

* Clean Cities Hotline, 9300 Lee Highway, Fairfax, VA 22031-1207; Tel 800-CCITIES; Fax 202-586-1558; E-mail < ccities@nrel.gov > ; Web < www.ccities.doe.gov > . Encourages use of alternative fuel vehicles and

development of alternative fuel stations. Associated with the National Alternative Fuels Hotline (see below).

Electric Vehicle Association of the Americas, 601 California Street, Suite 502, San Francisco, CA 94108; Tel 415-249-2690 or 800-4EV-FACT; Fax 415-249-2699; E-mail < ev@evaa.org > ; Web < www.evaa.org > . Serves as a central information source about electric vehicles. Website includes directory of U.S. EV charging stations and descriptions of EVs currently on the market.

* EV Rental Cars, 9775 Airport Boulevard, Los Angeles, CA 90045; Tel 877-EV RENTAL; Fax 310-642-4543; E-mail < info@evrental.com > ; Web < www.evrental.com > . First source of electric vehicle and natural gas vehicle rentals in the U.S.

* National Alternative Fuels Hotline, 9300 Lee Highway, Fairfax, VA 22031-1207; Tel 800-423-1363 in U.S.; 703-934-3069 from outside U.S.; E-mail < hotline@afdc.nrel.gov > ; Web < www.afdc.nrel.gov > . Comprehensive information source about alternative fuel vehicles in U.S. Provides access to documents distributed by the National Renewable Energy Laboratory's Alternative Fuels Data Center, which maintains websites including maps of alternative fuel stations at < www.afdc.nrel.gov/refuel/usmaps.html > , and links to the Alternative Fuel Vehicle Fleet Buyer's Guide at < www.fleets. doe.gov > .

Natural Gas Vehicle Coalition, 1100 Wilson Blvd., Suite 850, Arlington, VA 22209; Tel 703-527-3022; Fax 703-527-3025; Web < www.ngvc.org > . Promotes and tracks developments in the natural gas vehicle industry.

Partnership for a New Generation of Vehicles, PNGV Secretariat, U.S. Department of Commerce, Herbert Hoover Building, Room 4845, 14th Street & Constitution Ave. NW, Washington, D.C. 20230; Tel 202-482-6260; Fax 202-482-6275; E-mail < pngv-info@ta.doc.gov > ; Web < www.ta.doc.gov/pngv > . U.S. government-industry collaboration to develop alternatively-fueled and fuel-efficient vehicles.

Propane Vehicle Council, 1155 Connecticut Ave. NW, Suite 300, Washington, D.C. 20036; Tel 202-530-0479; Fax 202-463-8570; E-mail < jcolaneri@propanevehicle.org > ; Web < www.propanegas.com > . Promotes use of propane as vehicle fuel.

Rocky Mountain Institute, 1739 Snowmass Creek Road, Snowmass, CO 81654-9199; Tel 970-927-3851; Fax 970/927-3420; Web < www.rmi.org > and < www.hypercarcenter.org > . Originator of Hypercar™ concept.

WestStart-CALSTART, 3360 E. Foothill Boulevard, Pasadena, CA 91107; Tel 626-744-5600; Fax 626-744-5610; E-mail < feedback@calstart.org > ; Web < www.calstart.org > . Formerly CALSTART. Promotes adoption and use of alternative vehicles. Good source of alternative vehicle news and information.

Telecommunications

Canadian Association for Distance Education (CADE), Suite 204, 260 Dalhousie Street, Ottawa, Ontario K1N 7E4 Canada; Fax 613-241-0019; E-mail < cade@csse.ca > ; Web < www.cade-aced.ca >. Sponsors conferences and programs on distance education; publishes the *Journal of Distance Education* and *Communiqué.*

Canadian Telework Association, 52 Stonebriar Drive, Nepean, Ontario K2G 5X9 Canada; Tel 613-225-5588; Fax 613-225-0161 E-mail < info@ivc.ca > ; Web < www.ivc.ca >. Promotes telework in Canada.

European Telework Online, Web < www.eto.org.uk >. Part of the European Telework Development initiative of the European Union. Includes links to country-specific telework pages from throughout Europe, including the Telework Telecottage and Telecentre Assciation in the U.K.; U.K. Enquiries: 0800 616008 Outside U.K. + 44 1203 696986 Fax: + 44 1453 836174; E-mail < 100272.3137@compuserve.com >

International Telework Association and Council, 204 E. Street NE, Washington, D.C. 20002; Tel 202-547-6157; E-mail < tac4dc@aol.com > ; Web < www.telecommute.org >. Promotes and shares information about benefits and techniques of teleworking.

* June Langhoff's Telecommuting Resource Center, E-mail < june@langhoff.com > ; Web < www.langhoff.com >. Rich source of telecommuting information from the author of *The Telecommuter's Advisor.*

United States Distance Learning Association, P.O. Box 376, Watertown, MA 02471-0376; Tel 800-275-5162; Fax 781-453-2533; E-mail < webmaster@usdla.org > ; Web < www.usdla.org >. Promotes development of distance learning.

NOTES

To save space, these notes have been condensed. The first reference to a source contains full bibliographic information, and subsequent references to that source are abbreviated, unless the source is included in the bibliography within the "Selected Resources" section; for those references, full citations are found only in the bibliography. Where one note is given for a full paragraph, or at the end of a list, references are in order of the appearance of the facts or quotations in the text. Information widely available from sources consulted has not been cited. Where a reference is used more than once, it is sometimes cited only the first time it is used, with an accompanying note: "Unless otherwise cited, all [similar information] is from this source." Listed websites were accessible as of December 1999. Unreferenced quotes are from personal interviews.

Chapter 1

1. McShane, *Down the Asphalt Path*, 104-105; Flower and Jones, *100 Years on the Road*, 12; Flink, *Automobile Age*, 13.
2. Leonard Bruno, *On the Move* (Detroit: Gale Research, 1993), 80; McShane, *The Automobile*, 11, 22; Flink, *Automobile Age*, 2; Flower and Jones, *100 Years on the Road*, 10-11, 17.
3. Flink, *America Adopts the Automobile*, 15; Flink, *Automobile Age*, 17-18, 21-23.
4. Flink, *America Adopts the Automobile*, 8, 37; Flink, *Automobile Age*, 29-30; Goddard, Getting There, 50.
5. Jim Henry, "There wasn't a horse in sight at 1900 N.Y. auto show," *Automotive News* 2 (26 Jun 1996): 16; "Where the Charm Is," *Motor World* 2 (16 May 1901): 127; Musselman, *Get a Horse!*, 81.
6. Flink, *America Adopts the Automobile*, 22, 42.
7. Flink, *America Adopts the Automobile*, 106; Berger, *Devil Wagon in God's Country*, 178; Sachs, *For Love of the Automobile*, 5; Guillet, *Story of Canadian Roads*, 148; McShane, *The Automobile*, 26.
8. "100 events that made the industry," *Automotive News* 2 (26 Jun 1996), 17, 30; Flink, *Automobile Age*, 10-11, 23, 32; Flower and Jones, *100 Years on the Road*, 12, 25; McShane, *The Automobile*, 23, 27, 35; McShane, *Down the Asphalt Path*, 173-174; Pettifer and Turner, *Automania*, 99, 183.
9. William F. Dix, "The Automobile as Vacation Agent," *Independent* 56 (2 Jun 1904): 1259-1260; Kenneth and Blanche Schneider, eds., *The Quotable Car*, 21-22; Ibid., 10; Kenneth Schneider, *Autokind vs. Mankind*, 28.
10. Flink, *America Adopts the Automobile*, 50; McShane, *The Automobile*, 32; Daniel Yergin, *The Prize: The Epic Quest for Oil, Money, and Power* (New York: Simon & Schuster, 1991), 80; Flink, *Car Culture*, 157-158.
11. Flink, *Automobile Age*, 18-27, 41; Rae, *American Automobile*, 238.
12. Flink, *Automobile Age*, 25, 43-48; Rae, *American Automobile*, 62.
13. Flink, *Automobile Age*, 38-45; Pettifer and Turner, *Automania*, 93.
14. Sachs, *For Love of the Automobile*, 12-13.

15. Flower and Jones, *100 Years on the Road*, 37-38.
16. Musselman, *Get A Horse!*, 16-17, 20.
17. Flink, *America Adopts the Automobile*, 66-70; Berger, *Devil Wagon in God's Country*, 23; Guillet, *Story of Canadian Roads*, 149.
18. Sachs, *For Love of the Automobile*, 8-10; McShane, *The Automobile*, 10 (Duke of Wellington quotation).
19. Flink, *America Adopts the Automobile*, 65-66; Rae, *American Automobile*, 29.
20. Pettifer and Turner, *Automania*, 201.
21. Sachs, *For Love of the Automobile*, 15 and 22.
22. Flink, *Automobile Age*, 151; McShane, *Down the Asphalt Path*, 194.
23. McShane, *Down the Asphalt Path*, 226; Mark S. Foster, *From Streetcar to Superhighway* (Philadelphia: Temple University Press, 1981), 114.
24. Roger Rowand, "Early tires were as primitive as early cars," *Automotive News* 2 (26 Jun 1996): 12.
25. Flower and Jones, *100 Years on the Road*, 50-51.
26. Pettifer and Turner, *Automania*, 45.
27. Pettifer and Turner, *Automania*, 11-13.
28. Flink, *Automobile Age*, 31; Flink, *America Adopts the Automobile*, 99-100.
29. Flink, *Car Culture*, 165; Berger, *Devil Wagon in God's Country*, 20-21, 182.
30. McShane, *Down the Asphalt Path*, 221; McShane, *The Automobile*, 64-65.
31. McShane, *Down the Asphalt Path*, 217; Lincoln Highway Association, *The Lincoln Highway* (New York: Dodd, Mead & Company, 1988), 252-253; Goddard, *Getting There*, 3; Rae, *American Automobile*, 91.
32. Rae, *American Automobile*, 13; Sperling, *Future Drive*, 36; Berger, *Devil Wagon in God's Country*, 195; Ibid., 18.
33. Flower and Jones, *100 Years on the Road*, 43; Pettifer and Turner, *Automania*, 42; Sachs, *For Love of the Automobile*, 14.
34. Berger, *Devil Wagon in God's Country*, 31; Flink, *America Adopts the Automobile*, 94.
35. Flink, *America Adopts the Automobile*, 92, 94, 103.
36. Kay, *Asphalt Nation*, 196.
37. Flink, *Automobile Age*, 188-189.
38. Flink, *Automobile Age*, 189-191; McShane, *The Automobile*, 51; Charles Child, "'Buy now, pay later,' and car sales soared," *Automotive News* 2 (26 Jun 1996): 72.
39. Flink, *Automobile Age*, 188.
40. Musselman, *Get A Horse!*, 269-270.
41. Flink, *Automobile Age*, 191.
42. Flink, *Automobile Age*, 193, 212.
43. Flink, *Automobile Age*, 218, 221; Rae, *American Automobile*, p 109; Guillet, *Story of Canadian Roads*, 169.
44. Flink, *Automobile Age*, 129.
45. Kay, *Asphalt Nation*, 196.

Chapter 2

1. From publicity for James Klein and Martha Olson, *Taken for a Ride* (Hohokus, NY: New Day Films, 1996).

2. McShane, *Down the Asphalt Path*, 191; Flink, *Automobile Age*, 136; Pettifer and Turner, *Automania*, 49.
3. Flink, *America Adopts the Automobile*, 52-55; Pettifer and Turner, *Automania*, 36, 47 (peak horse numbers).
4. Pettifer and Turner, *Automania*, 56; Flink, *America Adopts the Automobile*, 110.
5. Flink, *Automobile Age*, 79, 153.
6. Berger, *Devil Wagon in God's Country*, 43-44.
7. Berger, *Devil Wagon in God's Country*, 51; Flink, *Automobile Age*, 153-154.
8. Williams, *Autogeddon*, 87.
9. Goddard, *Getting There*, 9. Unless otherwise cited, material in "Renouncing the Railroads" is from this source. See also 13, 14, 16, 23, 25, 31, 40, 98, 101, 147, 226-227, 231.
10. Flink, *Automobile Age*, 364.
11. James Vance, *Capturing the Horizon* (New York: Harper and Row, 1986), 394.
12. Rae, *The Road and Car in American Life*, 89.
13. Kay, *Asphalt Nation*, 212.
14. Smith, *Social History of the Bicycle*, 48-49, 54.
15. Smith, *Social History of the Bicycle*, 50-53; Perry, *Bike Cult*, 37.
16. Smith, *Social History of the Bicycle*, 218-219, 242.
17. Perry, *Bike Cult*, 37.
18. "100 events that made the industry," *Automotive News* 2 (26 Jun 1996): 86; Bruno, *On the Move*, 178, 198; Flink, *Automobile Age*, 37-38, 64-65, 122; Kay, *Asphalt Nation*, 183; Liebs, *Main Street to Miracle Mile*, 208; McShane, *The Automobile*, 52-53, 62; Peter Montague, "Bad Decisions Again and Again," *Rachel's Environment & Health Weekly* 541 (10 Apr 1997): 1; Pettifer and Turner, *Automania*, 242; Rae, *American Automobile*, 106.
19. Smith, *Social History of the Bicycle*, 246; Perry, *Bike Cult*, 37-38.
20. Burton J. Hendrick, *The Age of Big Business* (New Haven: Yale University Press, 1919), 122-123; Flink, *Automobile Age*, 3; Goddard, *Getting There*, 67, 76-77.
21. Goddard, *Getting There*, 73-75, 82-83, 120-121, 129.
22. Goddard, *Getting There*, 74-75; Flink, *Car Culture*, 142.
23. Flink, *Automobile Age*, 365.
24. St. Clair, *Motorization of American Cities*, 6, 32-53, 64, 72; Goddard, *Getting There*, 129-134.
25. Flink, *Automobile Age*, 364; St. Clair, *Motorization of American Cities*, 58; Goddard, *Getting There*, 132-135.
26. St. Clair, *Motorization of American Cities*, 63; Goddard, *Getting There*, 132-133.
27. Goddard, *Getting There*, 135.
28. St. Clair, *Motorization of American Cities*, 83.
29. Goddard, *Getting There*, 123, 248-249.
30. Jonathan Kwitny, "The Great Transportation Conspiracy," *Harper's* 262, no. 1569 (Feb 1981): 15.
31. Goddard, *Getting There*, 201.

Chapter 3

1. Lincoln Highway Association, *The Lincoln Highway*, vii.

2. Pettifer and Turner, *Automania*, 47.
3. Guillet, *Story of Canadian Roads*, 155; Goddard, *Getting There*, 46, 51.
4. St. Clair, *Motorization of American Cities*, 20; Flink, *America Adopts the Automobile*, 209.
5. Flink, *America Adopts the Automobile*, 163; Goddard, *Getting There*, 57-58.
6. Goddard, *Getting There*, 61; Lincoln Highway Association, *The Lincoln Highway*, 57.
7. Flink, *Car Culture*, 187; Goddard, *Getting There*, 155; Guillet, *Story of Canadian Roads*, 157-159.
8. Goddard, *Getting There*, 96-97, 112-113.
9. Flink, *Automobile Age*, 374-375; Goddard, *Getting There*, 155-56.
10. Goddard, *Getting There*, 149; Kay, *Asphalt Nation*, 199; McShane, *The Automobile*, 91; Bruce Seely, *Building the American Highway System* (Philadelphia: Temple University Press, 1987), 88.
11. Goddard, *Getting There*, 158, 160.
12. "The American Automobile: The First 100 Years," *The Wall Street Journal*, 26 Jun 1996, Supplement 4, 8, 9, 11; Flink, *Automobile Age*, 261-262; Goddard, *Getting There*, 116; Kay, *Asphalt Nation*, 234-235; Liebs, *Main Street to Miracle Mile*, 154-155, 212; John Robinson, *Highways and Our Environment* (New York: McGraw-Hill, 1971), 154.
13. St. Clair, *Motorization of American Cities*, 121-122, 130, 133.
14. Goddard, *Getting There*, 179-186; St. Clair, *Motorization of American Cities*, 157; Rae, *American Automobile*, 204.
15. St. Clair, *Motorization of American Cities*, 154-160; Goddard, *Getting There*, 184.
16. Mowbray, *Road to Ruin*, 14.
17. Tom Lewis, *Divided Highways: Building the Interstate Highways, Transforming American Life* (New York: Viking, 1997), 121-122; St. Clair, *Motorization of American Cities*, 160-161; Goddard, *Getting There*, 172, 184.
18. Helen Leavitt, *Superhighway-Superhoax* (Garden City, NY: Doubleday, 1970), 45.
19. Kay, *Asphalt Nation*, 233; Goddard, *Getting There*, 178.
20. Jackson, *Crabgrass Frontier*, 30-32, 184-185.
21. Jackson, *Crabgrass Frontier*, 203, 233.
22. Kay, *Asphalt Nation*, 180, 230, 245.
23. Jackson, *Crabgrass Frontier*, 168; Goddard, *Getting There*, 199, 216.
24. Mowbray, *Road to Ruin*, 34-35, 177, 200-201.
25. American Farmland Trust, "Farming on the Edge," Table 7, < http://farm.fic.niu.edu/foe2/report/foetab7.html >.
26. John Warbach and Mark Wyckoff, *Growth Management Tools & Techniques* (Lansing, Mich.: Michigan Coastal Management Program, Dept of Natural Resources, 1995), 2-3; Michigan Society of Planning Officials (MSPO), *Patterns on the Land* (Rochester, Mich.: MSPO, n.d.), 4.
27. Flink, *Automobile Age*, 173-177; Kay, *Asphalt Nation*, 172 (Yellowstone attendance).
28. Flink, *Automobile Age*, 173; Pettifer and Turner, *Automania*, 96 (1940 park attendance).

29. National Park Service, *Alternative Transportation Modes Feasibility Study Volume III: Yellowstone* (Denver, CO: National Park Service, Jul 1994), 34 and Appendix A; National Park Service, *Alternative Transportation Modes Feasibility Study Volume IV: Yosemite* (Denver, CO: National Park Service, Jun 1994), 26, 87, maps.
30. Paul Sutter, "Driven Wild," *The Road RIPorter* 2, no. 1 (Jan/Feb 1997): 4-5; Bethanie Walder, "The Problem with Temporary Roads," *The Road RIPorter* 3, no. 2 (Mar/Apr 1998): 12.
31. Hélène Cyr, *Handmade Forests* (Gabriola Island, B.C.: New Society Publishers, 1998), 127.
32. Dave Foreman and Howie Wolke, *The Big Outside* (New York: Harmony Books, 1992), 14.
33. Michael Renner, *Rethinking the Role of the Automobile* (Washington, D.C.: Worldwatch Institute, 1988), 46.
34. Mowbray, *Road to Ruin*, 100-101.
35. Federal Highway Administration, "TEA-21, A Summary," 1998, < http://www.fhwa.dot.gov/tea21/sumauth.htm > ; Cervero, *The Transit Metropolis*, 38.
36. Surface Transportation Policy Project, "An Analysis of the Relationship Between Highway Expansion and Congestion in Metropolitan Areas," Nov 1998, < www.transact.org/congestion/analysis.htm > .
37. Kay, *Asphalt Nation*, 15, 296.

Chapter 4

1. Unless otherwise cited, historical background on advertising in this chapter is drawn from James Playsted Wood, *The Story of Advertising* (New York: Ronald Press Company, 1958) and Frank Rowsome Jr., *They Laughed When I Sat Down: An Informal History of Advertising in Words and Pictures* (New York: Bonanza Books, 1959).
2. First quotation: Pettifer and Turner, *Automania*, 124; all others: Wood, *The Story of Advertising*, 305-306.
3. Rowsome, *They Laughed When I Sat Down*, 110, 165; McShane, *The Automobile*, 52, 61.
4. Allen D. Kanner and Mary E. Gomes, "The All-Consuming Self," *Adbusters* 3, no. 4 (summer 1995): 23; "The Sponsored Life," *Adbusters* 3, no. 4 (summer 1995): 83.
5. *Advertising Age*, "Ad Age Dataplace," Sep 1999, < http://adage.com/dataplace/ > .
6. *Advertising Age*, "Ad Age Dataplace," Sep 1999, < http://adage.com/dataplace/ > .
7. Jean Halliday, "General Motors slices spending in magazines," *Advertising Age* 69, no. 9 (2 Mar 1998): 1 + ; "Advertisers pose threat to free speech," *Adbusters* 3, no. 1 (winter 1994): 14; Evan Smith, "Jim Hightower: A Hellraising Texas Radio Personality Fights to Stay on the Dial," *Mother Jones* 20, no. 6 (Nov/Dec 1995): 58; Jeffrey Schrank, *Deception Detection* (Boston: Beacon Press, 1975), 16.
8. John Kenneth Galbraith, *The New Industrial State* (Boston: Houghton Mifflin, 1967), 29-30, 212.

9. Schrank, *Deception Detection*, 3-10.
10. "Automotive Industry Targets Minority Drivers With A Diverse Marketing Menu," *Minority Markets Alert* 9, no. 11 (Nov 1997): 1 + ; Cleveland Horton, "Cagey media tricks pay off in sales dividend: snaring boomers requires artful ad buys," *Advertising Age* 67, no. 14 (1 Apr 1996): s14.
11. McShane, *The Automobile*, plates following 147.
12. Unless otherwise cited, ads quoted are from 1993-1998 TV broadcasts or issues of *Food and Wine, Fortune, The New Yorker, Newsweek, Time, U.S. News and World Report, USA Today, The Vancouver Sun,* or *The Wall Street Journal.*
13. McShane, *The Automobile*, 83.
14. George Cantor, "Road rage becomes cliche for driving stupidity," *Detroit News*, 21 Nov 1998, C16.
15. Michael Frostick, *Advertising and the Motor-Car* (London: Lund Humphries, 1970), 64-68.
16. Bradford Wernle, "Jordan put the sizzle in pitch," *Automotive News* 2 (26 Jun 1996): 78.
17. Bradford Wernle, "Jordan put the sizzle in pitch," *Automotive News* 2 (26 Jun 1996): 78.
18. Pettifer and Turner, *Automania*, 130.
19. Frostick, *Advertising and the Motor-car*, 158.
20. Bob Mackin, "Autosaurus goes to court," *Adbusters* 3, no. 3 (winter 1995): 84; Chris DeVito, "Legal battle looms over Autosaurus," *Adbusters* 3, no. 1 (winter 1994): 12; "Autosaurus rises from the ashes," *Adbusters* 3, no. 2 (summer 1994): 77.
21. Leif Nielsen, "Auto shows mean big money," *Automotive News Europe* 3, no. 1 (5 Jan 1998): 4; Paul A. Eisenstein, "Expect the Unexpected," *WorldTraveler* (Jan 1995): 28; Jean Halliday, "Makers Target Buyers with Alternate Media," *Automotive News* 5737 (27 Oct 1997): 30; Jean Halliday, "Carmakers new models in public eye before ads," *Advertising Age* 68, no. 19 (12 May 1997): 76.
22. Sheila Harty, *Hucksters in the Classroom* (Washington, D.C.: Center for Study of Responsive Law, 1979), 12.
23. Reginald McIntosh Cleveland, "How Many Automobiles Can America Buy?" *World's Work* (Apr 1914): 36-37.
24. Flink, *Automobile Age*, 234; "100 events that made the industry," *Automotive News* 2 (26 Jun 1996), 79, 82.
25. Stephen Bayley, *Harley Earl and the American Dream Machine* (London: Weidenfeld and Nicholson, 1991), 93.
26. James Wren, "Advertisements," in George S. May, ed., *The Automobile Industry, 1896-1920 / The Encyclopedia of American Business History and Biography* (New York: Facts On File, 1990), 5.
27. Max Sutherland, *Advertising and the Mind of the Consumer* (St. Leonard's, Australia: Allen & Unwin, 1993), 132-133.
28. Allen D. Kanner and Mary E. Gomes, "The All-Consuming Self," *Adbusters* 3, no. 4 (summer 1995): 23.
29. "The American Automobile: The First 100 Years," *The Wall Street Journal*, 26 Jun 1996, Supplement, 9; "100 events that made the industry," *Automotive*

News 2 (26 Jun 1996), 129, 130; Kay, *Asphalt Nation*, 244; McShane, *The Automobile*, 113-115.

Chapter 5

1. David Pimentel et al, "Ecology of Increasing Disease," *BioScience* 48, no. 10 (Oct 1998): 819.
2. Paul Zajac, Ward's Communications, personal communication; The Polk Company, Dec 1999; U.S. Federal Highway Administration, *Our Nation's Travel: 1995 NPTS Early Results Report* (Washington, D.C.: Department of Transportation, 1997), 3-6.
3. Brian Akre, "Light truck sales pass cars," *Detroit News*, 4 Dec 1998, B2; Flink, *Car Culture*, 194-196.
4. Ralph Kisiel, "Trucks veered from work to fun and sales keep growing," *Automotive News* 2 (26 Jun 1996): 150.
5. Keith Bradsher, "Trucks, darlings of drivers, are favored by the law, too," *New York Times*, 30 Nov 1997, 1 + ; Jason Mark, "Turn Signals," *Nucleus* 20, no. 4 (winter 1998-99): 4; Motavalli, *Forward Drive*, 202.
6. Henry Diamond and Patrick Noonan, *Land Use in America* (Washington, D.C.: Island Press, 1996), 4; U.S. Federal Highway Administration, *Our Nation's Travel*, 9, 11-17; William A. Martin and Nancy A. McGuckin, *National Cooperative Highway Research Program Report 365: Travel Estimations Techniques for Urban Planning* (Washington, D.C.: Transportation Research Board, 1998), 21.
7. U.S. Department of Energy, *Transportation Energy Data Book, Edition 19* (Oak Ridge, Tennessee: Oak Ridge National Laboratory, 1999), 1-15, 1-17, 1-18, 2-4, 2-7, 2-9.
8. U.S. Federal Highway Administration, *Our Nation's Travel*, 13, 22; Texas Transportation Institute,*Urban Mobility Study 1998*, < http://mobility.tamu.edu/study/PDFs/Chapter4.pdf > ; U.S. Federal Highway Administration, *Our Nation's Travel*, 13.
9. "The American Automobile: The First 100 Years," *Wall Street Journal*, 26 Jun 1996, Supplement 10-11; Zuckermann, *End of the Road*, 95-96; McShane, *The Automobile*, 162; "A hundred years on the clock," *The Economist* 339, no. 7971 (22 Jun 1996): 53; U.S. DOE, *Transportation Energy Data Book, Edition 19*, 1-17.
10. Tamim Raad and Jeff Kenworthy, "Dimensions of Difference," *Alternatives Journal* 24, no.1 (winter 1998): 16-17.
11. John Pucher, "Back on Track," *Alternatives Journal* 24, no.1 (winter 1998): 26-34.
12. "More motors," *The Economist* 346, no. 8051 (17 Jan 1998): 5; European Conference of Ministers of Transport, *European Transport Trends and Infrastructural Needs* (Paris France: OECD Publications Service, 1995), 74; "All jammed up," *The Economist* 348, no. 8084 (5 Sep 1998): 4.
13. Paul A. Eisenstein, "Global Auto Sales Pick Up Speed," *Northwest Airlines WorldTraveler* (Mar 1996): 21.
14. "All jammed up," *The Economist* 348, no. 8084 (5 Sep 1998): 4; Mark Hertsgaard, *Earth Odyssey* (New York: Broadway Books, 1998), 89.

15. American Automobile Manufacturers Association (AAMA), *World Motor Vehicle Data 1998* (Washington, D.C.: AAMA, 1998), 23; Richard Russell, "Notes and Quotes," *Dow Theory Letters* 1266 (2 Dec 1998): 6.

16. Barry Newman, "Old East Bloc Sees New Freeways as Roads to Capitalist Advance," *Wall Street Journal*, 7 March, 1995, A1 + ; Ken Fireman, "American gridlock in Russia," *San Francisco Examiner*, 3 Jul 1994, Sunday Punch.

17. Fortune Magazine, 1999 Fortune Global 500, < http://www.pathfinder.com/fortune/global500/index.html >.

18. Richard Russell, "Notes and Quotes," *Dow Theory Letters* 1211 (23 Oct 1996): 4.

19. "Car firms head for a crash," *The Economist* 343, no 8016 (10 May 1997): 14; Richard Russell, "Notes and Quotes," *Dow Theory Letters* 1226 (21 May 1997): 4; "Making cars in Latin America: Trouble in Eldorado," *The Economist* 345, no. 8047 (13 Dec 1997): 57-58.

20. American Automobile Manufacturers Association (AAMA), *World Motor Vehicle Data 1998* (Washington, D.C.: AAMA, 1998), 10.

21. Alfred P. Sloan, *My Years with General Motors* (Garden City, New York: Doubleday, 1963), 315.

22. Automotive News, *1998 Market Data Book* (Detroit, Mich.: Automotive News, 1998), 17, 48; "Auto industry sells record 16.9 million vehicles," 5 Jan 2000, < www.cnn.com/2000/US/01/05/auto.sales.ap/ >

23. Cervero, *The Transit Metropolis*, 38; Paul A. Eisenstein, "Korea, Poland, typify global automotive boom," *Christian Science Monitor*, 18 Jan 1996, 8; "Cycle Rickshaw Persecution Persists," *Sustainable Transport* 8 (winter 1998): 12; Walter Hook, "Jakarta: A City in Crisis," *Sustainable Transport* 8 (winter 1998): 14 + ; "China aids carmakers," *San Francisco Chronicle*, 10 Jan 1994, B2.

24. Devra Lee Davis et al, *Urban Air Pollution Risks to Children* (Washington, D.C.: World Resources Institute,1999); R. Monastersky, "Pollution surge from new Chinese cars," *Science News* 152, nos. 25 and 26 (20 and 27 Dec 1997): 396; "Asia pollution reaches West Coast," 5 Mar 1999, < www.enn.com/enn-subscribe-news-archive/1999/03/030599/pollution_2006.asp > ; "China accelerates alternative fuel auto industry," 3 Dec 1998, < www.enn.com/news/wire-stories/1998/12/120398/fuels.asp >.

25. Michael Richardson, "Asia chokes on growing pollution," *International Herald Tribune*, 21 Aug 1997, 1; R. Monastersky, "China's air pollution chokes crop growth," *Science News* 155 (27 Mar 1999): 197; Lester R. Brown, *Who Will Feed China?* (New York: W.W. Norton, 1995), 26, 58-60.

26. Richard A. Kerr, "The Next Oil Crisis Looms Large — and Perhaps Close," *Science* 281 (21 Aug 1998): 1128, 1130; Walter Youngquist, *GeoDestinies* (Portland, Oreg.: National Book Co., 1997), 189; Worldwatch Institute, *Vital Signs 1998* (Washington, D.C.: Worldwatch Institute, 1998), 51.

27. Eric Freedman, "Goodbye gas guzzlers," *Automotive News* 2 (26 Jun 1996): 131; David Lewis, University of Michigan, personal communication.

28. Seth Dunn, "After Kyoto: A Climate Treaty With No Teeth?" *WorldWatch* 11, no. 2 (Mar/Apr 1998): 33.

29. Worldwatch Institute, *Vital Signs 1998*, 19; Tom Gray, American Wind Energy Association press release, 12 Dec 1996.

Part 2, Introduction

1. Brower and Leon, *Consumer's Guide to Effective Environmental Choices*, 86.

Chapter 6

1. McShane, *The Automobile*, 101.
2. Wyn Grant, *Autos, Smog and Pollution Control* (Aldershot, Hants, U.K.: Edward Elgar Publishing, 1995), 31.
3. OECD, *Towards Sustainable Transportation: The Vancouver Conference* (Paris, France: OECD, 1997), 21 (regarding CO_2 emissions).
4. U.S. EPA, "Automobile Emissions: An Overview," 20 Jul 1998, < http://www.epa.gov/oms/05-autos.htm >.
5. "Russian crisis has helped environment," 20 Jan 1999, < www.planetark.org/dailynewsstory.cfm?newsid = 1748&newsdate = 20-Jan-1999 >; "Pollution chokes Delhi as people look on," 20 Jan 1999, < www.planetark.org/dailynewsstory.cfm?newsid = 1751&newsDate = 20-Jan-1999 >.
6. U.S. EPA, *National Air Quality and Emissions Trends Report 1997* (Research Triangle Park, NC: U.S. EPA, 1998), 25; Bill Liebhardt, "Farms, Cities and the Environment," *Sustainable Agriculture News* 4, no.4 (summer 1992): 1; R. Monastersky, "China's air pollution chokes crop growth," *Science News* 155, no. 13 (27 Mar 1999): 197; Peter Jaret, "Air Quality: Unacceptable," *Health* (Mar 1989): 50.
7. U.S. EPA, *National Air Pollutant Emission Trends 1900-1996*, 1-1, 2-15; John Seinfeld, *Atmospheric Chemistry and Physics of Air Pollution* (New York: Wiley, 1986), 58; Environment Canada, "Automobile Emissions, Individual Health and the Environment," 1 Apr 1998, < www.ec.gc.ca/emission/2-6e.html >; Williams, *Autogeddon*, 122; OECD, "Selected Environmental Data and Indicators," < www.oecd.org/env/indicators/AnnexI.pdf >.
8. David Pimentel et al, "Ecology of Increasing Disease," *BioScience* 48, no. 10 (Oct 1998): 821; Makower, *Green Commuter*, 67; U.S. Bureau of Transportation Statistics, *Transportation Statistics Annual Report 1996* (Washington, D.C.: U.S. Department of Transportation, 1996), 143; "Car exhaust gets another indictment," *Science News* 135, no. 8 (25 Feb 1989): 123; California Air Resources Board, "Half of the mutagenic activity of ambient air is from derivatives of emitted PAHs," Research Notes No. 94-22, Nov 1994, < www.arb.ca.gov/research/resnotes/Notes/94-22.htm >; OECD, "Selected Environmental Data and Indicators," < www.oecd.org/env/indicators/AnnexI.pdf >; Environment Canada, "Automobile Emissions, Individual Health and the Environment," 1 Apr 1998, < www.ec.gc.ca/emission/2-6e.html >; U.S. Department of Energy, *Transportation Energy Data Book, Edition 19* (Oak Ridge, Tennessee: Oak Ridge National Laboratory, 1999), 4-7.
9. OECD, "Selected Environmental Data and Indicators," < www.oecd.org/env/indicators/AnnexI.pdf >; U.S. Department of Energy, *Transportation Energy Data Book, Edition 19* (Oak Ridge, Tennessee: Oak Ridge National Laboratory, 1999), 4-3; Richard P. Turco, *Earth Under Siege* (New York: Oxford University Press, 1997), 194-195; U.S. EPA, *National Air Pollutant Emission Trends, 1900-1996*, 1-1; J.H. Schulte, "Effects of mild carbon monoxide intoxication," *Archives of Environmental Health* (Nov 1963): 524-

530; Alan Wellburn, *Air Pollution and Acid Rain: The Biological Impact* (New York: Wiley, 1988), 175-180.

10. "Pollution kills 60,000 yearly, study says," *Los Angeles Times*, 13 May 1991 A24; Devra Lee Davis et al, "The Hidden Benefits of Climate Policy," *Environmental Health Notes* (Dec 1997): 1; Gerard Kiely, *Environmental Engineering* (London: McGraw-Hill, 1997), 868; Kay, *Asphalt Nation*, 87; U.S. EPA, *National Air Pollutant Emission Trends, 1900-1996*, 3-14.

11. Earth Summit Watch, "The Global Phaseout of Leaded Gasoline," 1999, < www.earthsummitwatch.org/gasoline.html > ; World Bank Group, "World Bank Recommends Global Phase-Out of Leaded Gasoline," 18 May 1996, < www.worldbank.org/html/extdr/extme/gaspr.htm > ; World Bank Group, "Phasing Out Lead from Gasoline," Jan 1998, < http://wbln0018.worldbank. org/essd/pmext.nsf/670c98692c42a13c852565e2005a58d8/ > .

12. Hilary French, *Clearing the Air* (Washington, D.C.: Worldwatch Institute, 1990).

13. "California water agencies act on MTBE," ENN, 3 Jun 1998, < www.enn.com/enn-news-archive/1998/06/060398/mtbe.asp > ; Stephen Hoffert, "Haze of Uncertainty Surrounds Gas Additive," *The Scientist* 12, no. 13 (22 Jun 1998): 1; S. Patton, "MTBE: A good idea backfires," ENN, 21 Sep 1998, < www.enn.com/enn-features-archive/1998/09/092198/mtbe.asp > .

14. "MMT," EDF, 1994, < http://www.edf.org/pubs/FactSheets/h_mmt1.html > ; "Gas Additive's Potential Toxicity Alarms Scientists." *Crime Times* 2, no. 2 (1996), < www.crime-times.org/966/w96bp4.htm > ; "EDF Blasts Rollback of Canadian MMT Ban," EDF, 21 Jul 1998, < http://www.edf.org/pubs/ NewsReleases/1998/Jul/b_MMTban.html > .

15. Seinfeld, *Atmospheric Chemistry and Physics of Air Pollution*, 94-95.

16. Legal advertisement, *San Francisco Chronicle*, 25 May 1993, A16.

17. Doyle, *Crude Awakening*, 97; U.S. EPA, "Nat'l Emissions Stdrds for Hazardous Air Pollutants," 1998, < www.epa.gov/reg3artd/enforce/toxics.htm > .

18. Healthy City Office, *Smog: Make It or Break It* (Toronto: City of Toronto, 1998).

19. U.S. EPA, "Motor Vehicle Industry Notebook," 1993, < www.csa.com/routenet/epan/motvehsnIVb.html > and < www.csa.com/routenet/epan/motvehsnIVa.html > .

20. U.S. EPA, "Motor Vehicle Industry Notebook: IV.C," 1995, < www.csa.com/routenet/epan/motvehsnIVc.html > ; U.S. EPA, *1996 Toxics Release Inventory* (Washington, D.C.: U.S. EPA, May 1998), 159, 257, 264.

21. California Air Resources Board and South Coast Air Quality Management District, "Measuring Concentration of Selected Air Pollutants Inside California Vehicles," Dec 1998, < www.arb.ca.gov/research/indoor/in-vehsm.htm > .

22. "EPA to screen products for invasive chemicals," ENN, 28 Aug 1998, < www.enn.com/news/wire-stories/1998/08/082898/chemscan.asp > .

23. Intergovernmental Panel on Climate Change, *Climate Change, 1995: Scientific-Technical Analyses* (New York: Cambridge University Press, 1996); Lester Brown et al, *Vital Signs 1998* (Washington, D.C.: Worldwatch Institute, 1998), 66; C.D. Keeling and T.P. Whorf, "Atmospheric Carbon Dioxide Record from Mauna Loa," Scripps Institute of Oceanography, 23 Jul 1999, < http://cdiac.esd.ornl.gov/trends/co2/sio-mlo.htm > .

24. R. Monastersky, "Earth's temperature shot skyward in 1998," *Science News* 155, no. 1 (2 Jan 1999): 6.

25. International Council for Local Environmental Initiatives (ICLEI) and U.S. EPA, *Saving the Climate — Saving the Cities* (Toronto: ICLEI, 1995), 32; "1998 a disaster for insurers, leading firm says," ENN, 30 Dec 1998, < www.enn.com/news/wire-stories/1998/12/123098/insurance.asp > .

26. R. Monastersky, "Satellite Detects a Global Sea Rise," *Science News* 146, no. 24 (10 Dec 1994): 388; "Trouble in Paradise Ecologic, Economic," ENN, 28 Sep 1999, < www.enn.com/enn-subscriber-news-archive/1999/09/092899/paradise_6011.asp > .

27. ICLEI and U.S. EPA, *Saving the Climate — Saving the Cities*, 40-42; David Pimentel et al, "Ecology of increasing disease," *BioScience* 48, no. 10 (Oct 1998): 819, 823.

28. Chris Thomas and Jack Lennon, "Birds Extend their Ranges Northward," *Nature* 399 (20 May 1999): 213; Janet Raloff, "Sea Sickness," *Science News* 155, no. 5 (30 Jan 1999): 72; Reuters, "Environmentalist says Seychelles coral dying," ENN, 22 Dec 1998, < www.enn.com/news/wire-stories/1998/12/122298/coraldie.asp > .

29. Brown et al, *Vital Signs 1998*, 68; M.H. Jones et al, "Carbon dioxide fluxes in moist and dry Arctic tundra during the snow-free season," *Arctic, Antarctic and Alpine Research* 30, no. 4 (Nov 1998): 373-380; "Arctic tundra pumping carbon into atmosphere," 19 Dec 1996, < www.enn.com/news/enn-news-archive/1996/12/121996/12199605.asp > .

30. R. Monastersky, "Sea Change in the Arctic," *Science News* 155 no 7 (13 Feb 1999): 104-106; "Melting of Antarctic ice shelves accelerates," 9 Apr 1999 < www.enn.com/news/enn-stories/1999/04/040999/iceretreat_2583.asp > ; Brown et al, *Vital Signs 1998*, 68; U.S. Office of Science and Technology Policy, *Climate Change: State of Knowledge* (Washington, D.C.: Office of the President, 1997), 15.

31. Andy Soloman, "Antarctic Ice Melt May Come In Next Generation," 29 Jan 1999 < http://www.planetark.org/dailynewsstory.cfm?newsid = 1587&newsdate = 29-Jan-1999 > ; U.S. Office of Science and Technology Policy, *Climate Change: State of Knowledge*, 12; Jim Motavalli, "2000: Planet Earth at the Crossroads," *E Magazine* X, no. 1 (Jan-Feb 1999): 31-32; J. Alan Pounds et al, "Biological response to climate change on a tropical mountain," *Nature* 398 (15 Apr 1999): 611-615; Richard A. Kerr, "Warming's Unpleasant Surprise: Shivering in the Greenhouse?" *Science* 281 (10 Jul 1998): 156-158.

32. International Council for Local Environmental Initiatives (ICLEI), *U.S. Communities Acting to Protect the Climate* (Toronto: ICLEI, 1998), 21.

33. "Landscape changes may alter climate," 31 Dec 1998, < www.enn.com/enn-news-archive/1998/12/123098/landscape.asp > .

34. Sharon Begley, "He's not full of hot air," *Newsweek* (22 Jan 1996): 24-29.

35. "The Automobile and the Environment," ICLEI Energy Fact Sheet, 1993, < http://www.iclei.org/efacts/auto.htm > ; "What's Wrong with the Car?", *The Watershed Sentinel* (Dec 1992/Jan 1993); Freon is a registered trademark of Dupont and Company.

36. Kay, *Asphalt Nation*, 112; Makower, *Green Commuter*, 11.

37. ICF Incorporated, *Supply and Demand of CFC-12 in the United States 1998* (Washington, D.C.: U.S. EPA, 15 May 1998), 5; Sue Stendebach, U.S. EPA, personal communication.

38. Elizabeth Levy, "No More Ozone Hole?" *E Magazine* X, no. 1 (Jan-Feb 1999): 22; "UV rays in New Zealand on the rise, study says," 10 Sep 1999, < www.enn.com/news/wire-stories/1999/09/091099/uvrays_5573.asp >.

39. A. Ferguson and D. I. Wardle, *Arctic Ozone* (Ottawa: Environment Canada, 1998), 15-18.

40. Randall S. Cerveny and Robert C. Balling Jr., "Weekly Cycles of Air Pollutants, Precipitation and Tropical Cyclones in the Coastal NW Atlantic Region," *Nature* (6 Aug 1998), summary, < www.asu.edu/clas/geography/nature/ >; Usha Lee McFarling, "The rain in Maine falls mainly on the weekends," *Seattle Times*, 6 Aug 1998, < www.seattletimes.com/news/nation-world/html98/altwett_080698.html >

41. Kurt Paterson, Michigan Technological University, personal communication.

42. U.S. EPA, *National Air Pollutant Emission Trends, 1900-1996*, 2-5; Turco, *Earth Under Siege*, 270-277.

43. J. Dillon, "Fading Colors," *Audubon* 100, no. 5 (Sep-Oct 1998): 49; "Acid Rain in Pennsylvania," Penn. Dept. of Env. Prot., 1 Mar 1999, < www.dep.state.pa.us/dep/deputate/airwaste/aq/Factsheets/fs2036.htm >; M. Forstenzer, "Cars kill trees," *High Country News*, 14 Apr 1997, 5; M. Horn, "The Vanishing Past," *U.S. News & World Report* 113, no.11 (21 Sep 1992): 80-89; Turco, *Earth Under Siege*, 260, 279, 281-284.

44. Peter Jaret, "Air Quality: Unacceptable," *Health* (Mar 1989): 49; David Pimentel et al, "Ecology of Increasing Disease," *BioScience* 48, no. 10 (Oct 1998): 819-820; U.S. EPA, *1996 Toxics Release Inventory*, 49; C. Schrender, "Chicago area children could use breathing space, study finds," *Chicago Tribune*, 28 Apr 1995, B1.

45. "Pollution linked to heart disease," BBC, 12 Aug 1998, < http://news.bbc.co.uk/hi/english/health/newsid_149000/149716.stm >

46. Makower, *Green Commuter*, 8; "Auto fumes linked with cancer," *GEO* (Nov 1981): 134; Peter Jaret, "Air Quality: Unacceptable," *Health* (Mar 1989): 51; AP, "U.S. government advised on carcinogens," 4 Dec 1998, < www.enn.com/news/wire-stories/1998/12/120498/cancer.asp >; Air Resources Board, "Toxic Air Contaminant Emissions from Diesel-Fueled Engines," Calif. EPA, Oct 1998, < www.arb.ca.gov/toxics/dieseltac/factsht1.pdf >; David Pimentel et al, "Ecology of Increasing Disease," *BioScience* 48, no. 10 (Oct 1998): 820.

47. Makower, *Green Commuter*, 6; David Pimentel et al, "Ecology of Increasing Disease," *BioScience* 48, no. 10 (Oct 1998): 820; Kay, *Asphalt Nation*, 111.

Chapter 7

1. Joanna Burger, *Oil Spills* (New Brunswick, NJ: Rutgers University Press, 1997), 35-36.

2. Interagency Coordinating Committee on Oil Pollution Research (ICCOPR), "Oil Pollution Research and Technology Plan," Apr 1997, < http://www.uscg.mil/hq/g-m/nmc/gendoc/coop/coop.htm >; Burger, *Oil Spills*, 29-30.

3. Jack Doyle, *Crude Awakening* (Washington, D.C.: Friends of the Earth, 1993), 105,145; Ted Williams, "Fatal Attraction," *Audubon* 99, no. 5 (Sep-Oct 1997):

24; Rob Edwards, "All at Sea," *New Scientist* (28 Nov 1998), < www.newscientist.com/ns/981128/news.html >.

4. Doyle, *Crude Awakening*, 195-196; B. Oyinbo, "Chevron Nigeria: Raid Kills Protestors," *Car Busters* no. 3 (autumn 1998): 7.

5. Minerals Management Service, "OCS Oil Spill Facts," U.S. Interior Dept, < www.mms.gov/eod/stats/oilsil.pdf >; Burger, *Oil Spills*, 30.

6. J. Cousteau, "Jean-Michael Cousteau Watch: The Challenge of Valdez," 12 Apr 1999, < www.enn.com/features/1999/04/041299/valdez_2601.asp >; Burger, *Oil Spills*, 51-55; ICCOPR, "Oil Pollution Research and Technology Plan," Apr 1997, < www.uscg.mil/hq/g-m/nmc/gendoc/coop/coop.htm >.

7. "Canada targets ocean oil dumpers," 14 Apr 1999, < www.enn.com/news/wire-stories/1999/04/041499/canadaoil_2662.asp >; "Illegal oil dumping taking toll on penguins," 12 Jan 1999; < www.enn.com/news/enn-stories/1999/01/ 011299/penguinaus.asp >.

8. "Bulgarian plant unharmed by Danube oil spill," 15 Jan 1999, < www. planetark.org/dailynewsstory.cfm?newsid = 1685&newsdate = 15-Jan-1999 >.

9. "Pipeline hole blamed for Alaska refuge oil spill," 19 Jan 1999, < www. planetark.org/dailynewsstory.cfm?newsid = 1711&newsdate = 19-Jan-1999 >.

10. "Tar balls floating toward Puerto Rico beaches," 28 Jan 1999; < www.enn.com/news/wire-stories/1999/01/012999/tarballs.asp >.

11. "Ship leaking oil threatens Oregon coast," 9 Feb 1999, < www.enn.com/news/wire-stories/1999/02/010999/oilbird.asp >.

12. Makower, *Green Commuter*, 13; Doyle, *Crude Awakening*, 19, 21, 36-37, 48-49, 55, 213.

13. ICCOPR, "Oil Pollution Research and Technology Plan," Apr 1997, < www.uscg.mil/hq/g-m/nmc/gendoc/coop/coop.htm >; U.S. General Accounting Office, *Pollution from Pipelines* (Washington, D.C.: U.S. GAO, 1991), 3; "Increase in oil pipeline accidents noted," 3 Feb 1999, < www.edf.org/pubs/NewsReleases/1999/Feb/a_pipeline.html >; Doyle, *Crude Awakening*, 92.

14. U.S. EPA, *Indicators of the Environmental Impacts of Transportation* (Washington, D.C.: U.S. EPA, 1996), 91; Philip Voorhees, *Perspectives on the Generation and Management of Used Oil in the U.S. in 1991* (Lexington, Mass.: Clayton Environmental Consultants, Nov 1992), 8, 11; Natural Resources Defense Council, *Burning Used Oil* (Washington, D.C.: NRDC, 1991), 1-5.

15. Doyle, *Crude Awakening*, 97.

16. Office of Underground Storage Tanks, "Corrective Action Measures for 2nd Half FY 98," U.S. EPA, 30 Sep 1998, < www.epa.gov/swerust1/cat/ camnow.htm >; "Colorado firm helps keep UST leaks in check," 18 Jan 1999, < www.enn.com/news/wire-stories/1999/01/011899/tankco.asp >.

17. "Individuals called biggest threat to oceans," 3 Dec 1999, < www.enn.com/news/enn-stories/1999/12/120399/oceanpoll_7801.asp >.

18. Reed Noss, "Ecological Effects of Roads," in Wildlands Center for Preventing Roads, *Road-Ripper's Handbook* (Missoula, Montana: Wildlands CPR, 1995), 13-14.

19. Noss, "Ecological Effects of Roads, 16.

20. Kay, *Asphalt Nation*, 90-92; Noss, "Ecological Effects of Roads, 14; David Ruben, "A Healthier Alternative to Road Salt," *New Age* (Nov-Dec 1990): 12; Schiller et al, *Green Streets*, 5.

21. Arnold Aspelin, *Pesticide Industry Sales and Usage* (Washington, D.C.: U.S. EPA, Aug 1997), 10, and personal communication.

22. Leslie Sinclair, Humane Society, personal communication, 13 Apr 1999; Makower, *Green Commuter*, 76.

23. Emily Green, Brett Hulsey and Pat King, *Southeastern Michigan: America's New Cancer Alley?* (Madison, Wisc.: Sierra Club Great Lakes Program, 1997), 7-8.

24. American Automobile Manufacturers Association, *Final Progress Report: U.S. Automotive Pollution Prevention Project* (Detroit: AAMA, 1998), 1.

25. U.S. EPA, *1996 Toxics Release Inventory*, 292; American Automobile Manufacturers Association, *Motor Vehicle Facts & Figures 1997* (Washington, D.C.: AAMA, 1997), 54.

26. ICLEI Energy Fact Sheet, 1993, < www.iclei.org/efacts/auto.htm > ; Personal communications: Jackson Nickerson, 12 Apr 1999; Fiona Osborn, Int'l Carwash Assoc., 13 Apr 1999; Ed Holbus, Car Wash Owners & Suppliers Assoc., 12 Apr 1999.

27. U.S. EPA, "Motor Vehicle Industry Notebook," 1993, < www.csa.com/routenet/epan/motvehsnIIIa.html > ; U.S. EPA, *1996 Toxics Release Inventory*, 290; Kiely, *Environmental Engineering*, 352; Kay, *Asphalt Nation*, 93.

28. Ward's Communications, *Ward's Automotive Yearbook* (Southfield, Mich.: Ward's, 1997), 19; Makower, *Green Commuter*, 144.

29. Mark Rust, *Automobile Shredder Residue Report* (St. Paul, Minn.: Minnesota Pollution Control Agency, 1995), p.v; U.S. EPA, "Motor Vehicle Industry Notebook," 1993, < www.csa.com/routenet/epan/motvehsnIIIa.html > .

30. Rust, *Automobile Shredder Residue Report*, ix, 4, 7, 12-22, 30-31.

31. U.S. EPA, *Indicators of the Environmental Impacts of Transportation*, 91-92; Scrap Tire Management Council, "Scrap Tire Facts & Figures," Rubber Manufacturers Association, 1999, < www.rma.org/scrapfctn.html > .

32. U.S. EPA, *Indicators of the Environmental Impacts of Transportation*, 93-94.

33. Lynda Lukasik, "Weak Controls Burn Hamiltonians," *Alternatives Journal* 24, no. 1 (winter 1998): 6.

34. David Bacon, "Good Idea, Bad Neighbor," *Alternatives Journal* 24, no. 1 (winter 1998): 11.

35. Kay, *Asphalt Nation*, 87-88; "Lightning ignites massive tire-dump fire in California," 24 Sep 1997, < www.enn.com/news/wire-stories/1999/09/092499/tirefire_5923.asp > ; Makower, *Green Commuter*, 100-103.

Chapter 8

1. Flink, *Car Culture*, 191-192; "Top Consumer 'Turn offs' in Buying a New Vehicle," JD Power and Associates, 30 Jun 1998, < www.jdpower.com/jdpower/releases/80630car.html > ; National Association of Consumer Agency Administrators and Consumer Federation of America, "Eighth Annual NACAA/CFA Consumer Complaint Survey Report," Nov 1999, < www.ncaanet.org/survey99.htm > .

2. "Targeted cars among most trouble-free," *Milwaukee Journal Sentinel*, 25 May 1995, 10D; J.D. Power and Associates, "1998 Intial Quality Study 2," 3 Jun 1998, < www.jdpower.com/jdpower/releases/80603ca2.html >; Tim Hurd, U.S. NHTSA, personal communication; Ward's Communications, *Ward's Automotive Yearbook* (Southfield, Mich.: Ward's, 1997), 103.

3. "Fraud widespread at auto body shops, state report says," *San Francisco Chronicle*, 14 Jul 1994, A18; "How car repair shops cheat women," *Good Housekeeping* (Mar 1995): 201; Kevin Clemens, "Can you fix my car?" *Reader's Digest* 151, no. 906 (Oct 1997): 87-92.

4. Pettifer and Turner, *Automania*, 17; "Auto thefts at lowest levels in 12 years," Consumer Insurance Guide, 12 Feb 1999, < www.insure.com/auto/thefts/thefts98.html >.

5. Mark Bricklin, "Walking, Thinking and Intellectual Angina," *The Commonwealth* 85, no. 25(24 Jun 1991): 453.

6. Preston Schiller et al, *Green Streets* (Washington, D.C.: STPP, 1998), 10; Frank Grad et al, "The Automobile and the Regulation of Some of its Non-Exhaust Impacts on the Environment," *Columbia Journal of Environmental Law* no.1 (1975): 217.

7. Galen Cranz, *The Chair* (New York: Norton, 1998), 164.

8. Kay, *Asphalt Nation*, 107-108.

9. National Institutes of Health, *Clinical Guidelines on Overweight and Obesity in Adults*, 1998, < www.nhlbi.nih.gov/guidelines/obesity/ob.home.htm >; "CDC's National Physical Activity Initiative," U.S. Dept. of Health and Human Services, n.d.; "The Link Between Physical Activity and Morbidity and Mortality," U.S. Centers for Disease Control, n.d.

10. Pettifer and Turner, *Automania*, 209; McShane, *The Automobile*, 45; "European Union Mandates Noise Maps for Cities," *New Scientist*, 19 Sep 1998, < www.nonoise.org/news/1998/sep13.htm >; James Geary, "Mad about the noise," *Time* 152, no. 4 (27 Jul 1998); OECD, *Fighting Noise* (Paris: OECD, 1986), 45; Kiely, *Environmental Engineering*, 391, 399; European Commission, "Future Noise Policy," 1996, < www.nonoise.org/library/eunoise/ greenpr.htm >; OECD, *Roadside Noise Abatement* (Paris: OECD, 1995), 9. Unless otherwise cited, web citations for the Noise section are from the Noise Pollution Clearinghouse.

11. Barbara Ruben, "On Deaf Ears," *Environmental Action* (Mar/Apr 1991): 16-19; Kiely, *Environmental Engineering*, 396, 401; OECD, *Roadside Noise Abatement*, 20, 25; OECD, "Selected Environmental Data and Indicators," 1997, < www.oecd.org/env/indicators/AnnexI.pdf >.

12. Barbara Ruben, "On Deaf Ears," 16-19; OECD, *Roadside Noise Abatement*, 20, 25; OECD, "Selected Environmental Data and Indicators," 1997, < www.oecd.org/env/indicators/AnnexI.pdf >; "European study shows city noise leads to serious ill health effects," *Evening Standard*, 9 Oct 1998, < www.nonoise.org/news/1998/oct4.htm >.

13. Kay, *Asphalt Nation*, 106; Steve Newman, "Tone Deaf," *Earthweek* (21 Jul 1995); "Road noise makes life unbearable in upscale Maryland planned community," *Baltimore Sun*, 16 Oct 1998, < www.nonoise.org/news/1998/ oct11.htm >; OECD, *Roadside Noise Abatement*, 28.

14. "Cairo's noisy citizens asked to hush up," *Christian Science Monitor*, 2 Jan 1997, 7; "Beijing takes measures to reduce noise pollution from car alarms," *China Daily*, 9 Apr 1998, < www.nonoise.org/news/1998/apr5.htm > .

15. "Texas city officials argue with nuns over erecting a noise wall and the purchase price of land," *Fort Worth Star-Telegram*, 23 May 1998, < www.nonoise.org/news/1998/may17.htm > ; "Nuns' plan acceptable to city," *Fort Worth Star-Telegram*, 5 Aug 1998, 1.

16. Sam Whiting, "A day in the life of a parking meter," *San Francisco Chronicle*, 26 May 1993, B1 + ; Roamy Valera, International Parking Institute, personal communication; "Downcity: Make it fun and they'll pay to park," *Rhode Ways*, 26 Apr 1998, < www.projo.com/special/rways/main.htm > .

17. "U.S. cities thrive, but poverty, congestion continue," 22 Jan 1999, < www.planetark.org/new/worldnews2.html > ; "Study shows traffic worsening in a variety of ways and places," Texas Transportation Institute, 16 Nov 1999, < http://mobility.tamu.edu/news_release/99newsrel.pdf > ; Gordon, *Steering a New Course*, 25.

18. Alan Boyd, "Bangkok Gridlock," *New World* 2 (Apr 1998): 29; "All jammed up," *The Economist* 348, no. 8084 (5 Sep 1998): 3-18; Oliver Tickell, "Death duties," *Guardian Weekly*, 5 Jul 1998, 23.

19. "Car commutes especially hurt women," *Urban Ecologist* 1 (1995): 16.

20. "All jammed up," *The Economist* 7; OECD, "Selected Economic Data and Indicators," < www.oecd.org/env/indicators/AnnexII.pdf > ; Oregon Environmental Council, Bicycle Transportation Alliance, and Coalition for a Livable Future, *An Expensive Love Affair* (Portland, Oreg.: OEC,1998).

21. "Study shows traffic worsening in a variety of ways and places," Texas Transportation Institute, 16 Nov 1999, < http://mobility.tamu.edu/news_release/99newsrel.pdf > ; Gordon, *Steering a New Course*, 42-43; Williams, *Autogeddon*, 134; "Weird News: Commuter Vehicle," *Comic Relief* 64 (Jun 1994): 30.

22. "An instant of anger, a lifetime of regret," *USA Today*, 23 Nov 1998, 19A; "Road rage takes a turn into the drive-through lane," *Atlanta Journal and Constitution*, 11 Dec 1998, 05E.

23. Scott Bowles, "Aggressive driving," *USA Today*, 23 Nov 1998, 17A; "About half of carjacking attempts succeed," 7 Mar 1999, < www.cnn.com/US/9903/07/carjackings/ > ; Louis Mizell, "Aggressive Driving," AAA Foundation for Traffic Safety, 1997, < http://raven.webfirst.com/aaa/Text/Research/agdrtext.htm#Aggressive Driving > ; Scott Bowles, "An expensive price tag," *USA Today*, 23 Nov 1998, 20A.

24. Mizell, "Aggressive Driving," < http://raven.webfirst.com/aaa/Text/Research/agdrtext.htm#Aggressive Driving > .

25. Carol J. Castaneda, "Violence by malicious drivers up 51% since '90," *USA Today*, 7 November 1996, 1A; Mizell, "Aggressive Driving," < http://raven.webfirst.com/aaa/Text/Research/agdrtext.htm#Aggressive Driving > .

26. "Auto Aggression," UCI in the News, 28 Nov 1995, < www.uci.edu/ ~ inform/media/951128.html > .

27. M. Joint, "Road Rage," Mar 1995, < http://raven.webfirst.com/aaa/Text/Research/agdrtext.htm#Aggressive Driving > .

28. Dominic Connell and Matthew Joint, "Driver Aggression," AAA Foundation for Traffic Safety, Nov 1996, < http://raven.webfirst.com/aaa/Text/Research/ agdrtext.htm#Aggressive Driving > .

29. "Rage starting to rule the nation's roads," *USA Today*, 29 Aug 1997, 3A; D. Connell and M. Joint, "Driver Aggression," Nov 1996, < http:// raven.webfirst.com/aaa/Text/Research/agdrtext.htm#Aggressive Driving > .

30. "Fury still the rage on roads," *Toronto Sun*, 17 Sep 1998, 3; "Road rage," *Journal of Commerce*, 10 Feb 1999, 4A; "Do kids notice road rage?" *USA Today*, 15 Sep 1998, 1A; "Lane Ranger," *Atlanta Journal and Constitution*, 4 Oct 1998, O20.

31. "Aggressive Driving: Are You at Risk?" STPP, 1999, < www.transact.org/ aggressivedriving99 > ; "Flame thrower now an option on S. African cars," CNN, 11 Dec 1998, < www.cnn.com/WORLD/africa/9812/11/flame. thrower.car > .

32. Donald Appleyard, *Livable Streets* (Berkeley: University of California Press,1981).

33. Jackson, *Crabgrass Frontier*, 279-280.

34. Kay, *Asphalt Nation*, 27-29.

35. Pamela Sebastian, "Business briefs," *Wall Street Journal*, 16 Apr 1998, A1.

36. Kay, *Asphalt Nation*, 48-49.

37. Rae, *The American Automobile*, 1.

38. Enere John, "Shell Is Killing Us," *Car Busters* 4 (early spring 1999): 11; "Rights group urges action by oil firms in Nigeria," 23 Feb 1999, < www.enn.com/news/wire-stories/1999/02/022399/oil.asp > .

39. John Vidal, "A tribe's suicide pact," *Guardian Weekly*, 12 Oct 1997, 8-9.

40. Dominique Gallois, "French oil firm plays down role in Africa," *Guardian Weekly*, 9 Nov 1997.

41. Ivan Illich, *Energy and Equity*, 30-31.

Chapter 9

1. Daniel Egan, "Car-Free, Care-Free, and On Our Bikes," *The BUGle* (n.d.).

2. American Automobile Association (AAA), *Your Driving Costs* (Heathrow, Flor.: AAA, 1999), 7-8.

3. "The Used Vehicle Department," National Automobile Dealers Association, < www.nada.org/nadadata/ > .

4. Litman, *Transportation Cost Analysis*, iv.

5. Alexandra Eadie, "Consumer purchases at retail stores," *Globe and Mail*, 22 Dec 1998, 15.

6. U.S. Bureau of Labor Statistics, "Consumer Expenditure Survey," < ftp://ftp.bls.gov/pub/special.requests/ce/standard/1998/age.txt > .

7. U.S. Bureau of Transportation Statistics (BTS), *Pocket Guide to Transportation* (Washington, D.C.: U.S. Dept. of Transportation, 1998), 19; Freund and Martin, *Ecology of the Automobile*, 46-49.

8. Kay, *Asphalt Nation*, 130.

9. AAMA, *Motor Vehicle Facts & Figures*, 1997, 57-62; Ronald J. Alsop, ed., *The Wall Street Journal Almanac 1998* (New York: Ballantine Books, 1997), 408; AAA, *Your Driving Costs*, 1999, 5, 7.

10. AAA, *Your Driving Costs*, 1999, 7.

11. Canadian Automobile Association (CAA), *Driving Costs, 1999 Edition* (Ottawa: CAA, 1999); CAA figures based on data from Runzheimer Canada Inc.

12. Litman, "Transportation Cost Analysis: Summary," 8 Jul 1999, < www.islandnet.com/ ~ litman > : 40; Litman, *Transportation Cost Analysis*, 6-2; Alan James, "Exploding myths about the cost of car transport," *World Transport Policy and Practice* 4, no.4 (1998): 10-15.

13. Litman, *Transportation Cost Analysis*, 3.2-5, 3.3-7.

14. Litman, *Transportation Cost Analysis*, vi.

15. Brian Ketcham and Charles Komanoff, *Win-Win Transportation*, 8; John Bailey, *Making the Car Pay Its Way* (Minneapolis: Institute for Local Self-Reliance, 1992), 1; Cora Roelofs and Charles Komanoff, *Subsidies for Traffic* (New York: Tri-State Transportation Campaign, 1994), 1.

16. Transport 2000 Canada,*The Highway ABCs for Taxpayers* (Ottawa, Ontario: Transport 2000 Canada, [1996]).

17. Kay, *Asphalt Nation*, 117, 254-255.

18. McShane, *The Automobile*, xi; U.S. DOT, *Highway Statistics 1996*, IV-14 and IV-15; Ketcham and Komanoff, *Win-Win Transportation*, 14; Litman, "Transportation Cost Analysis: Summary," 12 (figures showing that auto taxes and fees average 2.6 cents per vehicle mile, compared to an estimated 3.5 cents per vehicle mile of total roadway costs, are derived from U.S. Federal Highway Administration, *1997 Federal Highway Cost Allocation Study* (Washington, D.C.: U.S. Department of Transportation, 1997)); Litman, *Transportation Cost Analysis*, 3.6-5 - 3.6-6.

19. Cameron Smith, "The high cost of trucking," *CCPA Monitor*, (Nov 1998): 17.

20. Todd Litman, "Driving Out Subsidies," *Alternatives* 24, no. 1 (winter 1998): 39.

21. Tom Van Dan, Michigan Technological University, personal communication.

22. Nora Zamichow, "Most costly U.S. freeway opens in L.A.," *San Francisco Chronicle*, 15 Oct 1993, A5.

23. "Cypress Replacement," Caltrans, n.d., < http://tresc.dot.ca.gov/Cypress/ CypRep.html > ; Phillip Matier and Andrew Ross, "New stretch of freeway costs a bundle," *San Francisco Chronicle*, 19 Jul 1993, A1 + .

24. D. Chen, "Broken Promises Mar Big Dig," *Progress* 8, no. 4 (Oct 1998), < www.transact.org/oct98/bigdig.htm > .

25. Kay, *Asphalt Nation*, 118; Bonni McKeown, Corridor H Alternatives, personal communication.

26. U.S. Bureau of Transportation Statistics, *Transportation Statistics Annual Report 1999* (Washington, D.C.: Dept. of Transportation, 1999), 80.

27. Brian Laghi, "$17 billion fix sought for crumbling highways," *Globe and Mail*, 17 Dec 1998, A1 + .

28. Goddard, *Getting There*, 253; Litman, *Transportation Cost Analysis*, 12.

29. Oliver Tickell, "Death duties," *Guardian Weekly*, 5 Jul 1998, 23.

30. Freund and Martin, *Ecology of the Automobile*, 10; Kay, *Asphalt Nation*, 124; Litman, *Transportation Cost Analysis*, 3.8-1; MacKenzie et al, *The Going Rate*, 10.

31. Litman, *Transportation Cost Analysis*, 3.8-2.

32. McShane, *The Automobile*, 165.

33. MacKenzie et al, *The Going Rate*, 17.

34. Green Scissors Campaign, *Green Scissors '96* (Washington, D.C.: Friends of the Earth, Feb 1996), 13, 18.

35. Roland Hwang, *Money Down the Pipeline* (Boston, Mass.: Union of Concerned Scientists, 1995), ES-1.

36. Litman, *Transportation Cost Analysis,* 3.12-5.

37. Doyle, *Crude Awakening,* 219.

38. Neal Templin, "Finding gold in garages," *Wall Street Journal,* 18 April 1997, B14; Litman, *Transportation Cost Analysis,* 3.4-2.

39. Kay, *Asphalt Nation,* 63-64; Hart and Spivak, *Elephant in the Bedroom,* 31.

40. Roamy Valera, International Parking Institute, personal communication.

41. Litman, "Transportation Cost Analysis: Summary," 10; Litman, *Transportation Cost Analysis:* 3.4-2.

42. Litman, *Transportation Cost Analysis,* 3.4-3 – 3.4-7.

43. Oregon Environmental Council, Bicycle Transportation Alliance, and Coalition for a Livable Future, *An Expensive Love Affair: Are You Getting Taken for a Ride?* (Portland, Oregon: Oregon Environmental Council, 1998).

44. Mark Delucchi, *Annualized Social Cost of Motor-Vehicle Use in the U.S., 1990-1991* (Davis, Calif.: Institute of Transportation Studies, 1997).

45. Ketcham and Komanoff, *Win-Win Transportation,* 100; Kay, *Asphalt Nation,* 121; MacKenzie et al, *The Going Rate,* 18-19; "Study shows traffic worsening in a variety of ways and places," Texas Transportation Institute, 16 Nov 1999, < http://mobility.tamu.edu/news_release/99newsrel.pdf > ; Hans-Joachim Rehg, "Remote-Controlled Traffic," *New World* 2 (Apr 1998): 20; Alan Boyd, "Bangkok Gridlock," *New World* 2 (Apr 1998): 30.

46. Ketcham and Komanoff, *Win-Win Transportation,* 27, 103; Lawrence Blincoe, *Economic Cost of Motor Vehicle Crashes 1994* (Washington, D.C.: U.S. National Highway Traffic Safety Administration, 1995); "Accident Facts," National Safety Council, 1998, < www.nsc.org/lrs/statinfo/af78.htm > .

47. Oliver Tickell, "Death duties," *Guardian Weekly,* 5 Jul 1998, 23.

48. Mark Delucchi, *Annualized Social Cost of Motor-Vehicle Use in the U.S., 1990-1991* (figures in 1990 dollars).

49. Bank of America, Greenbelt Alliance, California Resources Agency, and Low Income Housing Fund, *Beyond Sprawl,* 1-8; Sierra Club, "The Dark Side of the American Dream," 1998, < www.sierraclub.org/sprawl/report98 > ; Henry L. Diamond and Patrick F. Noonan, *Land Use in America,* 38; Litman, *Transportation Cost Analysis,* 3.14-3; Kay, *Asphalt Nation,* 63-67, 306.

50. Robert W. Burchell et al., *The Costs of Sprawl — Revisited,* 140-141; Diamond and Noonan, *Land Use in America,* 35-40; Greenbelt Alliance, *Contra Costa County: Land Use or Abuse?* (San Francisco: Greenbelt Alliance, Apr 1996), 15; Michael Kinsley and L. Hunter Lovins, "Paying for Growth, Prospering from Development," *Planning and Zoning News* (Jul 1995): 12.

51. Litman, *Transportation Cost Analysis,* 3.14-4.

52. Tracy Baxter, "The Real Cost of Globe-Trotting Food," *Green Guide* 64 (Feb 1999): 1-2.

53. David Pimentel et al, "Economic and Environmental Benefits of Biodiversity," *BioScience* 47, no.11 (Dec 1997): 754; R. Costanza et al, "The value of the world's ecosystem services and natural capital," *Nature* 387 (1997): 253-260.

54. Based on Pimentel and Costanza's figures divided by world land area of approximately 60 million square miles.

55. Ketcham and Komanoff, *Win-Win Transportation*, 30.

56. Litman, *Transportation Cost Analysis*, 3.16-2.

57. MacKenzie et al, *The Going Rate*, 23; Moffet and Miller, *The Price of Mobility*, ii; Litman, "Transportation Cost Analysis: Summary," 44; Ketcham and Komanoff, *Win-Win Transportation*, 20; Litman, *Transportation Cost Analysis*, 4-6.

58. U.S. Bureau of Labor Statistics, "Consumer Expenditure Survey," < ftp://ftp.bls.gov/pub/special.requests/ce/standard/1998/age.txt > .

59. Go for Green, *Developing Communities for Active Transportation*. (Ottawa: Go for Green, 1998), 3.

60. Movement Transport Consultancy, *The Rush for Roads* (London: Alarm UK, 1994), 7.

61. UPI Umwelt- und Prognose-Institut Heidelberg e.V., UPI-Bericht #21, "Umweltwirkungen von Finanzinstrumenten im Verkehrbereich," Auftrag des Ministeriums fuer Stadtentwicklung und Verkehr des Landes Nordrhein-Westfalen (Department of Urban Development and Transportation), Jan 1991.

62. Ketcham and Komanoff, *Win-Win Transportation*, 55.

63. Ketcham and Komanoff, *Win-Win Transportation*, 78.

64. Newman, "Sustainable Transportation — In from the Cold?", 1, 18; Kay, *Asphalt Nation*, 128-129; Litman, "Transportation Cost Analysis: Summary," 36.

65. Litman, *Transportation Cost Analysis*, 6-14; Litman, "Transportation Cost Analysis: Summary," 33.

66. Litman, *Transportation Cost Analysis*, 3.3-10.

67. Litman, *Transportation Cost Analysis*, 4-6. Exchange rate of U.S.$1 = Cdn$1.48 from < www.bloomberg.com > on 4 Dec 1999.

Chapter 10

1. International Federation of Red Cross and Red Crescent Societies (IFRC), *World Disasters Report 1998* (New York: Oxford University Press, 1998), 20.

2. National Safety Council, *Injury Facts™, 1999 Edition* (Itasca, Illinois: National Safety Council, 1999), 80-81, 122-123.

3. McShane, *The Automobile*, 109, 125; "Thick fog, high speed: 11 killed in 300-car pileup," *Milwaukee Sentinel-Journal*, 13 Feb 1996; IFRC, *World Disasters Report 1998*, 20.

4. Oliver Tickell, "Death duties," *Guardian Weekly*, 5 Jul 1998, 23; "Road crashes to be third largest killer in 2020," IFRC, < www.ifrc.org > ; IFRC, *World Disasters Report 1998*, 21-22.

5. IFRC, *World Disasters Report 1998*, 22; National Safety Council, *Injury Facts™, 1999 Edition*, 16.

6. National Safety Council, *Injury Facts™, 1999 Edition*, 10-11, 100; "Statistics: Research on Youth," Mothers Against Drunk Driving, < www.madd.org/stats/stat_youth.shtml > ; U.S. DOT, *Transportation Statistics Annual Report 1998*, 79; Oliver Tickell, "Death duties," *Guardian Weekly*, 5 Jul 1998, 23; Right Of Way, *Killed by Automobile*, 9.

7. National Safety Council, *Injury Facts™, 1999 Edition*, 78-79, 104-111.

8. National Safety Council, *Injury Facts™, 1999 Edition*, 29.

9. AAMA, *Motor Vehicle Facts and Figures 1997*, 89.

10. Murray Ritchie, "Bid to make motoring cleaner but dearer; Europe to take on car culture," *The Herald* (Glasgow), 9 April 1997, 2; Oliver Tickell, "Death duties," 23.

11. Scott Bowles, "Healing comes slowly for family of crash victim," *USA Today*, 23 Nov 1998, 19A.

12. Sherwin B. Nuland, *How We Die* (New York: Random House, 1993), 145-146.

13. Kay, *Asphalt Nation*, 104.

14. E. Blanchard and E. Hickling, *After the Crash* (Washington, D.C.: Amer. Psychological Assoc., 1997), 24, 188-189; "Broken windshields, crumpled psyches," *Newsweek* 134, no. 11 (13 Sep 1999): 74.

15. This represents 98 percent of the average number injured in crashes each month, about 1.25 million (based on IFRC figures).

16. Brewster Bartlett, Pinkerton Academy, personal communication; "RoadKill '99," EnviroNet, < http://earth.simmons.edu/roadkill/roadkill.html >.

17. "Roadkills," Animal People, Sep 1994, < www.animalpepl.org/RoadKls.html >.

18. Mark Matthews, "Wildlife crossings cut down on roadkill," *High Country News*, 23 Nov 1998, 3.

19. Jim Armstrong, "Lost in Space," *Orion* 15, no. 2 (spring 1996): 26.

20. D. Wilcove et al, "Quantifying Threats to Imperiled Species in the United States," *BioScience* 48, no. 8 (Aug 1998): 607-615.

21. D. Wilcove et al, "Quantifying Threats to Imperiled Species in the United States," 613; Kay, *Asphalt Nation*, 195; Bruce Babbitt, U.S. Interior Secretary, personal communication.

22. Alan Durning, *The Car and the City* (Seattle: Northwest Environment Watch, 1996), 8, 24.

23. Surface Transportation Policy Project et al, *Mean Streets 1998* (Washington, D.C.: STPP, 1998), 4, 9, 11.

24. Peter Kilborn, "No work for a bicycle thief," *New York Times*, 7 Jun 1999, A1; Neal Templin, "The bicycle loses ground as a symbol of childhood liberty," *Wall Street Journal*, 10 Sep 1996, A11.

25. "Higher speed limits raise fatality risk," *New York Times*, 28 Jul 1995, A26; M. Herman et al, *Bicycle Blueprint* (New York: Transportation Alternatives, 1993), 42; "Motor vehicle deaths 15 percent higher on roads in 24 states that raised speed limits," Insurance Institute for Highway Safety, 14 Jan 1999, < www.highwaysafety.org/news_releases/1999/pr011499.htm >.

26. S. Sternberg, "Car phones jack up risk of collision," *Science News* 151, no. 7 (15 Feb 1997): 100.

27. "Statistics: The Impaired Driving Problem," Mothers Against Drunk Driving, < www.madd.org/stats/default.shtml >.

28. "Canada-Wide Statistics," MADD Canada, < www.madd.ca/library/stats.htm >.

29. Right Of Way, *Killed by Automobile*, 7.

30. "Statistics: Research on Youth," Mothers Against Drunk Driving, < www.madd.org/stats/stat_youth.shtml >.

31. J.F. O'Hanlon and J.J. de Gier, *Drugs and Driving* (London: Taylor & Francis, 1986), 255, 260, 261.

32. "Dieting impairs reaction time," *Science News* 151, no. 21 (24 May 1997): 327.

33. "Man run over by his own car," *San Francisco Chronicle*, 29 Jul 1994, A19.
34. "No license to drive," *San Francisco Chronicle*, 14 May 1993, A20.
35. "100 events that made the industry," *Automotive News* 2 (26 Jun 1996): 113.
36. "100 events that made the industry," 125, 129; Pettifer and Turner, *Automania*, 224.
37. Pettifer and Turner, *Automania*, 224.
38. Flink, *Automobile Age*, 384.
39. "To you ... and your car," *Bottom Line Personal*, 30 Mar 1993, 15.
40. David Everett, "Child seats often give false security," *Detroit Free Press*, 10 Feb 1995, 1A, 8A.
41. Oliver Tickell, "Death duties," *Guardian Weekly*, 5 Jul 1998, 23.
42. National Safety Council, *Injury Facts™, 1999 Edition*, 80-81, 122-123.
43. Bureau of Transportation Statistics, *Transportation Statistics Annual Report 1996*, 69.
44. Komanoff et al, *Killed by Automobile*, 43.
45. Komanoff et al, 12-13, 38.
46. Komanoff et al, 17, 37, 54.
47. Komanoff et al, 56-57.
48. Newman, "Sustainable Transportation — In from the Cold?" 14.
49. Williams, *Autogeddon*, 31-35.

Chapter 11

1. Emily Smith, "America's kids are more inactive than ever," Partnership for a Walkable America release.
2. J. Ralston, *Walking for the Health of It* (Washington, D.C.: AARP Books, 1986), 3, 69; R. Eugster, "The ABCs of Walking," *Living Healthy* 1, no. 1 (fall 1996): 10; M. Bricklin, "Walking, Thinking, and Intellectual Angina," *The Commonwealth* 85, no. 25 (24 Jun 1991): 452; Makower, *Green Commuter*, 114; A. Hakim et al, "Effects of Walking on Mortality among Nonsmoking Retired Men," *New England Journal of Medicine* 338, no. 2 (8 Jan 1998): < www.nejm.com >.
3. Kay, *Asphalt Nation*, 109.
4. Troy Holter, "Do you own your car or does your car own you?" *AERO Sun Times* (summer 1996): 9.
5. Ellen Jones, "Car-free living in Chevy Chase, D.C.," *Audubon Naturalist News* (Apr 1996): 8.
6. Heather Salerno, "Going on Shank's Mare," *Washington Post*, 10 Oct 1995, C05.
7. Peter Calthorpe, *The Next American Metropolis* (New York: Princeton Architectural Press, 1993), 9.
8. W. Gould, "Subdivision takes step back to ped-friendly times," *Milwaukee Journal Sentinel*, 19 Aug 1996, 2B.
9. Meredith May, "Berkeley cops leave cars and take to the streets," *San Francisco Examiner*, 2 May 1992, B-1, B-8.
10. Mike Alan Hama, personal communication, Sep 1997.
11. California Air Resources Board, *The Air Pollution-Transportation Linkage* (Sacramento: ARB, 1989), 4.

12. Makower, *Green Commuter*, 5, 116.
13. Cambridge Systematics, *Downtown Crossing* (Washington, D.C.: U.S. Department of Transportation, Jul 1982).
14. U.S. Federal Highway Administration, *National Bicycling and Walking Study*, 23.
15. Greenest City, *Safe Routes to School* (Toronto: Greenest City, 1997) (brochure).
16. Bureau of Transportation Engineering and Development, *Pedestrian Transportation Program* (Portland, Oreg.: Office of Transportation, 1996).
17. Ralston, *Walking for the Health of It*, 7.
18. Engwicht, *Street Reclaiming*, 67.
19. "The Mommy Lane," *Transportation Alternatives* 2, no. 6 (Nov/Dec 1996): 17.
20. Elise Houghton, "A new kind of bus afoot," *Green Teacher* 51 (spring 1997): 24.
21. Marjorie Alvord, personal communication, Jul 1997.
22. "Safe Routes to Schools," Sustrans, < www.sustrans.co.uk/srts/index.html >.
23. Engwicht, *Reclaiming Our Cities and Towns*, 143-144.
24. Engwicht, *Street Reclaiming*, 79.
25. Ellen Jones, "Car-free living in Chevy Chase, D.C.," *Audubon Naturalist News* (Apr 1996): 8.
26. Walkable Communities Inc., *Creating a More Walkable Las Vegas* (High Springs, Florida: Walkable Communities Inc., 1996), 6, 54.
27. Chris Bradshaw, Ottawalk, personal communication, Jan 2000.
28. Michael Hartmann, < http://ourworld.compuserve.com/homepages/mattiash/S1-eng.htm >.
29. "Our kind of towns," *Walking* 14, no. 4 (Aug 1999) 87-89.
30. Walkable Communities Inc., *Creating a More Walkable Las Vegas*, 4.
31. "Walkable Communities: Twelve Steps for an Effective Program," Florida Department of Transportation, 1995; Dan Burden, *Street Design Guidelines for Healthy Neighborhoods* (Sacramento, Calif.: Center for Livable Communities, 1999); and WalkBoston, *Walkable Communities* (brochure).
32. Walkable Communities, Inc., *Creating a More Walkable Las Vegas*, 6, 27-28, 30.
33. America WALKs, *America WALKs* (brochure).
34. Walkable Communities, Inc., *Creating a More Walkable Las Vegas*, 32.
35. Rodney Tolley and Les Lumsdon, "Developing a Model Local Walking Strategy," in Bicycle Federation of America, *ProBike ProWalk 98 Resource Book* (Washington, D.C.: Bicycle Federation of America, 1998), 23-27.
36. Burden, *Street Design Guidelines for Healthy Neighborhoods*, 7.
37. Ellen Vanderslice, "A Pedestrian Master Plan for Portland, Oregon," in Bicycle Federation of America, *ProBike ProWalk 98 Resource Book*, 123-127.

Chapter 12

1. Ben Swets, "City Bicycling," in Hackleman, *The New Electric Vehicles*, 92-93.
2. Lowe, *The Bicycle*, 21-22.
3. Perry, *Bike Cult*, 160.
4. W. Hook, "Economic Importance of Nonmotorized Transportation," *Transportation Research Record* 1487 (1995): 16; B. Burgess, "Shifting from Cars to Bikes," B*icycling Reference Book* (1993-94): 17.

5. M. Malaspina et al, *What Works: Air Pollution Solutions* (Washington, D.C.: Environmental Exchange, May 1992), 43; Lowe, *The Bicycle*, 20.
6. Malaspina et al, *What Works*, 43; Hal Zina Bennett, *The Complete Bicycle Commuter* (San Francisco: Sierra Club Books, 1982), 88-89.
7. Lowe, *The Bicycle*, 19.
8. Lowe, *The Bicycle*, 16; Phil Hammerslough, "Letters: Car-Crazed USA," *A to B* 12 (Jun/Jul 1999): 17; Makower, *Green Commuter*, 116.
9. Engwicht, *Reclaiming Our Cities and Towns*, 45; U.S. FHWA, *National Bicycling and Walking Study*, 24; Lester R. Brown et al, *State of the World 1996* (New York: W.W. Norton, 1996), 1.
10. U.S. FHWA, *National Bicycling and Walking Study*, 23; Go for Green, *Developing Communities for Active Transportation* (Ottawa: Go for Green, 1998), p.7; Lowe, *The Bicycle*, 18-19.
11. John Luton, "Golden Chariots," *Monday Magazine*, Nov 1998.
12. Urs Heierli, *Environmental Limits to Motorisation*, 1993, 121; Lowe, *The Bicycle*, 8.
13. Photo feature, *Guardian Weekly*, 26 Oct 1997.
14. Advertisement, *Monday Magazine*, 7-13 January 1999, 16-17.
15. Community Bicycle Network, *Put Bikes to Work for Your Business!*, Fact Sheet #1 (flyer).
16. Lester R. Brown et al, *Vital Signs 1996* (New York: W.W. Norton, 1996), 82; *Spoke N Word* (fall 1996): 3.
17. "Cops shift gears in crime fight," *San Francisco Chronicle*, 30 Aug 1993, A17.
18. Randy Ghent, "Brian Campbell's House Bikes," *Auto-Free Times* 11 (spring 1997): 14-15.
19. Railway Development Society, *Life Beyond Cars*, 6.
20. Jeffrey S. Olson, "Enhancing Liveable Communities: Five ISTEA Models in New York State," in Bicycle Federation of America, *Pro Bike Pro Walk 96* (Washington, D.C.: Bicycle Federation of America, 1996), 128.
21. "A Spotlight on Center for Appropriate Transport," *Re:Cycle* 5, no. 1 (spring 1998): 7.
22. Roy Bohn, "Earn-a-Bike Alumni ... Where Are They Now?" *Re:Cycle* 5, no. 1 (spring 1998): 1, 3.
23. Perry, *Bike Cult*, 259.
24. Gregory B. Rogers, "Bicyclist Deaths and Fatality Risk Patterns," *Journal of Accident Analysis and Prevention*, 27, no. 2 (1995): 215-223; Ross D. Petty, "The Federal Government and Bicycle Safety," *Bicycle Forum* 20:4.
25. U.S. FHWA, *National Bicycling and Walking Study*, Executive Summary, vii.
26. J.C. McCullah, "The Bicycle Can Save New York," in Herman, *Bicycle Blueprint*, 7.
27. U.S. FHWA, *National Bicycling and Walking Study*, 91 and Case Study 18, 33; Alderman Hasselaar, "Cycling in Groningen," *Velo-City Report*, 11; "What's Wrong with the Car?" *The Watershed Sentinel* (Dec 92/Jan 93).
28. Andy Clarke, "Bicycle-Friendly Cities," *Transportation Research Record* 1372 (1992): 71-75.
29. S. Martin, "Best Cities for Cycling," *Bicycling* (Nov/Dec 1995): 46+; Alan Coté, "10 Best Cities for Cycling," *Bicycling* (Mar 1999): 53+.

30. Lowe, *The Bicycle*, 35-36; U.S. FHWA, *National Bicycling and Walking Study*, Case Study 16, 11; Brown et al, *Vital Signs 1996*, 82; Malaspina et al, *What Works*, 43.
31. Lowe, *The Bicycle*, 10, 37; Malaspina et al, *What Works*, 43.
32. Brown et al, *Vital Signs 1996*, 82; H. Kaufman, "Revolution of Necessity," *E Magazine* (Dec 1993): 27-29.
33. Lowe, *The Bicycle*, 45.

Chapter 13

1. Jenise Doty, "Car-Free With Kids," *Auto-Free Times* 15 (early spring 1999): 19; Daniel Egan, "Car-Free, Care-Free, and On Our Bikes," *BUGle* (n.d.); Railway Development Society, *Life Beyond Cars*, 2; Ryan Mackenzie, "Living Car-Free in Cleveland," *Progress* VI, no. 2 (Mar 1996): 5.
2. Cervero, *The Transit Metropolis*, 17, 23, 31; U.S. Federal Transit Administration,*1996 Report: An Update* (Washington, D.C.: U.S. Department of Transportation, 1996), 2; Gerald Barber, "Aggregate Characteristics of Urban Travel," in Susan Hanson, ed., *The Geography of Urban Transportation* (New York: Guilford Press, 1995), 88.
3. U.S. DOE, *Transportation Energy Data Book*, Ed.17, 2-16; Nadis and MacKenzie, *Car Trouble*, 120; U.S. FTA, *1996 Report: An Update*, 3; "Statistics Summary," American Public Transit Association, < www.apta.com >.
4. Newman and Kenworthy, *Winning Back the Cities*, 22; note that consolidation around rail stations is less likely where transit stops are park-n-ride locations, with huge parking lots instead of homes and businesses around stations.
5. "National Impacts of Transit Capital and Operating Expenditures on Business Revenues," APTA, < www.apta.com > ; Goddard, *Getting There*, 273; Schiller et al, *Green Streets*, 19, 26.
6. APTA, *1998 Transit Fact Book*, 125.
7. U.S. Federal Transit Administration, *Intermodal Surface Transportation Efficiency Act: Flexible Funding Opportunities for Transportation Investments* (Washington, D.C.: U.S. Department of Transportation, 1996), 13; National Safety Council, *Injury Facts™ 1999*, 122.
8. Kay, *Asphalt Nation*, 346.
9. Personal communication, Amtrak public affairs office; VIA Rail website.
10. Susan Carey, "Even When It's Quicker to Travel by Train, Many Fly," *Wall Street Journal*, 29 Aug 1997, B1 + .
11. Mileages and car travel times from "Mileages and Driving Times Map," Rand McNally, *Rand McNally Road Atlas: United States, Canada, Mexico, 1991*, 128. Driving costs include both variable and fixed costs, based on figures from AAMA, *Motor Vehicle Facts and Figures 1995*, 58 and AAA, "Your Driving Costs," 1997 Edition. Travel time and costs for train and air travel are as reported in the *Wall Street Journal* (29 Aug 1997).
12. Goddard, *Getting There*, 265.
13. "The Taxi as Transit Mode," in *Transportation Options, Moving the Economy In-Print* (Toronto: Detour, 1999), 48.
14. Michael Torreiter, "Going My Way?" *Alternatives* 24, no. 1 (winter 1998): 19.
15. Makower, *Green Commuter*, 121.

16. Laurel Severson, 3M, personal communication; Jim Motavalli, "In Transit," *E Magazine* X, no. 1 (Jan/Feb 1999): 46; Makower, *Green Commuter*, 124.

17. National Station Car Association, 4 Jan 1998, < www.stncar.com > .

18. Ellen Jones, "Car-free living in Chevy Chase, D.C.," *Audubon Naturalist News* (Apr 1996): 8.

19. S. Shaheen, D. Sperling, and C. Wagner, "Carsharing in Europe and North America," *Transportation Quarterly* 52, no. 3 (summer 1998): 35-52.

20. Don Malcolm, "Car Sharing," *The Watershed Sentinel* (Dec 1994/Jan 1995): 27.

21. James S. Cannon, *Paving the Way to Natural Gas Vehicles* (New York: INFORM, 1993), 52-54.

22. "Walking Still Faster," *Mobilizing the Region* 47 (22 Sep 1995) (electronic ed.); *Mobilizing the Region* 69 (8 Mar 1996) (electronic ed.); Jonas Rabinovitch and Josef Leitman, "Urban Planning in Curitiba," *Scientific American* 274, no. 3 (Mar 1996): 46-53; Zilan Moura, "Profitable urban transit," *Sustrans Digest* 040 (19 Aug 1997) (electronic ed.).

23. K. Schneider and P. Capo, *California Transit Guide* (Davis, Calif.: California Transit Publications, 1991), 163.

24. Network for Efficient, Safe and Sustainable Transportation, *Citizen Advocacy: Working for Sustainable Transportation Alternatives in Your Community* (Washington, D.C.: Advocacy Institute, 1993), 13.

Chapter 14

1. R. Blumenstein, "Auto industry reaches surprising consensus," *Wall Street Journal*, 5 Jan 1998, A1 + .

2. MacKenzie, *Keys to the Car*, 55; "Clinton announces deal to develop 80-mpg cars," *San Francisco Chronicle*, 30 Sep 1993, A9.

3. MacKenzie, *Keys to the Car*, 23-24.

4. Makower, *Green Commuter*, 133; Sperling, *Future Drive*, 30; Gordon, *Steering a New Course*, 88; Pettifer and Turner, *Automania*, 117; MacKenzie, *Keys to the Car*, 27.

5. Makower, *Green Commuter*, 132; MacKenzie, *Keys to the Car*, 22-23; Sperling, *Future Drive*, 29; Gordon, *Steering a New Course*, 85.

6. < www.propanegas.com/consumer/vehicles.html > ; Cannon, *Paving the Way to Natural Gas Vehicles*, 6; Gordon, *Steering a New Course*, 80-82.

7. < http://206.168.70.144/bulletin2.html > ; < www.iangv.org/ngv/stats.html > ; "India to switch to eco-friendly fuels by October," 20 Jan 1999, < www.planetark.org/new/worldnews2.html > ; Makower *Green Commuter*, 134; Cannon, *Paving the Way to Natural Gas Vehicles*, 7; MacKenzie, *Keys to the Car*, 29; Sperling, *Future Drive*, 29.

8. Cindy Purfeerst, Clean Cities program, personal communication, 25 Aug 1999.

9. Makower, *Green Commuter*, 138.

10. Sperling, *Future Drive*, 44-47.

11. Makower, *Green Commuter*, 138-139.

12. "Study: Charging electric cars could drain power supply," 16 Apr 1998, < http://www.enn.com > .

13. "Ballard mum on fuel-cell orders," *Sunday Province*, 14 Nov 1999, A59; D. McGinn and A. Rogers, "Operation: Supercar," *Newsweek* 132, no. 21 (23 Nov

1998): 48-53; Motavalli, *Future Drive*, 123; Bill Visnic, "New Alliance Hastens Fuel Cell Development," *Ward's Autoworld*, April 1999, < www.wards.com >.

14. Motavalli, *Forward Drive*, 14, 66; D. McGinn and A. Rogers, "Operation: Supercar," *Newsweek* 132, no. 21 (23 Nov 1998): 52.

15. Paul F. Howard, presentation at Moving the Economy conference, July 1998, Toronto; Schiller et al, *Green Streets*, 20; Meredeth Willey, Alternative Fuels Hotline, personal communication.

16. "Getting Around," *Environment* 41, no. 7 (Sep 1999): 21.

17. "Spotlight on Niche Markets," *Alternative Fuel News* 2, no. 6 (Mar 1999): 8.

18. Hackleman, *The New Electric Vehicles*, 135-137, 142.

19. Paul Webster, "A car with a healthy air," *Guardian Weekly*, 8 Feb 1998; Paul Webster, "Air today, Mexico City tomorrow," *Guardian Weekly*, 21 Jun 1998; Heather McCabe, "Running On Empty," *Wired*, May 1999, < www.wired.com/wired/archive/7.05/mustread.html?pg = 19 >.

20. Marcy Rood, Clean Cities Program, personal communication.

21. "Denver Takes Charge!" *Alternative Fuel News* 3, no. 1 (May 1999): 17.

22. Motavalli, *Future Drive*, 85.

Chapter 15

1. Survey by Challenger, Gray & Christmas, *Christian Science Monitor* (31 Aug 1999)(electronic ed.); Langhoff, *Telecommuter's Advisor*, 27; "NUA Analysis: How Many Online Worldwide," NUA Internet Survey, 1999, < www.nue.ie/surveys/analysis/graphs_charts/comparisons/how_many_onlin e.html > ; "Internet Domain Survey, July 1999," Internet Software Consortium, < http://www.isc.org/dsview.cgi?domainsurvey/WWW-9907/report.html >.

2. Patricia L. Mokhtarian, "The Information Highway: Just Because We're On It Doesn't Mean We Know Where We're Going," *World Transport Policy and Practice* 2, nos. 1-2 (1996): 24-28.

3. Langhoff, *Telecommuter's Advisor*, 22.

4. Langhoff, *Telecommuter's Advisor*, 21.

5. Langhoff, *Telecommuter's Advisor*, 18, 22-23.

6. Donaldson and Weiss, "Health, Well-Being and Organization Effectiveness in the Virtual Workplace," in Tan and Igbaria, *The Virtual Workplace* (Hershey, Penn.: Idea Group Publishing, 1998), 34.

7. Patricia L. Mokhtarian, "Now that Travel can be Virtual, will Congestion Virtually Disappear?" *Scientific American* 277, no. 4 (Oct 1997): 93.

8. Robert M. Johnston, MD, Richard L. Nevins, MD, and Michael L. Weaver, MD, "Another kind of tele-home health: Medical Call Centers," *Telemedicine Today*, < http://telemedtoday.com/articlearchive/articles/anothertelehome.htm >.

9. Oregon Office of Energy, *Telework* (Salem, Oregon: Oregon Office of Energy, 1997), 6; Oregon Office of Energy, *Telecommuting* (Salem, Oregon: Oregon Office of Energy, 1996), 1; Commuter Connections,*Washington Metropolitan Telework Demonstration Project* (Washington, D.C.: Metropolitan Washington COG, 1999), 8.

10. Union of Concerned Scientists, *Transportation Options: Telecommuting* (Fact Sheet), 1; Langhoff, *Telecommuter's Advisor*, 18; Amelia Kassel, MarketingBase, personal communication; Melvin Levin, *Teleworking and*

Urban Development Patterns (Lanham, Maryland: University Press of America, 1998), xiii; "The Broader Impacts of Telework," Canadian Telework Association, < www.ivc.ca/part15.html > ; "Gartner Group predicts 50% failure rate for telecommuting programs," < www.langhoff.com/surveys.html#failure > .

11. Langhoff, *Telecommuter's Advisor*, 26.
12. Minnesota Public Radio Broadcast, 8 Oct 1997.
13. Langhoff, *Telecommuter's Advisor*, 237-238; Bredin, *Virtual Office Survival Handbook*, 36.
14. Langhoff, *Telecommuter's Advisor*, 227.
15. "Programs and Services," Canadian Association for Distance Education, < www.cade-aced.ca/english/prog_set.html > .
16. Langhoff, *Telecommuter's Advisor*, 182-183.
17. "Distance Learning Fact Sheet," U.S. Distance Learning Association, 10 May 1999, < www.usdla.org/Pages/dl.html > .
18. "Internet Statistics," < www.netcard.net/netstats.html > .
19. Makower, *Green Commuter*, 125-126.
20. Ellen Jones, "Car-free living in Chevy Chase, D.C.," *Audubon Naturalist News* (Apr 1996): 8.
21. Langhoff, *Telecommuter's Advisor*, 231.
22. Patricia L. Mokhtarian, "The Information Highway: Just Because We're On It Doesn't Mean We Know Where We're Going," 24-28.
23. Patricia L. Mokhtarian, "Now that Travel can be Virtual, will Congestion Virtually Disappear?", 93.
24. Patricia L. Mokhtarian, "Now that Travel can be Virtual, will Congestion Virtually Disappear?", 93.

Chapter 16

1. Newman and Kenworthy, *Sustainability and Cities*, 170-172, 175-176.
2. Newman and Kenworthy, *Winning Back the Cities*, 8.
3. Cervero, *The Transit Metropolis*, 418-419, 424.
4. "Fruitvale BART Transit Village Progress Report," Unity Council, 1 Sep 1999, < www.unitycouncil.org/html/ftvupdate.html > ; Jenny Kassan, personal communication.
5. John King, "Starting from scratch," *San Francisco Chronicle*, 22 Apr 1999, E1.
6. Cervero, *The Transit Metropolis*, 88.
7. Urban Ecology, *Blueprint for a Sustainable Bay Area*, 44.
8. Eno Foundation, *Parking*, 16-17.
9. Maryland Office of Planning, *What You Need to Know About Smart Growth and Neighborhood Conservation* (Baltimore: Maryland Office of Planning, 1997), 1-20.
10. Richard Untermann, *Reshaping Our Suburbs* (Seattle, Wash.: Bullitt Foundation, n.d.).
11. "Dirty Little Secrets," Friends of the Earth, Update 1998, < www.foe.org/DLS/Update98.html > .
12. Cervero, *The Transit Metropolis*, 168; Newman and Kenworthy, *Sustainability and Cities*, 195.

13. Keith Harper and Paul Brown, "Prescott heralds transport revolution," *Guardian Weekly*, 26 Jul 1998, 9.
14. Kay, *Asphalt Nation*, 353-354; Todd Litman, "Driving Out Subsidies," *Alternatives* 24, no. 1 (winter 1998): 40; Schiller et al, *Green Streets*, 19-20.
15. Wayne Roberts and Susan Brandum, *Get A Life!* (Toronto: Get A Life Publishing House, 1995), 72.
16. U.S. Federal Transit Administration and Federal Highway Administration, *Intermodal Surface Transportation Efficiency Act: Flexible Funding Opportunities for Transportation Investments* (Washington, D.C.: U.S. Department of Transportation, 1996), 9.
17. "Belgium experiments with free public transportation," CNN Today, 14 Jul 1998, Transcript #98071409V13.
18. Makower, *Green Commuter*, 149.
19. John Pucher, "Back on Track," *Alternatives* 24, no. 1 (winter 1998): 33.
20. Dan Burden and Peter Lagerway, *Road Diets: Fixing the Big Roads* (Walkable Communities Inc., Mar 1999), 8, < www.walkable.org/download/rdiets.pdf >.
21. Livable Oregon Inc., *Skinny Streets: Better Streets for Livable Communities* (Portland, Oreg.: Livable Oregon and the Smart Development Project, 1996).
22. Newman and Kenworthy, *Sustainability and Cities*, 176.
23. Go for Green, *Developing Communities for Active Transportation* (Ottawa: Go for Green, 1998), 8.
24. Walkable Communities Inc., *Creating a More Walkable Las Vegas*, 18.
25. Go for Green, *Developing Communities for Active Transportation* (Ottawa: Go for Green, 1998), 8.
26. Cervero, *The Transit Metropolis*, 417-422.
27. Donald H. Camph, *Dollars and Sense: The Economic Case for Public Transportation in America* (Washington, D.C.: Campaign for Efficient Passenger Transportation, 1997), 77.
28. U.S. FTA, *1996 Report: An Update*, 2.
29. Jim Olivetti, American Public Transportation Association, personal communication.
30. WalkBoston, *Walkable Communities: 5 Steps to Making Your Community Safe and Convenient on Foot* (Boston: WalkBoston, n.d.).
31. Schiller et al, *Green Streets*, 6.
32. Pettifer and Turner, *Automania*, 276.
33. Patrick Siegman, "Pedestrian malls," 21 Dec 1998, < www.tlcnetwork.org/_Email/000000a7.htm >.
34. "Paris urges European cities to ban cars for a day," 15 Jan 1999, < www.planetark.org/new/worldnews2.html >.
35. Cornell University Office of Transportation Services, *Commuting Solutions: Summary of Transportation Demand Management Program (TDMP)* (Ithaca, New York: Cornell University, Oct 1997), 1, 2, Attachment 6.
36. Engwicht, *Street Reclaiming*, 59-60, 125-126.

Chapter 17

1. Kay, *Asphalt Nation*, 304.
2. WalkBoston, *Improving Pedestrian Access to Transit*, 9.

3. U.S. Federal Transit Administration, *Bicycles and Transit: A Partnership that Works* (Washington, D.C.: U.S. Department of Transportation, 1998), 10-11; Rails to Trails Conservancy and the Association of Pedestrian and Bicycle Professionals, *Improving Conditions for Bicycling and Walking: A Best Practices Report* (Washington, D.C.: U.S. Federal Highway Administration, 1998), 42.
4. Metro Rideshare, < http://transit.metrokc.gov/bike/racks_on_vans.html >.
5. U.S. Federal Highway Administration, *Leaving a Place Better Than We Found It* (Washington, D.C.: U.S. Department of Transportation, 1996), 2.
6. Schiller et al, *Green Streets*, 19.
7. Brower and Leon, *The Consumer's Guide to Effective Environmental Choices*, 90.
8. Mary Sawyer, Mayflower Transit, personal communication (based on U.S. Census Bureau figures).
9. Railway Development Society, *Life Beyond Cars*, 1-2.
10. Brower and Leon, *The Consumer's Guide to Effective Environmental Choices*, 100.
11. Ellen Jones, "Car-free living in Chevy Chase, DC," *Audubon Naturalist News* (Apr 1996): 8.
12. Ellen Jones, "Car-free living in Chevy Chase, DC," 8.

Chapter 18

1. John Akre's Car-Free Pages,
   < http:home.earthlink.net/ ~ jakre/carfree/freelif.htm >.
2. Devra Lee Davis et al, *Urban Air Pollution Risks to Children* (Washington, D.C.: World Resources Institute, 1999).
3. Whitelegg, *Critical Mass*, 4-5.

INDEX

ABOUT THE AUTHOR

KATIE ALVORD was born and raised in northern California. She has been a transportation reform advocate for more than 15 years. A freelance writer and former librarian, her work has included stints with several non-profit organizations involved in transportation, land preservation, and other environmental issues. Her writing credits include articles and reviews in *Auto-Free Times, Buzzworm, Car Busters, E Magazine, The Road-RIPorter, The Urban Ecologist, Wild Earth,* and several regional periodicals. In 1992, she began writing (as Katie Scarborough) about her experience of embarking on a car-free car divorce while living in a rural part of Sonoma County, California. Her efforts earned her a Clean Air Champion award from the San Francisco Bay Area Air Quality Management District, and related public education work gained her other honors. She also served on the Sonoma County Bicycle and Pedestrian Advisory Committee and Congresswoman Lynn Woolsey's Environmental Advisory Committee. In 1994, she moved to rural Upper Michigan, where she and her husband currently live car-lite. To keep their driving down, they've been known to put snow tires on their bikes for winter riding, carry bikes on their kayak, haul groceries home in bike trailers, and ski to parties.

Katie is a graduate of the University of California at Davis, where she bicycled to classes and received a B.A. with honors in Biological Sciences. She also spent a year studying at Smith College, and she holds a Master's degree in Library and Information Studies from the University of California at Berkeley.

If you have enjoyed *Divorce Your Car!* you might also enjoy other

BOOKS TO BUILD A NEW SOCIETY

New Society Publishers' mission is to publish books that
contribute in fundamental ways to building an ecologically sustainable
and just society, and to do so with the least possible impact on the
environment, in a manner that models this vision.

Our books provide positive solutions for people
who want to make a difference.
We specialize in:

Sustainable Living

Ecological Design and Planning

Environment and Justice

New Forestry

Conscientious Commerce

Resistance and Community

Nonviolence

The Feminist Transformation

Progressive Leadership

Educational and Parenting Resources

For a full list of NSP's titles, please call 1-800-567-6772
or check out our web site at: www.newsociety.com

NEW SOCIETY PUBLISHERS